THE ECONOMICS OF LATIN AMERICA

THE ECONOMICS OF LATIN AMERICA

Development Problems in Perspective

RAWLE FARLEY
State University of New York
College at Brockport

1973 **HARPER & ROW, PUBLISHERS**
New York   Evanston   San Francisco   London

To Ena, Jonathan, Christopher, Felipe, Anthony,
Jeremy, Jay, and to my father and mother

CONTENTS

PREFACE

This book attempts to meet the need for a comprehensive study of the problem of economic development in Latin America from the viewpoint of a development economist. The book is intended to improve perspectives on the realities of the Latin American economy, the character of conditions affecting speedier economic advance in Latin America, the achievements which have been registered (particularly over the last decade), and the complicated uncertainties which will continue to affect predictions about time-horizons and development paths in Latin America.

An appreciation of the massive dimensions of the development challenge in Latin America is impossible without a grasp of the conditions from which Latin America seeks escape. In Latin America, an emergency situation exists, primarily because of the uncheckable growth of the population, a growth which is not paralleled by the speed with which the economy grows and changes. Since, in my view, it will be impossible to check the growth of the Latin American population in the foreseeable future, the transformation of the quality of human life in Latin America must depend on the rapidity with which economic development can take place. The initial conditions are such and the boundary conditions to be overcome are so severe that, barring unexpected technological discoveries, rapid transformation in the economic status of Latin America is not a short-run possibility.

I have divided the book into four parts. In Part I, I set out, against the background of Latin America's uncheckable population growth and spatial disequilibrium, the socioeconomic parameters of the development dilemmas of Latin America and the objectives of development as determined by the Latin American milieu. In Part II, given the parameters of the condition to be changed, I evaluate the performance of the Latin American economy as a whole, the performance of the agricultural sector, and the relation of the agricultural setting in Latin America to the problem of over-all economic change. In Part III, I assess Latin American industrialization, the financial dimensions of Latin American development, and the problems confronting Latin American economic integration. In Part IV, I review the economic status of Latin America at the end of the first decade of the Alliance for Progress, illustrating the difficulties of economic transformation through a case study of Venezuela.

As a further aid to the reader's appreciation of the development effort required in Latin America, I have included 112 statistical tables, in addition to necessary figures, diagrams, and maps. Quantification must be used with considerable caution when talking about Latin America since the statistics may vary even from one official document to another. Nonetheless, despite possible shortcomings, it is better to have the statistics as they are and be able to arrive immediately at some quantified expression than to have no statistics at all. It is better too that interpretation be guided by available statistics than to have no quantitative constraints on interpretative analyses. Besides, the statistics allow the reader to immediately detect areas for further research and enable him to make his own conjectures about future development paths in Latin America.

Although I offer no general model for Latin American development, I conclude with a generalization on the relation between economic development, social consensus, and political leadership. I have also taken the view that while no imported model can be imposed on Latin America and that while successful approaches used in one Latin American country do not guarantee similar success in another, much common ground is being discovered through hemispheric cooperation and common ideas will continue to be shared.

This book is written for use by undergraduate and graduate students in Latin American economics and political science, as well as by students of economic development. The material can readily be adapted to a one- or two-semester course. The book is also intended for the intelligent layman and for other individuals whose day-to-day business is with Latin American economic affairs.

I must thank a number of people who contributed to the writing of this book. My wife, Ena, stands out—for immense and continuously constructive contributions to this book, despite her own domestic responsibilities and her academic duties as assistant professor of American History at the State University College at Buffalo. Richard Schroeder, Alfred Wolf, and a large number of distinguished University specialists in Latin America gave encouraging support. I received remarkable help with source materials from many United States and Latin American government departments and private agencies and through the librarians at the State University College at Brockport. My neighbor, Mrs. Margaret Ketchum, was most patient throughout the job of typing and retyping my manuscript and helping me in the desperate race against time pressures. Finally, there are the students in my Latin American development and economic development classes and many, many other people to whom I owe so much for their observations. I take, of course, sole responsibility for errors of omission or of perspective in this work.

Rawle Farley

PART I

POPULATION GROWTH AND THE SOCIOECONOMIC
CONSTRAINTS ON DEVELOPMENT IN LATIN AMERICA

CHAPTER 1

THE DIMENSIONS OF THE DEVELOPMENT CHALLENGE

The term *Latin America* is used in this book to mean all those countries of the Americas which lie south of the Rio Grande. Of these countries, 23 are members of the Organization of American States (OAS)—namely, Mexico, Guatemala, Honduras, El Salvador, Nicaragua, Costa Rica, and Panama in Central America; Colombia, Venezuela, Ecuador, Peru, Bolivia, Chile, Argentina, Uruguay, Paraguay, and Brazil in South America; Jamaica, Haiti, the Dominican Republic, Barbados, and Trinidad and Tobago in the Caribbean archipelago. The United States is of course also a member of the OAS.

Cuba might still be a member of the OAS, but since Castro's take-over, it remains an ideological alien outside of the OAS. The ideological stance of Cuba, however, inevitably comes under consideration in relation to the development objectives of Latin America.

The other territories south of the Rio Grande which are not members of the OAS include the following: the independent Cooperative Republic of Guyana, with institutional links to Latin America, and the members of Caribbean Free Trade Association (CARIFTA), comprised principally of former or presently British-linked Caribbean territories, of which the Cooperative Republic of Guyana is a member. To these must be added British Honduras, Martinique, Guadeloupe, Curaçao, Surinam, Cayenne, Saba, St. Martin, St. Croix, Bonaire, the Bahamas, Bermuda, and the British Virgin Islands, all of which continue in one form or another interesting constitutional relationships with Britain, France, and the Netherlands. Reference to the development problems of these countries as well as to those of Barbados, Trinidad, Jamaica, and the U.S. Virgin Islands will be only marginal in this book.

The last remaining major country south of the Rio Grande—Puerto Rico—enjoys a special constitutional relationship with the United States. Although the constitutional and cultural position of Puerto Rico remains unique, the transformation of the island from poverty to comparative prosperity has been spectacular. The Puerto Rican experience however receives only passing reference in this book.

The geographical definition of Latin America is, of course, used simply as a matter of convenience. Latin America so defined is comprised of 23 independent countries, the rest being dependencies or countries specially related to metropolitan areas. Of these, Jamaica, Barbados, and Trinidad and Tobago are dominions within the British Commonwealth.

It is possible to group Latin American countries according to the language used; we might distinguish between Spanish-speaking Latin America, Portuguese-speaking Latin America, and the rest. This rest includes the English-speaking, independent countries of Guyana, Trinidad and Tobago, Barbados, and Jamaica; the French-speaking republic of Haiti; the English-speaking, British-associated states in the Leeward and Windward Islands (Antigua, St. Kitts–Nevis–Anguilla, Montserrat, St. Lucia, Dominica, St. Vincent, Grenada, and the Grenadines); the English-speaking territories of British Honduras, Bermuda, the Virgin Islands (British), and the Bahamas; the French-speaking territories of Martinique, Guadeloupe, and St. Martin (French); and the Dutch-speaking territories of Surinam, Curaçao, Saba, Bonaire, and St. Martin (Dutch).[1]

THE LATIN AMERICAN IDENTITY

Geographical, political, or linguistic boundaries, however, do not adequately define the uniqueness of Latin America. In fact, geographical, political, and linguistic boundaries may emphasize differences rather than the broad similarity implied in the term *Latin America.* Although Latin America is on the whole conspicuously poor, poverty does not distinguish it from the rest of the developing world—Africa, Asia, the Middle East—or from countries under the command of socialist systems. In fact, even the term is under dispute in some quarters, where the more distinctive term *Indo-America* is favored.[2]

There is no need to debate the relative merits of *Latin America, Pan-America, Ibero-America, or Indo-America.* Suffice it to say that the essential Latin America has a distinct cultural identity. The predominant ingredients of that identity are generally referred to as *Hispanic,* for the origins of this identity go back to Latin America's historical connections with Spain, Portugal, and France. The essential Latin America has, however, an identity of its own above and beyond its inherited cultural ingredients. European Latin America, Afro–Latin America, and Indo–Latin America are all integral parts on an independent and distinctive Latin American identity.[3]

The Hispanic and Indian inheritance, in so far as it is reflected in the basic institutional life of Latin America, remains relevant to all major development considerations in modern Latin America. The hacienda, for instance, endures in Latin America as one of the major obstacles to economic development.

To sum up, the essential Latin America has a distinctive personality which differentiates it from the English- and Dutch-speaking newcomers into the political-economic orbit of the OAS and into the military-economic orbit of the Americas. This distinctive personality, forged by the process of history, must be taken into account in any development analysis, decisions, recommendations, or programs of action for Latin America. That this distinctive personality must be considered was reflected in the affirmations by the member states of the Special Committee on Latin American Coordination (CECLA), meeting at ministerial level in Viñá del Mar, Chile, to propose, among other things, that new development approaches reflect the realities of the continent. CECLA affirmed that it was imperative for Latin American countries to reach solutions "born of their own criteria, which reflect their national identity" (1969, p. 2). The historical

---

[1] Preston James (1964, p. xi) divides Latin America into Spanish-speaking countries, Portuguese-speaking countries, and the Antilles and Guianas.

[2] See Haya de la Torre (1963, pp. 282–289).

[3] Cf. Silvert (1968, pp. 3–9); Glade (1969, pp. 3–25); Zea (1968, pp. 3–16); Davis (1968, pp. 23–44); Chilcote (1969, pp. 125–136); U.S. Senate, (1960c pp. 62–69).

background and the contemporary milieu of Latin America make it essential to latinize the work of development on this continent. Yet this indispensable construction of development programs on the basis of local and national criteria is a general principle applicable to all developing countries and even to many developed countries. Therefore, Latin America is not unique in demanding this kind of pragmatism in development approaches.

There is another fact which, however interesting in itself, does not make Latin America unique in the developing world. This is the startling contrast between the cultural richness of the Latin American civilization and the general economic poverty of the whole area. Latin America enjoys world-wide distinction for its contribution to the arts, the sciences, and the humanities. Every country in Latin America has won its quota of glory for its contribution. At the level of economic development, however, Latin America is confronted with problems shared by the most backward countries in the world. The paradox of unique cultural achievement and economic poverty is not peculiar to Latin America. Consciousness of cultural richness, however, explains to a significant extent the complicated reactions and sensitivities to proposals for transforming Latin America from its state of underdevelopment. These sensitivities cannot be ignored at international economic bargaining tables; but again, this is true of many developing countries with culturally rich backgrounds.

Demography and Development

The uniqueness of Latin America in the developing world derives from the fact that it has the fastest growing population in modern times. This phenomenon in turn confronts the Latin American economy with the task of generating a rate of economic advance which will permit it not only to meet the minimum needs of its explosively expanding population but also to satisfy the demand for an increasingly higher standard of living. The magnitude of the challenge is predetermined by (1) the rate at which the population increases; (2) the present economic status of Latin America; (3) the intensity of rising expectations in Latin America; and (4) a variety of obstacles, past and present, to structural transformation to increasing productivity, and to bridging the gap between development requirements and actual performance.

The issue is that of securing an effective upgrading of the quality of life in Latin America. The quality of life is not wholly dependent on economic development, but economic development is clearly a significant determinant of the quality of life. The practical task here is that of achieving this development within the context of an emergency situation generated by (1) widespread poverty; (2) chronic inequities in distribution and in social chances, (3) oligarchical institutional arrangements; (4) the peripheral standing of Latin American economies in relation to the international economy; (5) severe shortcomings in fiscal and managerial skills; and (6) inappropriate political arrangements; and, of course, (7) population pressures.[4]

THE ORIENTATION OF THIS TEXT

Our concern throughout this book is the identification of obstacles to accelerating the rate of economic development in Latin America to provide an increase in

---

[4]See Coale (1964, pp. 125–140) and Hirschmann (1964, pp. 140–146).

real income per individual and in productive employment of the population proportionate to the needs of the Latin American situation. It is axiomatic that the objective of any development effort is to improve the human condition. On the other hand, despite unresolved mysteries surrounding the development process, we assume as axiomatic that the quality of the population is more important than any other productive factor in determining the initiation, maintenance, and success of the development process.[5] I describe, therefore, in Part I of this book the human condition in Latin America, setting out first the dimensions of the demographic phenomena, which conditions, in turn, the over-all speed at which Latin American economic development must take place.[6]

To avoid making a mystique of development, it is essential to define what we mean by development. It is possible to use Furtado's view of underdevelopment and define development as a process of correcting "a state of factor unbalance"; which reflects a "lack of adjustment between the availability of factors and the technology of their use" (1967, p. 142). Development as a process of correction must in terms of this view "achieve full utilization of both capital and labor simultaneously" (1967, p. 142).[7] In terms of Latin American realities, however, the simultaneous and full utilization of both capital and labor, while maximizing national income, may still leave much to be desired in the sphere of income distribution. Very few tests on development attempt to define it;[8] Furtado's perceptive thesis is one of the few which does but even he defines development by

---

[5]Cf. U.S. Senate (1960, p. 584):

> Human beings are both the end and the most significant means of economic development. The quality of human resources, including education, training, health, initiative, and the will to work, far outweigh all other determinants of economic growth. . . . The rate of growth and composition of the population, the level of education and training, the population distribution as between cities and rural areas, and the levels of living and social conditions of various groups within the country, must all be taken into account in the formulation of a development program.

[6]Cf. McNamara (1970, p. 7): "we cannot content ourselves with the mere quantity of man's life on the planet. And if our investments are to meet this wider goal, we and other investors need to add to the patterns of analysis a new dimension of social concern. This concern must, of course, be as rigorous, factual and informed as any of our other economic analysis and forecasts."

[7]Cf. Hopkins (1969, p. 8): "The concept of equilibrium in utilization and remuneration of the factors of production is, nevertheless, useful in setting goals at which to aim and standards against which to measure performance."

[8]But see Singer (1964, p. 41): "An underdeveloped country then may be defined as a country with 80 percent of its people in agriculture and a developed country as one with only 15 percent of its employment in agriculture, in both cases give or take a little according to foreign trade." Also see Kindleberger (1965, p. 1): "economic growth means more output, and economic development implies more output and changes in the technical and institutional arrangements by which it is produced"; Adelman (1967, p. 1): "definitions are necessary to establish ground rules for discussion. . . . We shall define economic development as the process by which an economy is transformed from one whose rate of growth of per capita income is small or negative to one in which a significant self-sustained rate of increase of per capita income is a permanent long-run feature." See Viner (1964, pp. 4–9), Lewis (1964, pp. 10–22), and Letvin (1964, pp. 23–29). Finally, see Reynolds (1969, pp. 401–408), and Villard (1963, pp. 27–28).

way of defining underdevelopment. Stated more positively for Latin America, development must secure a transformation of the economy in such a way that a number of objectives are achieved simultaneously. These are (1) an increase in per capita income which steadily and significantly exceeds the increase in population; (2) a transformation of the backward sector to a level of efficiency equal to that of the most modern sector of the economy and, beyond that, to a level of international competitive competence; (3) the full utilization of the labor force; (4) the correction of the chronic inequities in income distribution; (5) the stabilization of price levels; (6) balanced growth; (7) the ending of dependence upon a single product; (8) the modification of external dependence and exogenous stimuli; (9) the creation of equitable social opportunities for all and of conditions for the emergence of local entrepreneurship, which will play a far more decisive role in the development process than foreign entrepreneurship; and (10) the achievement of full economic integration for Latin America.[9]

It is a misinterpretation of the dimension of the development problem in Latin America to confine the meaning of development to "a significant self-sustained rate of increase of per capita income as a permanent long-run feature."[10] For one thing, there is no choice other than to push up the rate of growth per head faster than the rate of growth of the population as a whole. The population advance in Latin America, as we shall see, is unstoppable and will continue to be unstoppable for a long time. For another, the rate of population advance conditions the speed at which development must be pushed. The social pressures in Latin America permit no other conception but that development must represent a definite break with the past—one so dramatic that the poverty and stagnation of the past will be completely obliterated. Again, the development problem involves the transformation of archaic political structures, which militate against individual freedom as they do against the modernization of the economy.[11]

Latin American nationalism requires and demands that neocolonialism be rejected and that a Latin American development ideology sustain the Latin American determination to secure an internalized industrial revolution to end the traditional state of foreign dependence.[12] Development, in light of the ideological drive in Latin America, is not simply a matter of achieving a better level of income. Development involves a systematic determination to close the

---

[9] See also Mora (p. 83).

[10] Quote is from Adelman (1967, p. 1); see also Adelman and Morris (1968, esp. pp. 1184–1185). See also Mamalakis (1969, pp. 9–46); Seers (1969, pp. 2–6); Pan American Union (1970); and Commission on International Development (1969, p. ix): "There is far more to development than economic and material progress, and gross national product is no assurance of the possession of other values and qualities."

[11] Cf. Johnson (1968a, pp. 44–45); Enke (1963, esp. pp. 537–540); and Alexander (1962).

[12] See Hirschmann (1969, p. 3). In this excellent study of the "principal weaknesses of present institutional arrangements concerning private international investment," Hirschmann gives a number of ways in which current institutions and practices could be restructured; the essay is written "against the backdrop of rising nationalism and militancy in the developing countries, particularly in Latin America and of an astounding complacency, inertia, and lack of institutional imagination on the part of the rich countries." See also Stein and Stein (1970, pp. 190–198); Madrigal-Nieko, in Inter-American Development Bank (1969b, pp. 212–217); and Street (1967, pp. 45–62).

gap between the prevailing level of income in Latin America and the prevailing level of income in North America. The wish for an endogenous economic revolution in the performance of the Latin American economy is perfectly explicable. Affluence lies just north of the Rio Grande and the demonstration factor is at work with the newspaper, the radio, the cinema, the television, and the tourist—all communicating the vision of the affluent society north of the Rio Grande. Despite exciting differences in economic capacity, no logic can presuppose that there is one standard of living possible for North Americans and another for Latin Americans.

The desire to equalize the standard of living in Latin America, where the majority are poor, to that in North America, where the minority are poor, is one thing. The economic capacity to bridge this gap is another. In light, however, of the population explosion and the present economic status of Latin America, it is clear that Latin America cannot retreat from making this effort. In this book, we attempt on the one hand to see how far Latin American development ambitions have succeeded, especially during the years of the Alliance, and on the other hand, to identify the major factors affecting Latin American economic performance. In Part II, I examine the structure of the economy, the achievement in over-all growth in recent years, and the problems confronting development ambitions, especially in the agricultural sector. In Part III, I assess the problems and prospects for Latin American industrialization and economic integration; in Part IV, I assess the relevance of the economic development experience of Venezuela to the development ambitions in Latin America. In the final chapter, we attempt to reach some general conclusions on the relationship between political leadership and the fulfillment of development goals.[13]

Indicators of Economic Performance

Quantitative indicators of the status and performance of the Latin American economy are now becoming more and more available. It is readily admitted, however, that despite the increasing availability of data, existing data needs to be tested further and correlated with similar data assembled by various agencies.[14] Nonetheless, we assume that it is better to use such indicators as are available than to disregard them.

As a matter of convenience, we use the specific and general goals set out by the Charter of Punta del Este (August 17, 1961) as the basic criteria for judging Latin American economic performance in recent years.[15] President Kennedy, in announcing the Alliance for Progress on March 13, 1961, before Latin American diplomatic representatives and the U.S. Congress, expressed the general development goals in language approved by Latin America. "I have called," he said, "on all the people of the Hemisphere to join us in a new *Alliance for Progress—Alianza para el Progreso*—a vast cooperative effort, unparalleled in magnitude and nobility

---

[13]Cf. Prebisch: "[past actions of Latin American governments] were rarely based on a major political strategy in which economic and social development was a fundamental and persistent element" (1970a, p. 2).

[14]The reader may wish to refer to: Higgins (1968, chap. 1); Kuznets (1962, esp. pp. 3–26); Beckerman and Bacon (1966, pp. 519–536); and UN (1959).

[15]U.S. House, (1966, pp. 101–114); Pan American Union (1968f); Mora (pp. 11–23); U.S. Department of State (1965).

of purpose, to satisfy the basic needs of the American people for home, work and land, health and schools—*techo, trabajo y tierra, salud y escuela.*" The fundamental Alliance goals, which in the charter of Punta del Este the American republics agreed to achieve within the decade, can be summed up as follows:

1. Achieving a rate of economic growth in every Latin American country of not less than 2.5 percent per capita per year, to give Latin America the assurance of self-sustained development
2. Disseminating the benefits of economic progress through a more equitable distribution of the national income, simultaneously raising the level of income of the neediest sectors of the population while increasing the savings–income ratio
3. Balanced diversifying of the national economic structures, making for less dependence on a few primary products and the importation of capital goods, at the same time stabilizing both the prices of exports and export-derived incomes
4. Accelerating national industrialization, fully utilizing the public and the private sectors, providing productive and gainful employment for the unemployed, and giving priority to the development of capital goods industries
5. Decisively improving the level of agricultural productivity and output and related support institutionalism
6. Accelerating programs of agrarian reform and putting an end to unjust agrarian structures and systems of land tenure and use
7. Eliminating adult illiteracy, assuming by 1970, as a minimum, access to six years of primary education for each school-age child in Latin America; modernizing the educational system; developing research; and increasing the provision of trained personnel
8. Increasing life expectancy at birth by a minimum of five years and improving the levels of individual and public health; providing towards this end adequate potable water supply and sewage disposal to not less than 79 percent of the urban and 50 percent of the rural population; reducing by at least 50 percent the mortality rate of children under five years of age; controlling or eradicating illness and communicable diseases; upgrading national health levels, through the provision of trained personnel and scientific research efforts
9. Providing increased housing for low-income groups and replacing deficient and inadequate housing
10. Maintaining stable price levels to avoid inflation or deflation
11. Strengthening existing agreements on economic integration to accelerate the achievement of a Latin American common market
12. Strengthening cooperation to avoid excessive fluctuations in foreign exchange earnings derived from primary products exports, at the same time taking active steps to facilitate the access of Latin American exports to international markets.

That development was to be a matter of self-help was clearly built into the provisions of the Charter. Out of an anticipated total cost of $100 billion (U.S.) over the decade to fulfill these goals, Latin America obligated itself to supply $80 billion. The remaining $20 billion was to be supplied from outside, with the United States undertaking, in a variety of ways, to supply $1 billion a year in public funds.

The goals have undergone expected change as the dimension of the development confrontation have become apparent. For the 1970s, for instance, the needed over-all rate of development has been put at 8 percent. To accomplish this, per capita income must be increased by 42 percent in the 1970s and 62 percent in the 1980s. So far as the savings capacity of Latin America is concerned, Prebisch estimates that this must be increased from 18 percent to 26.5 percent to meet needed investment requirements (1970a, p. 2).

It must be emphasized again that Latin American development aspirations will not have been satisfied if they are not achieved within a democratized political framework. The fulfillment of the development goals implies an economic transformation inseparable from a democratized social and political framework—a transformation in which the number and power of Latin American entrepreneurs are decisively greater than the number and power of foreign entrepreneurs within Latin America. Sensitivity to foreign entrepreneurship as well as entrepreneurial limitations certainly make the regionalization of entrepreneurship an important qualitative indicator of development.[16]

One Region or Several Republics?

As should be expected, the Latin American countries differ in many respects. Table 1.1 illustrates wide differences in area, population, and gross domestic product (GDP) per capita. Beyond these are differences in geographical structure, local political settings, local historical backgrounds, population sizes and mix, economic and educational status, resources, and even linguistic backgrounds. Geographically, Latin America contains some of the highest mountains in the world and some of the flattest plains; some of the richest agricultural lands in the world as well as vast deserts; cool temperate climes and hot steamy jungles; solidly entrenched dictatorships achieving little by way of economic transformation and a few vitalizing democracies facing the confrontations of development with discipline and imagination; industrial complexes that are as sophisticated as any in the world and vast stagnant economic sectors; a multitude of some of the world's greatest intellectuals, scientists, and administrators and an alarmingly great number of people who need to be educated. Despite these differences, Latin America is a single, coherent economic region. The countries of the region share a common historic background, common traditions and cultural ties, and common economic problems and social aspirations—a Latin American identity which transcends the expected differences among the countires. Out of this common identity emerges a desire to regionalize development policies and to create a Latin America in which development is geared to human welfare and in which national development plans bring about uniform development for all sections of Latin American society.[17]

In the next chapter, we examine the population problem in Latin America—a problem the solution of which is described by Prebisch as one of the fundamental prerequisites to achieving an effective development policy.

---

[16]Cf. Plaza (1969, p. 2): "For the foreign investor, the message should be clear: the brightest opportunities lie in multinational joint ventures with Latin American participation." See also Sayigh (1964, pp. 9–13); and Leff (1968, pp. 59–76).

[17]See CEPAL (1969j).

TABLE 1.1

Area, Population, and Gross Domestic Product Per Capita

	Area (in square miles)	Estimates of total mid-year population, 1969 (in thousands)	Gross domestic product per capita, 1968 (in 1963 dollars)
Argentina	1,072,068	23,983	660
Barbados	166	254	420
Bolivia	424,163	4,804	135
Brazil	3,286,473	92,282	290
Chile	292,257	9,566	360
Colombia	439,513	20,463	280
Costa Rica	19,653	1,700	430
Dominican Republic	18,703	4,174	265
Ecuador	104,506	5,890	215
El Salvador	8,083	3,326	280
Guatemala	42,040	5,015	310
Haiti	10,714	4,768	75
Honduras	43,277	2,495	250
Mexico	759,530	48,933	470
Nicaragua	53,668	1,904	360
Panama	29,208	1,417	565
Paraguay	157,047	2,314	215
Peru	494,293	13,172	300
Trinidad and Tobago	1,980	1,039	815
Uruguay	72,172	2,852	530
Venezuela	347,029	10,035	905

Source: Inter-American Development Bank (1969a).

CHAPTER 2

DEMOGRAPHY AND DEVELOPMENT

The poorest continents and countries in the world have, on the whole, the highest rates of population increase, as Table 2.1 indicates. Latin America is outstanding among them. It is difficult to anticipate any change in the demographic explosion in the foreseeable future. Given the present development status of Latin America, the absolute size of the population and its present rate of increase determine the speed with which economic development must be accelerated. If matters continue at the present demographic pace, Latin America faces a disastrous deterioration of its already depressingly low standard of living, unless two conditions are fulfilled to counteract the situation: (1) the birth rate must decline, and (2) per capita incomes must increase dramatically. The historical experience of developed countries indicates that the former followed the latter. In the complex world of population dynamics, it is difficult to establish with certainty what will arrest demographic disaster. The economic evolution of developed countries, however, demonstrates that an industrial revolution did accompany a dramatic increase in the population and that lower birth rates eventuated under conditions of sustained growth. In Latin America, as in most developing countries, modern health science has led to a dramatic reduction in mortality rates without any appreciable reduction in birth rates, generating an increase in population long before any significant change in the structure of the economy or in aggregate output. The population problem obviously complicates the problem of development.

Overpopulation is, of course, relative to the state of development. An argument could be adduced that there are potentialities for development in Latin America which make the prospect for the population–total output relationship far more optimistic than it appears to be at present. We will later examine in detail these potentialities. Our concern now is with the contemporary problem of increasing the aggregate economic output. Such an increase, which would enable Latin America to enjoy a rising per capita income sufficient to make a decisive change from the present quality of living, is functionally dependent on new combinations or new injections of technical knowledge, capital accumulation, and labor. GNP per capita is admittedly not a comprehensive development indicator; but clearly, other things being equal, economic performance must be such—in any society—that the rate of increase in output must continuously exceed the rate of population growth to give that society basic chances for progressive improvement in the quality of life. The redistribution of existing poverty cannot bring about this result. On the other hand, the sequence of increased output, increased income, increased savings, increased investment, increased output—dependent fundamentally on the quality of the population

12

and its innovational and productive genius—can be subverted by the quantity of the population.

A disproportionate increase in population in relation to the increase in total output negates the development effort in several ways. It pulls down per capita gains, leaving individual incomes where they were before or even less than before. Investment capital which could have been used to advance output must be diverted to meet the needs of the new population. The excessive population growth results in an increased dependency ratio and in general deterioration of the quality of life. Underemployment and unemployment increase or at least remain at the same level. Illiteracy increases absolutely if not relatively. It becomes more difficult to provide for improved education, housing, and health and, since per capita income is adversely affected, the utilization of domestic savings becomes a more difficult matter. From a development point of view, resources are wasted, the problem of transforming the economy to meet development goals becomes even greater, the brain drain out of the country gets a bigger push, and the disparity between life in the poor nations and that in the rich nations grows even wider.[1]

The continuing magnitude of the problem in Latin America can be readily illustrated. In 1955, the United Nations Economic Commission for Latin America (UNECLA), interpreting the acceleration of growth as meaning "that the income level attained by more developed countries should be approached more rapidly than at present," attempted to answer the question of whether the Latin American growth rate was satisfactory "in terms of the time required to attain that level" (1955, p. 11). Using one-third of the average per capita income in 1953 in the United States ($2000) as an attainable target "within a reasonable period of time", UNECLA estimated that it would take 42 years for the per capita Latin American income of $248 (at 1950 prices) to reach $666 if the Latin American average per capita income continued to grow at a rate of 2.4 percent a year. However, if the per capita income in the United States was assumed to continue to grow at 2.0 percent a year, it would take Latin America 252 years to reach one-third of the per capita income of the United States. This period could be shortened only by a decisive and determined acceleration of economic growth rates in Latin America together with a reduction in the growth rate of the population.

The implications of this situation were graphically brought out a decade later in the testimony of Dr. Alberto Lleras Camargo, former president of Colombia. Speaking on July 9, 1965, before the U.S. Senate Sub-Committee on Foreign Aid Expenditures on the effects of the population explosion to economic advance in Latin America, he observed:

As we know, the amount of goods and services that were available or were being produced in the developing countries prior to this burst of fertility has not grown at the same or even comparable rate. These countries that were making solid and in some cases surprisingly good progress, like the great majority of the Latin American republics, suddenly discovered new problems. There were not even

---

[1] See Meade (1967, pp. 233–242); Enke (1963, pp. 335–355); Currie (1967, pp. 25–38); Population Reference Bureau (1969); U.S. Department of State (1969a, pp. 1–3); and Ohlin (1967, pp. 53–60). Cf. Meade (1968, pp. 47–54).

TABLE 2.1
Selected Population Data and Selected Comparisons

	Population estimates mid-1970 (in millions)[a] (1)	Births per 1000 population[b] (2)	Deaths per 1000 population[b] (3)	Current rate of population growth (4)	Number of years to double population[c] (5)	Infant mortality rate (deaths under one year per 1000 live births)[b] (6)	Population under 15 years (in percent)[d] (7)	Population projections to 1985 (in millions)[a] (8)	Per capita gross national product (in U.S. dollars)[e] (9)	Population increase 1965-70 (in millions)[a] (10)
Latin America	283.f	38	9	2.9	24		42	435		37
Middle America	67	43	9	3.4	21		46	112		10.5
Costa Rica	1.8	45	8	3.8	19	70	48	3.2	410	0.3
El Salvador	3.4	48	13	3.4	21		45	5.9	270	0.5
Guatemala	5.1	46	16	2.9	24	89	46	7.9	310	0.7
Honduras	2.7	49	16	3.4	21		51	4.6	240	0.4
Mexico	50.7	44	10	3.4	21	64	46	84.4	490	8.0
Nicaragua	2.0	47	16	3.0	24		48	3.3	360	0.3
Panama	1.5	42	10	3.3	21	43	43	2.5	550	0.2
Caribbean	26	35	11	2.2	32		40	36		2.7
Barbados	0.3	29	9	0.8	88	54	38	0.3	420	0.01
Cuba	8.4	28	8	1.9	37	38	37	11.0	330	0.8
Dominican Republic	4.3	48	15	3.4	21	73	47	7.3	260	0.7
Guadeloupe[g]	0.4	32	8	2.4	29		42	0.5	470	0.04
Haiti	5.2	45	20	2.5	28		42	7.9	70	0.6
Jamaica	2.0	39	8	2.1	33	30	41	2.6	460	0.2
Martinique[g]	0.4	30	7	2.0	35		42	0.5	540	0.2
Puerto Rico[g]	2.8	25	6	1.4	50	28	39	3.4	1,210	0.03
Trinidad and Tobago	1.1	30	8	1.8	39	42	43	1.3	790	0.1

Tropical South America	151	39	9	3.0	24		43	236		20.8
Bolivia	4.6	44	20	2.4	29		44	6.8	170	0.5
Brazil	93.0	39	11	2.8	25	170	43	142.6	250	12.3
Colombia	21.4	44	11	3.4	21	78	47	35.6	300	3.3
Ecuador	6.1	47	13	3.4	21	90	48	10.1	210	1.0
Guyana	0.7	40	10	2.9	24	40	46	1.1	330	0.1
Peru	13.6	44	12	3.1	23	62	45	21.6	350	1.9
Venezuela	10.8	46	10	3.4	21	46	46	17.4	880	1.6
North America	228[f]	18	9	1.1	63		30	280		13.2
Canada	21.4	17.7	7.4	1.7	41	22.0	33	27.3	2,380	1.8
United States[h]	205.2	17.6	9.6	1.0	70	21.2	30	241.7	3,670	11.4
Africa	344.2	47	20	2.6	27		44	530		41
Asia	2,056[f]	38	15	2.3	31		40	2,874		223
Europe	462[f]	18	10	0.8	88		25	515		18
U.S.S.R.	242.6	17.9	7.7	1.0	70	26.5	28	286.9	970	12.1
Oceania	19[f]	25	10	2.0	35		32	27		2.0
World	3,632[i]	34	14	2.0	35		37	4,933		343

[a] Estimates from United Nations. World Population Prospects, 1965–85. As assessed in 1968, United Nations Population Division Working Paper No. 30, December 1969.

[b] Latest available year. Except for North American rates computed by PRB, world and regional estimates are derived from World Population Prospects (see Source note). The country estimates are essentially those available as of October, 1969 in United Nations Population and Vital Statistics Report, Series A, vol. 21, no. 4, with some adjustments that were necessary in view of the deficiency of registration in some countries.

[c] Assuming continued growth at current annual rate.

[d] Latest available year. Derived from World Population Prospects (see Source note) and United Nations Demographic Yearbook; 1967.

[e] 1967 data supplied by the International Bank for Reconstruction and Development.

[f] Regional population totals take into account small areas not listed on the Data Sheet.

[g] Nonsovereign country.

[h] United States figures are based on data from the U.S. Bureau of the Census and the National Center for Health Statistics. The total mid-year population has not been adjusted to accommodate the estimated 5.7 million "undercount" of the U.S. population in the 1960 census.

[i] Total reflects U.N. adjustments of discrepancies in international migration data.

N.B.: In general, for many of the developing countries, the demographic data including total population, age reporting and vital rates are subject to deficiencies of varying degrees. In some cases, the data are estimates of the United Nations Secretariat.

Source: Population Reference Bureau (1970).

*schools or hospitals, not enough land, insufficient food supplies, inadequate law
enforcement, and not even enough cemeteries to take care of the rising population. . . . the cities became breeders of hitherto unknown problems. Water
supplies, electric power, sewage systems, and telephone services—all were inadequate. . . . Latin America is breeding misery, revolutionary pressure, famine, and
many other potentially disastrous problems in proportions that exceed our
imagination even in the age of thermonuclear war.* [2]

Only a massive and unprecedented acceleration of economic growth involving
a revolutionary transformation of the economy, of values, and of the social and
political structure, accompanied by a fall in the birth rate, can significantly
ameliorate the situation. Population indicators in Latin America are, in fact,
basic indicators of the quality of life in Latin America which must be immediately
transformed through development. We will look now at the general indicators of
the status and performance of the Latin American economy in relation to the
complex population problems. Although the official figures vary widely, they
illustrate respective relative situations.

THE POVERTY LINE

It is assumed that a country with an average per capita GNP of $500 dollars (U.S.)
can be regarded as poor. This figure is less than 14 percent of the 1968 U.S. per
capita GNP of $3,670. [3] If a per capita GNP of $500 is used as a criterion,
Latin America with its per capita GNP of $418 is clearly very poor. [4] As the
selected figures in Table 2.1 show, the GNP per head ranges from a high of
$1210 for Puerto Rico and $880 for Venezuela to a low of $70 for Haiti. Except
for Puerto Rico, Venezuela, Panama, Martinique, Trinidad and Tobago, Argentina, and Uruguay, the GNP per capita of every Latin American country is
below the $500 figure. Even in Puerto Rico, the GNP per capita was less than
one-third that of the United States. Brazil, the giant of Latin America in terms
of size and population, has a GNP of $250 per head, lower than that of El
Salvador, which has the smallest area in Spanish Latin America. Obviously, the
level of development indicated by the per capita GNP can hardly satisfy the
revolution of rising expectations.

Growth of GNP, Population, and Per Capita Product

The depressing effect of the rate of population growth on the per capita product
of Latin America can readily be demonstrated. Table A.1 (in the Appendix)
shows that for the period 1950–55, the average annual percentage change in the
total GNP of Latin America slightly exceeded that of the developed countries
including the United States and almost equalled that of the developed countries
excluding the United States. The rate of population growth was, however, nearly
three times that of the developed countries, a situation which resulted in a lower

[2] U.S. Senate (1967a, pp. 108–109).
[3] Figure taken from Organization for Economics Cooperation and Development (1970,
   p. 22).
[4] This figure (in U.S. dollars and at constant 1966 prices) is for 1967 and for 18 Latin
   American republics. See U.S. Department of State (1968c, p. 9). The figures given in
   this document vary from the figures supplied in Table 2.1. This is a problem which only
   further research can resolve.

average annual percentage change in the GNP per capita for Latin America as compared with the developed countries. For 1950-55, for instance, despite the fact that the average percentage change for Latin America was 5.1 and for developed countries including the United States was 4.7, the percentage change in GNP per capita for Latin America was only 2.3 percent as against 3.5 percent for the developed countries including the United States. The indicators for 1967 are even more interesting. In that year the total GNP of Latin America increased by 4.5 percent as against 3.4 percent for the developed countries including the United States. Despite a superior rate of economic advance, however, the differences in the population growth rates were such—3.0 percent for Latin America as against 1.1 percent for developed countries—that the percentage change in the GNP per capita for Latin America was only 1.5 percent as against 2.4 percent for the developed countries including the United States. Latin America's rate of population increase for the period 1960–68, as Table 2.2 indicates, remained higher than the rates for Africa, Asia, and Europe. But per capita product for Latin America for the same period, as shown in Table 2.3, expanded at a rate less than one-third that of Europe and at a slower rate than that of Asia. The growth rate of Latin America's GNP for the period 1961–67 averaged 4.5 percent a year—as compared with a rate of 4.3 percent for the countries of the Organization for Economic Cooperation and Development (OECD).[5] With an average growth rate of the GNP of 5.7 percent in 1968 and 5.8 percent in 1969, the growth of the Latin American economy remained superior to that of the OECD countries which registered a rate of 5.7 percent in 1968 and 5 percent in 1969.[6] However, though per capita product for Latin America increased by 2.9 percent in 1969, higher than the rate

TABLE 2.2

Rate of Population Increase in Developing Countries by Regions (In percent)

	1960–65	*1966*	*1967*	*1968*
Africa, total	2.4	2.5	2.6	2.6
North of Sahara	2.6	2.6	2.8	(2.8)
South of Sahara	2.3	2.5	2.5	2.5
Latin America, total	2.9	2.9	2.9	2.9
North and Central	3.3	3.3	3.3	3.3
South	2.8	2.8	2.8	2.8
Asia, total	2.6	2.5	2.6	2.6
Middle East	2.6	2.5	2.7	2.7
South Asia	2.6	2.5	2.5	2.5
Far East	2.7	2.7	2.7	2.7
Europe	1.4	1.4	1.5	(1.5)
Over-all Total	2.5	2.5	2.5	(2.4)

Source: OECD Development Centre quoted in Society for International Development (1970).

[5]Calculations by AID are reported by Pan American Union (1969b). Felipe Herrera (1970, p. 2) puts the Latin American figure at 4.7 percent.
[6]Once again the problem of a precise figure. CEPAL (1970c) gives figures for Latin America of 6.1 percent for 1968 and 6.4 percent for 1969.

TABLE 2.3

Per Capita Product by Main Developing Regions (In percent)

	1960–65	1966	1967	1968	1960–68
Africa, total	1.0	-0.3	1.1	1.3	0.8
North of Sahara	-0.3	-2.6	1.1	2.5	-0.06
South of Sahara	1.6	0.9	2.0	0.7	1.5
Latin America, total	1.7	1.5	1.4	2.5	1.7
North and Central	3.5	3.8	2.7	3.2	3.4
South	1.4	0.3	0.6	2.2	1.3
Asia, total	2.1	2.2	4.9	3.0	2.6
Middle East	5.0	3.6	4.9	6.5	5.0
South Asia	1.0	0.2	6.7	2.2	1.7
Far East	2.7	4.7	2.0	2.4	2.8
Europe	6.0	7.1	2.1	3.5	5.3
Over-all total	2.4	2.3	2.8	2.6	2.5

Source: OECD Development Centre quoted in Society for International Development (1970).

of 1.8 percent for the period 1961-67, it was inferior to the per capita growth in OECD countries.

In 1968 and 1969 the rate of growth in per capita product of Latin America actually exceeded the 2.5 percent minimum target set by the Alliance for Progress. Indeed, as shown in Table 2.4, Mexico, Nicaragua, Panama, and Trinidad and Tobago achieved over the period 1961-69 per capita rates of growth superior to the 2.5 percent goal of the Alliance. But no other Latin American country did so. For Latin America as a whole, with a population growth rate averaging 2.8 percent over the period, the average annual rate of increase of per capita product from 1961-69 was only 1.9 percent, an achievement well below the Alliance goal.[7] In view of the immediate pressure of popular expectations for a better level of living and the uncertainties to be overcome in order to meet these expectations, the case for limiting the birth rate in Latin America is obvious.

Using the Simple Seventy Rule to calculate the length of time required for growth rates to double, we arrive at a number of interesting approximations for Latin America in terms of time perspective.[8] Given a 2.3 percent increase in the per capita product between 1950-55 (see Table A.1), it would take a little more than 30 years to double the product per head. With the per capita product increment of 2.1 percent achieved between 1955-60 and 1.7 percent between 1960-65, it would take respectively 33.4 and 42 years to double the per capita product. With the per capita product increase of 1.4 percent achieved between 1966-67, it would take 50 years to double the per capita product. European

---

[7]The reader may wish to refer to Kindleberger (1965, pp. 269-291). See also Urquidi (1968, pp. 2-8).

[8]See Urquidi (1968, p. 5). The reader may also refer to Suits (1970, pp. 128-129) for a brief review of the Simple Seventy Rule.

TABLE 2.4

Growth of Per Capita Product, 1961–69

	Percentage increase		Percentage increase
Argentina	1.9	Honduras	2.0
Bolivia	2.6	Mexico	3.2
Brazil	1.9	Nicaragua	3.4
Chile	1.7	Panama	4.3
Colombia	1.5	Paraguay	1.4
Costa Rica	2.3	Peru	2.3
Dominican Republic	-0.8	Trinidad and Tobago	3.3
Ecuador	1.1	Uruguay	-1.1
El Salvador	2.2	Venezuela	1.1
Guatemala	1.9	*Total: Latin America*	1.9
Haiti	-0.6		

Source: Inter-American Development Bank (1969a, p. 2).

countries, however, with average annual per capita growth rates of 6 percent in the period 1960–65 could double their per capita product in under 12 years. Latin America with an average per capita increase of 1.9 percent over the period 1961–69 (see Table 2.4) would double the per capita product in just under 37 years. On the other hand, the population, growing at nearly 3 percent per annum, would double itself in under 24 years. Other things being equal, a lower rate of population increase would obviously give Latin America a better chance to achieve a higher economic growth rate in a shorter time.

POPULATION VERSUS POTENTIALITIES

It is possible to explain, as Stycos does, the paradox of the Latin American population problem as rooted in the incapacity of the Latin American culture to exploit an immense territory and its considerable natural resources for the benefit of a relatively "small population" (1968, p. 2). The development of Latin American potentialities through the expansion of the frontier is a permanent part of the Latin American dream. Three matters, however, must be taken into account: (1) There is no comprehensive and accurate quantification of these potentialities or of the cost of developing them now; (2) The development of these potentialities is a long-run proposition; and (3) An economic growth rate of 8 percent a year is a goal for the 1970s and not a realized rate of advance for the 1960s. Other things being equal, these developments may yet take place. We cannot presume to have reached the end of technological and organizational revolutions in economic life. But on present evidence, Latin American demographic expansion weakens further an economic situation described by Prebisch as one of "dynamic insufficiency" (1970, p. 2).

We have already indicated that the Latin American population is growing at a rate of approximately 2.9 percent a year. This is almost three times the current rate of growth of the population of the United States and, over three and one-half times the current rate of growth of the population of Europe (see Table 2.1).

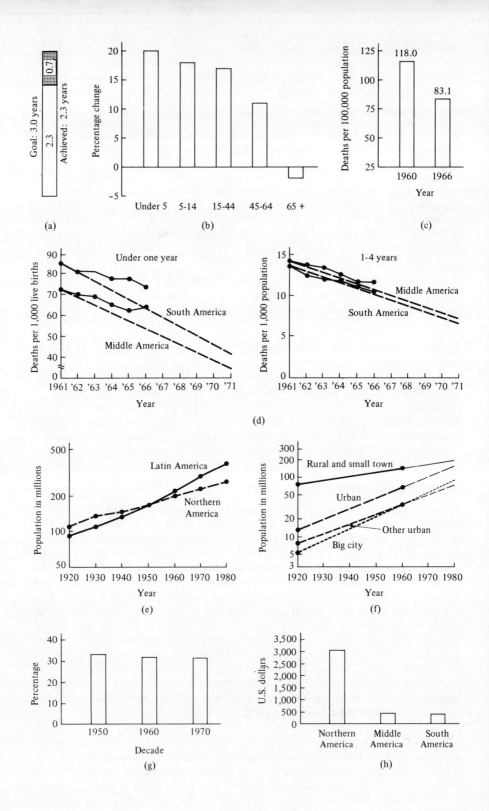

Goal: 3.0 years
Achieved: 2.3 years
2.3
0.7

(a)

Percentage change

20

15

10

5

0

-5

Under 5   5-14   15-44   45-64   65 +

(b)

Deaths per 100,000 population

125

100

75

50

25

118.0

83.1

1960   1966

Year

(c)

Deaths per 1,000 live births

90
80
70
60
50
40
0

Under one year

South America

Middle America

1961 '62 '63 '64 '65 '66 '67 '68 '69 '70 '71

Year

Deaths per 1,000 population

15

10

5

0

1-4 years

Middle America

South America

1961 '62 '63 '64 '65 '66 '67 '68 '69 '70 '71

Year

(d)

Population in millions

500

200

100

50

Latin America

Northern America

1920 1930 1940 1950 1960 1970 1980

Year

(e)

Population in millions

300
200
100
50
20
10
5
3

Rural and small town

Urban

Other urban

Big city

1920 1930 1940 1950 1960 1970 1980

Year

(f)

Percentage

40

30

20

10

0

1950   1960   1970

Decade

(g)

U.S. dollars

3,500
3,000
2,500
2,000
1,500
1,000
500
0

Northern America   Middle America   South America

(h)

It is also over two and one-half times the rate of growth of the population of mainland China. As Table 2.1 shows, the average rate of growth of the Latin American population far exceeds the average rate of growth of the total world population. By present projections, the rate of growth of the Latin American population is likely to increase to 3.5 percent a year by the year 2000.[9]

This rapid population growth reflects the net results of a dramatic fall in the mortality rates (see Figure 2.1) without a corresponding reduction in the birth rate. Mortality rates fell dramatically as a result of the introduction of modern health techniques into Latin America after 1915, principally by the Rockefeller Foundation and the Pan American Health Organization, assisted by American foreign aid and domestic Latin American agencies. The result was that in a country like Costa Rica mortality rates fell by 50 percent within 20 years—a reduction which took Britain, starting in the eighteenth century, over 150 years to accomplish.

In Costa Rica, as shown in Table 2.1, the death rate is 8 per thousand population, lower than the 9.6 per thousand population of the United States. On the other hand, the birth rate in Costa Rica is over two and one-half times that of the United States. Yet Costa Rica's per capita income in 1967 was one-ninth that of the United States and the growth rate of the economy for the whole period 1961–67 fell below the minimum goals set by the Alliance for Progress. Indeed, according to some calculations, Costa Rica's population growth rate could be set as high as 4.5 percent a year while the death rate per thousand population may be the even lower figure of 7. Within a century, its present population of around 1.8 million, given the current rate of advance, may increase to 75 million, 44 times the present total.[10] In Mexico, the annual net addition to the population more than doubled over a period of 20 years. In 1939, there were 865,000 births and 446,000 deaths, giving a net addition to the population of 419,000. By 1959, with fewer deaths and twice as many births, the net addition to Mexico's population totaled 1,195,000.

In Latin America, as a whole, the Ten Year Health Program brought about, after only five years, significant reductions in the mortality rates among children 1–4 years of age, reducing these rates between 1961–66 by 17.1 percent in

[9]Ohlin (1967, p. 22).
[10]See also Denton (1969, pp. 43–45); Pan American Union (1969a).

FIGURE 2.1 (opposite)
General Indices of Health Progress, Population Growth, Percentage of Economically Active Population, and Per Capita National Income in Latin America from 1960
Health Progress:
(a) Increase in life expectancy; (b) Percentage decrease in death rates by age; (c) Reduction in death rates from infectious diseases (per 100,000 population); (d) Decreases in child mortality [Dashed lines indicate the projected decreases wanted in Latin America and Middle America; the solid lines indicate the actual decreases over the past decade]
Population Growth:
(e) Growth of population in Northern and Latin America; (f) Growth of urban and rural populations in Latin America
Economically Active Population:
(g) Percentage of population economically active in Latin America
Per Capita National Income:
(h) Per capita national income in the three regions of the Americas, 1966

Middle America and 23.3 percent in South America. The mortality rates for infants fell by 11.1 and 12.3 percent, respectively, between 1961-66 (see Table A.2). Though these reductions fall short of the goals set by the Alliance for Progress, steady advancement is being made toward these goals. It is estimated that a minimum of 999,000 children under 5 years of age die annually in Latin America. If death rates in this group were the same as those for the United States, the figure would only have been 258,000. In other words, 741,000 or more of these deaths are preventable, which would make for further increases in the rate of population growth.[11]

Consequences of Population Growth

Apart from depressing the per capita product, three major consequences follow the current rate of growth in the net population of Latin America—with serious implications for economic development. First, the absolute numbers of the Latin American population are expected to expand so rapidly that in the year 2000 the total population, according to the U.N. projections in Table 2.5, will be almost twice that of North America and certainly much greater than that of Europe. Estimates in Table 2.5 show that in mid-1970 the population of Latin America exceeded that of North America by 55 million. In the year 2000, calculated on the basis of constant fertility rates, the excess of Latin America's present population over that of North America would become some 368 million. Latin America's mid-1970 total population is 179 million less than that of Europe. By 2000, it is projected that the Latin American population will exceed that of Europe by some 185 million. The projections in Table A.3 differ slightly but support the picture in more detail. The contemporary position is that the Latin American population doubles every 24 years. Compared with this, the population of North America doubles every 63 years, that of Europe every 88 years, and the world population, at current rates of growth, every 35 years. The Costa Rican population doubles the fastest in the world—every 19 years.

A second consequence of the rate of growth of the present net population is the increase in the dependency ratio, that is, the number and proportion of the population under 15 and over 64, if the potentially productive population is defined as the population between the ages of 15 and 64. As shown in Table 2.1, 42 percent of the Latin American population is under 15 years old as against 30 percent of the population of North America. Again, approximately 5.7 percent of the Latin American population is 60 years or older and 1.2 percent is 75 years or older in comparison with an estimated 13 percent and 3.1 percent, respectively, for North America. Except for Uruguay, Argentina, Barbados, Puerto Rico, Chile, and Cuba, over 42 percent of the population of every country in Latin America consists of children under 15 years old. Honduras with 51 percent, has the largest proportion of children to adults not only in Latin America but in the world.[12]

The low ratio of adults to the total population puts a burden on the adults

---

[11] Pan American Health Organization (1968a, p. xii). From the estimates made, 680,000 of the 999,000 deaths are under one year of age; 450,000, or two-thirds of them, are excess deaths. Of the 319,000 deaths which occur in the 1–4 age group, 291,000 are preventable—that is, more than 90 percent.

[12] CEPAL figures differ somewhat from those in Table 2.1: 38 percent for Haiti as against 42 percent, for example, and 47.8 percent for Honduras and 48.2 percent for Nicaragua. See CEPAL (1969c).

TABLE 2.5

World and Regional Population (In millions)

	World	Africa	Asia	North America	Latin America	Europe	Oceania	U.S.S.R.
Mid-1970	3,632	344	2,056	228	283	462	19	243
Projection for 2000, U.N. constant fertility	7,522	860	4,513	388	756	571	33	402
Projection for 2000, U.N. medium estimate	6,130	768	3,458	354	638	527	32	353

Source: Population Reference Bureau (1970).

to maintain the GNP and to divert their savings to support the increasing number of children. The GNP per capita, other things being equal, tends to remain depressed. The burden on the adult population could be relieved somewhat, of course, by the recruitment of additional children into the labor force. It is estimated that some 5 percent of the total active population of Latin America is made up of children in the age group 10–14, a ratio equal to 15 percent of all the children in this age group.[13] Given the low income levels and the need to survive, these children have no choice. But the use of child labor adversely affects the long-run productivity potential of the economy, since longer years of education mean a better trained and a more productive worker. The question of education and its effect on Latin American economic development will be considered in greater detail later in this book.

The depressant effect of the dependency ratio becomes clearer when we examine labor force participation rates. The number of people working, willing to work, able to work, and looking for work is always less than the total labor force. Labor participation rates differ at various age levels, between sexes, and of course under differing conditions and time periods.[14] In Latin America, the ratio of the economically active population has remained fairly stable, amounting to 34 percent of the total population in 1950 and 33 percent in 1960 (see Figure 2.1). The estimate remained unchanged for 1965 and for 1970. The economically active population grows at 2.9 percent a year, almost the same rate as the general population. Thus, one-third of the population produces in order to support the whole population. Put another way, one active worker supports two inactive people in Latin America. A lowering of the dependency ratio, through lowered fertility and reduction in the number of children under 15, would improve the ratio of the active population and, other things being equal, raise per capita gains. The low per capita output is related to another ingredient in the situation. Although, as Figure 2.2 shows, the ratio of the labor force in agriculture has declined from 50 percent in 1950 to an estimated 44 percent in 1970, the fact is that the majority of the labor force—with the inevitable problem of a high dependency ratio—is still concentrated in agriculture. Yet output in agriculture remains lower than in any other sector. The low per capita output in the backward agricultural sector, in turn, drags down the average per capita gain for the whole economy.

[13]UNECLA (1968a, p. 19).
[14]See Fleischer (1970, pp. 72–90).

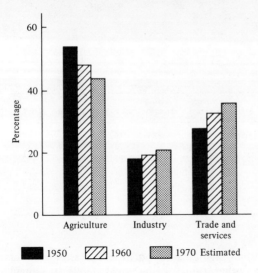

FIGURE 2.2
Percentage Distribution of Labor Force by Sector in Latin America
Source: Pan American Health Organization (1968b, p. 5).

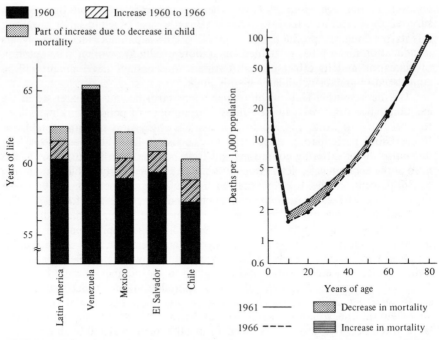

FIGURE 2.3
Increases in Life Expectancy in Four Countries and in Latin America
Source: Pan American Health Organization (1968b, p. 46).

FIGURE 2.4
Changes in Death Rates by Age in Latin America, 1961–66
Source: Pan American Health Organization (1968b, p. 46).

The third and expected concomitant of the rate of growth of the net population is that public health measures associated with the dramatic fall in mortality rates have brought about a significant extension of life expectancy in most countries of Latin America as Figures 2.1, 2.3, 2.4, and Table A.4 show. Uruguay and Barbados, for instance, enjoy life expectancies of 69.2 and 69 years, respectively. Argentina, Costa Rica, Panama, Trinidad and Tobago, and Venezuela have life expectancies of over 63 years. Longer life expectancies in principle mean longer years of contribution to economic output. But in Latin America longer life expectancy tends to maintain the output–population ratio (since in these countries a greater number of old people does not correspond to a greater output). Women withdraw early from the active labor force. Two-thirds of the female labor force begins to withdraw before the age of 35.[15]

POPULATION GROWTH, TECHNICAL PROGRESS, AND PER CAPITA INCOME

Up to this point we have been considering the effect of rapid population growth on average per capita income in Latin America. The relationship between population and economic development brings to mind the old question of the chicken and the egg. Does economic development influence the rate of population growth or does population growth influence the rate of development?[16] The question becomes more complicated if the growth of population is ignored on the assumption that increased investment and technical progress are really the key strategic determinants for achieving, say, an 8 percent annual rate of growth in aggregate Latin American output, with the very satisfactory per capita gain of 5 percent. There is no end to the possibilities for debate about what comes before what. However, although no finite evidence exists of an axiomatic correlation between the rate of population growth and the rate of economic growth, empirical evidence suggests that the rate of population increase in Latin America does retard the rise in per capita income.[17] Simple subtraction of the rate of population increase from the rate of increase in aggregate output, $(\Delta y/y) - (\Delta p/p)$, gives the unsatisfactory result of 1.9 percent as the average per capita product for Latin America for the period 1961-69.

Yet the savings–investment coefficients for the period were not unsatisfactory as judged by comparing the indicators for developing and developed countries. Average savings and investment rates for Latin America for the period 1960-67 equaled the rates for developing countries, while the average savings–investment ratio exceeded that of all developing countries.[18] Again, only three countries in Latin America had a rate of capital formation of less than 15 percent during the period 1961-67.[19] But the rate of population growth modifies the picture in the following way. Assume a marginal capital–output ratio of 4:1.[20] With a population

[15]UNECLA (1968a, p. 20).

[16]See Coale and Hoover (1958, pp. 9–28). See also Kuznets (1960, pp. 337–338).

[17]See Hagen (1968, pp. 247–271).

[18]See Inter-American Development Bank (1969a, pp. 62–63).

[19]Guatemala, Haiti, Uruguay.

[20]The marginal capital–output ratio is the ratio of extra additions to the stock of capital in relation to the extra output secured by that addition. See Van Arkadie and Frank (1966, pp. 297–299); Tinbergen (1958, pp. 70–76); and Byé (1963, pp. 110–124).

growth of 3 percent a year, net savings and investment would have to be at least 12 percent of the total product to maintain the same per capita income for the increased population. A higher per capita income would require more than 12 percent. If we add another 3–5 percent to take care of depreciation, then the 15 percent rate of capital formation does not make much immediate difference, if any, to per capita gains. The gains from a lower rate of population growth can be demonstrated very simply. If population growth were 1 percent and the marginal capital-output ratio 4:1, then the investment ratio need only be 4 percent of total product to maintain per capita income at the same level. An investment of 12 percent, with a population growth rate of 1 percent, would obviously mean a tremendous advance in per capita gains. The effect of population growth in Latin America obviously introduces a difference in the per capita gains from a savings–investment ratio as high as 15 percent. It is obvious that with the present population growth rate, an increasing share of scarce capital must be invested merely to keep per capita income where it is.

Historical evidence points to no permanently valid relationship between population growth rates and economic growth rates. In industrialized countries, however, high rates of population growth and high industrial growth rates did go together until the point of demographic transition was reached. In Latin America, as a result of public health measures, population expanded rapidly before the start of the structural transformation associated with rapid advance of the economy. The net population increased; the per capita product did not. This was not because the economy did not advance at rates which compared favorably with the rates in developed countries, but because the population of Latin America grows much faster than the population in the advanced countries.

This is all, of course, a first approximation in the explanation of the Latin American situation. We could very well have put the blame on the slow change in the rate of technical progress and on all the variables associated with accelerated economic growth. But, population in Latin America outdistanced the rate of output long before the onset of the structural shifts associated with economic modernization.[21]

Prospects for Population Growth

The prospects for a reduction in the rate of population expansion in Latin America are not easily determinable. In order to evaluate these prospects, we

---

[21]Cf. Kuznets (1960, pp. 337–338):

By definition [underdeveloped countries] suffer from an acute shortage of capital, not only for material investment but also for adequate raising and education of their younger generation; and the whole structure of their society is unfavorable to the adoption of many potentials of modern technology, since it necessitates major changes that no living society can absorb within a short period. It is, therefore, unrealistic to assume that population increase in an underdeveloped country is followed by the adequate investment in both human beings and material capital, by the advantages of greater mobility, and by the stimulus of a wider and more responsive market associated with population increase in developed countries and which contribute to greater product per capita. This is particularly true in view of the actual (or threatening) acceleration of rates of national increase in the underdeveloped countries, resulting from the maintenance of, or even slight rise in, the already high birth rates combined with the remarkably rapid reduction in death rates made possible by recent revolutionary changes in public health and control of diseases.

will first summarize the causes of the rapid expansion and then attempt to give a brief account of the attempts to limit fertility.

As has been indicated, the spread of public health measures in Latin America increased the net population by a dramatic reduction in the death rate, a reduction not balanced by a corresponding reduction in the birth rate. The death rate is likely to fall still further because of the persistent dedication of the Pan American Health Organization and Latin American domestic public health agencies. It is difficult, however, to forecast changes in the birth rate because health measures reinforce attitudes and factors which persistently support high birth rates in Latin America. These factors are Latin American nationalism, the vanity of machismo, religious beliefs, the dependence–in–reverse attitude, illiteracy, and the deteriorating environment of the cities.

Nationalism generates considerable ideological resistance to family planning efforts. On the one hand, there are Latin Americans who regard family planning as another imperialist imposition to keep Latin America colonial. Under this assumption, large populations are somehow equated with the possibility of a bigger voice in world affairs. On the other hand, nationalism supports the necessity for a large population to conquer the vast empty spaces of Latin America (see Map 2.1) and, at the same time, create through numbers a larger internal market. The equating of population rise to world power is a difficult thesis to uphold in a world where economic power may be necessary to support political leverage in world affairs. The conquest of the empty spaces of Latin America still awaits researched assessment of the possibilities. It could be that, in time, the mythical wealth of the empty spaces of Latin America would become actual reality. The passion for development accompanied by appropriate technology, capital, entrepreneurship, and social organization may eventually conquer the frontiers as happened in the United States. Solving the development problems of Latin America is, however, an immediate issue.

The question of colonizing the empty lands will be considered later in this book. For the present, three practical deterrents may be noted. The first is the scarcity of trained personnel to meet the administrative, organizational, and technical requirements of the situation. The second is the absence of infrastructure, reflecting, of course, the over-all scarcity of capital. The third problem is the uncertainty of the degree to which reverse immigration away from the coast can be stimulated. The evidence on the cost of settling new lands is slim. The Inter-American Development Bank (IDB) reported in 1966 that total expenditures of $20,000 (U.S.) to $30,000 (U.S.) per family were "not infrequent in such programs." Averages for nonirrigated projects appeared to be lower—about $5000 (U.S.) to $10,000 (U.S.) per family.[22] There is little information, however, on the rate of return over the costs. Theoretically, adding increasing amounts of land and labor where capital is scarce results in diminishing returns after a time. But this theoretical limitation can be reversed or avoided by technological progress. To anticipate the future in technological progress is foolhardy. The important point is that the development of the empty lands of Latin America is not an immediately viable proposition offering an instant solution to the problem of a low average per capita income. Long-term

[22]Inter-American Development Bank (1966, p. 47).

hope, rather than immediate reality, is a significant factor supporting high birth rates in Latin America.[23]

Machismo is another factor supporting high rates of population growth in Latin America. To be *muy macho* is to be very masculine and very virile.

---

[23]See also U.S. Senate (1967b, pp. 8–11). See also Bell and Todaro (1969, pp. 375–399), and Stycos (1969, pp. 2–6).

MAP 2.1
Population Density of Latin America (City populations based on 1965 data)
Source: Chase Manhattan Bank (1967a).

Machismo demands proof in terms of fathering large families. Machismo is regarded as a widespread lower class compulsion in Latin America. Again, the large majority of Latin Americans are Catholic, and birth control by contraception is not an accepted doctrine. Further, the poor of Latin America, like the poor in many developed and developing countries, regard children as an economic asset. This dependence-in-reverse attitude is likely to persist in the absence of those social security levels which can come rationally only through increased productivity.

Two further factors which militate against reducing the growth of the net population are illiteracy and the deteriorating social environment of the towns. Despite the reduction of illiteracy from 47.9 percent in 1950 to 27 percent in 1970, as shown in Table 2.6, nearly 80 million Latin Americans are still illiterate. In many countries, the number of illiterates has increased in absolute numbers. Illiteracy, of course, affects the success of family planning education in obvious ways. In the cities and towns of Latin America, living conditions for significant proportions of the urban population continue to deteriorate because of the extremely rapid growth of the urban population (see Figure 2.5). This in turn creates a negative environment for birth control.

Population Growth and the Towns

The population of the rural areas of Latin America grows at a steady average of about 1.5 percent a year. The population of the cities, however, grows at a rate of about 7 percent a year, over twice the annual average growth rate of the population as a whole. The phenomenal urban growth rate results partly from the rate of natural increase in the towns and much more significantly from the massive immigration of the rural population into the towns and cities.[24] Map 2.1 indicates the demographic disequilibrium which characterizes the distribution of the Latin American population. Although estimates differ, taken together they give a relatively good picture of the astonishing expansion of the urban population. In 1950, it has been estimated, 25 percent of the Latin American population was urban while 75 percent was rural.[25] In 1960, the urban population had increased to 33 percent of the total population, the growth in the urban population between 1950-60 amounting to some 25.4 million people, according to the census count in 16 Latin American countries. In absolute terms, the increases were largest in Brazil (9.4 million), Mexico (4.2 million), Colombia (3.7 million), and Argentina (317 million), and smallest in Paraguay (100,000) and Honduras (100,000). Half of the new population of the cities over the decade 1950-60 were migrants from the rural areas.

The next decade witnessed even higher rates of urban population growth. An estimated 54 percent of the Latin American population was urbanized at the end of the 1960-70 decade. In one year, 1969-70, the urban population of

[24]The reader may wish to refer to: Inter-American Development Bank (1965a, pp. 97-100; 1968a, pp. 333-380); Chase Manhattan Bank (1967a, pp. 5-8); Dorselaer (1967, pp. 263-279); CEPAL (1970a).

[25]Inter-American Development Bank (1968a, p. 335). Localities with a minimum population of 20,000 or more are considered urban. But Chase Manhattan Bank (1967a, p. 5) gives the following figures: 1950 urban population estimated at 39 percent of the total population; 1950-60 urban population grew by 30 million.

TABLE 2.6
Literacy Rates

	Circa 1950	Circa 1960	1970[a]
Argentina	86.4 (1947)	91.4	94.0
Barbados	91.1 (1946)	98.2 (1967[a])	98.0
Bolivia	32.1	39.5	47.0
Brazil	49.3	60.5	71.0
Chile	79.8 (1952)	83.6	90.0
Colombia	49.4[a]	72.9 (1964)	78.0
Costa Rica	79.4	84.4 (1963)	89.0
Dominican Republic	42.9	64.5	70.0
Ecuador	57.7	67.5 (1962)	73.0
El Salvador	38.4	49.0 (1961)	58.0
Guatemala	29.4 (1951)	37.9 (1964)	45.0
Haiti	10.5	20.0 (1965[a])	24.0
Honduras	35.2	47.3	57.0
Mexico	55.9	62.0	73.0
Nicaragua	38.4	49.8 (1963)	60.0
Panama	69.0	76.6	83.0
Paraguay	65.8	74.6 (1962)	78.0
Peru	47.0[a]	61.1 (1961)	71.0
Trinidad and Tobago	73.9	88.4	93.0
Uruguay	85.0[a]	90.3 (1963)	93.0
Venezuela	51.0	63.3 (1961)	70.0
Latin America	52.1	66.8	73.0

[a] Estimate.

Source: Inter-American Development Bank (1969a, p. 137).

Venezuela increased by 5.6 percent (see Table A.5). In the period 1965–80 the Latin American urban population may possibly increase by over 100 million. As shown in Figure 2.5, close to 80 percent or more of the populations of Venezuela, Argentina, or Uruguay may be urbanized by 1980. One estimate suggests that, by 1980, 60 to 70 percent of the population of Latin America may be urbanized, the urbanized population then equaling the whole Latin American population in 1960.[26] Under a population pressure which outdistances the capacity of the cities to keep pace with the demand for adequate living conditions, overcrowding increases rapidly and an environment develops which accelerates the rate of population growth. Slum dwellers can hardly be expected to assume the burden of limiting the population. It is estimated that at least one-fifth of Latin America's population live in slums.

CONCLUSIONS

The picture of net population growth in Latin America is somewhat modified by low rates of population growth in a few Latin American countries, by compar-

[26] See Roberts (1969, p. 10).

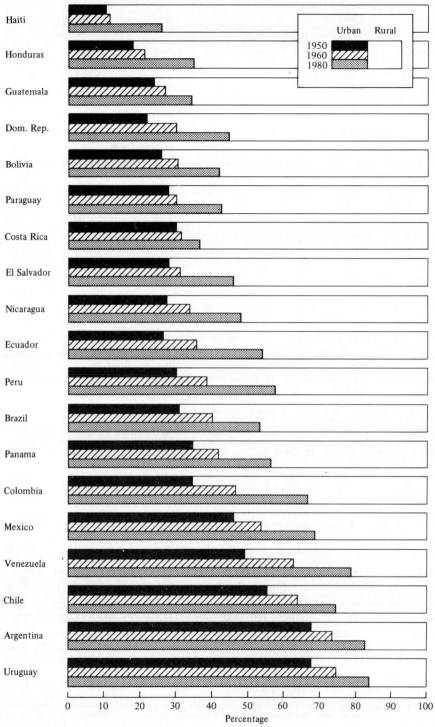

FIGURE 2.5
Percentages of Rural and Urban Population for 1950 and 1960 and Projection for 1980 (By countries)
Source: Population Reference Bureau, October 1969, p. 2.

atively low ratios of urban to total population in other places, and by the prospects for family planning. The population of Barbados increases only 0.9 percent a year; that of Uruguay 1.2 percent; Argentina 1.5 percent, and Puerto Rico 1.1 percent. The ratio of the urban to the total population is still below 30 percent in Bolivia, Haiti, and Honduras. Family planning clinics have been operating in Latin America since 1925, beginning with Mexico. By 1969 there were 882 such clinics, 65 percent in hospitals and governmental clinics. The fact that clinics are now established in every major country in Latin America represents a tremendous breakthrough.

Prospects for immediate limitation of the rate of population increase are not very good, however. Even if they were, there is no axiomatic correlation between low population growth and high output per capita. The per capita product of Argentina for the period 1961-68 averaged only 1.9 percent and that of Uruguay a negative 1.1 percent. Again, although the ratio of the urban to the total population was less than 30 percent in a few countries, the urban population in Haiti and Honduras, for instance, expanded in 1969-70 at rates of 3.8 percent and 5.2 percent, respectively. With regard to family planning efforts, it was estimated that of 55,432,000 women of childbearing age in the period 1965-69, only 690,120 (as Table A.6 shows) or 4.62 percent were protected against further reproduction. Enke reached the important conclusion for policy makers that economic resources of a given value which were devoted to slowing down population growth rather than accelerating production growth "could be 100 or so times more effective in raising per capita incomes in many L.D.C.s [less developed countries]."[27] He further calculated that an adequate birth control program in the less developed countries might cost as little as 10 cents per capita yearly. These are certainly remarkable findings. But their implementation as part of a general deliberate policy in Latin America is only a long-term possibility in view of the political and cultural barriers to family planning control.

We are dealing here with an area of great uncertainty. We assume that after a certain stage of industrial advance a demographic transition generally takes place with a decline in fertility rates catching up with the declines in mortality rates. It is clear that a decline in fertility rates, given the present Latin American population–resource balance, would mean a higher per capita income, giving Latin America a better chance to advance.[28] Modern health science clearly assists in lowering the mortality rate and, in many instances, may contribute to an increase in fertility rates. Since Latin American development has an immediacy about it, the question of how long it will take for reduced fertility rates to begin to be in balance with reduced mortality rates is important. According to Ohlin's data, this demographic transition in Europe was far from rapid.[29] In the case of Latin America, Table A.7 shows steadily declining birth rates for Argentina in the periods 1860-64 and 1955-59. The trend, however, is not that stable for the

[27]Enke (1966, p. 56). Julian L. Simon of Hebrew University and the University of Illinois reached basically similar conclusions (1970).

[28]The reader may refer to some basic general observations on population stability in relation to the "carrying capacity" of "spaceship Earth" in Boulding (1970, pp. 149–157). See also Kingsley Davis (1968, pp. 270–271).

[29]Ohlin (1967, p. 14).

other countries. In Venezuela, for example, estimated birth rates declined in the periods 1900–04 and 1920–24, but then began to rise again. There is a similar pattern for other countries in the table.

A clear conclusion can be drawn. The needs of the population are presently so vast and urgent that Latin America cannot wait for the long-term prospect of a reduced fertility rate, even if such a prospect could be forecast with certainty. Starving people cannot be persuaded to wait for the assumptions of a theory to be tested.[30] While experiments are being carried out to remove the inhibitions to the reduction of fertility rates, the Latin American determination to transform the present economic status of the region and eradicate mass poverty can be fulfilled only through the alternative path of intensifying the mobilization of human, material, and organizational resources for more rapid economic growth. Under the present population pressures, the impossible has to be made possible if an improvement in the standard of living is to be secured. Mexico, with a gross domestic product which expanded in the period 1961–68 at a rate of 6.8 percent a year, and with an average per capita product of 3.2 percent for that period, demonstrates so far that economic escape is possible through determined development.

Obviously, a lower fertility rate, other things remaining equal, would mean a higher per capita income, generating in turn (other things remaining equal) the usual sequence—more savings, more investment, more production, more income, more savings—breaking the vicious cycle of poverty (low income, low savings, low investment, low productivity, low income).[31] The numerical growth of the population is clearly a depressant, under present circumstances.

The analysis of population along with the three other economic fundamentals—natural resources, capital formation, and technology—does assist in identifying the dimensions of the development problem and the obstacles to more rapid development, and in working out what can be done to accelerate growth and development.[32] But analytical tools for Latin America, as has been pointed out, go beyond these fundamentals. Economic development in Latin America cannot be divorced from geography, or history, or indeed the whole social and institutional complex that is Latin America.

Therefore, in the next chapter we consider the geographical setting of Latin America, and in Chapter 4, the quality of the Latin American population.

[30] Cf. Samuelson (1961, p. 775): "history teaches us that men do not always starve quietly."
[31] See Nurkse (1955, pp. 4–5).
[32] See Samuelson (1961, p. 782).

CHAPTER 3

THE GEOGRAPHY OF ISOLATION
AND DISEQUILIBRIUM

Economists who follow the traditional analytical approaches to the discipline rather than common sense tend to ignore geography and so lose perspective on the major factors affecting a country's rapid development.[1] The geographical background of Latin America may not be so ignored for it is a prerequisite to any appreciation of the dimensions of the development problem. Geographical factors have an obvious original relationship to the amount and distribution of natural resources, the location of settlements, transportation costs, and the general level of economic activity. Geographical factors can support or obstruct development. In many instances, of course, geographical limitations may be temporary, because of the possible future changes in technical progress. But in the case of Latin America, forecasts for the future depend very much on the results of scientific research and the policies carried out on the basis of research findings.

GEOGRAPHY AS A CONSTRAINT

Geographical factors dominate the continent, as Map 3.1 clearly indicates. Geography, then, is an unavoidable constraint to economic development in Latin America. The physical and human geography of Latin America can, with reasonable accuracy, be described as a geography of isolation and disequilibrium. The situation undoubtedly complicates the development problem for Latin America. A physical cross-section of South America from the Pacific Coast in Peru to the Atlantic Coast in Brazil typifies the uneven distribution of physical features. Going from west to east, we find narrow, harborless desert coasts; complicated mountain barriers with few passes and equally complicated foothills; hot, wet, flood-ridden plains and basins; dry plateau country ending abruptly in sharp escarpment drops backing another narrow, though fertile, coastal plain.[2]

---

[1] For instance, Maritano and Obaid (1963, pp. 92–93): "The vastness and riches of Latin America can make the visitor, as well as the enthusiastic Latin politician, forget the vagaries of geography and its unfriendliness to man and progress. . . . [Physical and climatic] elements still are a handicap to development today." In addition to articles in the standard geographical journals, there are many texts dealing with geographical aspects of Latin America. The following are only a few which the reader may wish to consult: James (1959, pp. 18–30; 1964, pp. 3–32); Robinson (1967, pp. 1–41); Cole (1965); Whitbeck and Williams (1940, pp. 3–23); Hanson (1951, pp. 36–62); Alexander (1962, pp. 15–28); and Tannenbaum (1966, pp. 3–34).

[2] For instance, Hagen (1966, pp. 65–114). Valuable supplementary data can also be obtained from various Latin American governments and agencies.

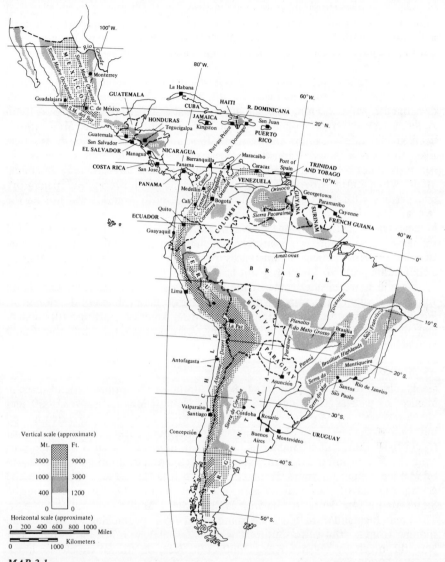

MAP 3.1
Physical Features of Latin America
Source: U.S. Department of State (1968b).

In terms of size, the total area of Latin America is an impressive 8 million square miles, more than twice the size of Europe. Two countries, namely, Brazil and Argentina, take up more than half the land area of South America, while Mexico dominates Central America. In the Caribbean CARIFTA countries, if we omit Guyana and British Honduras, Jamaica takes up more than half the area of the island archipelago. More important than size is the availability of immediately utilizable agricultural land, which in Latin America is severely limited by its physical features. Disequilibrium characterizes the distribution of arable land, of other natural resources, and of population, thus increasing transportation costs and adding to the difficulties of spatial planning and economic integration as envisaged under the Latin American Common Market (LACM).[3]

Latin America, of course, is historically accustomed to isolation. In relation to the developed world, Latin America was isolated by geography. South America, the greatest part of the land mass of Latin America, faces developing Africa, not developed Europe. So long as Spain and Portugal exercised hegemony over Latin America, the external geographical isolation was not noticeable. Mercantilism decreed mandatory sailings between the Iberian peninsula and South America. Even this was a hardy exercise of transporting goods over long stretches to a central point of collection in Panama, and sailings were in any case only an annual affair. When Latin America gained her independence, however, the mandatory connections with the Iberian peninsula ceased. South America was not on the regular Atlantic trade routes and its external isolation stood out as a clear fact. Modern transportation connections with North America and Europe have ended this external isolation. Air transportation has similarly modified internal isolation, but the geographical circumstances of Latin America make internal isolation a continuing problem which may not be solved in the immediate future.

We will now consider some of the principal physical characteristics of Latin America in order to gain some further perspective on the problem of development. We will look first at the spatial structure in Central America, starting with Mexico, and then at South America with passing references to the Caribbean island archipelago.

Mexico and Central America

Geographical features impose rather severe limitations on utilizable land space in Mexico, as well as affecting transportation. Half of Mexico is over 3000 feet above sea level; two-thirds consists of steep slopes. One-third of Mexico is level but even so the level land consists largely of intermont basins. In consequence of its configuration, half of Mexico is deficient in moisture. A great highland area from the American border to the Isthmus of Tehuantepec dominates the breadth of Mexico taking up some 30 percent of the total land area. Bordering the central plateau of the highland area, and part of the whole structure, are the Sierra Madre Occidental to the west and the Sierra Madre Oriental to the east. The great highland thrust is itself punctuated by a spectacular volcanic region running from northwest to southeast. The central plateau is not flat, broken as it is in the north by bolsons rising 3000–4000 feet, on top of which rise block ranges of 3000 feet. In the south, the mountain basins are as high as 7000–8000 feet and above these basins rise volcanoes of more than 18,000 feet. The borders of the plateau are split open by north-south streams, deep longitudinal valleys, and narrow gorges which make travel and penetration from the coast to the interior extraordinarily difficult. The Sierra Madre Occidental, over 100 miles in width, with peaks rising over 10,000 feet, is almost impassable. It firmly separates the highland from the Pacific. The Sierra Madre Oriental is hardly a less formidable barrier. The southern borders of the plateau are similarly dissected and terminate in steep scarp slopes standing up above the Pacific and the Isthmus

[3]For an extended investigation of this topic, the reader may consult Brown (1966).

of Tehuantepec. Northwest of the great highland is arid country of block mountains and basins. East of the highlands and south of Tampico, the broader coast continuing the Gulf Coast of Texas narrows out, squeezed out by big extensions of the Sierra Madre Oriental right up to the Isthmus of Tehuantepec. South of the flat isthmus is the dissected highland region of the Chiapas, with its crystalline ranges, rift valleys, block mountains, and stream dissection patterns.[4] Flat land is clearly at a premium in agricultural Mexico.

The mountainous terrain and the climatic pattern combine to split the population into lonely clusters dotted across this great country of nearly 760,000 square miles and 50 million people. Half the population of Mexico is concentrated therefore in the Central Region which accounts for only 14 percent of the total land area of Mexico and 20 percent of all the agricultural land. Even here the population is split up into separate clusters located in the seven separate inter-montane basins determined by the physical character of the surface configuration. Central Mexico is a focus for internal migration while mountainous southwestern Mexico remains underdeveloped and its inhabitants, because of the lack of surface communications, are practically unintegrated into the national economy. Southeast Mexico, an area of tropical rain forest, remains underpopulated while Lower California Sur is practically uninhabited.[5]

The cordillera dominating Central America induces similar isolation and transportation difficulties in almost all the Central American republics. In Guatemala, Indians live in small isolated centers in the innumerable basins of the highland. The Petén, as northern Guatemala is called, represents one-third of the national territory, but, flat though it is, the rain-forested Petén has a population of less than 1 percent of the total population of Guatemala. The Petén is agriculturally unproductive, because of poor soil.[6] The 200-mile stretch of Guatemala along the Pacific Coast has no natural harbors.

Highlands also dominate the geography of Honduras, producing the political and social isolation which is now under change. In the eastern part of the country, there are highlands of just under 10,000 feet. Around the capital, Tegucigalpa, peaks reach over 6000 feet above sea level, and in the north, despite lower heights, the terrain is equally rugged. Nearly two-thirds of Honduras is mountainous. Isolated clusters of people have been part of the social scene over long centuries. Indeed, much of northeastern Honduras is coming only slowly under national control. The Meskito savannas are part of the disputed common territory between Honduras and Nicaragua, but they are practically uninhabited. Even in colonial times, the road between Guatemala City and Nicaragua bypassed Honduras because of the steep highland climb, just as the Inter-American Highway does today.

In Nicaragua, although split by a northeast to southwest mountain chain, some 70 percent of the land area is potentially utilizable for agriculture. But only 30 percent is being used. Disease-ridden virgin forests and swamps near the

[4]For further details, see James (1959, pp. 594–649).
[5]Inter-American Development Bank (1966, pp. 271–272). The population density in Central Mexico is about 25 persons per square mile; but in Quintano Roo and Lower California the density is around 3.1 and 2.9 persons per square mile, respectively. See also Cline (1963, esp. pp. 37–67).
[6]Inter-American Development Bank (1966, pp. 271–272).

Atlantic make further development costly. Most of Nicaragua's population is in the western half of the country.

Between Panama and Colombia, the rugged, wet, rain-forested Darien Gap constituted a formidable obstacle to the completion of the Pan American Highway. The average estimated cost of completing 741 kilometers of the road over the Darien Gap was put at $321,000 (U.S.).[7]

The airplane and the determined road construction during the Alliance years, however, are steadily modifying the historic isolation of many Central American territories.[8]

South America

In South America, there are three dominant mountain systems. On the west coast, the Andes run southward for a distance of over 4000 miles from Panama to Tierra del Fuego, constituting the largest mountain barrier in the world and splitting the narrow coastal region from the rest of South America. Across the north of South America are the east-west Guyana Highlands, less formidable in height, but a separating barrier between much of northern South America and the Orinoco and Amazon lowlands. On the east coast, the Brazilian Highlands, bounded on one side by a steep, abrupt escarpment running north and south, leave only a narrow coast 30 to 60 miles in width between the scarp edge and the sea. This scarp edge is itself a formidable transportation barrier since it separates the coast from the vast interior plateau and the plains of Brazil and the rest of South America. Although approximately only 6 percent of South America is over 10,000 feet above sea level while over 60 percent of the continent is less than 1000 feet in elevation, the location of the mountainous areas is such that the vast interior plains of the Amazon and Orinoco suffer from severe drawbacks of climate and inaccessibility.

The Andean mountain system affects the economic development of every country in western South America. It contains the highest mountain in the Western hemisphere—Aconcagua in Argentina—which is over 23,000 feet and has at least 50 peaks of over 20,000 feet. The Andes average about 200 miles wide, reaching their broadest width of about 400 miles in the bleak altiplano region of Bolivia.[9] Passes are few and far between, and the most useful of them are over 10,000 feet above sea level.[10]

In Colombia, the Western, Central, and Eastern Cordillera, three massive ranges of the Andes, with their high river valleys, tablelands, and peaks over 18,000 feet, directly contribute to one of the most serious problems in Colombia, namely, internal transportation. The Inter-American Development Bank summed up this situation in 1966:

The Andean Zone where the bulk of the population is concentrated is isolated by high, unbroken mountain ranges that are almost insurmountable barriers to

[7]UNECLA (1969b, p. 236).
[8]For a more detailed background, see Kalijarvi (1962); Latin American Reports (1964).
[9]Estimates of the width of the Andes differ. Robinson (1967, p. 10), gives an estimate of nearly 300 miles as the maximum width. James (1959, p. 208), gives an estimate of approximately 400 miles.
[10]James (1959, p. 26).

the efficient movement of goods within the nation. The topographical factors that facilitate diversification of agricultural output have made it difficult to settle extensive regions east of the Andes, along the Pacific coast and in the lower Magdalena river valley. [11]

In Ecuador, the two ranges of the Andes split the country into three regions. The mountains reach heights of over three miles, with the intermont basins occupied by isolated clusters of people. The difficulties of communication are immense. The coast and mountain basins have practically no connection with the Oriente, the section east of the Andes, reinforcing the already complicated traditional problem of social cohesion in the country.

Peru is similarly split into three separate regions by the Andes. The narrow coastal plain in the "rain shadow" area of the Andes is practically a desert except where the rivers debouch into the sea. The Andes, some 200 to 250 miles wide in Peru, reach heights of 20,000 feet and more, and below the high levels are complicated canyons separating isolated valley sides. The lowest passes are 14,688 and 15,665 feet. Mountain and jungle impose natural limitations on the development of the Amazonian selvas (tropical forests) of Peru, although this region has potential and accounts for some 60 percent of Peru's area and most of its forest resources.

Bolivia is similarly affected by the Andes and is additionally isolated since it lost its Pacific Coast territory to Chile in the 1880s. The Andes are widest in Bolivia. The Western Cordillera, with its numerous volcanic peaks, the broad bleak altiplano, with average heights of 12,000 to 14,000 feet, and the Eastern Cordillera, reaching heights of over 21,000 feet, occupy the western half of Bolivia. Between the Eastern Cordillera and the Santa Cruz plains and Chaco lowlands of Bolivia is the rugged yungas country, deeply gorged by the Madeira and other rivers of the Amazon system. The rugged terrain is clearly a hindrance to communication and climatic factors contribute further to the country's isolation and economic stagnation.

Chile is a stringbean country stretching for some 2630 miles. Physical features and climatic factors also impose severe limitations on its economic development, rendering unusable some 75 percent of its nominal land area of 286,396 square miles. Northern Chile is no more than the Atacama Desert backed by the towering Andes. Southern Chile is largely a network of rain-bleached mountains, forests, glaciers, and fjorded coasts. The real Chile is therefore reduced to the Central Valley where population pressures intensify the explosive problems of land tenure and land use.

On the east coast of South America, the escarpment below the Brazilian plateau, like the Andes in Chile, leaves only a narrow Atlantic coastal plain interrupted in places by extensions of the plateau itself. The scarp face runs for over a thousand miles north and south, making communication a costly and difficult exercise. Flat land along the 2500-mile-long Atlantic Coast is a mere 60 miles wide. Behind the scarp face is the one million square mile Brazilian plateau, but the scarp face isolates northeastern Brazil from rainfall, producing frustrating problems of irrigation and development.

[11] Inter-American Development Bank (1966, p. 148). In 1964, Colombia had a national average of 40 persons per square mile but in the five departments where 52.6 percent of the population lives, the density averaged some 194 persons per square mile.

Agricultural Land

We will now consider the effect of geographical factors on agriculture in Latin America. In Table A.8 the effect on available agricultural land can be seen, while the figures for agricultural land per capita reveal the effect of population. In Bolivia, Nicaragua, Brazil, Peru, Chile, Colombia, Panama, Ecuador, and Guatemala, agricultural land amounts to less than one-fifth of the total land area. The United States has proportionately almost twice as much agricultural land as Latin America. The constraints become more marked if we take population growth rates into account. In 1965, land per head of the Latin American agricultural population was estimated at 2.11 hectares as against 6.14 hectares for developed countries. By the year 2000, land per head for developed countries is estimated to more than double to 12.90 hectares, while the average for Latin American will have fallen to 1.88 hectares.[12] The relative scarcity of land, determined in the first instance by geographical factors, becomes progressively worse under conditions of rapid population growth. This in turn brings pressures for increased input of capital and accelerated technical progress to improve productivity from the progressively more scarce land. If we take into account soil resources and soil properties in Latin America, new limitations emerge, barring technological change. The Food and Agricultural Organization of the UN (FAO) reported in 1965:

It is no accident that much of the yet uncultivated land in Latin America lies within the humid tropics. The history of man's penetration of this region has been marked by high hopes often followed by failure. Endemic diseases, the difficulty of transportation and communications in general and the lack of markets have made those farmers who have remained emulate the primitive system of shifting cultivation. Under such circumstances, few indeed are examples of successful and efficient agricultural industries established in the humid tropics and most of these are associated with special crops on favorable soils better supplied with nutrients than the rest.[13]

CONCENTRATION, DISPERSION, DISEQUILIBRIUM, AND REGIONAL CONTRASTS

Geographical factors contribute markedly to the disequilibrium that Comisión Económica Para América Latina (CEPAL) calls the spatial structure of Latin American development.[14] Concentration, dispersion, divisiveness, and regional inequality were dominant characteristics of the Latin American economy at the end of the 1960s, just as they were in colonial times. If Latin America's internal resources are to be fully developed by means of economic integration, the problems created by the concentration or dispersal of geographical features, natural resources, and human location must be solved by spatial planning.

The physical configuration of Latin America divides coast and interior, ports and hinterlands, resource locations and the developed areas requiring their

---

[12] See Organization for Economic Cooperation and Development (1968, p. 70).
[13] Wright and Bennema (1965, p. 113).
[14] See Brown (1966, pp. 2–5), for some very useful comments on the omissions of Latin American planning in this respect. See also CEPAL (1970a).

use. Major cities, ports, and industrial centers, and a high proportion of the population and total product of most Latin American countries are on the coast. The major centers of settlement and development, as shown in Map 2.1, are concentrated around the capitals and principal ports. In western South America, the enclaves of modern development in Colombia include the densely populated high basins of the Eastern Cordillera around Bogotá, Chuquinquira, and Sogomosa, Cucuna and Ocana, the dynamic Antiquoian region, the industrialized Cali area, and the rival areas of Santa Marta, Barranquilla, and Cartagena; in Ecuador, the capital Quito and its port of Guayaquil on the coast; in Peru, Lima and its port of Callao; in Bolivia, La Paz; and in Chile, the restricted Central Valley. On the east coast, the corresponding enclaves include conspicuously in Argentina the Greater Buenos Aires area; in Uruguay, Montevideo; and in Brazil, southeastern Brazil and in particular the great industrial area around the Rio de Janeiro-Santos–São Paulo axis. On the northern coast, Georgetown, Guyana, and the La Guaira–Caracas area stand out. These concentrations are largely on the coast except in countries like Bolivia, Paraguay, Mexico, and Colombia, where climate and other factors contribute to the regional disequilibrium.

Demographic disequilibrium is a characteristic regional condition. The distribution of population in Latin America, particularly in South America, makes it a continent surrounded by islands of people. It is estimated that 26.2 percent of the population occupy 2.6 percent of the land area while only 4.9 percent of the population of Latin America occupy 52 percent of the land area.[15] This population distribution reflects several conditions in contemporary Latin America, among them, the extent of nonutilizable land, the extent of underutilization of available land, and the various factors leading to the intense concentration of population on the coastal areas and in the towns.

Table A.9 gives some indication of regional imbalance in population distribution in some of the major countries of Latin America. In Venezuela, for instance, the Guayana region, with 45 percent of the land area, is occupied by only 3 percent of the total population. In Argentina, the loneliness of Patagonia thrusting 1000 miles south of the Rio Colorado is redeemed only by sheep grazing over vast estancias and by the location of the oil industry at Comodoro Rivadavia and the mediocre coal deposits at Rio Turbio. In this vast area bounded on the west by the Andes and on the east by the cold South Atlantic, 2.5 percent of the total population of Argentina occupy over 28 percent of the land area of the country.[16] The table shows other examples of demographic disequilibrium.

Latin America has no Midwest and no Chicago. Yet the frontier challenge is

[15] See CEPAL (1969h). See also Chase Manhattan Bank (1967a, p. 5). In this article it is estimated that Latin America has an area of 29 people per square mile and that more than 50 percent of the population lives on approximately 5 percent of the land area. CEPAL (1970a) estimates that in 40 percent of the Latin American territory, the density of population is less than one person per square kilometer and in 66 percent of the territory population density is under five persons per square kilometer.

[16] In 1960, 65 percent of the Argentinian population of 20 million was concentrated in the Pampa region. Argentina then had an over-all density of 18.2 per square mile; but the density in the Pampa was 46.8 as against 13.0 in the Northeast region and 2.6 in Patagonia. For excellent descriptions of disequilibrium and geographic isolation in Argentina, see McGann (1966, pp. 9–21); and Scobie (1964, pp. 11–35).

there constantly sparked by the El Dorado myth and by nationalist aspirations. Juan Batista Alberdi, the Argentinian intellectual, coined a slogan which still holds sway in Latin America: "To govern is to populate." But the westward movement of peoples pushing aggressively against the frontier in U.S. history does not find an equivalent in Latin America. People keep moving to the coast from the rural areas. In Argentina, even the newly arrived immigrants stayed in Buenos Aires. In Brazil, new immigrants from Portugal, Italy, Germany, France, Japan, and elsewhere, despite every possible persuasion to go west, concentrate in Rio de Janeiro, São Paulo, and the south, again mainly on the coast. However, the building of Brasilia between 1957 and 1960, at heavy cost and at fantastic speed, under President Kubitschek, in the midst of the semiarid, thinly populated highlands of the state of Goiás, 600 miles away from Rio de Janeiro, may induce a reverse migration of Brazilians away from the coast.[17]

Brazil's hot, wet, forested, flood-ridden Amazon basin, despite an estimated area of 2,700,000 square miles, some 80 percent of the land area of Brazil, has a density of less than two persons per square mile.[18] The population is mainly lonely clusters of nomadic Indians, shifting groups of rubber and gold speculators, and the widely separated settlements of Iquitos, Manaus, and Belém which have seen better days in the times of the gold and rubber booms. The isolation and loneliness described in Charles Wagley's *Amazon Town* continue to dominate the landscape of interior Brazil, although they are being modified under the modernizing impact of SPVEA, the official Amazon Economic Development Authority.[19] (See Appendix B.)

This pattern repeats itself in almost every major country in South America. In the Republic of Guyana, for instance, the interior accounts for some 98 percent of the area of the country (83,000 square miles) but houses less than 10 percent of the population of over 750,000. Beyond the confluence town of Bartica on the River Essequibo, Mackenzie on the Demerara River, and Kwakwani on the Berbice River are found the sites of some of the largest bauxite deposits in the world. The interior of Guyana, despite its fabled potential wealth, belongs to a few vaqueros at Lethem, gold and diamond speculators, forest workers, and small groups of Amerindians. As in Brazil, hinterland development is now part of active national planning.[20] The interiors of the other two Guianas, Dutch and French, parallel the situation in Guyana. In Venezuela, the Orinoco basin is still largely empty land despite major discoveries and developments

[17]Brazil in 1960 and an over-all population density of only 24 per square mile, but on the narrow Atlantic coast the population density was over 130 per square mile. See Jaguaribe (1968, pp. 158–159), Brazilian Government Trade Bureau (1970), and Ludwig (1969, pp. 101–113). Ludwig gives a higher figure for anticipated costs of Brasilia than Sir William Holford's 1962 estimate of $840 million (U.S.).

[18]The reader may also wish to consult Poppino (1968, pp. 9–39).

[19]See also Wagley (1964, p. 5), and Brazilian Government Trade Bureau, (1968). Following the declaration of Manaus as a free trade zone, the population increased from 242,000 to 300,000 between 1967 and 1968. See Center for Inter-American Relations (1969, pp. 45–48); also see Table A.11 in Appendix A.

[20]See for instance, British Guiana (Guayana) Development Program (1966–1972). This plan is being revised, but emphasis on interior development remains. The population density on the coast is over 1,000 per square mile, the over-all population density is less than 10 per square mile.

from 1958. The largest center of the llanos is Ciudad Bolívar with a growing but still small population. The character of the Guayana Highlands of Venezuela, distant and practically empty until recently despite the mining of gold, diamonds, manganese, and iron ore, is being transformed by a large steel plant and the initiation of the enormous Caroni Hydroelectric Scheme with a potential of some 10 million kw. In Colombia, less than 3 percent of the total population live in the eastern half of the country. In Paraguay, less than 4.2 percent of the population occupies the plains of the Gran Chaco, which accounts for 68 percent of the total area of the country. The population density there is less than one person per square kilometer.

Contrasting Economies

In every Latin American country, the two basic regional contrasts to which geographical factors, among others, contribute are the hollow, in many cases stagnating, interior lands and the economically advanced and densely populated concentrations on the coast or around the main cities.

The interior territories of the Guyanas, the Orinoco plains, the Amazon lowlands, the Gran Chaco, Patagonia, and the eastern provinces of the countries split by the Andes may all be called the "hollow lands" of Latin America. In fact, almost all the frontiers of South America are hollow frontiers, drawn across lonely, almost uninhabited territory, sometimes outside of political control and at best in only tenuous contact with the administrative centers of government.[21]

The contrast between the hollow lands and the densely populated sections is likely to widen, unless reversed by development planning which has come to terms with the spatial implications of the Latin American setting. The potential widening of the gulf between these contrasting economies stems from the fact that concentration tends to induce more concentration. Where there are dense concentrations, the original geographic advantages are reinforced by the economic advantages of a larger market outlet. More investment, more services, and more people are attracted into these areas, and so the process continues, sharpening the contrasts between the regions of the country through increasing differences in external and other economic advantages. Table A.10 gives some indication of the degree of imbalance of the contribution of various developed areas to the value of industrial production and shows the distribution of personal incomes and the contribution to gross domestic product. Outside of the metropolitan areas, one of the most striking cases in all Latin America is that of northeastern Brazil. Here the character of the topography, soil, climate, and inherited practices in land utilization and other factors combine to make this vast region of over 11 percent of the total area of the country the almost perennial calamity area for Brazil. The 26 million Brazilians who inhabit the northeast have an average income of less than $100 (U.S.) a year.[22] The highly significant work of the

[21] We have used the term *hollow frontier* to describe territories occupied by a sparse and widespread population. James (1959, pp. 459 and 491–492), used the term to describe "earlier settled lands [which] declined in the value of production and in the density of the population."

[22] There are numerous studies of this section of Brazil. These references are highly eclectic: Robock (1962, pp. 65–89), Singer (1964, pp. 221–290), Higgins (1968, pp. 736–741), and Furtado (1965, pp. 264–270). The following are among special research studies put

Northeast Development Authority (SUDENE), the official Brazilian agency, in promoting industrial development in the area has only created further disparities to be resolved.[23]

Transportation and Disequilibrium

The difficulty and the cost of accelerating over-all development within each country of Latin America and of promoting integrated development within the boundaries of the whole continent have been increased by the spatial dimensions of the problem. Geographic isolation, division, and dispersion, reinforced by developments which only added to the difficulty have made for the initially weak articulation of the economies of Latin America. In a special study in 1960, the Institute of International Studies and Overseas Administration of the University of Oregon recognized, as we have here, that "the economic integration of various regions within Latin America is regarded as an important condition for the economic progress of the area."[24] In relation to the factors identified in this chapter, the study noted:

Natural barriers in the form of mountains, deserts, and impenetrable rain forests, together with the political history of Latin America, have conspired to produce an area of isolated islands of economic activity. Economic growth emanated from the port cities to the hinterland which produced the commodities destined for export to the United States and Western Europe. Highways and railroads connected the hinterland with the coastal cities, but because of geography, political boundaries, and economic orientation, lines of communication between centers of activity in different countries have failed to develop. As a consequence, trade between Latin American countries has not developed as has trade between Canada and the United States or among the countries of Western Europe.[25]

Details have become inevitably modified in varying degrees in various countries since these observations were made, but the fundamental thesis continues to hold good. Indeed, the realities of the Latin American situation make it clear that it will be some time before there is any substantive change in the situation. A solution to the problems emanating from this physical and economic polarization is easy to theorize. If a Latin American country wants to end disparities in the development and welfare status of each region, the unbalanced concentration of economic activity must be altered. If equalization of welfare is the goal, islands of modernity cannot continue to support the vast areas of stagnation. The conceptual solution is macroeconomic transformation of the situation through over-all programing, involving articulation of national, sectoral, and continental objectives and policies. Over-all programing involves detailed working out and establishment of a vast system of horizontal and vertical

---

out by the Banco do Nordeste do Brasil: (1968) and (1967–1969).
See also Pan American Union (1968d), and Hirschmann (1963, pp. 11–92).
[23] For a summary comment, see Center for Inter-American Relations (1969, pp. 42–44, 46–47, 148–152). See also Daland (1967).
[24] U.S. Senate (1960a, p. 564).
[25] *Ibid.* See also Nystrom and Haverstock (1966, pp. 9–14).

linkage, with an immense demand on the administrative, economic, physical, and social resources of Latin America.

Qualitative descriptions of the Latin American economies indicate the existent situation and the direction and scale of the transformation necessary. Conventional epithets apply. The economies are regionally and technologically dualistic. They are largely enclave economies, peripherally dependent on the highly industrialized countries to which their economic activity is linked. Enclave economic activity, necessarily externally oriented, has a low level of linkage with the rest of the economy, emanating from accidental spill-overs of their exogenous connection. In using this conventional terminology from the literature on development, we might even employ Byé's epithet, "non-communicating" (1963, p. 119).[26] The need for over-all planning to modify the situation is recognized in every major economic declaration from the Punta del Esté to the Consensus of Viña del Mar. The Latin American cannot retreat from over-all planning. Nationalism and reality demand an endogenous economic revolution. The 1965 Declaration of the Presidents of America that "the economic integration of Latin America demands a vigorous and sustained effort to complete and modernize the physical infra-structure of the region" is a restatement of a recognized truth. (See Appendix B.) If Latin America wants an indigenous economic revolution, a land transport network must be built, all types of transport systems must be improved "to facilitate the movement of persons and goods throughout the hemisphere," and other measures are essential to implement the larger objectives.[27] Those who are impatient for more rapid progress may be tempted to say that the Alliance for Progress is dead, or at least has failed, but it is too early for this kind of judgment. The planned conquest of space is not as simple a matter as building a railroad across Castro's Cuba where three-fourths of the terrain is absolutely level land. It is not as simple as building Route 90 across the affluent United States with its much less forbidding physical restraints, its favorable disposition of population concentrations, its industrial activity and profitable traffic potential, and with no political sensitivities to take into account.[28]

The realities in Latin America go further. Distances are huge and empty spaces vast. Ports are separated from the hinterlands. Resources which should occur together, with advantages for competitive industrial utilization, are widely separated. Rivers are numerous but there are severe limitations to their utilization. Consideration of these factors compels a more balanced appreciation of the economic achievements and economic complexities in Latin America's development thrust.

Let us take the question of distances. Chile is about the size of Texas but

---

[26] See also UNECLA (1964aa, pp. 10–11).

[27] Cf. Herrera (1969): "I feel [regional nationalism] represents one of the few ways out for Latin America in the world of the future. . . . Regional nationalism has had a double expression in recent years: one has been the movement toward economic integration as a mechanism for stimulating a dynamic rate of growth; the other is the movement toward the adoption of a common bargaining position rooted in commercial policy and foreign trade."

[28] For comparative purposes, the reader may find it useful to refer to Pegrum (1968, pp. 77–103).

lengthwise would extend from New York to San Francisco or from mid-Ontario to the southern border of Mexico.[29] Bogotá in Colombia is 4514 and 4667 air kilometers from Rio de Janeiro and Buenos Aires respectively, farther than from Bogotá to New York (4230 air kilometers). Given the topography of Latin America, the development of air transportation obviously represents a vital contribution in linking the various parts of Latin America. Ocean transportation has traditionally performed a similar function, connecting port to port around the long sea haul of the continent. In fact, before the coming of the airlines, the sea route was practically the only link between Latin American countries themselves and between Latin America and the industrial world beyond. In the Caribbean, it was impossible except by accidental circumstances to travel directly through the eastern Caribbean to Jamaica and British Honduras—a long haul of 3000 miles—until the establishment of British West Indian Airways and the federal boats, which still carry on although the Federation of the West Indies collapsed in 1962.

At the beginning of the Alliance years maritime transport was dominant. In 1962, waterborne traffic in Latin America accounted for 97 percent of the exports and imports of 10 major Latin American countries and for 89–100 percent in nine others. This was the inevitable consequence of concentration of economic activity on the coast, the relative absence of industrial centers beyond the coast, the lack of international surface transport, the immense distances across a huge continent, and the equally immense physical barriers to development of internal and international surface transport.[30]

All forms of transportation—air, sea, river, road, and rail—suffer from deficiencies in administration, coordination, and from technical and financial drawbacks.[31] During the Alliance years, remedial policies were intensified to correct these deficiencies. There are, however, some fundamental problems related to air and sea transport. In the case of air transport, the demand for international operations generally exceeds the demand for domestic operations.[32] This is partly the result of the relative low volume of freight traffic on domestic services, which, in turn, reflects in significant measure the hollowness of the hinterland. There is also a political push toward Latin American ownership and control of both air and sea transport. The cost effect of such a change has yet to be fully determined.[33] Most important of all, however, air and sea communication tend to be profitable only between already existing areas of industrial concentration. This fact contributes to increased concentration rather than otherwise. Rivers suffer from several major limitations, among them natural limits to navigability, resulting from the physical structure of Latin America and the

---

[29] See Gill (1966, pp. 1–3). Sea distances are of course even greater. From Valparaiso to Montevideo, via Callao, Guayaquil, Barranquilla, La Guiara, and Rio de Janeiro, it is over 8300 nautical miles. The distance from Valparaiso to Buenos Aires (traveling counterclockwise) is over 2700 nautical miles (Brown, 1966, p. 257).

[30] UNECLA (1963a, pp. 95–96).

[31] See UNECLA's *Economic Survey of Latin America,* from 1960 on.

[32] UNECLA (1967a, p. 238). Between 1966 and 1967, international air operations increased 16.6 percent (world average, 15.5 percent), as against 4.8 percent for domestic operation (world average, 22.6 percent).

[33] See, for instance, CEPAL (1969d, 1969f, and 1970b).

underdeveloped state of the hinterland. Since highways are far more viable than the railway, the promotion of road construction is of highest priority in counter-acting existing conditions of isolation and disequilibrium. The experience of Brazil is illuminating. The Social Progress Trust Fund made the following observations in 1969:

Brazil's transport system is one of the principal bottlenecks in economic develop-ment. Since few rivers flow from the interior to the east coast, railroads and roads were built to connect coastal population centers with the agricultural producing areas in the hinterland. Oceangoing ships, in turn, for many years provided the only linkage among coastal settlements. However, the deterioration of rail and ship service since World War II and an active program of highway construction brought about a marked shift in the traditional transport mix.

Improvement in the transport picture since 1950 has been limited almost exclusively to road construction and paving, for the carrying capacity of the coastwise fleet and railroads has declined. This has resulted in the almost total predominance of road transport over ship and rail shipping, but since trucking normally is economical for only relatively short or medium distances, high transport costs remain a serious barrier to the realization of potential benefits from greater internal integration of the Brazilian economy.

A general transport survey was initiated in 1965 to provide the basis for preparation of an integrated ten-year plan. The first phase of the survey, already completed, contains master plans for highways in Minas Gerais, Parana, Santa Catarina and Rio Grande do Sul, and for the railroads and ports of Rio de Janeiro, Santos and Recife. The second phase, expected to be finished in 1969, will provide master plans for highways in most of the states not considered in the first phase.[34]

It might be noted at this point that the physical configuration of Latin America, regardless of past and future improvements in transportation, makes it impossible in some places to replace the mule, the yak, and the human back as the means of transport.

Rivers and the Problem of Isolation

The river complexes of Latin America, despite their appearance on the map, do not resolve the problems of isolation. In Central America, the majority of the rivers dry up seasonally or become too silt-laden to offer natural harbors for ocean-going ships. In South America, the major river systems are the Magdalena in Colombia, the Orinoco in Venezuela, the Amazon in Brazil, the São Francisco, and the Parana-Plata system. The course of the Magdalena is broken by rapids, although railway links between the navigable parts have somewhat modified the disadvantages of this obstacle. Physical features similarly limit the navigability of the São Francisco. Despite a total of some 6000 miles of navigable waterways

---

[34] Inter-American Development Bank (1969a, p. 237). See also Cárdenas (1968, p. 314):

Latin America's traditional ties to the world markets and the nature of the trade flows have contributed to the establishment of a transportation system that has served mainly to connect the countries and their small centers of economic activity to the industrial nations, maintaining isolation between one country and another within the region. This explains why the structure of transportation in Latin America is still mostly limited to national borders with predominance of maritime transportation for intraregional traffic, antiquated railroad systems, and a small volume of river traffic.

offered by the Orinoco system, the region has until recently remained under-developed. The Amazon system offers some 40,000 miles of navigable water, and is the most navigable river in the world. Ocean-going vessels can reach Manaus, 1000 miles upstream, and smaller craft can reach Iquitos, 2000 miles from the Atlantic. But because of physical and climatic factors the whole basin remained isolated until the recent efforts to promote development were initiated. On the Brazilian plateau, most rivers flow inward away from the coast. On the other hand, the rivers crossing the Brazilian escarpment into the sea are expected-ly rapids-obstructed and useless for navigation.

In Argentina, the economic advantages of water transport must be balanced against natural disadvantages. The Panama, the Paraguay, and the Uruguay unite to form the River Plata system. These are all navigable rivers and constitute an immense commercial asset to Argentina, Uruguay and their neighboring countries. But the streams which form the Plata system are not without shifting channels, liability to flood, and interruption by rapids. In any case, the Plata system does not really penetrate the great fertile heartlands of Argentina. The rivers of Patagonia obstruct rather than aid transportation development. They cut deep into the plateau, they flood when the melting snow arrives, and when the floods are gone they flow deep below oversize canyons.

On the narrow west coast of South America, the rivers flowing into the Pacific may, with an occasional exception, be similarly dismissed as decisive contributors to communication. On the northern coast of the continent, Guyana has a number of great rivers. The Demerara and the Berbice are highly navigable, but beyond the bauxite mines at Mackenzie and Kwakwani there is the usual undeveloped hinterland. The Essequibo, 620 miles long, is navigable for only 100 miles. Beyond that it is obstructed by rapids.

Undoubtedly, the development of river transport could make an invaluable contribution to interior development in Latin America and to the promotion of economic integration. The basin of the Plata covers an area as large as that of the Amazon, involving the territories of five countries, and has a population of over 80 million. It is an obvious case for "a coordinated action in the regulation of the rivers, the infrastructure, the systematic exploitation of the natural resources, the problems posed by the landlocked situation of Bolivia and Paraguay and the provision of access to the interior of the continent."[35] However, the potential for developing more effective river transport cannot be readily realized without overcoming a multitude of physical, financial, and political obstacles. Even if these obstacles were overcome, river transport, because of natural limitations, could not solve the problems of regional unbalance.

Road Transportation

We have seen the limitations of sea, air, and river transport as means of counter-acting regional imbalance in Latin America. The relative merits of rail and road development are also worth discussion. Indeed, since the whole transportation picture involves the use of scarce resources, it becomes a question of deciding to which of the various competing systems to allocate the resources. It is a

[35] See Cárdenas (1968, p. 318).

matter of alternatives. Specific studies have come up with valuable preliminary data.[36] The physical terrain of Latin America, the low population density of the hinterland, and the scattered location of even this small population can be said to give the highway immediate economic priority. Roads can connect scattered centers to an extent that the railway cannot. Roads can develop centers which may in turn attract the airlines. Roads can bring passenger and freight traffic to the rivers. The development of the interior through road construction, judiciously supported by other elements in the transport mix, would counteract both isolation and the present patterns of economic disequilibrium.

Once again, however, topography and the spatial factor of distance as well as other impediments must be considered in any evaluation of the problem of highway development. Historically, at the beginning of the Alliance for Progress, road development in Latin America lagged behind, even in contrast with other developing countries. Table A.13 shows total Latin American road mileage in 1962 amounted to only 3.2 percent of the world total as compared with 6 percent for Africa and 14.1 percent for Asia and the Middle East. Haiti had a total all-weather road mileage of only 501 miles. Honduras had a total of only 344 miles of paved roads in a total road network of 3131 miles. Uruguay was even worse off, with 277 miles of paved roads in a total road network of 8934 miles. Huge Bolivia had a total of 571 miles of paved road as against a figure of 1035 miles of paved roads for little El Salvador. Brazil, the giant of Latin America in size and population, had a total of 16,441 miles of paved roads in a total network of 76,400 miles of roads, less than Mexico with its 30,300 miles of paved roads in 59,000 miles. Venezuela had only 11,718 miles of paved roads in a total of 27,671 miles.

Topography obviously enters into the picture. The montana region of the eastern Andes obviously poses a problem for any transportation development. But in Argentina, where the flat land constitutes an apparent advantage, road building comes up against unhelpful natural dilemmas. Neither gravel nor stone is available on the great pampas for surfacing. The road network is therefore largely confined to the Buenos Aires area, and vast regions of the countryside are practically without roads. In Brazil, 75 percent of the road network is confined to the southeastern region. In Colombia, topographical factors traditionally heighten road costs as well as retard construction.[37]

The case for the acceleration of highway construction is clear, and highway construction is being accelerated internally and internationally throughout Latin America. For the period 1958-66, road mileage more than tripled in Argentina and practically doubled in Costa Rica, Guatemala, Panama, the Dominican Republic, and Venezuela. There were significant percentage improvements in Colombia, Ecuador, Honduras, Nicaragua, and Peru.[38] International highway developments, under Alliance efforts, are succeeding in breaking up isolation and creating new frontiers for settlement and development. (See Map 3.2 and Figure 3.1). The Carretera Marginal, for instance, an Alliance for Progress project

[36] See, for instance, CIAP (1967, pp. 19–20).
[37] Cf. Whitbeck and Williams (1940, p. 41).
[38] See Pan American Union (1968b, pp. 303–308).

MAP 3.2
Proposed Roads in South America
Source: U.S. Department of State (1968d, p. 27).

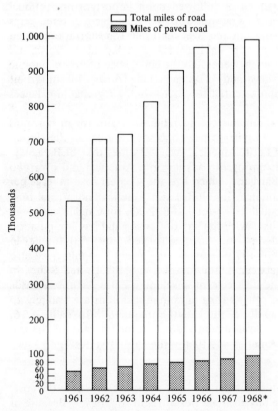

*Preliminary data only available for number of miles of paved roads.

FIGURE 3.1
Actual Highway Construction in South America, 1961–68
Source: U.S. Department of State (1969c, p. 55).

sponsored by Colombia, Ecuador, Peru, and Bolivia and constructed along the eastern slopes of the Andes, runs for a distance of over 3500 miles. It was designed to open up vast areas of virgin land and make accessible the wealth of the Amazon and Orinoco basins. The Carretera Marginal will link up with the Trans-Chaco Highway running 400 miles from Asunción, Paraguay, to the Paraguay-Bolivia border, and connecting with numerous feeder roads. Table A.14 shows some of the major international highways under study and construction in Latin America. The most dramatic of these, of course, is the building of the 43,500-mile Pan American Highway. The completion of the Pan American Highway has made major modifications in the geographical and human isolation of all Latin America. It provides new mobility for men, goods, and ideas; new stimulus to markets and an increase in the number of trucks and other vehicles; and new feeder connections to unify and expand market interrelations and strengthen political coherence, both internally and externally.

The Highway Development Gap

Road construction has accompanied or followed upon important institutional changes in the field of transport.[39] Transportation by road has registered gains over traditional railway transportation and over maritime transportation, which has suffered from the high cost of port and harbor dues, delays at the ports, and from the fact that road development generated the emergence of new economic centers in the interior with new and increased trade flows. In important respects, the transport revolution essential for transforming regional imbalances is taking place.

The transport gap, however, remains considerable. In 1966, for instance, as Table A.12 shows, improved road mileage per 1000 square miles in the United States was nine times that of Latin America, over 40 times that of Paraguay, which had the fewest miles of improved roads in Latin America, and over two and one-half times that of El Salvador, which had the greatest road mileage per 1000 square miles in Latin America. In 1968, Latin America had a total road mileage of 804,000, just about equal to the total of 802,000 for Canada, although Latin America is nearly more than twice the size of Canada and has a population nine times as great. Paved roads in Latin America totaled only 75,000 miles in 1968, less than half the total of 157,677 miles for Canada.[40] Table A.12 also shows the development gap between Latin America and the United States in terms of cars and railroads. The high cost of developing Latin America's roads is indicated in Table A.15, and other forms of communications are unlikely to redeem physical isolation as rapidly as the situation requires.[41] In Table A.16, the figures on communications development indicate some measure of the gap between the situation in Latin America and that in the United States.

Alternative Costs

The railways, perhaps more than any other mode of transport, illustrate the costs and difficulties imposed by the physical features of Latin America.[42] Because of the topography and the limited productivity of the hinterlands, railway networks in Latin America are primarily in coastal regions. Mexico is an exception in that its railway network is largely in the Central Plateau, with extensions to ports on the Mexican Gulf. A number of historical factors have affected the development, rationalization, and modernization of the Latin American railway system. Built expediently to serve the export centers and avoid the cost of construction over difficult terrain, the railways also suffer from low technical standards, obsolescence, and a variety of operational defects. Because of the lack of an over-all policy, even the railway gauges within a single country are different. In Brazil, for instance, the railways built in the nineteenth century do not constitute an

---

[39] See UNECLA (1964, pp. 152–153).
[40] See U.S. Department of State (1968d, p. 24), and Pan American Union (1968b, p. 303).
[41] Cf. Hanson (1951, pp. 316–368), Benham and Holley (1960, pp. 43–50), and Currie (1966, pp. 198, 228–230).
[42] Whitbeck and Williams (1940, p. 15) give the following altitudes for railways crossing the Andes: Guyaquil and Quito Railroad, Ecuador—11,841 ft.; Central Railroad of Peru—15,665 ft.; Southern Railroad of Peru—14,688 ft.; Africa-La Paz Railroad in Chile and Bolivia—13,986 ft.; Antofagasta and Bolivia Railroad—13,000 ft.; and Chile-Argentine Trans-Andean Railroad—10,452 ft.

integrated system.[43] Changes are of course taking place, but costs and difficulties imposed by topography remain inescapable retarding influences, as in the highways, in much of Latin America.

We have already pointed out that the development of air communication revolutionized transport connections throughout the continent. The transport mix which will emerge as time goes on will depend very much on competitive capacity and circumstances. For instance in Brazil, studies of transport development for the period 1960–66 indicate that air transport is more economical than highway transport. On the other hand, in addition to suffering from an inadequate volume of bulk and carload freight, the railways have steadily lost the more profitable types of revenue traffic to air and highway transportation.[44] As Currie observes in respect to transport policy in Colombia:

The fewer the transport routes and the more heavily utilized they are, the lower the transport costs per unit of goods moved. Therefore, the more the population is concentrated in the cities, and the more the exploitation of natural resources is carried on near cities, or near main heavily used lines of transport, the lower will transport costs figure in the final price of goods.[45]

There are, however, two qualifications to this analysis. The first emerges from the geographical arrangements: resources are not always near the cities in Latin America. The Amazon basin, for instance, is estimated to have at least one-half of the timber resources of the world in addition to extensive mineral deposits at the headwaters of the tributaries of the lower Amazon. The revealed resources of the Guayana region of Venezuela are enormous. The timber, forestry, mineral, and hydroelectric potentials of the hinterland of the Republic of Guyana are impressive. Similar potentialities exist in the Andean regions of Argentina. The lumber potentialities of the Péten in Guatemala are well established, as is the natural resource potential of the Oriente sections of the countries of western South America. In all these cases, resources are distant from the cities and the areas of industrial concentration. A second qualification to Currie's observation stems from the need to secure economic integration in Latin America as the "collective instrument for accelerating Latin American development."[46] These two qualifications indicate the necessity of developing a transport network to link up isolated centers and interior regions with centers of industrial concentration if regional disequilibrium is to be corrected and a national market forged. This may require the development of a transport network long before profitable returns materialize. Transportation already accounts for a large share of the public budget; geography and regional imbalance can add further to its cost.[47]

THE CONQUEST OF ISOLATION AND DISEQUILIBRIUM:
THE GUAYANA EXAMPLE

The factors we have described constitute basic realities to be taken into account in any appreciation of the problem of development in Latin America. Isolation,

[43] See Pan American Union (1967f, p. 25).
[44] Whitbeck and Williams (1940, pp. 23, 26).
[45] Currie (1966, p. 229). See also Roberts and Kresge (1968, pp. 341–359).
[46] Pan American Union (1967g, p. 6).
[47] See Great Britain, Colonial Office (1948, pp. 163–189), for some estimates of transport construction costs at that time in interior Guyana.

however, need not necessitate a retreat from the challenge of development. The hinterland of the Republic of Guyana, one of the richest areas in the world in terms of mineral, power, and agricultural resources, is already being opened up through significant investment of social overhead capital, specialized institutionalization, and the efforts of private enterprise.[48] The impossible is being made possible under the impact of new governmental direction and in the years of the Alliance for Progress. The transformation of the Guayana region of Venezuela represents one of the most dramatic instances in Latin America of overcoming natural deterrents to structural transformation and development.[49]

Physical Characteristics of the Guayana Region

The Guayana region, a complex of rounded hills and narrow valleys covered by forests and savannas, is an upland area capped by plateaus and mesas, the edges of which are dissected by many streams. It lies south of the Orinoco River and accounts for nearly half the area of Venezuela. Up to the 1940s, various adjectives could be applied to the area—wild, lonely, swampy, unmapped, almost unexplored, remote, roadless, neglected, and inaccessible. For all practical purposes the region was outside the effective national territory. Yet it is actually only 300 miles from the densely populated mountain areas of the coast. Between the Guayana region and those areas lie the flat, wide Orinoco plains (los llanos). These plains are part savanna and part dense jungle. They are alternately flood-ridden and dessicated, according to the season. Although the plains account for one-third of the area of Venezuela, they are sparsely populated. To the southeast lies the Gran Sabana, a 14,000-square-mile plateau, with a scarp face of sheer cliffs 2500 feet high rising steeply from the surrounding jungle in the north. The Gran Sabana is a wilderness of grass, bush, palm trees, waterfalls, and lagoons, with massive flat-topped bluffs emerging to heights of over 9000 feet above sea level. Eight of the nine streams which rise in this area flow into the Rio Caroni.

The geographical characteristics of the Guayana region represent at once both natural deterrents and immense economic promise. The Venezuela government deliberately set out in 1960 to transform this region into a Ruhr-type industrial complex.

Guayana's Potentials

The sequence of events in the development of the Guayana region underlines several important features in the initiation of any development, particularly regional development. These are: the importance of preliminary surveys and systematic analysis of economic possibilities as prerequisites to implementing planned intentions; the importance of institutionalizing, with the purposes and

[48] See National Advertising Co. (n.d.) and Guyana Ministry of Information (1968). Cf. Great Britain, Colonial Office (1948, pp. 127–128, and following chapters).

[49] The material in this section is drawn from the following Corporacion Venezolana de Guayana (CVG) publications: (1963) (1968a, b, and c). See also the following issues of Venezuela, Embassy of: Spring (1968, p. 7); Summer (1968, p. 6); and Winter (1969–70, p. 11).

powers of the newly created development institutions specifically and unam-
biguously defined; and the importance of constructively adjusting national
sensitivities to a policy of economic realism once it becomes clear that foreign
capital and foreign technical assistance are unavoidable.[50] Official determination
to develop the Guayana region took account of four factors: the stage reached in
Venezuela's economic development in 1960; the need for balanced growth; the
extraordinary resource endowment of the region; and decreases in the supply of
high-grade ores from the mines of Minnesota.

By 1960, changes in Venezuela's economic needs necessitated the planned
exploitation of the extraordinary resources of the Guayana region. It was anticipated that the annual economic growth rate of 7 percent a year over the past 25
years could not continue, largely because of diminished prospects for the growth
of the petroleum industry. These calculations of course had implications for
anticipated foreign exchange earning levels, public revenues, and the level of
over-all investment. Concomitantly, Venezuela's population of approximately
8 million was growing at a rate of over 3 percent a year, implying a doubling of
the population every 23 years. It was necessary to quadruple the output of goods
and services in the next 20 years to maintain the rate of economic growth. To
achieve this goal, industrial production had to expand at least 12 percent a year;
manufacturing had to be substantially diversified; and Venezuelan industry had
to develop substantial new exports. Industry, despite its scale, dynamism,
advantages for employment, and total product growth, remained too dependent
on imports of basic and intermediate products. The increase in import demand
was not being counterbalanced by an increase in export earnings. Venezuela had
to increase its production of metals, petrochemicals, electrochemicals, and
heavy and light machinery to eliminate its dependence on imported basic and
intermediate products. In these circumstances, developing the potential resources
of Guayana became of priority importance.

The principle of securing a more balanced growth between the regions of the
country through the decentralization of economic activities and through a more
rational utilization of the natural and human resources of each region is an
accepted principle of Venezuelan planning.[51]

The Guayana region has sufficiently impressive basic resources to justify
the ambitions of the Venezuelan government to make it a key area in the plans
for accelerated economic advance. Although there were known gold and iron
ore deposits the region remained undeveloped because of the lack of transportation and because the leading U.S. steel companies were, until the end of World
War II, using high-grade ores from Minnesota. The end of the Minnesota ores,
the beginning of road construction, and the development of oil in the llanos and
Guayana combined to give economic significance to Guayana.

One of the region's greatest assets is Cerro Bolívar, the iron mountain of
Venezuela, 7½ miles long and 2631 feet high. Cerro Bolívar yields some 420,000

---

[50]In 1961, the CVG recruited professional resident personnel from the Joint Center for
Urban Studies of the Massachusetts Institute of Technology and Harvard University to
advise CVG on various special aspects of development in the Guayana region. See, for
instance, Rodwin and Assoc. (1969).

[51]See Venezuela, Central Office of Coordination and Planning (n.d.).

tons of high-grade ore a year with an iron content of some 60 percent. It is estimated that the Guayana Highlands have proven reserves of iron ore amounting to 1.3 billion tons. Diamonds and manganese are already being mined and there are possibilities for bauxite, nickel, sulphur, kaolin, salt, and coal.[52] The development of the nearby petroleum industry supports the incipient industrial activity in the area. The proven reserves of the petroleum fields are put at over 2.2 billion barrels and over 11 trillion cubic feet of gas. The power potential of the Rio Caroni is put at over 10 million kilowatts. Fresh water for industrial and domestic purposes and abundant forests add to the region's basic assets.

The Approach to Regional Development in Guayana

As a basic first step, the Venezuelan government in December, 1960, created a special public authority, Venezuelan Corporation of Guayana (CVG), with the broad responsibility and power to carry through an integrated development program in the Guayana region. This program included simultaneous research in basic reserves, industrial promotion and management, the development of human resources, regional planning, and urban design.

The regional development program involved a systematic analysis of regional resources and their geographical accessibility; an assessment of the potential contribution of the Guayana region to the total economy of Venezuela in terms of the diversification and expansion of the country's exports; and an assessment of the implications of centralizing development in the city of Santo Tomé de Guayana (Ciudad Guayana). This systematic approach included the following essential steps: selecting a preliminary list of industries geared to utilize Guayana's resources; refining the initial list in terms of national and world demand, minimum scale of operation, whether they would be complementary, competitive costs, transportation factors, and electric power capacity; establishing production goals for selected industries based on projections for world and domestic demand; and using these goals as a basis for calculating aggregate production values, investment, labor, electricity consumption, and space requirements.

This data was basic to estimates of employment effect and the development of complementary industrial activity and services and in order to make population projections and do urban planning. It was needed for projections of regional demand and supply and for estimates of the financial implications of the program and the availability of public, private, and international capital. This detailed programing allowed for a refining of parameters where indicated by the special studies and by circumstances and experience, and facilitated the framing of short-run, medium and long-run programs. It also improved financial coordination and allowed for control, evaluation, and adjustment in the program.

---

[52]The iron ore reserves may be bigger. Proven deposits of other minerals are as follows: salt—1,130 million cubic tons, with a possibliity of 400 million tons more; sulphur-bearing minerals—700,000 tons; and kaolin—700,000 tons. In 1968, the Venezuelan Government signed a contract with the Orinoco Mining Company to construct a plant to produce annually one million tons of 86.5 percent pure iron ore briquettes for export. The Orinoco Mining Company is an affiliate of U.S. Steel and holds a government concession to develop the Cerro Bolivar iron ore deposits.

Under the regional development plan for Guayana, the public sector assumed an important role both in the initiation of planned transformation of the region and in the allocation of national investment. For the first five years, 10 percent of the national investment was allocated to the Guayana region, in the expectation that the region would, by 1975, be contributing 20 percent of the gross industrial product of Venezuela and 20 percent of the total value of the country's exports. Despite its deliberately defined role, the government of Venezuela provided from the beginning every possible encouragement to investment and production under private enterprise. Indeed, offical preference was for substituting private enterprise for public initiative wherever possible.

Some of the data amassed through the careful planning just described is shown in the accompanying maps and tables. The center of the new regional development is Ciudad Guayana. Map 3.3 shows the location of the city and the boundaries of the industrial area and supplies a general picture of the distribution of population and natural resources. Map 3.4 concentrates on the economic resources, locational advantages, and spatial relationships of the region around Ciudad Guayana. Table 3.1 sums up the annual production targets set for Guayana by the national development program. Tables A.17–A.21 give tabulations of estimated fixed investment requirements for the Guayana region in the

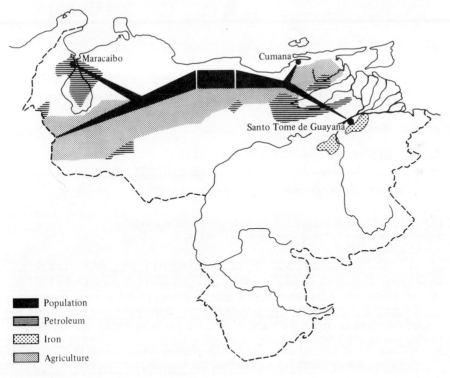

■ Population
≡ Petroleum
▨ Iron
▨ Agriculture

MAP 3.3
Population and Natural Resources of Venezuela
Source: U.S. Department of State (1969c).

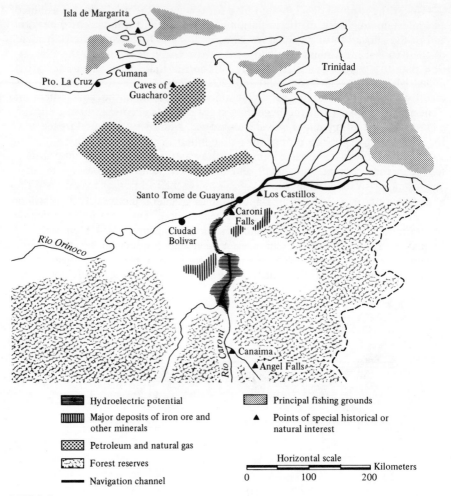

Hydroelectric potential

Major deposits of iron ore and
other minerals

Petroleum and natural gas

Forest reserves

Navigation channel

Principal fishing grounds

▲ Points of special historical or
natural interest

Horizontal scale

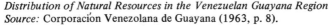

Kilometers

0   100   200

MAP 3.4
Distribution of Natural Resources in the Venezuelan Guayana Region
Source: Corporación Venezolana de Guayana (1963, p. 8).

period 1963-75; projections of the value of exports from the Guayana region
from 1960-75; projections for Guayana's contribution to manufacturing production in relation to aggregate value of manufacturing production for Venezuela
for the period 1960-75; and projections of the population and labor force in
Cuidad Guayana from 1966-75 and of housing needs by family income groups
for the period 1962-80.

An Evaluation of the Development Plan for Guayana

Our theme in this chapter and throughout the book is that impulsive judgments
on the rate of development in Latin America under the Alliance for Progress
often fail to take into account the original economic status of Latin America and

TABLE 3.1

Venezuela: Annual Production Targets for Guayana, 1975[a] (In thousands)

Installed electric power capacity [b]	2,100
Finished steel products[c]	3,860
Reduced iron ore[c]	10,000
Aluminum ingots[c]	200
Magnesite[c]	20
Manganese[c]	30
Elemental phosphorous[c]	60
Ammonia[c]	80
Nitric acid[c]	15
Ammonium nitrate[c]	20
Chlorine and caustic soda[c]	20
Oxygen[c]	400
Pulp and paper[c]	130
Heavy machinery[d]	500,000
Construction materials[d]	50,000
Light manufactures[d]	100,000

[a]Set by the National Development Program.
[b]In kilowatts.
[c]In metric tons.
[d]In dollars.

Source: Corporación Venezolana de Guayana (1963, p. 4).

the extraordinary range of obstacles to be overcome. Included in this range of obstacles, of course, are the physical and spatial dimensions with which we have been concerned so far. A consideration of the regional economic approach in Guayana can contribute constructively to practical reflections on the spatial aspects of economic development throughout Latin America.[53]

In the first place, it is clear that spatial obstacles and regional unbalance in Latin America are not necessarily permanent characteristics of the economic landscape. These deterrents are in many cases modifiable given appropriate policy determinations, quantitatively and qualitatively supported by new capital, new technology, additional labor, new skills, new organization, and constructive changes among the noneconomic variables. The distinguishing line between the so-called hard and soft variables is not that clear-cut at regional or national levels anywhere in Latin America.[54]

In the second place, decisions to institutionalize and adopt measures to stimulate the flow of capital, increase the labor supply, and introduce technical

[53] See Higgins (1968, p. 479):

The neglect until very recently of the spatial aspects of economic development is all the more unfortunate because it is generally being realized that the spatial relationships are at the very core of the development problem. There are almost no 'underdeveloped countries.' There are only underdeveloped areas, and an underdeveloped country is one in which the underdeveloped areas are a very large proportion of the total economy. Also see Siebert (1968).

[54] See Powelson's illuminating observations in "Towards an Integrated Growth Model" (1968, pp. 57–59).

change emerged, as we have seen, from carefully assembled and tested data—a prerequisite to the formulation of the model which followed and for decision-criteria as well for the selection of instrument variables.[55]

In the third place, a priori dogmatism, if any, vis-à-vis foreign investment and private enterprise surrendered to the economic realities of Venezuela's development needs.

Let us now look at some indicative changes in the economic landscape of the Guayana region. We have already seen that the complex of towns which makes up Ciudad Guayana is the locus of the new industrial area. Its locational advantages include its situation at the confluence of the Caroni and Orinoco rivers, its proximity to natural resources and hydroelectric power, and its tourist potential. The Orinoco allows year-round access to the Atlantic Ocean, and ocean-going ships drawing up to 30 feet can sail up the Orinoco for 215 miles to pick up the products of the new industrializing region. U.S. Steel, located on the western side of the river, and Bethlehem Steel, on the eastern side, ship ore via the Orinoco to their plants in the United States. The expansion of industrial capacity under public and private enterprise cooperation is demonstrated in the CVG-owned and -managed steel mill (SIDOR) in Matanzas on the Orinoco and the CVG-managed aluminum plant (ALCASA) in Ciudad Guayana.[56] SIDOR's iron ore supply from nearby deposits is mined by private enterprise, and power for the ore-reduction furnaces is supplied from the CVG Macagua hydroelectric plant on the Caroni. SIDOR's products are sold to domestic oil and construction industries and exported to Japan, Mexico, Argentina, Italy, Colombia, and even the United States. ALCASA, built on an equal partnership basis with Reynolds Metals International, had an initial capacity of 10,000 tons.[57]

An increased demand for energy inevitably accompanied the expansion of industrial capacity and the anticipation of future expansion. The Macagua hydroelectric plant on the Caroni put in operation in 1959 generages 500,000 kw. The gigantic Guri plant when fully in operation has an anticipated capacity of 3 million kw. Power from this plant may well be supplied to Brazil, Colombia, and the Republic of Guyana, as well as to the eastern and central parts of the country.

Obviously, increased regional output is functionally dependent on an increased supply of labor. The population of Ciudad Guayana in 1950 was only 4000. Three main factors have influenced rapid increases in labor supply since then. These are migration, technical training, and the provision of a planned urban environment not only conducive to the retention of the labor force but also an incentive to labor performance. The creation of the city of Ciudad Guayana has introduced several exceptional aspects into the spatial landscape of

[55] See Siebert (1968, pp. 185–200).

[56] In 1962 SIDOR started production of seamless pipes, structural shapes, rods, bars, and wire. The mill has an ingot capacity of 750,000 tons and can produce 600,000 tons of finished products a year. In 1968, SIDOR embarked on a $150 million enlargement program to make rolled plates and coil and sheet steel.

See also Meier (1965, pp. 145–152) on the "resource-oriented" organization of space.

[57] The first phase involved a battery of 70 reduction cells producing 10,000 tons a year of 99.5 percent pure aluminum ingots. With 70 more units added, production rose to 22,500 tons in 1969. Plans call for the development of a mill producing pulp for shipment to Caracas and for an enriched-ore plant utilizing natural gas with an annual capacity of one million tons of pellets with an iron content of from 80 to 85 percent.

Latin America. Like Brasilia, the creation of Ciudad Guayana expressed a deliberate act of policy, but, unlike Brasilia and other urbanization in Latin America, the expansion of Ciudad Guayana has proceeded concomitantly with industrial expansion. The population of Ciudad Guayana stood at 50,000 in 1962, and is expected to expand to 415,000 in 1975 (see Table A.20) and exceed 600,000 in the 1980s.[58] It is by design a coherently planned industrial city. By 1975, 70 percent of the production of goods and services will originate from manufacturing. As Table A.19 shows, Ciudad Guayana by 1975 will produce 95.2 percent of the total value added of metal products for all Venezuela and 37.6 percent of the total value added of machinery and transportation equipment. The labor force working in heavy manufacturing between 1966 and 1975 will have increased numerically over 5½ times. Much of the industry is large-scale and capital intensive and because of this, official calculations estimate the productivity of the labor force of Ciudad Guayana by 1975 at twice the average for Venezuela. In turn, changes in industrial structure and labor productivity are reflected in changes in the levels of family incomes. In 1962, 72 percent of the 8650 families of the city belonged to the low income group earning an average annual income of $2667 (U.S.). It is projected that by 1975 this figure will be reduced to 28 percent.

The economic interrelationships of the city with the national and international economy have prevented the city from being an isolated spatial point, a characteristic prevailing in much of Latin America's empty spaces. According to official calculations, 40 percent of the goods and services generated in the area will be exported, 35 percent consumed, and 25 percent invested. Imports will account for 27 percent of the needs of the city. Ciudad Guayana, in becoming the incipient Pittsburgh of Venezuela, begins to belie the observation that Latin America has no Chicago away from the coast.[59]

It is projected that the population of Ciudad Guayana will expand approximately 150 times between 1950 and the 1980s. Migration has been stimulated by publicity about expanding economic horizons, work opportunities, favorable wage levels, and increased provision for education, technical training, housing, health, and sanitary and recreational facilities. The organized flow of official information makes it abundantly clear that the city seeks to create an atmosphere "that will attract and hold the entrepreneurs and technicians necessary to initiate and manage its growing industrial base, since excellence in these fields will be an essential ingredient in keeping Guayana competitive in the world market."[60] The majority of the migrants come from within the state of Bolívar (where Ciudad Guayana is located) and from neighboring states, the migration

[58]Cf. Tannenbaum (1966, p. 21): "In the next few generations only a miracle could populate the now empty spaces of the eastern Andes and that half of South America that roughly falls within the Amazonian belt, and make them flourish. And this judgment is but slightly affected by such developments as the iron mines on the Curane River in the Orinoco delta in Venezuela. . . ."

[59]Ibid., p. 12: "The vast majority of the 135,000,000 people in South America live within 200 miles of the coast. The great urban centers face out toward the sea and not toward the interior. There is no St. Louis, Chicago, Minneapolis, Denver, and Salt Lake City in the center of South America."

[60]See Corporación Venezolana de Guayana (1963, pp. 37–38). For a theoretical comment on the information aspects of labor mobility between regions, see Siebert (1968, pp. 55–59).

flow being stimulated further by the marginality of the position of the migrant before migration.[61] Improved transportation to Ciudad Guayana as well as the intense impact of official information flows, have created, as Hans Singer puts it, "a general sense of moving forward" (1964, p. 54).

The Impact on Agriculture

Industrial concentration and changing income levels in the Guayana region inevitably meant an increased demand for food. Transportation costs for food were high and food itself was scarce and costly. It became necessary to increase food production within the region, import it from another region, or import it from abroad. The first alternative was impossible because of severe natural limitations. The large area of empty land around Ciudad Guayana, with its thin layer of soil overlying a granite structure, is unsuitable for large-scale agriculture. The third alternative would have been self-defeating in terms of wasting foreign exchange and weakening endogenous transformation ambitions. The second alternative remained the only rational choice. Massive investment in industrial change, accompanied by institutional and other innovations, had to be repeated in the neighboring Amacuro delta in eastern Venezuela to meet the increased demand for food in Guayana.[62] Once again the methodology of the approach to secure a transition from a state of agrarianism to dualism (to use Fei's and Ranis's descriptive distinctions), is important.[63] It was simply a repeat of the approaches used to effect a regional industrial transformation in Guayana.

Once again geographic factors imposed higher than usual costs in overcoming obstacles to the spillover effects of industrial change. The Orinoco delta, made up of 26 channels flowing into the Atlantic, occupies some 50 percent of the Amacuro delta. Agrarianism obviously dominated until CVG, given the power to develop agriculture in the territory, initiated a massive investment effort to improve agricultural output. The delta, an area of 7000 square miles, cut up into innumerable islands by a meandering river, had a population of only 40,000 in 1961, 10,000 of whom lived in the territorial capital of Tucupita. The rest were spread out in several villages, growing a variety of crops in flood-menaced areas where the only transportation was by small craft through shallow river channels. Agricultural transformation in the Amacuro delta, therefore, has involved massive

---

[61] A consequence of the declining demand for unskilled labor in the eastern oilfields and of long-standing depressed conditions in agriculture in the state of Sucre. It should be noted, however, the Ciudad Guayana faces the old problem of slums (barrios) being erected by unskilled and impecunious migrants—a cultural import!

[62] Studies initiated by the CVF in 1959 and continued in 1960 showed that the soils of the llanos north of the Orinoco were unsuitable for large-scale agricultural development.

[63] See Fei and Ranis (1964, p. 4):

The central feature of agrarianism is the overwhelming preponderance\of traditional agricultural pursuits. The agrarian economy is essentially stagnant, with nature and population vying for supremacy over long periods of recorded history. Moreover, the prognosis for the future is 'more of the same.' The central feature of dualism, on the other hand, is the coexistence of a large agricultural sector with an active and dynamic industrial sector. Its inherent condition is one of change, and its vision of the future is the ultimate graduation into economic maturity.

inputs—particularly intrastructural investment for drainage dikes, canals, roads, housing, and of course for agricultural experimentation and support services.[64]

CONCLUSIONS

Spatial obstacles must be considered in any analysis or evaluation of development in Latin America where the dissemination of growth impulses and the securing of regional articulation are the object. It is not sufficient, however, to simply mention spatial obstacles and ignore the implications of imposed alternative costs, the pressures on scarce resources, and the retarding effect on the development process of a situation where population pressures cannot be readily reduced in the near future.[65] Physical structure and regional disequilibrium clearly dominate Latin America and demand massive investment and organizational and technological initiative of tremendous dimensions to fulfill the development visions of Latin America. We cannot accept these boundary conditions as insuperable, despite their undoubted significance. Yet the myth of impossibility— a myth which population pressures and the prospects for technological change disallow—can persist. Consider the following observations on the Guayana region:

. . . the Guayana Highlands are the most remote and undeveloped geographic section of Venezuela. . . . Mineral deposits are believed to be great, but the problems of exploitation and transportation are extreme. While the potential for development is large, the future remains fairly dim. Most of the highlands are unpopulated except for a few small groups of primitive Indians, and the entire region is little known and largely unmapped.[66]

Although we might argue, as data emerge, about the induced allocation of scarce resources in terms of the ideals of economic efficiency, the point is that internal economic policies did evolve to break the constraints regarded by too many as permanently insuperable.[67]

Other things being equal, appropriate approaches can emerge to suit appropriate situations. Changed economic characteristics make it obvious that this has been the case in the Guayana and Orinoco delta regions of Venezuela. The integrated approaches and the outward push of the transformation curves

[64]The first investments included the building of a dam across the Mánamo channel of the Orinoco with three locks to regulate the water flow and prevent flooding in the rainy season. Next, 62 miles of flood control dikes had to be built along other channels to save half the delta area from being flooded. A 20-mile road was built to connect Tucupita with the rest of Venezuela, and displaced farmers were provided with substantial housing.

[65]See Domar (1957, p. 18): "a comprehensive theory of growth should include physical environment, political structure, incentives, educational methods, legal framework, attitude to science, to changes, to accumulation—just to name a few."

[66]Burnett and Johnson (1968, p. 201). Cf. Leontieff (1963, pp. 116, 123–124), and Mansfield (1968). See also Street (1969, pp. 39–47), and Enke (1963, pp. 91–106, 107–123).

[67]See Lipsey and Steiner (1966, p. 7–11). Also see Kohler (1968, pp. 316–347, 470–471).

followed the internal discovery of method and reconciliation to politically admissible terms in respect of private enterprise, foreign capital, and imported technology.

The limited substitution of government intervention for private entrepreneurial penetration may cause classical and even neoclassical eyebrows to lift. But with the pressures and the immediacy of the goals under the Alliance for Progress, development by laissez faire on the evidence of the pre-CVG status of the regional economies we have examined could not fill the bill. Nor could development through a complete command approach fill the bill, given the sociopolitical values of post-Jiménez Venezuela and of the Alliance for Progress to which Venezuela subscribes.[68] Accelerating the speed of development under a limited command approach was the only alternative.[69] There may be argument about the applicability of the approach to other Latin American countries, but the results clearly demonstrate that, despite the dimensions, geographically imposed spatial deterrents can be modified.

We turn now to an examination of development-related aspects of the status of the principal agent and, of course, the object of the economic transformation, namely the Latin American people.

[68]Pérez Jiménez was dictator of Venezuela in the period 1948–58.
[69]Cf. Vernon (1964).

CHAPTER 4

THE HUMAN CONDITION IN LATIN AMERICA

In this chapter we examine the social dimensions of the problem of development in Latin America. Even a brief appraisal of the problem will point up the inadequacy of the human resources to meet the immediate development requirements of Latin America and the magnitude of the demand on economic performance if the human condition in Latin America is to be decisively improved. If we take into account the almost uncheckable population pressures, the spatial dimensions to be overcome, and the social boundary conditions, the cumulative picture begins to add up to an unusually anxious economic situation. Unless the economy is appropriately speeded up and the development steps we have outlined implemented, other solutions might be found which would produce a far more complex situation.

SOCIAL CONSTRAINTS ON DEVELOPMENT

We focus first on the relationship between social conditions and economic development, since social factors affect human skills.[1] Among those factors which constitute constraints on economic development in Latin America are: social arrangements and social values; health, nutrition, and environmental sanitation; housing; education; and entrepreneurship. We deal in this chapter with the status of health, nutrition, and environmental sanitation in Latin America. In the following two chapters we discuss housing conditions and the status of education. Empirical evidence of conditions in selected countries has been included to assist the reader in coming to terms with the reality of the situation in one or two particular countries. Quantitative indicators, however, are only relative estimates.

The General Relationship

In Latin America, the need for transformation of social values and of the social structure is as fundamental to economic development as the accumulation of capital and advances in technical progress. Where people are concerned, to concentrate merely on human skills is to ignore the realities of the social context. Latin American economists, who live with the realities, cannot afford to play the game of blind man's bluff, factoring out noneconomic variables under the residual umbrella of *ceteris paribus* (other things being equal) or ignoring them altogether to meet the traditional formalities of economic analysis. The functional

---

[1] Cf. Bruton (1965, pp. 110–117, 240–253).

65

relationship between the social milieu and economic advance is actively recognized by concerned leadership in most developing countries. Traditionally, however, this relationship has remained marginal territory for the sophisticated economist or has been relegated to the sociologist, psychologist, anthropologist, historian, or even the novelist.[2]

The differences between Latin American economists and economists from developed countries, and between economists in general and other social science specialists, are, however, being significantly reconciled where noneconomic variables are concerned. Tomás Roberto Fillol, for instance, in an important study of the Argentine case, sought "to demonstrate [that] the nature of Argentina's basic problem is fundamentally, though not exclusively, *social* rather than economic." According to Fillol:

The fact that the Argentines are a "conglomeration" of people rather than an organic "community," together with the fact that those same cultural traits also constitute a powerful barrier to the appearance of "western-capitalistic-like" economic initiative in the bulk of the society's members, is and has been in the past a fundamental impediment retarding the nation's economic growth (1961, pp. 2–3).[3]

Latin American specialists meeting in Mexico in 1969 chose to view the development process as "the result of the interplay of economic, social and political factors."[4] Changes in attitudes, values, and patterns of behavior were regarded as essential prerequisites to development in Latin America.

The (planned) importance of *ex-ante* changes in noneconomic variables in order to accelerate economic development (together with the traditional economic inputs) derives empirical support from the experience of development during the Alliance years. The Inter-American Development Bank noted in its report in March, 1963, that "during the past two decades, political, economic, and social events have gradually brought about a realization in the Hemisphere that the development of Latin America could not achieve proper balance and the necessary momentum unless a share of resources were allotted to social investment programs to supplement traditional investments." As a result, social investment programs have become "conceived of as an integral and essential part of a policy of economic development of the Latin American area, and as a means of rapidly incorporating Latin America's masses in the growth process" (1963, p. 1).[5]

Sociologists have expectedly come to terms with the recognition of the functional relationship between social factors and accelerated economic develop-

---

[2] See Okun and Richardson (1962, pp. 334–416).

[3] Cf., however, Prebisch (1970, p. 5): "It is frequently argued that this internal social integration [of the underprivileged masses] must first be achieved, and then industrial integration at the Latin American level. A great mistake. Internal integration calls for the acceleration of development."

[4] Stavenhagen (1970, pp. 57–58). Stavenhagen wrote as senior staff associate of the International Institute for Labor Studies, which sponsored the Symposium on Social Participation in Latin America held at El Colegio de Mexico in Mexico City, October 14–16, 1969.

[5] In September, 1960, the Special Committee called by the OAS to meet in Bogota recommended that an Inter-American Program for Social Development be set up *inter alia* to carry through "as considered appropriate in each country" measures for the improvement of the conditions of rural living, of housing and community facilities, of educational systems and training facilities and of health. At the same time, a special Inter-American Fund for Social Development was set up by the United States, with the Inter-American Development Bank as "the primary mechanism for its administration."

ment.[6] This is no more than a return to the assertions of John Stuart Mill.[7] For economists, *ceteris paribus* may have implied recognition of the importance of social factors. As we have said, however, the gap between Latin American economists and North American economists in the treatment of noneconomic variables is no longer as persistent as indicated in John Powelson's observations (1968, pp. 57-85). The reconciliation has not been however without some hesitancy. In speaking of health factors, James McKenzie Pollock gives expression to this *détente* when he points out:

Not so long ago many of the classical economists regarded investment in health as a consumer service which contributed little to development and in fact syphoned off resources which they considered could be better expanded in other ways to achieve that magic figure of 5 percent annual economic gain. A few rearguard exponents of this point of view still remain but the experience of the last few years has convinced most development economists that the creation of a social as well as an economic infrastructure is necessary for balanced development (1966, pp. 14-17).

It is worth repeating that the social milieu including attitudes, social organization, and a whole spectrum of social factors cannot be factored out as prerequisites to accelerating development. Singer, for instance, comes to terms with this fact when he recognizes that improvements in health, education, nutrition, housing, and social security are "the keys to growth."

This raising of the level of people's life is both the objective of development and also its instrument. Improvement in people's level of life can be achieved both directly ["social development"] or indirectly via income and economic resources ["economic development"]. But a rational development policy must be able to look at these things as a single entity; where they are taken apart for analytical or descriptive purposes, where they must be put together again in policy as well as in final analysis (1965, p. 5).[8]

Changes in social attitudes, values, and organization, of course, follow modernization, but the social milieu in Latin America represents such a deterrent to accelerated development that social transformation cannot be postponed if the human resources are to be mobilized for speeding the development thrust. Three observations are essential here. First, in the long run the distinction between noneconomic and economic variables may fade out, as has happened in the course of economic evolution in the developed countries.[9] A country can wait hopefully for noneconomic factors obstructing the development momentum to disappear ultimately. However, population pressures in Latin America and the generally low level of life necessitate the overturning of retarding social factors in the interest of development now. Yet these are factors of immense dimensions, and deeply ingrained social inhibitions cannot be changed overnight.

---

[6]See Moore (1951), Hoselitz (1962, pp. 337-348), Brenner (1966, p. 177), and Lipset and Solari (1967).
[7]For a comment on John Stuart Mill's treatment of the role of noneconomic phenomena, see Spengler (1960, pp. 118-124).
[8]Cf. Hagen (1962) and Bruton (1965, pp. 241-262).
[9]Cf. Habakuk (1968, pp. 33-48).

Second, if we admit the importance of social transformation in Latin America, we get caught up in the old problem of circularity. The opportunity cost of changing social values and arrangements is high. Development is essential to pay for social transformation and social transformation is essential for development. Resources in Latin America are limited and uncertain, making for an excruciating allocation problem between social expenditures and other sectoral claims. Political overtones inevitably intrude, frequently causing misallocation or overallocation and generating unhelpful conflicts. Even if decision-making were eminently rational, the fundamental dilemma of the incapacity of many Latin American countries to finance the social sector still remains. The U.N. Economic Commission for Latin America, in its report for 1967, noted bluntly that in the Latin American countries with a low per capita output, low level stagnation spells not only a low capacity to meet the enormous educational and other social needs, but also the loss through migration of the few professionals and technicians produced by the countries (1969, p. 49).

Our final observation reveals the formidable dimension of the task confronting Latin America where noneconomic variables are concerned. We know the constraints exist not only as hallowed cultural peculiarities but also as severe deterrents to economic development. The situation appears even more grave if we regard Denison's analysis of economic growth in the United States as relevant to Latin America; during the first half of the twentieth century capital and land contributed only around 12 percent to U.S. development. Other factors, including increased education of the labor force, contributed 85 percent.[10] We do not know how limiting the constraints are in Latin America since researched data is scarce. Yet the persistence of these uncertainties may be a factor in producing an unbalanced growth, defeating Latin America's aspirations for balanced growth.[11] These constraints are not easy to change, and their continuation inhibits social participation and effective and rapid decision-making in the development process.

The functional relationship of health, nutrition, housing, and education to accelerated economic development can be readily appreciated. As we have seen, there is growing agreement between Latin American and North American economists that existing cultural norms can adversely affect economic growth and inhibit economic progress unless endogenously changed.[12] This is not a new discovery. Moreover, modern empirical evidence overwhelmingly supports the blunt observation that:

Economic theorists are coming to recognize that the central process of economic growth is not so much accumulation of material resources as upgrading of human resources along with technology. People must acquire modern horizons, working habits and, above all, technical skills. As they do, the economy increases in productive capacity and flexibility.[13]

---

[10] See Michaelis (1968, pp. 492–501), who indicates that even the United States is not exempt—though at a different economic level—from social conditioning factors. Cf. U.N., Department of Economic Affairs (1951, pp. 13–16).

[11] Cf. Bhatt (1965, pp. 88–97).

[12] Consideration of the effect of social constraints on growth is now appearing in modern basic principles of economics texts. See, for example, Lipsey and Steiner (1966, pp. 685, 697).

[13] Keesing (1967, p. 306). See also Meier (1970, pp. 5, 598–633). Cf. Kerr et al. (1964).

That the quality of the population is a basic correlate to the capacity of the economy to expand has never been doubted by Latin America economists. Latin American social scientists have continuously rejected imposed economic development models as inappropriate for Latin America. On the other hand, they have never underestimated the tenacity of traditional social factors and the extent to which these noneconomic variables constitute an obstacle to economic development.[14] We can now bring the relationship between cultural factors and economic growth into focus.

Noneconomic variables as constraints to the accelerated economic advance that Latin America requires must not be ignored. If we accept the human factor as the dominant development determinant, we can see that the continuing resistance of values, attitudes, and social organization to modernizing necessities, combined with substandards in health, nutrition, housing, and education, means continued undermobilization of potential human resources which are critical to accelerated growth in Latin America. In a comparison of factor endowments and per capita income between Mexico and the United States, for instance, one calculation suggests that for Mexico, with a per capita income in 1958 14.2 percent that of the United States, 85.8 percent of the difference was explicable in terms of differences in human capital stock.[15] The human capital stock differential was such that, according to Krueger's calculation, "even if Mexico had had the United States' endowment per head of land, capital and other resources, Mexican per capita income would have been less than 45.6% that of the United States." With the same aggregate productions functions, Mexico's human capital stock differential had to improve to raise Mexico's per capita income above 45.6 percent that of the United States (1968, pp. 650–651). Other results of the Krueger compu-

tation $y^O = \sum_i f_i x_{i0}$ are presented in Table 4.1, and the gap between Latin

American countries and the United States in health, nutrition, and education is shown in Table 4.2. The initial conditions of the social sector clearly demand dramatic transformation to allow dramatic economic change, but dramatic transformation in the social sector is a formidable proposition which could hardly have been achieved in a single decade under the Alliance for Progress.

The question of a specific time period for overcoming the constraints of the social sector is unavoidable because of the desperate human conditions in Latin America, the low levels of per capita income, and the inexorable pressure of a population which doubles every 23 years or so. Fillol estimates that, with appropriate changes in the noneconomic variables and enlightened policies to promote rapid economic growth, it might still take Argentina "two or three generations for the new industrial environment to exert lasting effect on the dominant value orientations of the society at large" (1961, p. 111). Since Argentina is among the most advanced countries in Latin America, Fillol's estimate indicates the basic realities involved in the task of socioeconomic change in other Latin American countries.

Development: Consensus Versus Alienation and Separatism

In considering some of the salient features of the Latin American social situation

[14] See Veliz (1965, pp. 1–8). See also Sunkel (1969, pp. 21–22, 25–28).
[15] Krueger (1968, pp. 650–651).

TABLE 4.1

Per Capita Product and Importance of Human Capital Variables

	Per capita GDP as percentage of U.S. per capita GDP (1)	$\dfrac{\sum_i f_i' x_i{}^o}{\sum_i f_i' x_i{}'} \times 100$ (2)	Percentage difference explained $[100 - (2)]/[100 - (1)]$ (3)
El Salvador	7.5	45.5	58.9
Honduras	7.5	36.6	68.5
Jamaica	16.2	56.7	51.7
Japan	14.4	93.2	8.0
Mexico	14.2	45.6	63.4
Panama	15.0	51.5	57.1
Peru	7.3	51.0	52.9
Puerto Rico	23.2	59.8	52.3

N.B.: f_i' = median income in the United States in the ith class; x_{io} = fraction of population in the ith class in the country under consideration. Index i "ranges over all the age-sex-educational attainment sector classifications."

 Column (1) is U.N. estimates of country's per capita gross domestic product as a percent of the U.S. per capita gross product.

 Column (2) is estimate of $\sum_i f_i' x_i{}^o$ as percentage of U.S. income.

 Column (3) is "the percentage of the observed per capita income difference explained by differences in human capital stock." (1968).

Source: Krueger (1968).

which affect development, we start with the premise that an assimilated and enterprising population belonging to an open society, well housed, appropriately skilled, nourished, and educated, with a modern democratic government, is likely to subscribe more effectively to economic development than a population with exactly the opposite qualities.[16] In that model population, support of the development process would be rather spontaneous.

 To achieve any such spontaneous support in Latin America would mean overcoming immense social obstacles. Although social changes are taking place, Latin American society remains in the main rigidly stratified; class distances are virtually impassable. While vertical mobility is a distant hope, the society is also splintered laterally into practically noncommunicating groups. At nearly all levels, there are massive traditional constraints to rapid cultural adaptation to a modernized economy. The reality of the situation differs very much from any idealized image of a nationalist Latin America subscribing to assimilation and spontaneously predisposed to economic modernization.[17] The rigidities of history obviously cannot be loosened in a decade; yet delay invites explosive and potentially destructive political solutions.

The Oligarchy

The Latin American social structure has been largely dominated by the landed oligarchy. Historically, this has been a natural concomitant of agrarian

---

[16] Cf. Rostow (1960, pp. 26–28). See also Adelman (1961, pp. 9, 11–23).
[17] Cf. Mörner (1967).

TABLE 4.2

Selected Indicators of Health and Education

	Date	Comparable United States	Total for 19 Latin American Republics	Venezuela	Haiti
Population (in millions)	1969	203.2	257.7	10.1	5.1
GNP per capita (1967 prices in U.S. dollars)	1967	3,966	422	911	61
Health					
Life expectancy (in years)	latest	71	59	66	47
Infant mortality (per 100,000 births)	latest	22	79	46	130
Hospital beds (per 100,000 population)	latest	840	300	320	70
Inhabitants (per physician)	latest	650	1,750	1,200	16,000
Per capita caloric intake (per day)	1966	3,200[a]	2,550	2,490	1,780[b]
Education					
Primary students, ages 5–14 (in percent)	1965	81[d]	54	61	26
Secondary students, ages 15–19 (in percent)	1965	100	26	34	11
Students, ages 5–19[c] (in percent)	1965	87	47	54	23
Literacy rate (in percent)	latest	98	69	76	10

[a] 1967.
[b] 1959–61.
[c] As reported by UNESCO.
[d] Secondary figures including some primary students.

Source: U.S. Department of State (1969d).

dominance in an economy in which exclusive power accrued to the owner of the *latifundia* (the large landowner) whose power was traditionally supported by every major social institution of the society.[18] The hierarchical

---

[18] See Stavenhagen (1970, pp. 62–63) and Edelman (1965, pp. 55–84). At this point the reader may wish to note the broad interchangeability of the names *latifundia, fundo, fazenda,* and *estancia.* Economist Thomas Balogh (1965, p. 68) puts forward a sociological definition of *latifundia* as follows:

Latifundia *can be defined as a type of landownership which, whether worked directly or through tenant farmers, is sufficiently large to bring its owner a comfortable, often lavish income without much exertions. . . . The desire on the part of the landowners to increase luxury spending will increase the minimum size of the* latifundia; *conservatism and the traditional ways of behavior will decrease the size. Under these conditions, landowners are not concerned with maximizing income over a short period through a strenuous search for new techniques; all they want is to maintain income with as little effort and as little political risk as possible. This attitude is obviously an obstacle to the full development of agriculture. . . .*

arrangements of society were not, however, an invention of the Spaniards and Portuguese as is popularly imagined. Rigid social hierarchies existed before Columbus under the Incas, the Aztecs, and the Mayas. The Spanish and Portuguese simply erected in Latin America the hierarchical system which conditioned their lives in Spain and Portugal, thus reinforcing an arrangement that was already part of the great pre-Colombian civilizations of Latin America. The patron–peon relationship in agricultural activities and in mining continued after Columbus as it had been before Columbus.

Paternalism has not been unchallenged. There were Indian revolts and peasant protests which continue to the present day. Indeed, the Mexican Revolution of 1910 uprooted the power of the *hacendado* (traditional large landholder), ushered in the *ejido* (state-created peasant), and accelerated the modernization of the Mexican economy. The Bolivian Revolution of April, 1952, modified the power of the oligarchy and mobilized and consolidated a continuing influence for the peasants.[19] These examples can be multiplied. Even the armed forces in Peru, once keys defenders of the power of the oligarchy, are now in several places eroding the historic dominance of the oligarchy. In fact, the Alliance for Progress can be interpreted as a hemispheric attempt to put a peaceful end to the hegemony of the landed oligarchy.

Stavenhagen optimistically forecasts that "oligarchical domination in Latin America is running its historical course, and the crisis of the hegemony of the oligarchy simply foreshadows the latter's eventual disappearance from the political scene" (1970, p. 65). The disappearance of the oligarchy is one of the key preconditions for economic transformation in Latin America, but the central issue is not its eventual disappearance. It is that while the need for economic transformation is immediate, ending the dominance of the landed oligarchy is far from being an immediate possibility.

Put another way, the power and the attitudes of the landed oligarchy combine to represent in most of Latin America one of the most formidable basic constraints to accelerated economic development. The values of the landed oligarchy make up the major variables of what has been called the fundamentalist model which dominates the typology of value systems in Latin America.[20] These traditional values are regarded as fixed and unchangeable, and they form the criteria for judging all progress. Traditional and unchangeable roles are assigned to each group with the indigenous Latin American Indian in a position of contempt, except in Mexico. This credo of conformity and unquestioning acceptance of the traditionally dominant group serves to enhance the importance of the landowners and of social groups associated with them.[21]

Obviously what is needed is the complete substitution of an industrialist system of values with entrepreneurship and factor-augmenting technological progress at the core. A recent UNECLA study concludes that no such system has emerged to displace the fundamentalist model.[22] However, the landed oligarchy in many of the more developed countries now reluctantly share the upper echelons of the social pyramid with the new industrial elite, composed of a group of individualists

[19] See, for instance, Anderson (1967, esp. pp. 296–306).
[20] See UNECLA (1968a, pp. 77–95). See also Gillin (1960, pp. 34–38).
[21] UNECLA (1968a, p. 83).
[22] *Ibid.,* p. 83.

determined to push economic development. The tendency of this industrial elite is to combine with the new urban bourgeoisie and with organized labor against the landed oligarchy, but the latter still survive, even though uneasily.

The Middle Classes

We need not pursue the nature of the conflict between these various social groups, except to note that an immediate transformation of traditional attitudes to industrial attitudes cannot be expected from the Latin American urban middle class who, some social scientists claim, bear little resemblance to "the frugal, enterprising middle class supposed to have contributed so much to the development of nineteenth century Europe."[23] The size of the middle class varies from one Latin American country to the next, apparently according to the degree of urbanization. Inconclusive statistics give figures of 10 percent of the total population where the degree of urbanization is low up to 50 percent where the degree of urbanization is very high.

The economic role and attitudes of the middle classes are a matter of controversy. There is evidence that the middle classes are determinedly challenging the oligarchy for political and economic dominance in some countries. Other evidence indicates that the middle classes do no more than ape the ostentatious consumption patterns of the upper classes, attempting to forge business relationships and secure government jobs and protection against competition. This is obviously not an example of entrepreneurial initiative. The middle classes which form a high proportion of the populations of Argentina, Chile, and Uruguay are considered the least dynamic economically.[24] However the conflicting evidence is weighed, the middle classes have registered no decisive over-all victory over the still-prevailing fundamentalist ideas.

Oligarchical Attitudes as Development Constraints

It can be seen that although the oligarchy may eventually be uprooted, its influence still dominates much of Latin America. Oligarchic values in Latin America constitute development constraints in a number of areas. Of particular importance is the fact that oligarchic values limit the vertical mobility that is basic to the emergence of entrepreneurship and to extended economic participation. In the fundamentalist model, the patron is the patron and the peon is the peon. With this system of traditionally supported obligations, the landed oligarchy are hardly under pressure to become entrepreneurial. Oligarchic beliefs in individualism, *personalismo*, and *dignidad* have a different meaning from the interpretation of these values in North America. Each person is distinct in the Latin American view, but a maid is a maid, a floor worker a floor worker. Neither is equal to the company president nor could he ever conceivably be the company president.[25]

Individualism and *personalismo* impose severe boundary conditions on the size and structure of business organization, since the corporate structure of

[23] Wolfe (1965, p. 21).
[24] UNECLA (1968a, pp. 59-60). See also Gillin (1960, pp. 28-34), Stokes (1967, pp. 68-69), and Simplicity (1970, pp. 22-31).
[25] See Davis (1969, pp. 88-98). Cf, U.S. Senate (1967b, pp. 10-14), and Millikan and Blackmer (1970, pp. 142-152).

business implies large-scale impersonalized organization, ownership by unknown stockholders, and day-to-day direction and delegation by hired professional managers. Latin American value preferences predicate a family business, owned and managed by the family, the size of the business being determined by the importance of not losing personal touch with each employee. In recruitment of employees, of course, membership in the family takes precedence over objective qualifications. Empire-building, therefore, in the sense that the business is dominated by the patronal personality of the owner-manager, rather than organization-building impersonally defining business relationships and structure characterizes most of Latin America's business outlook. Despite considerable achievements in industrialization, the continuing dominance of the fundamentalist model slows down the adjustment of Latin American traditional values to immediately necessary industrial and technological change.

Historically, the political context has hardly been a counteractive force. After the successful revolts against Spain and Portugal, the Creoles (*hijos de algo*) replaced the Peninsulares. Independence came but it did not bring with it individual political liberty nor social fluidity.

The Rigidities of Differentiation

The persistence of the rigidities of vertical differentiation complicate the problem of communication and economic cooperation even in the most tolerant of social situations. In Brazil, for instance, with its massive Negro admixtures in the majority of the population, ethnic differences are presumed to be irrelevant. "There is a saying in Brazil," Silvert reports in a study of Chile, "that a Negro with a high position is white and that a white with a low position is Negro" (1965, p. 20). But the problem of "pigmentocracy" persists despite a gigantic attempt to overwhelm it by an *indigenismo* (nativization) ideology.[26] Chile is credited with a high degree of social tolerance, but there are rigid social gaps between "persons on the bottom of the social heap and those in the middle or on top."[27] The *roto* is the poor urban worker (equivalent to some 20 percent of the population) eking out an existence in the slums of the *poblaciones callampas* or *conventillos*. The *inquilinos* are the rural poor barely surviving on the traditional *fundos* of Chile. Silvert also observes that:

Whether or not sociologists can agree on a definition, Chileans themselves use many words to designate different class positions. They commonly speak of upper class persons, the aristocracy, the oligarchy, and so forth. Society persons are often amusingly (to an American) called members of the jailaif—*Spanish phonetic spelling for "high life." Such ideological terms as bourgeoisie are also in daily use to refer to the middle class persons who may also be called* acomodados *or "comfortable ones". . . . the poor . . . are also often called* gente humilde—*"humble people." The poor sometimes refer to themselves as* gente honesta *and to all others as* gente decente, *terms which mean just what they look like. (1965, p. 20).*

These differentiations enter into the bitter Chilean debates over alternative economic development ideologies.[28] The conflict, whatever the merits of the debate, inhibits development.

[26] See Mörner (1967, pp. 54, 147–148).
[27] Silvert (1965, p. 20).
[28] See *Time* (1970, p. 30).

The Splintered Society

The point at which economic development begins and the rate at which it is accelerated are obviously affected by the homogeneity of attitude to the development challenge, the spontaneity of popular response to common development objectives, as well as other conditions. In Latin American society, there is a high degree of social segmentation, a difficult factor to measure, but one which certainly inhibits the response of the masses to the challenge of accelerating development. Emphasis has centered largely on the vertical social profile in Latin America and its growth-inhibiting effects. However, there are also horizontal separatisms in terms of cultural outlook and economic status, in terms of linguistic differences, and of course in terms of geography, all of which add to the dimensions of the development problem in Latin America. The way in which these factors inhibit Argentina's economic development has been dealt with by Fillol (1961, pp. 2-3). We now consider some major aspects of the horizontal profile which inhibit response to development in Latin America in general.

Table 4.3 gives an indication of the polyglot composition of the Latin American population. Racial identification, however, is not as easily discernible. In much of Latin America, differences appear to be sociocultural rather than racial; racial classification is frequently a matter of individual choice. The Latin American population can alternatively be divided into those who were there before Columbus and those who came after Columbus. The former includes the Mayas, Incas, and Aztecs who built great civilizations; the latter includes the Spanish, the Portuguese, Africans, Italians, Germans, French, Dutch, Middle Easterners, Jews, Asians, and other groups. In the case of the latter group, as we have seen, there are still inhibitions to the assimilation of the Negro. There are also, in the case of other groups, boundary conditions to their absorption because of barriers to vertical mobility. This applies to *mestizos* (the mixture of European and Indian) and the *mulatto* (the mixture of European and African) in areas where these groups are not dominant.

TABLE 4.3

Population of Latin America: Area Concentration

Amerindian	thinly populated interior of South America (Amazonia)
	densely populated rural sections of southern Mexico, parts of Central America, Andean countries, parts of Paraguay and Chile
Mestizo	almost all towns, villages, rural areas; most cities
European	rural areas of southern Brazil, most of Argentina, Cuba, Costa Rica, Uruguay
	throughout much of urban Latin America
Mulatto	European dominant mulatto: parts of Cuba, Puerto Rico, Dominican Republic, Brazil
	European weak mulatto: Jamaica, parts of northeast Brazil
Negro	small sections of northeast Brazil, interior of Haiti, smaller West Indian islands.
Asian	Trinidad, Guyana, French Guiana, São Paulo (Brazil)

Source: Roberts (1969).

Viewed horizontally, these groups are splintered in a way which retards what Kindleberger calls the "aptitude for development" (1965, p. 25). Speaking of Spaniards and Indians, Tannenbaum spells out the situation as one in which "the two races met as billiard balls do on a billiard table. They met but did not penetrate" (1962, p. 37). Benton divides the Latin American population into the Vociferous Ones, the Resisters, and the Silent Ones (1961, pp. 6–9). The first group want the industrial and scientific revolution now. They include the intellectuals and professionals, the modern commercial classes, and the trade unions. They "often speak with opposing voices" but "they are all impatient." The Resisters are the traditionalists, who oppose modernization as they do nationalism and trade unionism. They comprise largely the landed oligarchy, vertically unyielding patronal defenders of an archaic agrarian structure that must yield to modernism. The Silent Ones, "silent and voiceless," include the Indians and "the silent lost people of the cities," the slum dwellers. Benton might have called the last group "the excluded ones," for they are virtually shut out by the other groups from political, economic, and broad social participation.

The Latin American Indian

The Indian population of Latin America is splintered by geography, language, and culture. It is homogeneous, however, in one major respect. The large majority live at the economic level of Rostow's traditional stage of economic growth. Yet the Indian population constitutes a majority of the total population of Bolivia, and Guatemala, nearly half the population of Peru and nearly one-third of the population of Chile and Ecuador, and over one-fifth of the population of British Honduras, if the figures in Table A.22 are correct. Figures, however, are highly unreliable. Benton reports that between one in every six and one in every 14 Latin Americans is an Indian (1961, p. 4). James has said that more than 80 percent of the people of Mexico are Indians "of one kind and another," 29 percent of the total Mexican population being pure-blooded Indian (1959, p. 587). Table A.22 suggests a figure of 8.8 percent for Mexico. A 1948 estimate puts the Indian population of Honduras at 40 percent, Paraguay at 65 percent, Colombia at 12 percent, as against 5.5 percent, 3.8 percent, and 1.6 percent in the table.[29] According to an official Brazilian estimate,[30] around 30 million of Brazil's 94 million people could claim some degree of Indian ancestry as compared with an estimate of 1.5 percent in Table A.22. Despite these discrepancies, the relative significance of the Indian population is clear.

The Indian population includes nomads, fishermen, and subsistence farmers scattered all over Latin America.[31] Linguistic differences isolate not only Indian from Indian but combine with geographical and cultural factors to isolate the Indian population from the rest of society. In Mexico, in 1950, 50 languages had to be used to complete the census; 7 percent of the Mexican population neither spoke nor understood Spanish.[32] In Bolivia, in 1960, 38 percent of the Indian population spoke only Aymara and 54 percent spoke only Quechua. Dialects

[29] Stokes (1967, p. 62).
[30] Brazilian Government Trade Bureau (1970, p. 8).
[31] Araucanians (Chile); Chibchas (Colombia); Jivaros (Peru); Onas, Yagans, and others (southern tip of South America); Tupi, Ges, and others (Brazil); Arawaks, Wapisiani, and others (Guyana).
[32] James (1959, p. 587).

further subdivide these languages creating a maze of communication barriers. Only 6 percent spoke some Spanish.[33] Brazilian Indians, who speak an estimated 90 different languages and some 300 dialects, can be classified by language.[34] Linguistic difference and geographical separatism obviously militate against rapid and effective communication and add to the range of development constraints.

In a good deal of Latin America, geography supports cultural separation. In Peru, for instance, the Sierra is a greater cultural divide than geography. The Sierra is the home of the majority of the Peruvian Indians, who are descended from the Incas and make up some 50 percent of the Peruvian population. The Social Progress Trust Fund of the Inter-American Development Bank reported in 1966:

One of the principal features of life in the Sierra is the survival of pre-Columbian cultures, with distinct languages, strong communal ties, attachment to ancestral land, the prevalence of subsistence farming, and resistance to the values and practices of modern life because the benefits of socioeconomic progress that has taken place elsewhere in Peru did not reach the Sierra until recently. These features and the relative isolation of the indigenous communities have made the integration of Peru a difficult task . . ." (Feb. 28, 1966, p. 515).

Agricultural productivity is highest on the coast where the European and the *mestizo*—the upper and middle strata of Peru—are located. In comparison, agricultural productivity is low and crops are principally for domestic consumption. Output per agricultural worker on the coast is an estimated three times that of the worker on the Sierra.[35]

To the European and the *mestizo*, the Indian of the Sierra is permanently inferior, and the *mestizo* left behind in the Sierra only slightly less so. To move back to the Sierra is considered a form of social sickness. But the *campesinos* (peasants), deprived of land, repeatedly move down to the coast in violence, invading the haciendas and commandeering private property.[36]

In Guatemala, the population is similarly segmented into Indians and *ladinos*, the counterpart of the *mestizos*. As in Peru, the Indians are relegated to permanent inferiority by the *ladinos*. The Indians themselves are split into several communities by geography, language, and custom, with communities spreading out into the eastern highlands, the southeast coast, and the northern third of Guatemala, the Petén. They live at near-starvation levels. In Brazil, the economic status of the Ge tribes illustrates the economic backwardness which is part of the economic transformation problem. The Ge tribes inhabit the area between the Amazon Valley and the Parana Basin. Their farmlands are not productive; they live by hunting. They are nomadic and clannish, and their economic and social behavior

---

[33] Adams et al. (1960, p. 113).

[34] Brazilian Government Trade Bureau (1970, p. 8).

[35] The coast accounted for some 83 percent of Peru's agricultural exports. Output per person in the 1950s is estimated to have increased by 20 percent; output per worker employed in agriculture for domestic consumption fell by 6 percent.

[36] See Inter-American Development Bank (1963, p. 263) and Kitty (1967, pp. 23, 51, 67, 119, 141–142). It is said that an Indian in Peru ceases to be an Indian simply by wearing sandals instead of shoes and by speaking Spanish instead of Quechua. In Brazil, an Indian becomes Brazilian simply by putting on pants, a shirt, and shoes and joining the general population.

is governed by rigid cultural norms. Because of language differences, one variety of the Ge tribes cannot even communicate with another. They have not even reached the pottery-making stage, and their capital equipment seems limited to arrows and stones.[37] Given these initial conditions, even reactive nationalism would find modernizing the Ge tribes a formidable task.[38]

Marginality

Another social phenomenon which serves to arrest the growth of the economy is marginalism. Latin America still remains a continent of submerged millions who in turn remain largely factored out of any contribution or any decisive contribution to the process of development. This phenomenon is now receiving considerable analytical attention[39]—in terms of quantifying the phenomenon. Marginalism has always been an embedded constraint to changing the behavior of the economy and yet it is dependent on economic change for its solution.

Although the term is subject to differing interpretations, the problem centers on the extent to which all sections of the population participate in the development process. The International Labor Office views participation as the contribution of individuals and groups of the economically active population to the speeding up of economic and social development. Stavenhagen, while accepting this view, goes further. He sees participation as including organized action to reject and replace the existing economic and social system. He regards the marginal mass in Latin America as nonfunctional in relation to the prevailing economic system.[40] The Chilean-based organization DESAL (Center for the Economic and Social Development of Latin America) suggests that the distinguishing characteristic of the marginal population resides "in lack of participation; as derived from the lack of belonging which is, in turn, a product of the lack of receptivity, i.e., rejection by participating society."[41] According to DESAL, marginal groups are further characterized by low levels of productivity and production, low standards of living, low educational and cultural levels, and low incomes— all signifying an enormous gap between the access to resources and benefits enjoyed by the traditionally privileged, participating Latin American sectors and the marginal groups. If society is considered as a network of social decisions, the marginal groups of Latin America are factored out of contributive or active participation. They do not participate in any policies directed at solving their own particular problems. The marginal groups lack organizational linkages with the rest of society and are unrepresented in the institutions of participating society. As DESAL puts it, the marginal mass is structurally and functionally nonintegrated vis-à-vis the requirements of modernization. Because of this, they become increasingly isolated and alienated.

It is important at this stage to look at the quantitative estimates of the marginal problem. The marginal population includes the Indian communities, peas-

---

[37] See Brazilian Government Trade Bureau (1970, p. 8).

[38] See Rostow (1960, p. 26): "As a matter of historical fact a reactive nationalism . . . has been a most important and powerful motive force in the transition from traditional to modern societies, at least as important as the profit motive."

[39] See, for instance, UNECLA (1969, pp. 43–45).

[40] Stavenhagen (1970, pp. 60–61, 72).

[41] See DESAL (1967, 1968).

ant conglomerates, slum dwellers, and subproletarian aggregates.[42] DESAL estimates the marginal population at some 180 million Latin Americans and characterizes them as living under inhuman living conditions—the components of which include a life expectancy of 35 years; an annual income level of little more than $100; an illiteracy rate of some 80 percent; illness and, above all, despair. UNECLA calculations put the urban marginal group at some 25 percent of the urban population of Latin America.[43] This group, according to UNECLA, grows 10–15 percent a year, a rate of growth obviously higher than the already high urban population growth rate.

It can be argued that Stavenhagen's nonfunctional definition of the marginal mass is not entirely accurate. For rural workers, even though feudally dominated by the hacienda, are playing a traditional economic and social role. They perform a function. Urban marginal workers do have organizations and do have jobs, even though at the lowest levels of security and pay. There is evidence of governments and political parties reaching out in varying degrees to the marginal mass stimulating them into participation in the process of change. On the other side, there is controversy about approaches to solve the problem of marginality. One view is that the marginal population is incapable of self-improvement. Another view is that the increasing degree of marginality emerges from a pattern of economic growth in which the dynamic sectors of the economy cannot, without a change in the present economic structure, provide enough job opportunities to allow the whole population to participate fully in the market.

For our argument, two points are important. First, it is not that the role of the marginal population is nonfunctional. It is that the traditional functions fulfilled by the marginal population in agriculture contribute only to the maintenance of its traditional backwardness; in the towns their jobs, such as they are, make no contribution to the modernization of the economy. Second, and this is the basic point, whatever the reasons and whatever the solutions for marginality, the initial condition is that an estimated 60–75 percent of the Latin American population remains excluded from any significant contribution to the acceleration of economic development.[44] They remain as an untapped input; they remain as an unexploited market.

We turn now to health and housing as development constraints in Latin America.

[42] See UNECLA (1969, pp. 44–45).

[43] The marginal population figure includes some 115 million of the rural population but excludes 50 to 60 million Latin Americans, a group termed by Toynbee as "herodianos," people who are better integrated with Europe or the United States than with their own hinterland. This group is not part of the demographically exploding poor, but, as pointed out earlier, they are part of the problem. They have failed to develop a home-grown ideology for the solution of home-based poverty in the rural countryside and in the towns.

[44] Cf. Prebisch (1970, p. 5). A study conducted in 1966 by DESAL's Agrarian Section and the Center for Economic Research of the Catholic University (CIELIC) showed that in greater Santiago only 2 to 2.4 percent of the marginal population participated in political organizations. Only 2.1 to 2.9 percent of those over 15 were in cooperatives; 7.4 to 14.7 percent in trade union groups; 2.2 to 12.1 percent in neighborhood councils; and 9 to 17.7 percent in mothers' centers. The slum dwellers earned an average of $12.75 (U.S.) monthly while the national average monthly income per person in Chile then stood at $31 (U.S.).

HEALTH AS A DEVELOPMENT CONSTRAINT

We have already recognized that improvements in health, sanitation, nutrition, housing, and education are keys to growth, along with the other traditional variables, capital and technology. Better health, like better education, causes an improvement in output since it improves the quality of the labor force. It is not that simple, however, in Latin America. Improved health facilities, which have reduced the death rates dramatically, have also caused a phenomenal increase in the population. In turn, the added population has been a depressant to per capita gains. As we have noted earlier, if the increased rate of growth of outputs steadily exceeded that of the population growth caused by better health, or if better health somehow caused a reduction in the birth rates, economic prospects might have been more promising. Possibilities for immediate reduction of birth rates to match the reduction of death rates in Latin America, however, are not promising. Despite this, for normal humanitarian reasons and because health standards are still inadequate, Latin America must continue to expand health facilities. The hope is that improvements in health along with other inputs will add so much extra output that the net growth of the economy will regularly and substantially exceed the net growth in population. A reduction in the birth rate is essential but the fact must be faced that, despite heroic efforts, this is only a long-term prospect.

The opportunity costs of improving health conditions are also very high, which add to the difficulties of allocation decisions. Investment in health implies the sacrifice of consumption as well as alternative investment priorities. Table 4.4 shows the proportion of central government expenditures allocated to health in various Latin American countries. Accurate and detailed investment estimates are not fully computed but it is clear that the financial constraints are severe. Table 4.2 gives some indication of the health gap between Latin America and the United States. This wide gap contributes, of course, to the wide differences in labor productivity. Infant mortality rates in Latin America point to an immense wastage of resources while, at the other end of the scale, the increase in life expectancy implies the increasing burden of maintaining people past working age who continue to need medical care, continue to consume, but have ceased to add to output. The economy is once again caught in a circular dilemma. Massive health inputs are essential for increased productivity and increased productivity is essential to pay for these health inputs.

An enormous investment is involved. According to one estimate, if we adopt a ratio of 4.5 hospital beds per 1000 population, the average cost of installing a bed in Latin America would lie between $10,000 and $12,000 (U.S.).[45] Another estimate[46] projected that to retain a hospital bed ratio of 2.1 beds per 1000 population to meet the needs of the increased population would require a capital investment of at least $820 million (U.S.) between 1966 and 1980 and an additional annual current expenditure of $611 million (U.S.) a year. A ratio of 4 beds per 1000 population would probably need a capital outlay of $2 billion (U.S.) and an additional current expenditure of $1.5 billion (U.S.) a year. To maintain the ratio of physicians at 1 to 2000 population in Latin America for

---

[45]Pan American Health Organization (1968, p. XVIII).
[46] See Pollock (1966, pp. 14–17).

TABLE 4.4

Expenditures for Public Health

	Total central government expenditures (in percent)
Puerto Rico[a]	22.7
Argentina	6.4
Bolivia	4.0
Brazil	2.5
Chile	7.9
Colombia	4.2
Costa Rica	6.9
Dominican Republic	7.4
Ecuador	1.9
El Salvador	14.0
Guatemala	10.3
Haiti	11.7
Honduras	9.8
Mexico	4.5
Nicaragua	11.3
Panama	14.0
Paraguay	4.1
Peru	5.2
Trinidad and Tobago	9.6
Uruguay	5.7
Venezuela	8.4

[a] For Puerto Rico, the figure is for health and welfare. From statistics of the Chemical Bank (1970).

Source: Inter-American Development Bank (1969a).

the next 20 years could mean a capital investment of $3.6 billion (U.S.) for training costs alone. A minimum rural health service utilizing largely auxiliary personnel could require a capital outlay of $5 billion (U.S.). These are immense sums of money requiring planning and international and bilateral assistance on an ever-widening scale. Enormous amounts have already been supplied under one form or another of American and World Health Organization aid.

An evaluation of the status of health, nutrition, and environmental sanitation will reveal both the progress made in Latin America and the difficulties remaining.

Health Goals Under the Alliance for Progress

Under the Charter of the Alliance for Progress, the cooperating governments set up a 10-year goal of increasing life expectancy at birth by a minimum of 5 years and of raising the capacity for learning and producing by improving individual and community health. Attaining these goals required providing adequate potable water supply and sewerage disposal to not less than 70 percent of the urban and 50 percent of the rural population; reducing the mortality rate for children under five years of age by at least 50 percent; controlling the most serious communicable diseases; ending mortality from certain specific illnesses, particularly malaria; improving nutrition; training medical and health personnel to meet minimum health needs; improving basic services; and generally harnessing science and research to prevent and cure sickness more effectively. These objectives were reaffirmed in the Declaration of the Presidents of America at Punta del Este in April, 1967.

Any attempt to assess the status of health and other related variables in Latin America is hampered by the continuing problem of defective or nonexistent statistical data. The records of death registration are poorly kept in some countries but not in other parts, particularly in the rural areas. Infants may die without ever having been registered. Defective data similarly affects the measurement of other major areas related to the health profile of Latin America.[47]

The Effect of Population Growth

The basic contemporary anxiety in the Latin American situation is the demographic explosion. The population is expected to increase by 174 percent between 1969 and 2000, compared with a world increase of 112 percent in the same period and an increase of 72 percent in North America, 25 percent in Europe, 74 percent in Oceania, 150 percent in Africa, and 67 percent in the USSR.[48] As we have seen, the rate of population growth in Latin America, generated by improved health measures, represents an enormous threat to the already not very satisfactory health status of the population. The demographic surge brings into the spotlight two particular areas of anxiety; the larger proportion of persons under 15 years of age, whose health status is of critical importance; and the disproportionate distribution of health services between the urban and the rural population.

The first situation gives rise to the problem of an increasing dependency ratio, which in Latin America now stands at a figure of 85.6 dependents per 100 persons of working age (see Table A.5). At the same time, a high mortality rate in the group below the minimum working age of 15 means nonreturns in terms of expected production output after age 15. To waste these scarce resources is an alternative cost Latin America cannot afford.

In the second case, though the rapid increase of the urban population is a potential source of increased health hazards, since health provision in the towns is far from adequate, in the rural areas, where the population is increasing at an absolute rate of 1.5 percent a year, faster than the population of the United States, the danger of health deterioration is even greater because health facilities are concentrated in the urban areas.

Despite the rapid population growth which has generated persistent pressure on existing health services, and despite defective record-keeping, it is known that life expectancy in Latin America increased from 25 to 30 years in 1900 to 60.6 years in the period 1965–70.[49] Table A.4 shows that 10 Latin American countries have a life expectancy higher than the average for Latin America. Eleven countries, however, do not, life expectancy in Bolivia being as low as 45.3 years. If we use the estimates of the Pan American Health Organization, average life expectancy in Latin America increased in the period 1960–66 by 2.3 years. Had

[47] See U.S. House (1969, p. 39).
[48] Population Reference Bureau (1969).
[49] See Prebisch (1970, p. 25).

all countries shown the same average increase, the average gain during the period would have been 3 years. Even so, however, Latin America would have achieved only 75 percent of the goal set by the Alliance for Progress.[50] The average life expectancy in Latin America is clearly above the world average of some 53 years but it is still well below the North American average of 72 years.

Initial Conditions in Health

The extension of life expectancy is dependent on a number of factors, among them, the reduction of childhood mortality, protection from disease, the eradication of disease, and changes in environmental conditions affecting human health. Research data on the relation between health inputs and health outputs is rather incomplete.[51] Nonetheless, useful general insights are possible from such data as exists. As Table 2.1 indicates, in both North America and Latin America the death rate per 1000 stands at 9. An examination of the causes of death, however, reveals important differences in the health status of the two regions.

For example, mortality of children under five accounts for 44 percent of all deaths in Latin America as against a figure of less than 7 percent for North America. There is a downward trend in childhood mortality in Latin America but, as Table A.2 shows, the goals of the Alliance are yet to be achieved in several countries. The causes of death of children under five include diarrheal diseases, measles, whooping cough, nutritional deficiencies, influenza, pneumonia, gastroenteritis, and other diseases that have largely lost significance in North America.[52] A comparative picture of the infant mortality rates in Latin America and in North America is shown in Table 2.1.

Taking the population as a whole, the level of illness and mortality caused by infectious diseases continues to be very high in Latin America, as can be seen in Tables 4.5, 4.6, and A.23. Despite significant reductions in the major epidemic diseases, they continue to affect health and economic development in Latin America, especially in newly settled areas.[53]

Nutritional Status

The Alliance for Progress recognized the necessity of improving nutritional standards in Latin America.[54] Nonetheless malnutrition still remains a major constraint to labor productivity. Comparison with the United States readily indicates the initial conditions. In the United States vitamin deficiencies and other nutritional deficiencies caused, in the period 1961-63, an annual mortality rate of 0.5 per 100,000 children under one year and 0.5 among children 1-4 years; anemias caused a death rate of 2.7 per 100,000 population under one year, and

---

[50] U.S. House (1969, pp. 39–40).

[51] See Enke (1963, pp. 398–418), an exceptional and realistic analysis of the causes of growth in less developed countries. See also Horowitz and Burke (1966, pp. 145–195), Bruton (1965, pp. 241–262), and Inter-American Development Bank (1969a, pp. 113–135).

[52] For instance, diarrheal diseases, measles, and whooping cough caused 226,000 deaths of children under five in Latin America; 98 percent of these deaths would have been avoidable in North America. Of the deaths from nutritional deficiencies, 80 percent were avoidable. See Pan American Health Organization (1968b, pp. 10–11).

[53] Pan American Health Organization (1968b, p. 13).

[54] Cf. also U.S. Department of State (1967) and Leibenstein (1957, pp. 63–66).

TABLE 4.5

Deaths From Disease, 1964

	INFECTIVE AND PARASITIC DISEASES			GASTROINTESTINAL DISEASES		
	Number	Rate[a]	Percent[b]	Number	Rate[a]	Percent[b]
North America	19,758	9.4	1.0	8,928	4.2	0.5
Middle America	70,370	106.0	10.6	67,267	101.3	10.3
South America	56,960	84.8	8.9	44,030	65.5	6.9

[a] Per 100,000 people.
[b] Percentage of total number of deaths.

Source: Pan American Health Organization (1965).

1.1 per 100,000 population 1–4 years. But in Colombia, for example, the corresponding figures were 142.3; 119.9; 27.8; 27.0. Essential foods continue to be short in Latin America and the ability to buy these foods remains limited. Understanding of nutrition is also defective. The Food and Agricultural Organization puts the minimum per capita daily requirement at 2550 calories and 71 grams of protein, of which 25 should be of animal origin. Despite nutritional improvements, as Table A.24 shows, there are still wide differences between the average nutritional status of Latin America and the United States. Thirteen countries failed to achieve the minimum daily calorie requirement, and the position with regard to protein intake was worse.

Environmental Sanitation

Water supply and sewerage systems are among the basic factors in health and labor productivity. Bad water is a direct source of disease, particularly gastroenteritis. Restricted water and sewerage provision also affects industrial expansion. Hence the recognition in the Charter of Punta del Este that by 1971, there must be potable water and sewage disposal for at least 70 percent of the urban population and 50 percent of the rural population. In 1960, only 61 percent of the urban population of Latin America had water service. Within the decade, 70 percent or more of the urban population had piped water in their homes, fulfilling one of the preliminary goals of the Alliance.[55]

Nonetheless, the provision of adequate water supplies and sewerage systems remains a serious problem in the rural areas. In 1961 only 7 percent of the rural population had water service. At the same time sewerage services were virtually absent in the rural areas, while only 29 percent of the urban population had this advantage. The backward situation of the rural areas lowered the average for the population as a whole. By 1968, only 44 percent of the total population of Latin

[55] This achievement conceals, of course, situations below this level of provision in several Latin American countries. Water service reached the following proportions of the urban population in 1968 in the countries or cities named: Haiti—20 percent, La Paz (Bolivia)—30 percent, Asuncion (Paraguay)—40 percent (see Inter-American Development Bank, 1969a). For Brazil, the Pan American Health Organization gives a figure of 44 percent (1968a, p. 46).

TABLE 4.6

Death Rates from Disease, 1966 (Per 100,000 people)

	North America	Middle America	South America
Tuberculosis	3.8	19.8	27.9
Whooping cough	0.0	12.1	12.1
Measles	0.2	18.5	15.1

Source: Pan American Health Organization (1968a).

America was served by water supply systems, since only 16 percent of the rural population was covered. By 1969, 36 percent of the urban population had sewerage services, but the position remained substantially unchanged in the rural areas except for the addition of a few septic tank and other disposal systems.[56]

There are other key constraints affecting the expansion of water and sewerage services. This expansion is functionally related to the rate of population growth, the availability of financial and physical resources, the emergence of appropriate institutions, and the availability of technical personnel and efficient administrators. The opportunity cost involved in providing these services to the rapidly growing population is high. In the period 1961-68, national and international funds for the construction of urban and rural water supply totaled more than $1468 million from all sources. Nearly 60 percent of this amount was in national funds. At the same time, it has been difficult to change traditional resource allocation which favors urban rather than rural areas. For instance, in the period 1961-67, it was estimated that $600 million was needed to meet water supply investment requirements in the rural areas; actually only $214 million was invested. To meet the cost of new water supply services for the period 1968-71 meant a total expenditure of $1343 million or $38.90 per capita for an expanded urban population of nearly 35 million, and $23 per head for an expanded rural population of 23 million. In Chile, the cost was $65 per capita for the urban population and $52 for the rural population.[57]

Without external financing, the population pressure would have caused the deterioration of already existing services, and without foreign financial insistence, the tradition would have continued of not changing appropriate user rates to make investments self-liquidating. Foreign financial assistance also enabled various Latin countries to attract investment resources into water and sewerage and to develop appropriate financial institutions. These developments in turn determined the necessity to establish appropriate regulatory agencies as well as to increase the supply of technically trained and administratively competent staff.[58]

It is an indication of the dimensions of the problem that, despite remarkable investments in water and sewerage facilities, at the end of the decade more than half of the population of Latin America remained without water and without sewerage services.

[56] See Pan American Health Organization (1968a, p. 46) and Inter-American Development Bank (1969a, pp. 127-128).
[57] See Pan American Health Organization (1968a, p. 47 and 1968b, p. 32).
[58] See Inter-American Development Bank (1969a, pp. 133-134).

Health Personnel

It is hardly fruitful at this point to attempt to set up an order of importance among the various factors affecting the health picture. But certainly a critical determinant of health and therefore of labor productivity is the supply of doctors and auxiliary health personnel in relation to the demands of the situation. For obvious reasons, the health situation cannot be readily modified in the short run—a situation which in turn affects the speed of Latin America's escape from underdevelopment. Quantitative shortages are severe. Despite the advances over the decade, the record of professional resources in health still remains defective.

Table A.25 shows that North America had far more doctors, more dentists, more graduate nurses, and more nursing auxiliaries per 10,000 population than Latin America in 1966. Similar shortages exist in the case of sanitary engineers, sanitary inspectors, veterinarians, pharmacists, laboratory technicians, X-ray technicians, and physiotherapists. Short-run solutions on present indications appear highly improbable. The minimum dimensions of the problem of medical inadequacy appear to be as follows. In 1967, it was estimated that Latin America needed more than 200,000 doctors by 1980 just to maintain its inadequate ratio of doctors to population.[59] In terms of absolute figures, the number of doctors increases year by year. In 1965, it was estimated that Latin American universities graduated some 7000 doctors a year. By 1969, following an expansion of medical training, the number of doctors graduating increased to 9200 a year. But the minimum number required was 17,000 a year.[60] The position in regard to dentists is hardly better. In the period 1960–68, the ratio of dentists remained at less than one per 10,000 population in Central America and less than 3 per 10,000 in South America. The rate of increase was less than that of the population.

Solving these deficiencies is complicated. Most of the medical personnel, like most of the medical facilities, are concentrated in the urban areas, and the economic and social deterrents of the rural areas—poor living conditions, low incomes, lack of hospitals and of transportation—may worsen the disequilibrium. As a result, the health profile of millions of Latin Americans in the rural areas could deteriorate rather than improve.

CONCLUSIONS

We have spoken in this chapter of a wide range of constraints which either prevent or slow down economic development in Latin America. Discounted at one time by economists, under the *ceteris paribus* umbrella, they are now accepted as deterrents to be taken into account when countries, particularly the less developed countries, really want to initiate the development process.[61] Determining the degree to which attitudes, social values, and low health status constitute limitations to starting development or to accelerating development is an elusive

---

[59] U.S. Department of State (1968a, p. 4).

[60] See Inter-American Development Bank (1965, pp. 75–76 and 1969a, p. 122).

[61] Bruton (1965, p. 11), uses the symbol S to equal "the social and cultural characteristics of the society, that affect the ability of the economy to produce." Adelman (1967, p. 13), uses the symbol U, representing "the entire social, cultural, and institutional complex of society." See also Leibenstein (1957, pp. 109–110).

exercise in quantification. But the general evidence is there as hard data that the emergence of entrepreneurship, the seizure of economic opportunities, the maximization of individual contribution to modern productive effort are all severely limited by the constraints we have described. They should not be ignored in assessing the dimensions of the development problem in Latin America.

We turn now to the question of housing, a deterrent as formidable as any of the other traditional variables.

CHAPTER 5

HOUSING AS A DEVELOPMENT CONSTRAINT

Housing as a development input can be considered in the same way as education, with which we deal in the next chapter. It can be treated as a consumer good or as a productive investment. Since the housing deficiencies with which we are concerned relate largely to the low income groups, we are considering housing at this level as a productive investment. Dwelling construction is part of capital formation and the United Nations has argued that fixed capital formation in dwellings should appear as a separate item in a table showing the composition of gross capital formation by type.[1] Dwelling construction in few countries accounts for more than one-third of domestic expenditure for capital formation of all kinds, but employment in construction in developed countries accounts for 20 to 30 percent of total employment in manufacturing and housing and for some 50 percent of the total direct and indirect employment in construction. Table A.26 shows that conditions in Latin America do not reach these levels. In addition to the link between housing and capital formation and employment, housing conditions relate to increased productivity because better housing has an effect on labor productivity. This functional relationship is similar to that of investment education and of health, except that in the case of health, the resulting increase in population may have a dampening effect on per capita gains, as we have seen.

HOUSING AS A BOUNDARY CONDITION

The precise relation between additional housing and additions to aggregate output is difficult to determine, but empirical experience confirms that bad housing conditions are a severe deterrent to increased labor productivity. In this chapter, we examine the extremely low level of housing in Latin America and note the extent to which housing conditions constitute a constraint to accelerated development. Because of the many ways in which housing is related to development in Latin America, the status of housing cannot be ignored in judging economic performance under the Alliance for Progress.

Housing constitutes a boundary condition to changing the initial status of the economy in several respects. The scarcity of housing severely limits the mobility of labor and the expansion of economic activity, and it generates social conflict affecting economic advance. Scarce housing results in high rents, which in turn generate pressures for higher wages. On the one hand, high rents weaken the ability to save and so weaken capital formation. On the other hand, high

[1]See UN (1963b, p. 55).

88

rents followed by high wages increase production costs, affecting not only the housing supply but also economic development in general. Beyond this, the opportunity cost of improving housing conditions is high. As in the case of all social overhead capital, investment in housing is lumpy; the returns in the short run are low; the gestation period is long; and housing investment yields no foreign exchange benefits. Without external assistance, solutions to the housing problem would be impossible. The deficit in housing is so great that attempting to correct it using domestic resources alone would introduce severe allocation problems.

Additional housing makes for increased output, but on the other hand increased housing depends on accelerated output. We have, however, treated housing in this chapter as a factor in economic growth in order to make more apparent how housing acts as a constraint in Latin America.

The Housing Deficit

We start with a primary difficulty. There are no accurate estimates of the total housing needs of Latin America. Despite discrepancies in the estimates, however, it is clear that the housing deficit is enormous. The Agency for International Development estimated in 1967 that over a million new houses will be needed annually simply to match the growth of population.[2] In March, 1963, it was estimated that the total housing shortage—urban and rural—for all Latin America stood at nearly 14 million units.[3] A 1951 estimate put the deficit in private housing units at 19,449,000—4,282,000 for the towns and 15,167,000 for the rural areas.[4] This was 63.6 percent of all existing dwellings. A Pan American Union estimate put the deficit in the same year at 25 million housing units—15 million new rural houses, 4.2 million rural dwellings needing replacement, and an additional 5.6 million dwellings soon to need replacing. Another estimate suggested that 80 million Latin Americans lack the "most elementary type of adequate housing." Under this estimate, 18 million new houses were needed at a minimum cost of some $25 billion.[5] An examination of the first five years of the Alliance for Progress, 1961-65, supported an estimate of upward of a million new housing units required to meet population growth in the towns alone.[6] In 1964, a calculation was made that the deficit stood at 8 million rural housing units and that to meet the growth of population nearly 440,000 new housing units were needed annually.[7]

Missed opportunities in the past put pressure on the present. Largely through the initiative of the Alliance for Progress and the Inter-American Development Bank it has become recognized that housing is a productive investment contributing to economic growth, increasing the ability of the worker to produce more, creating opportunities for unutilized or underutilized resources, and capable of attracting savings from even the small man. Before the Alliance, housing institutions were nonexistent, or too localized, unadventurous, or underadministered for effective performance. The statistics of the housing situation, incomplete as

[2] U.S. Department of State (1968a, p. 4).
[3] Inter-American Development Bank (1963b, p. 23).
[4] UNECLA (1963a, p. 161).
[5] UNECLA (1966, p. 16).
[6] Pan American Union (1967e, p. 184).
[7] Pan American Union (1967e, p. 198).

they are now, were even worse before 1950. The major fact was that, except for the select market among the upper and middle income bracket, housing was not a paying proposition and could not compete with profit-making alternative investment opportunities, especially in an inflationary climate.

Neoclassical economic attitudes toward housing, combined with institutional inadequacies, political indifference, the concentration on building for the small group who could afford to buy houses, and the greater and quicker profits outside the housing field, dampened housing development before 1950. After that date, the critical housing situation became further compounded by mounting population pressures and accelerated urbanization, and by social pressures for increased and better housing especially for the lower income groups. Despite massive attempts under the Alliance for Progress and significant efforts by several individual countries, the housing constraint increases in severity because the deficit in many cases becomes greater year by year (see Table A.27).

A brief look at the housing situation in Venezuela, which has an outstandingly action-oriented development context, is illuminating in assessing the Latin American situation generally, especially in countries at a less developed level.[8] According to census figures, the housing shortage in Venezuela in 1961 amounted to 540,000 units, and was expected to rise to 575,000 housing units by 1962.[9] The population in the meantime, totaling 7,900,000 in mid-1962, was increasing at the rate of 3.6 percent a year. The Venezuelan Plan for 1963–66 anticipated building 260,000 housing units, half of them in the urban areas and half in the rural areas.[10] Immediately after the Act of Bogotá, Venezuela created a number of powerful agencies committed to nothing else but housing construction. These were the Banco Obrero (Workers Bank), (Urban); the División de Vivienda Rural (Rural Housing Division); Ministerio de Sanidad y Asistencia Social (Ministry of Health and Social Welfare); the Oficina Central de Ahorro y Prestamo (Bureau of Savings and Loans); the Savings and Loan Committee; and a National Savings and Loan Bank. Every incentive was given to private enterprise to join government in the construction of houses. Venezuela pushed housing investment in the rural areas as an integral part of the development determinations of the nation. The government granted the peasant interest-free loans to pay for his house over a 20-year period. The Inter–American Development Bank further supported the attempts to transform housing in the countryside.[11] Venezuelan housing construction exceeded even the new goals set under the 1965–68 National Housing Plan. The achievements are shown in Table 5.1.

Yet, despite these forthright efforts and the enormous advances, Venezuela's housing deficit still stands at over 800,000 units. Over 20 percent of the population of Caracas still lives in slums. By the year 2000, Venezuela must build 3,918,740 new housing units to accommodate its population. This estimate

---

[8] As Bertram Gross points out, the "pragmatic, action-oriented style" of the Venezuelan planners is backed "by the fortuitous combination of material poverty of the masses, vast oil resources that provide a margin for experiment, resourceful leaders with the will to develop new means of action ... [and] experience in relating planning to annual program budgets." Gross, Preface to Friedmann (1965, p. xxii).

[9] Inter–American Development Bank (1963b, p. 286).

[10] Venezuela, Central Office of Coordination and Planning (n.d.).

[11] See Lernoux (1967).

TABLE 5.1

Venezuela: New Housing, 1959-68

	1959	1963	1966	1968
Housing	1,870	15,835	24,692	60,436
Financed directly	1,378	11,474	21,200	–
Loan system	492	4,361	3,492	–

Source: Venezuela (1967); Venezuela, Central Office of Coordination and Planning (n.d.).

assumes the same density per dwelling as at the time of the last housing census and includes the deficit at that time.[12]

The mounting housing deficit is persistent throughout most of Latin America. Trinidad and Tobago, for example, with a population growing over 2.5 percent a year, need 6000 new houses a year. For the period 1964-68 only 3500 a year were built. Taking into account dilipidated housing that should be replaced, Trinidad and Tobago need 10,000 new houses a year.

In the years 1950-60, Latin America as a whole, according to a UNECLA estimate, needed a minimum of 960,000 new housing units a year to meet population growth and replacement needs.[13] The total housing needs after 1960 rose to over 1.1 million units a year, the urban needs outpacing the rural needs. By 1975, it is estimated, 2.6 million housing units a year will be needed, urban needs having risen from 630,000 new units a year in the 1950s to 785,000 in the 1960s, and to at least 1.8 million by 1975. Apart from meeting the needs of a rising population, if the quality of housing is to be improved, the rate of building per year could range from 2.5 to 3.3 million units to meet needs by the year 2000. This would mean building 11 or 12 units per 1000 of the population for the next 30 years, a rate of construction about twice that of the developed countries. In fact, Latin America has been building only an average of two houses per 1000 of the population.

Qualitative Status of Housing

The quality of existent housing is apparent from the kind of material used in building and from the mushrooming urban slums in the main cities of Latin America. In Honduras and El Salvador, nearly three-quarters of the houses are of wattle and adobe and have dirt floors. Over one-third of the urban houses in Ecuador in 1962 had only one room, and roof or walls were in a state of deterioration and 70 out of every 100 houses in the rural areas were in this condition. In Guatemala 80 percent of the rural housing and more than half of the urban housing was in no better condition in 1964. Over 70 percent of the population of Peru in 1961 lived in mud or cane huts. Over 83 percent of the rural houses of Venezuela in 1950 had earth floors. Obviously, initiating change from these low levels adds to the magnitude of the job.

Since the agricultural sector is the backward yet dominant sector of the

[12]See Inter-American Development Bank (1969a, p. 102).

[13]Inter-American Development Bank (1966, p. 11).

Latin American economy, and since nearly half the population is rural, rural development and rural housing are matters of priority. Yet the development of rural housing has unique aspects which introduce further dilemmas. As we noted in Chapter 3, the rural areas are isolated, small, and scattered over wide distances. Houses are largely constructed of mud, thatch, cane, or almost anything that can be put together. The densities per room are high and ventilation is normally absent, as are sewerage, water, and electricity. The need is obviously there, but the nuclear distribution of the rural population adds to the difficulty of attracting capital for housing construction and for integrated and efficient housing planning.

Qualitative deficiencies are at their most conspicuous in the slums of Latin America. These slums have different names in various parts of Latin America, but there is a qualitative uniformity about them. In Chile, one fifth of the total population lives in *poblaciones callampas* (urban shanty towns) or in *conventillos*, tenement shacks without plumbing, water, electricity, or sewerage. More than one-fifth of the population of Caracas lives in *ranchos*, the urban shanty towns of Venezuela. In Brazil, over one-third of the population of Rio de Janeiro (more than a million people) and half of the population of Recife live in *favelas*. Peru has its *barriadas*, housing more than 20 percent of the population of Lima; Argentina has its *villas miserias*, housing more than 10 percent of the population of Buenos Aires; Colombia has its *tugurios*, housing more than 80 percent of the population of Buenaventura. One-third of the population of Panama City lives in the slums. Since population growth is generally ahead of new housing provision, the urban slums continue to grow. However, while the slums of the city are clearly visible to all, housing in the rural areas, hidden from the eye, is far worse than in the case of the city slums.

BOUNDARY CONDITIONS TO THE SUPPLY OF HOUSING

We deal now with three of the major obstacles to increasing the supply of housing in Latin America. These obstacles are (1) the level, distribution, and stability of personal incomes in Latin America; (2) the inadequacy of institutional provision for financing housing construction and the purchase of housing; and (3) the formidable financial requirements of the housing situation in relation to competitive demands on the public budget and on external funds.

Income Levels and the Effective Demand for Housing

The need for housing is greatest among low income families in Latin America, who cannot afford to buy decent housing. Expectedly, private enterprise in Latin America, other things being equal, gears the supply of housing to those who can afford to buy decent housing. The private entrepreneur does what is natural; he responds to the profit prospects at the upper and middle income brackets. The housing gap in Latin America reflects, therefore, to a large extent the state of income distribution in Latin America. Thus income distribution is a key explanatory variable in the housing situation.

The major characteristic of income distribution in Latin America is the concentration of income at the top. As shown in Figures 5.1 and 5.2, income is far more inequitably distributed in Latin America than in the United States and the

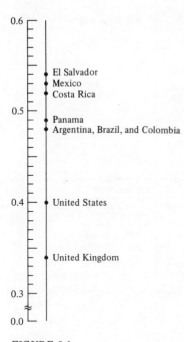

FIGURE 5.1
Coefficients of Income Concentration in Selected Countries
Source: UNECLA (1967b, p. 39).

United Kingdom.[14] The Latin American data is far from reliable but it is sufficiently indicative. During the Alliance years, changes have taken place in income
distribution, but these changes have not changed the initial situation very much.[15]
Figures 5.1 and 5.2 apply to 7 Latin American countries. In 1961, 5 percent of
all families in Argentina received 29.4 percent of the total personal income for
that year. The poorest 20 percent of all families received 7 percent of total
personal income, the average income in the first group being nearly six times the
national average and 17 times the average of the poorest 20 percent of all
families. In Brazil in 1960, 80 percent of the population received less than the
average national income, then about $34 (U.S.) per head.[16] Even in Mexico, as
shown in Table A.28, the bottom 50 percent of the total number of families
received only 15.4 percent of the total personal income of the country in 1963,
while the top 6 percent, received 41 percent of the total income. The top 6 percent could more clearly afford to buy decent homes.

[14] See UNECLA (1967b, pp. 38–60). In Figure 5.1, the Gini ratio of income concentration
was used. This ratio expresses the relationship between the area enclosed by the Lorenz
curve and the diagonal (equal distribution line) as a percentage of the total area of the
triangle.
[15] Cf. UNECLA (1969a).
[16] UNECLA (1967b, pp. 39–40).

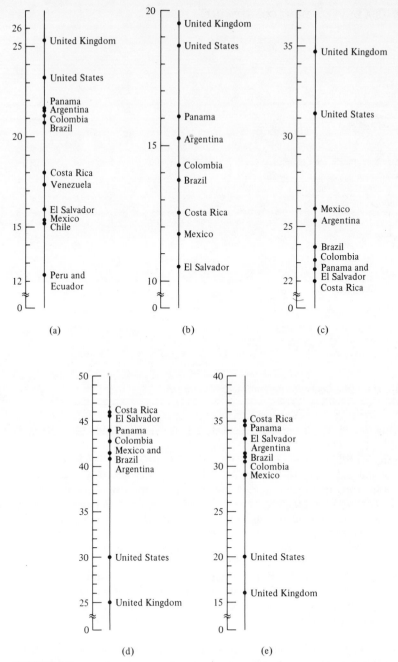

FIGURE 5.2
Percentages of Total Income Accruing to Specific Groups of Recipients: (a) *Fifty percent of population in lower income brackets (1st and 2nd deciles);* (b) *Thirty percent of population in 3rd, 4th, and 5th deciles;* (c) *Thirty percent of population in 6th, 7th, and 8th deciles;* (d) *Ten percent of population in higher income brackets (9th decile);* (e) *Five percent of population in higher income brackets (10th decile).*
Source: UNECLA (1967b, p. 41).

TABLE 5.2

Conjectural Distribution of Annual Income in Latin America

	Percentage of population	Percentage of total personal income	Percentage of average per capita personal income to general average	Annual income per capita (in dollars)	MONTHLY INCOME PER FAMILY (IN DOLLARS)		
					Average	Lower limit	Upper limit
Group 1	50	16	30	120	55	0	100
Group 2	45	51	110	400	190	100	500
Group 3	3	14	470	1,750	800	500	1,300
Group 4	2	19	950	3,500	1,600	1,300	0
Total	100	100	100	370	170		

Source: UNECLA (1963d), Vol. 2.

Income distribution for Latin America as a whole was not very different. Table 5.2 and Table A.29 are indicative of continuing concentration at the top. The validity of the figures needs further corroboration, but the picture is clear. Those who needed housing most were least able to afford it. In 1960, the bottom half of the population of Latin America existed on an average personal income of $120 a year, and accounted for only one-fifth of the total personal consumption, while the top 5 percent accounted for some 30 percent of total personal consumption.[17] The bottom half lived under substandard conditions in respect to nutrition, clothes, health, and education, and they obviously could not afford the houses they so clearly needed. It was simply not profitable to produce houses for the low income group. Yet it is this half of the population which reproduces itself most in Latin America.

Tables A.30 and A.31 give data for selected countries on general wage levels and on wages in agriculture at the beginning of the Alliance years. Table A.32 gives average wage data for various categories of the labor force in Central America six years after the start of the Alliance. Wages were low at the beginning of the Alliance years and, despite some changes, remained much too low to enable the lower income group to acquire decent housing.

Robert Alexander in a trail blazing book had little doubt that the Argentine industrial workers around 1950 were "among the best paid of their kind in Latin America" (1962, pp. 228, 229). Wages for a foreman in the metallurgical industries under Péron had increased from 0.94 peso per hour in 1942 to 6 pesos in 1954, and for the ordinary laborer from 0.60 peso to 4.75 pesos per hour. But even without taking inflation into account, these improved rates were far below the equivalent earnings in the United States—in 1954 U.S. dollars, $1.88 an hour in the metal products industries, $2.00 an hour in the machinery (nonelectrical) industry, and $2.10 an hour in basic metal industries.[18] Though manufacturing wages were low in all countries of Latin America, wages in agriculture were far lower.

[17]See UN, Economic and Social Council (1963, p. 1).

[18]International Labor Office (1962). In 1954, $1 (U.S.) equaled 5.00–13.95 pesos (Argentine).

On the haciendas, the workers may actually be wageless, being kept at a subsistence level of survival by traditional patronal kindnesses. A case study made by Whyte and Williams revealed that Indian *colonos* on one hacienda near Pisaro in Cuzco, Peru, were getting less than four cents a day. When the Indians unionized and won a contract after an extended and many-sided battle, the pay was raised to 12 cents a day.[19] In Central America average wages per hour and ordinary current wages and salaries even for the skilled in 1967 were still far less than the wages for the unskilled agricultural laborer in the United States a decade ago (see Table A.32). Even supplemented by overtime pay and fringe benefits, total earnings fall very short of the pay for equivalent skills in the United States.

The difficulty a family at these low pay levels would have in buying even a low cost house can be readily illustrated from some recent data. A family with a monthly income of $45 (U.S.) would have to pay $14 (U.S.) a month (nearly a third of the monthly income) for a house costing $2000, with a 25-year mortgage at 7 percent interest. In Venezuela, the average price of a house for an industrial worker making about $186 (U.S.) a month is $21,111. The mortgage interest rate is 7 percent. If we take into account other necessary expenditures, we can see that it becomes almost impossible for an average worker to buy a house. Some 50 percent of his monthly salary is spent on food, 10 percent on clothing, and 10 percent on transportation, leaving very little for such necessities as housing and education.[20]

The purchase of a house depends not only on the level of the individual's income but on the steadiness of that income. In Latin America as a whole, regressive tax structures weaken purchasing power; unemployment and underemployment make for an uncertain income base or for no income base at all; and incomes are persistently eroded by inflation which has become almost an integral part of the economic nexus. The tax structure is mentioned in Part II of this book, but it may be noted here that in 1967, indirect taxes on international trade accounted for 46 percent of the total tax collections of Ecuador. In 1968, import taxes accounted for some 40 percent of the ordinary revenues of the Dominican Republic.[21]

Unemployment and Income Stability

Buying a house is a long run proposition extending over a period of some 20 to 30 years. Obviously, carrying the purchase of a house requires a stable income over a considerable period of an individual's working years. Unemployment and underemployment make for instability of incomes or for a total lack of income for significantly large numbers of the Latin American population. Although consistent and established data is lacking, the available indicators are significant (see Table 5.3). In El Salvador, for example, one-third of the farm laborers are seasonally unemployed. In Guatemala, widespread unemployment is characteristic of the rural area.

The situation has not changed much over the years and, in fact, it may get worse. According to UNECLA estimates, the economically active population

---

[19]Whyte and Williams (1968, pp. 40–41).

[20]See Inter–American Development Bank (1969a, pp. 103, 108).

[21]Inter–American Development Bank (1969a, pp. 302, 315).

TABLE 5.3

Unemployment Indicators in Selected Countries

	Year	Section to which estimate refers	Percentage of economically active population unemployed
Argentina	1963 (July)	Buenos Aires	8.8
El Salvador	1961	whole country	5.3
Honduras	1961	whole country	5.7
Panama	1964	urban population	10
Peru	1964	whole country	20–30
Uruguay	1963	whole country	10

Source: Pan American Union (1967e).

will grow absolutely from 51 million in 1950 to 116 million by 1980.[22] The urban population during this period may increase from 61 million in 1950 to 216 million in 1980, more than three times in 30 years. The housing shortage will probably remain as severe as ever, since agriculture and urban employment are unlikely to provide sufficiently secure jobs and stable incomes over the next decade to change the picture. We will be able to evaluate the possibilities in greater detail when we analyze the performance of the Latin American economy. It can be seen, however, that after a decade of significant effort, agricultural development still stagnates in much of Latin America, distinguished only infrequently by improved job chances or by an environment offering an improved quality of life. The continuing cultural backwardness, technically and socially, keeps the rural population moving into the cities in search of jobs and the chance of a better life. But this is on the whole another road to disillusionment. The city grows in vast numbers, but the city is not an opportunity giving or opportunity creating frontier allowing these vast numbers to acquire decent housing. Though the industrial sector may advance, the towns simply cannot provide the jobs to meet the needs of an urban population growing at such phenomenal rates. Ecuador, for example, had an industrial growth rate of 8.1 percent a year in the period 1950-61, but the manufacturing industry could absorb only 9000 people, while the active urban population had increased by some 410,000.[23] While the growth of capital intensive industries may strengthen some income levels, low income levels may be weakened even further.

Inflation and Low Incomes

We have already noted that inflation is another factor which persistently weakens the ability of the low income groups to buy decent housing. Inflation depresses the real value of the already low nominal wages. At the same times, house rentals and the cost of housing in general and of land for residential construction are constantly increasing. Inflation, a Latin American problem long before the Alliance for Progress, persists—cutting harshly into low wages, especially in

[22] Pan American Union (1967a, p. 19).
[23] Pan American Union (1967a, p. 22).

Argentina, Bolivia, Brazil, Chile, Paraguay, and Uruguay. In 1958, for instance, the cost of living index (base year 1950 = 100) in Bolivia stood at 9566 and in Chile at 1561. The indices for Brazil and Uruguay stood at 268 and 414 respectively in 1958.[24] Between 1951 and 1960 prices in a sample 10 out of 20 Latin American republics rose by over 50 percent. Table A.33 shows the persistence of price inflation in the 1960s. Table 5.4 shows the annual percentage change in the cost of living for the period 1960-69.

Changes in the nominal exchange rates with the American dollar dramatize the inflationary pressures. In 1960, one American dollar was worth 83 Argentinian pesos, but in 1967, it was worth 350 Argentinian pesos. One American dollar, worth 475 Brazilian cruzeiros in 1962, was worth 2715 Brazilian cruzeiros in 1967. One American dollar worth 1.053 Chilean escudos in 1960 exchanged for 4.65 Chilean escudos in 1967.[25] In Uruguay, one American dollar exchanged for 100 pesos in November, 1967, but in May, 1968, it was worth 250 pesos. Between March, 1967, and May, 1968, the Uruguayan peso was devalued five times. Price tags disappeared from practically all goods since shopkeepers found it tiresome to change price tags every day as inflation soared. Uruguayan civil servants could not even afford to paint their houses.[26] Table A.34 shows the rise in house rentals in Latin America over the period 1960-69.

In an inflationary situation, the upper income groups can best defend themselves; the middle group gets caught in the vise of fixed salaries and the low income group gets caught also—clamped down below by their illiteracy, their low productivity in agriculture, their lack of skills in the ghettos of Latin America, and by the rigidities of a slowly changing social caste system, and an industrial advance which is nonexistent in some places and much too slow in others to open out better income chances fast enough. The urban worker can form trade unions or orgainze other forms of pressure and he does this. What he gains, however, is passed on in higher prices to the consumer. This is easy in tariff-protected countries where foreign competition is shut out and where minimal internal competition makes it unnecessary for the industrial elite to be efficient or to deliver goods at the competitive price and quality levels of North America. The greatest sufferers, therefore, are the rural workers, unorganized into trade unions, unskilled, illiterate, scattered, unprotected by social security, and nonbeneficiaries, in the main, of state privileges in the towns.[27]

The Financing of House Ownership

We have seen that the magnitude of Latin America's housing problem is such that quantitative and qualitative deficiencies are actually increasing despite massive efforts over the last decade to overcome this development constraint. Largely under the influence of the Alliance for Progress and the Inter-American Development Bank, national housing plans emerged as part of the national development plans, housing institutionalization developed in the public and

[24] See Institute of International Studies and Overseas Administration of the University of Oregon (1960, p. 638). See also Stark (1963, p. 122), Matthews (1963, p. 102).

[25] See also Chase Manhattan Bank (1967c, pp. 6, 7).

[26] See Browne (1968, p. 20).

[27] UN, Economic and Social Council (1963, p. 3). Cf. Herrick (1965), Beyer (1967).

TABLE 5.4

Percentage Increase in Cost of Living in Selected Countries, 1960–69

	1960	1961	1962	1963	1964	1965	1966	1967	1968	1969
Argentina	27.1	13.6	28.0	24.4	22.1	28.7	31.8	29.2	16.2	7.6
Bolivia	11.2	7.7	6.0	-0.7	10.0	2.6	7.3	–	5.5	2.1
Brazil	34.5	38.5	52.4	73.6	87.0	61.7	46.6	29.5	24.2	23.2
Chile	11.4	7.8	13.8	44.3	46.0	28.8	22.9	18.1	26.6	30.7
Colombia	5.6	8.5	4.2	27.2	17.8	7.0	16.7	8.0	7.4	6.9
Costa Rica	0.8	3.4	2.6	3.0	3.3	-0.6	0.0	1.2	4.0	2.7
Ecuador	1.5	4.2	2.8	5.9	4.0	3.1	–	3.8	4.3	6.3
El Salvador	-0.2	-2.7	0.1	1.5	1.7	0.6	-1.2	1.4	2.5	-0.2
Guatemala	-1.2	-0.6	2.1	0.1	-0.2	-0.8	0.7	0.5	1.5	2.5
Guyana	–	1.1	4.1	1.3	0.8	2.2	2.4	2.7	2.4	14.1
Honduras	-1.8	1.7	1.0	3.0	4.5	3.3	1.7	2.6	2.4	3.2
Mexico	4.9	1.8	1.0	0.6	2.3	3.6	4.2	3.0	1.6	2.8
Panama	–	0.1	0.4	0.5	2.4	0.5	0.2	1.4	1.6	1.8
Paraguay	11.0	–	–	–	–	3.8	2.9	1.4	0.6	2.0
Peru	8.6	4.5	6.6	6.4	10.5	17.0	9.4	–	19.1	6.2
Uruguay	38.6	22.6	10.9	21.2	42.4	56.6	73.5	89.3	125.3	20.9
Venezuela	–	–	–	1.1	2.2	1.7	1.7	0.0	1.3	2.4

Source: Inter-American Statistical Institute (1970).

the private sector, and national and international financial aid has flowed in significant quantities into the housing industry. Despite this, the limiting factors we have identified continue to operate as powerful boundary conditions. Public support of housing involves once again excruciating alternative costs. The size of the allocation problem—if housing were to be totally subsidized from domestic resources—can be judged, to some extent, by the size of the external support to housing. In the period 1961-69, the Inter-American Development Bank contributed a total of $322.7 million (U.S.) towards the financing of housing and urban development programs. In 1967, the U.S. Congress amended the Foreign Assistance Act of 1961 to add "home ownership and decent housing" to the three previous AID priorities of health, education, and agriculture, and included slum clearance, urban development, and cooperatives among the purposes of capital assistance. Congress also added $50 million to investment guarantees authorized for Latin American housing, bringing the amount up to $500 million. By 1969, direct U.S. government dollar loans to housing totaled some $176 million (U.S.) and investment guarantees amounted to $314 million. There were of course other forms of assistance. If local currency housing and urban development loans, Inter-American Development Bank loans, and the investment guarantee authorization level of $500 million are counted together, the United States, over the last nine years authorized or committed more than $1 billion to Latin American housing.[28]

External assistance on this scale certainly modified the situation to some significant extent. But despite the stimulation of mortgage institutionalization impetus for improved housing in every Latin American country, initial obstacles continued. Low incomes prevent the average family from paying outright for a house, as is sometimes expected, and on the other hand, endemic inflation adversely affects the mortgage market. The mortgage banks are closely connected with the commercial banks and the latter expectedly pursue cautious commerical policies, preferring to support loans to middle and upper income groups for obvious reasons. In any case, lower income groups cannot meet the down payments, the high interest rates, and the long-term repayment commitments. Similarly saving and loan associations benefit the middle income groups far more than the lower income groups. Cooperatives have developed, but cooperative effort is itself limited by financial support and by administrative and technical limitations. Self-help and mutual aid efforts in housing construction have increased, but again confront problems of financial support, of obtaining advantageous locations near to work, and of payment collections from low income families whose income and employment are subject to the instabilities we have described.[29]

Low and unstable incomes account largely for the difficulty of inducing a reallocation of investment in housing to favor these groups. Loans from the Inter-American Development Bank and the U.S. Agency for International Development for low income needs meet resistance from national housing institutions which favor middle income housing—a natural market preference. The insistence that these loans be on a self-liquidating basis impose further boundary conditions

---

[28] See U.S. Department of State (1967d, 1968d, and 1969b); Inter-American Development Bank (1969a, p. 112).
[29] See Inter-American Development Bank (1969a, pp. 105–111).

since payment schedules are difficult to meet. Even direct tearing down of slums, as evidenced from the experience of Brazil and of Peru, proves not only socially disruptive but an expensive imposition on the budgets of these countries.[30]

CONCLUSIONS

The quantitative and qualitative deficit in housing in Latin America is likely to remain a formidable constraint to development for a very long time to come. Since the level of income and its stability are key elements, it follows that, other things being equal, the housing gap will be solved when all Latin American families can afford to buy decent housing. But this general condition depends on the rate at which economic development takes place. At this point, the problem of circularity emerges again. Given the variables involved, it is clear that the housing status of Latin America cannot be changed within any forseeable specific time period. Yet, if this key constraint is not removed, the development status of Latin America remains adversely affected. The problem may even get worse in the future unless there are enormous internal and external changes supporting the transformation of the status of housing. Without these changes, the allocation of scarce resources to low cost housing is likely to be given a subordinate place in relation to other priority needs.[31]

We turn now to education as a development constraint in Latin America.

[30] See U.S. Department of State (1969b, pp. 43–44).
[31] U.S. Department of State (1969b, p. 43).

CHAPTER 6

EDUCATION AND DEVELOPMENT

EDUCATION AS A BOUNDARY CONDITION

This chapter attempts to evaluate, as far as the limited data allow, education as a boundary condition to economic development in Latin America. We first review the well-established theoretical relations between educational inputs and productive output. We follow this analysis with a case study of education and development in Chile and in Guatemala, to support the contention that, despite the contrasting status of literacy and development in these two countries, the confrontations so far as education and development are concerned are basically similar. Then we supply a quantitative and a qualitative picture of the status of education in Latin America as a whole, to indicate to some measurable extent the gap between the initial state of education and the changes required for accelerated economic development. We then attempt to identify the key factors which limit educational development in Latin America. We then draw conclusions pertinent to the problem of changing the educational status of the region in the interest of more rapid economic development.

Theory and Research

That education contributes to economic development is no new discovery. Higgins notes succinctly that for three centuries economists have emphasized the importance of "human investment" (1968, p. 410). Schultz, however, expressed the view that although it was obvious that people acquired useful skills and knowledge, it was not obvious that these skills and knowledge are a form of capital (1962, p. 106). But the latter observation would not hold good today, for Schultz's work, along with that of others like Denison, Abramovitz, Fabricant, Kendrick, Becker, Harbison, Myers, Kuznets, Lewis, and Balogh, helped to end the capital-is-everything approach to development.[1] Enke brings accepted facts together when he observes that "national resources can often be invested advantageously in improving people as well as in accumulating physical capital" and that "in fact one is not much use without the other" (1969, p. 1130). Although, few studies have been made from a historical point of view of the relationship between education and the beginnings of development, controversy continues to flourish.[2] Johnson senses a counterrevolution in favor of merging the current concentration on the role of human capital into "a generalized capital

---

[1] For easy reference, see the bibliography in Blaug (1968, pp. 425–430). See also Meier (1970, pp. 674–675).

[2] Cameron (1967, p. 318).

accumulation approach to economic development (1968, pp. 35-39). Shaffer
contended, like many others, that "it is generally inadvisable to treat man as
human capital" (1968, p. 45). It is not easy to separate the boundaries between
education as investment and education as a consumer service. Arguments inevitably continue on alternative choices in education in relation to development
objectives, on the alternative costs of education, and on problems of allocation in
relation to the educational mix. Quantifying the economic value of education
will remain an elusive challenge for a long time to come.

These issues are pertinent to Latin America. Consensus on the role of education in economic development in Latin America does not have to wait on a general theory of capital accumulation or on esoteric arguments surrounding the
term *human capital*. Economic common sense and experience indicate that the
obvious has to be accepted and acted upon because of the urgency of the Latin
American situation. For instance, it would be a miracle if a community with no
education at all (if this is imaginable) produced more than a community in which
every member was fully and formally educated. Again, obviously, in terms of
material productivity, other things being equal, a community in which each member was fully and formally educated in business administration and in science
should produce more than a community in which each member was fully and
formally educated say in classical Greek, however noble that exercise may be.[3]

Development involves decision-making all along the line. The more educated
the decision-makers, other things being equal, the more productive and profitable
the results. This applies even to the political climate and to the social climate,
which are of such importance to entrepreneurship and investment. The more
educated the decision-makers whose views add up to the abstraction called "climate," the more appropriate their decisions are likely to be in terms of the
realistic needs of the situation.

Even more realistically, the necessity and advantages of education in Latin
America as productive investment need not be argued pedantically from the high
bench of theory for at least one basic reason. Sufficient research has been undertaken to establish meaningful and convincing correlations between educational
inputs and increased productivity. Hence the repeated affirmations at all hemispheric meetings of a commitment to the vigorous promotion of education for
development.[4] Empirical evidence supports these commitments.

The relation of education to economic development in the United States has
become accepted textbook material. Bach, for instance, writes that investment
in human capital—better education, training on the job, healthier workers, and
the like—"may have accounted for a quarter of our economic growth during the
last quarter century, and is growing in importance." Indeed, he asserts that no
other factor has been more important to U.S. growth since 1929 (1966, p. 252).[5]
The case of Japan is equally instructive. The state, under the Meiji rulers, invested heavily in education in order to promote rapid industrialization, the training of engineers and scientists being given preference to the proliferation of law

---

[3] Cf. Harbison and Myers (1964, p. 31). Harbison and Myers use as an indicator of orientation of higher education the number of students enrolled in faculties of humanities, fine
arts, and law as a percentage of total third-level enrollment.

[4] Cf., for instance, Pan American Union (1967g, p. 4).

[5] See also Bruchey (1965, pp. 178–179).

schools.[6] Drucker contributes an important declaration of faith in the "learnability and teachability [through education] of what it means to be an entrepreneur and manager" (1962, pp. 783-784).

On the Latin American side, the distinguished economist Victor L. Urquidi underlines the universal recognition of education as a key determinant of economic development. As he puts it, an educational system designed primarily to train men for the liberal professions cannot possibly promote steady increases in productivity (1965, p. 79).[7] From the whole range of studies now available, Meier draws conclusions of relevance to our reflections on education and development in Latin America. Investment in human beings has been a major source of growth in advanced countries, but "the negligible amount of human investment in underdeveloped countries has done little to extend the capacity of people to meet the challenge of accelerated development" (1964, pp. 266-284). A move to merge concentration on human capital formation into a generalized capital accumulation approach may be a useful academic exercise. But it cannot invalidate the accumulated evidence that investment in education is a critical determinant of development.

The question of education in Latin America goes beyond the effects of increased education on output. To meet our development criteria, education must increase the opportunities for democratic mass participation in the whole process of social change, of which economic development is only a part. It can fairly be presumed at this point that an educational take-off is an essential element of any economic development and of social change in general.

We shift now from these general relationships to examine more closely the difficulties of bringing about rapid changes in education, using Chile and Guatemala as illustrations. We have chosen these two countries because although they stand in contrast to one another in terms of their respective educational and development status, the factors affecting their educational advance are basically no different. The time periods over which we examine educational development in these two countries are sufficiently long to illustrate the point that the confrontations to educational advance are obviously so immense that an immediate change in educational status would be a matter of utmost difficulty. Yet the urgency of the present economic situation requires immediate change.

THE CASE OF CHILE

Comparatively speaking, Chile enjoys a very favorable educational position in Latin America. As shown in Table 2.6, the literacy rate for Chile in 1970 stood at 90 percent. Chile therefore has a lower rate of illiteracy than any country in Latin America except for Barbados, Argentina, Uruguay, and Trinidad and Tobago. A special study of education and social change in Chile noted that: "Unlike many other Latin American countries where revolutions have been frequent, Chile presents the image of a people with deep respect for established government, a healthy tolerance for differing points of view, and a sincere dedication to the democratic processes."[8] The capacity of Chile to maintain a stable political

---

[6] Harbison and Myers (1959, pp. 260-261). See also Kerr et al. (1964, p. 99).
[7] See also Farley (1962, pp. 49-58).
[8] Gill (1966, p. 6).

structure may be a subject of controversy since the election of its Marxist president, Salvador Allende.[9] But even ideological uncertainty does not invalidate "the natural vitality and intelligence" Kaldor attributes to the Chilean population (1964, esp. pp. 233-287). In terms then of its level of literacy, traditional social sophistication, tradition of peaceful political accommodation, and possession of perhaps the largest middle class in Latin America, Chile appears to possess a very favorable profile for economic development.[10]

Under Eduardo Frei, the former Christian Democratic president, Chile was determined to pursue revolutionary advances in liberty.[11] Given the economic status of Chile, we must presume that economic development, despite the changed ideological stance of the government, remains the basic essential and that in turn education remains a key essential to the solution of Chile's urgent economic and social situation. Chilean economist Sergio Underraga Saavedra, for instance, regards education as "among the most important factors influencing the economic, political and social development of Chile." In his analysis, educational programs provided "a large part of the population with basic schooling, which is indispensable for achieving higher levels of efficiency in labor and in the economy as a whole." In addition, "another positive educational factor which should be singled out is the training of technicians and specialists, without whom it would have been impossible to reach the levels of industrialization and mineral and agricultural development achieved by the country" (1967, p. 116).[12]

Despite high literacy, impressive increases in school enrollments, and other quantitative indicators in Chile, the economy of Chile has been in trouble over the last two decades. Table 2.4 shows not only that the Chilean economy failed to achieve the minimum per capita target of 2.5 set under the Alliance for Progress, but also that the average per capita product for the period 1961-69 was lower than that of Guatemala where barely 45 percent of the population is literate. The explanation of the paradox, where education is concerned, is an instructive comment on the relation of education to development requirements. The Chilean population is highly literate, but it is not highly skilled for the Great Ascent, to use the title of Heilbroner's text (1963). The traditional classical education which dominates Chile is to a large degree inappropriate to the skills demanded in an industrializing society. Despite the high literacy level, therefore, and the significant educational advances, Chilean education must undergo enormous reform to meet the urgent needs of economic advance. It is never easy to modify, however, the legacy of history, particularly a history of rich endowment in abstract values.

The Legacy of History: A Nonquantifiable Constraint

In 1895, 72 percent of the Chilean population was illiterate. By 1970, this figure was reduced to 10 percent. This appears to be an enormous achievement. But in

[9] See, for instance, *New York Times* (1970a, p. 1).
[10] Cf. Adelman and Morris (1968, pp. 1208, 1209). See also Gillin (1960, p. 26).
[11] See Duncan and Goodsel (1970, pp. 407-414, p. 422).
[12] Saavedra supplies the following indicators of the "successful" advance of Chilean education: annual average growth of population—2.5 percent; annual average growth of enrollment in primary education—6.6 percent; in secondary education—15.2 percent; in specialized education—9.7 percent; and in university education—9.3 percent.

terms of the relation between educational content and development needs, Chile's progress might well be called concealed underdevelopment in education. The historical deficiencies which Chilean education inherits are immense and difficult to quantify. But they are real constraints which are still far from being transformed. The conquistadores who took Chile in 1540 were largely illiterate. In the colonial period ending in 1810, education was primarily directed to training for priestly functions, the curriculum consisting of Latin and philosophy, with learning by memory the principal method of teaching. Expectedly, children of peons, slaves, and servants were excluded from the educational process. During the Republican period, the aristocratic traditions in education became even more firmly cemented with the coming of German teachers in 1885.[13] Traditional inelasticities were still dominant when the Alliance for Progress began. Education continued to be feudal, formal, academic, aristocratic, and abstract, with almost no technical and vocational training. In all aspects it was largely unrelated to the development requirements of modernization.

Indicators of Concealed Underdevelopment in Chilean Education

The traditional qualitative deficiencies that characterized initial conditions in Chilean education at the beginning of the Alliance years have continued as bottlenecks, even though the Chilean government began to tackle them more seriously after 1960.

In 1957, for instance, 82.3 percent of the school population of Chile was enrolled in primary schools. The enrollment at other levels was much smaller— 8.9 percent in secondary schools; 7.2 percent in vocational schools, and 1.6 percent at university level. Even so, an estimated 90 percent of those enrolled in primary or general secondary schools were pursuing a general or academic type of education. Fewer than 10 percent were preparing for vocations or for professions in vocational schools and the universities. In 1962, at secondary school level, almost three-fourths of the enrollment was in the general university preparatory courses and only 30.4 percent of the total time at this level was devoted to sciences. Enrollment in agricultural schools amounted to less than two percent despite the importance of agriculture in Chile.[14] Middle-level manpower was in short supply in Chile. Yet vocational education was not coherently related to development needs. Indeed, these needs were yet to be established. At university level, the traditional curriculum prevailed so that the status of science and technology remained marginal.[15]

Table 6.1 supplies some selected indicators of educational progress in Chile during the period 1960-69. In terms of meeting the needs for Chilean development, educational advance in Chile still has to be rapidly accelerated to overcome the initial conditions in 1960. Education is free and compulsory at primary levels, but not all children of primary school age are at school, nor could they be accommodated under present physical conditions. The dropout rate is high. Despite vigorous efforts, particularly after 1964, it was impossible to solve this problem quickly. In 1962, more than 50 percent of the primary school students dropped out before completing first grade to join the ranks of the functionally illiterate.

[13] See Gill (1966, p. 17).
[14] Gill (1966, pp. 23, 33, 70).
[15] Cf. Myers (1959, p. 184) and Blitz (1965, pp. 73-107).

TABLE 6.1

Indicators of Educational Progress in Chile, 1960–69

	1960	*1969*
Literacy rate (in percent)	83.6	89.5
Average years of schooling for age 15 and older	4.92	5.5
Elementary school enrollment (in thousands)	1,202.8	2,121.8
Secondary school enrollment (in thousands)	226.6	245.6
Higher education-students matriculated (in thousands)	24.7	67.1
Adult education average (in number of students)	262,067 (1958)	311,470
General secondary school teachers employed (in all schools)	6,000	12,400 (1967)
Share of public expenditures for education (in percent)	10 (1959)	18.7
Index of central government expenditures on education (in constant 1966 prices)	100 (1961)	171.8 (1967)
Total public expenditures for education as percentage of GNP	2.7	3.65 (1965)

Sources: Figures for 1967 from U.S. Department of State (1969b).
Figures for 1965 from UNESCO (1961, 1965).
Remaining figures: Inter-American Development Bank (1961, 1962a, 1965a, 1966, 1967, 1968, 1969a).

In 1960, more than 95 percent of the students at secondary level dropped out. In 1965, only 2.7 percent of the economically active population held university degrees. The average level of schooling of the population by 1969 was still half that of the United States. Needless to say, education in the rural areas is at a much lower level than in the towns.

Technical and vocational training remains limited and a novelty. Secondary and higher education are exclusive and high cost, sharing also the curricular shortcomings of the primary and secondary stages. Educational administration and co-ordination have more than an average share of shortcomings. The inherited deterrents to educational advance continue despite continuous official efforts since 1961 to eliminate these formidable educational obstacles. In 1961, a survey of educational organization and administration revealed an anomalous state of affairs under which primary, secondary, and vocational school authorities supervised some university programs; primary school authorities supervised some secondary school programs; and secondary schools offered primary level studies and professional training![16] On the other hand, the primary school curricula were geared neither to employment nor to admission requirements at the secondary level. Technical and vocational education was not geared to development requirements.

[16] Inter-American Development Bank (1966, pp. 137–138).

In 1965, deliberate broad based initiatives were promulgated to end absenteeism affecting some 200,000 children at the primary level; to increase physical accommodation and the number of trained teachers; to expand vocational and technical education; and to align university training and research behind the development needs of the country.[17] International aid rallied to the support of these innovations, particularly at the level of higher education.

The disadvantages of tradition, as we have observed, cannot however be suddenly overcome. Table 6.2 supplies some indication of initial conditions in a key area, namely, the size and quality of the teaching profession in 1962. If we take into account teacher attitudes towards entrepreneurship, productivity, and material development in general, and the adverse effect of traditional teacher attitudes on children, the situation becomes far more serious.[18] Table 6.3 shows the stubbornness of tradition in the distribution of university students in specialized fields of study. The humanities, education, and medicine dominate so much that Blitz, in an interesting study, anticipated the shortage of architects, forestry engineers, engineers, and nurses, particularly in the middle strata of the last two, by 1970 (1965, p. 95).

THE CASE OF GUATEMALA

The complexities of an educational take-off in sophisticated Chile become far more compounded in Guatemala, where educational levels are the lowest in Latin America, except for Haiti. With a literacy ratio of around 45 percent (see Table 6.4) and a gross domestic per capita product in 1968 of only $310 (U.S.) Guatemala is a clear case of a low literacy ratio correlating with a low level of development. Once again, despite the economic potential of Guatemala and significant developments in education (see Table 6.4), educational underdevelopment remains a formidable constraint to more rapid development. Given the

TABLE 6.2

Chile: Teachers without Titles or Degrees, 1962

		PUBLIC		PRIVATE	
School	*Total teachers*	*Total teachers*	*Without titles*	*Total teachers*	*Without titles*
Elementary	32,100	26,017	8,053	6,083	5,366
Secondary	12,209	10,216	4,447	1,993	822
Agricultural	440	252	62	188	63
Commercial	2,154	1,498	577	656	436
General	5,195	5,195	2,552	–	–
Industrial	3,790	2,727	1,184	1,063	310
Normal	630	544	72	86	13
Total	44,309	33,233	12,503	8,076	6,188

Source: See Gill (1966).

[17]Inter-American Development Bank (1965, pp. 217–220).
[18]See, for instance: Gouveia (1967, pp. 484–510) and Farley (1962, pp. 49–58).

TABLE 6.3

Chile: Distribution of Students Attending Universities and Other Institutions of Higher Learning, by Field, 1966

	Percentage of total students
Humanities and Education	27.2
Other careers	21.2
Medical and Health Sciences	11.9
Engineering	9.3
Other social and political fields	8.4
Law	6.3
Administration and Economics	5.7
Agricultural Sciences	3.1
Architecture	2.9
Visual Arts and Music	2.6
Physical, Chemical, and Mathematical Sciences	1.4

Source: Inter-American Development Bank (1967).

TABLE 6.4

Selected Indicators of Educational Progress in Guatemala, 1960–69

	1960	*1969*
Literacy (in percent) (15 years and over)	37.9 (1964)	45.0 (1970)
Average years of schooling for population	1.2 (1964)	n.a.[a]
Elementary school enrollment (in thousands)	315.0	562.8
Secondary school enrollment (in thousands)	26.2	72.8
Higher education, students matriculated (in thousands)	5.3	13.4
Total enrollment in educational system	346.5	649.0
General secondary school teachers employed (in all schools)	1,857	3,507 (1967)
Share of public expenditures of education (in percent)	16.2 (1961–62)	17.9 (1968)
Index of central government expenditures on education (constant 1966 prices)	100 (1961)	120.8
Public expenditures as percent of GNP	2.3	

[a] Not available.

Sources: Figures for general secondary school teachers employed and index of central government expenditures on education: U.S. Department of State (1969b).
Figures for public expenditures as percent of GNP: Sylvain Lourié (1965, p. 41).
Remaining figures: Inter-American Development Bank (1961, 1962a, 1965a, 1966, 1967, 1968, 1969a).

initial conditions in education, it is not likely that the bottlenecks to educational advance can be removed as rapidly as a changed economic status for Guatemala would require.

Economic Potential

The tourist potential of Guatemala is strikingly obvious. The country is one of the famous centers of the great Mayan civilization which flourished for over 26 centuries, but declined and disappeared before the arrival of the Spanish conquistadores under Captain Pedro de Alvarado in 1524. Mayan achievements in astronomy, medicine, agriculture, mathematics, architecture, commerce, and political organization still astonish the world. The famous Mayan ruins at Tikal, Uaxactún, Piedras Negras, Sayaxche, Quirigua, Zacalen, Misco Viejo and other places, the Spanish monuments, the volcanoes, the lakes, the rivers and the beaches of Guatemala combine to form an immense though underexploited tourist potential. More than half the population of Guatemala is still Mayan and at humbler levels, the Mayas still contribute articles of matchless originality for domestic trade in Guatemala.

Guatemala's significance in the Central American Common Market as well as the potential resources of the country heighten the economic importance of the country. Smaller in area than Nicaragua (53,668 square miles) and Honduras (43,277 square miles), Guatemala has a larger population than any other member of the Central American Common Market.[19] The country has been called the focal point of Latin America and the gateway for the Central American Market.[20] An imposing number of Central American Common Market and other development institutions are located in Guatemala, justifying its claim to importance.

The potential resources of the country are significant. One-third of Guatemala's population lives in the cool highlands 3000–5000 feet above sea level but Guatemala's jungle-covered west coast, shunned by local farmers in favor of the cooler highlands, is reportedly covered by topsoil scores of feet thick.[21] The mineral potential in Guatemala includes coal, sulphur, iron, antimony, chromite, copper, lead-zinc, tungsten, manganese, nickel, asbestos, quartz, mercury, magnesium, chromium, barium, gold, flourine, cobalt, silver, gold, titanium, marble, mica. The International Nickel Company has invested over $100 million in Guatemala.

Nor is this the end. The possibility exists of developing a modern fishing industry off the coasts and in the lakes of Guatemala, which also provide a valuable source of electrical power. In the Petén, Guatemala has an immense area of great potential wealth. Fourteen thousand square miles in area, about one-third of the whole country, the Petén is estimated to have a forest reserve of over 21 million board feet of lumber, among them cedar, mahogany, primavera, lignum vitae, and pine, valued at over $2 billion (U.S.). The potential is there for an enormous prefabricated housing industry. The Petén has potentially enough mahogany to supply half the world's needs for an indefinite period of time. Indeed, the government has set up an official agency FYDEP

[19] The members of the Central American Common Market (CACM) are Guatemala, Nicaragua, Honduras, El Salvador, and Costa Rica.
[20] See *New York Times* (1968, pp. 60–61L, 64L).
[21] Stroetzel (1966, p. 4).

(Empresa Nacional de Fomento y Desarrollo del Petén) for the development of
the Petén.[22]

Human Resource Development

Despite these economic possibilities, human resource development in Guatemala
remains at a particularly low level, severely limiting increased productivity. At
first glance, the indicators in Table 6.4 seem to be a dramatic movement away
from the desperate indicators of 1950 (see Table A.35). In that year, 71 out of
every 100 Guatemalans 15 years and over were illiterate. Except for Haiti's 89
percent, Guatemala's illiteracy ratio was the highest in Latin America. Only 22
percent of the population aged 5-14 years were enrolled in primary schools—
although legally education was free and compulsory at this level. In contrast to
Guatemala, 88 percent of this age group were enrolled in schools in the United
States at that time and 66 percent in Argentina. The position was even worse for
the age group 15-19 years, the secondary school area. Exclusive of those enrolled
in vocational schools, only 7 percent of this age group was enrolled in Guatemala
as against 60 percent for the United States, and 21 percent for Argentina. The
position was equally bad in higher education. Out of every 100,000 persons, 84
were enrolled in higher education in Guatemala as against 1511 for the United
States and 480 for Argentina.

The Guatemalan government at the end of 1959 was spending only $3 per
capita and 1.9 percent of the GNP on education as compared with $97 per capita
and 4.6 percent of the GNP in the United States. Around this time, some 88 percent of the children had dropped out of school by the time they reached sixth
grade. Despite this abortive thinning out of the human resource pipeline, the
allocation for public education in Guatemala in 1963-64 was only 2.4 percent
of planned investment—less than one-fourth of the allocation in Venezuela.[23]

Against this background, therefore, the educational changes registered by
Guatemala between 1950 and 1970 represented spectacular progress in terms of
the objectives of the Alliance for Progress. Indeed, under a four-year program ending in the middle of 1963, Guatemala built more public school classrooms than had
been built for the whole period since the Spanish Conquest in 1524. Guatemala
even innovated a program called Operacion Escuela (Operation School), under
which old school buildings were renovated.[24] These advances received significant
financial and other support from regional organizations and institutions committed
to Central American integration. The Inter-American Development Bank, for instance, provided financial support to the five national universities of Central America for teaching basic sciences and strengthening the general studies program.

The advances made in Guatemala, however, conceal the magnitude of the task
remaining in the area of human resource development. The United States Agency
for International Development reported in 1968 that few of Guatemala's people
benefited from economic development, since over one-half of the population
were impoverished Indians and nearly two-third could neither read nor write.
With an educational level so low, few can contribute effectively to the needed
economic advance of Guatemala.

[22] See also Banco de Guatemala (n.d.) and Ministerio de Economia, Guatemala (1966).
[23] See UNECLA (1962; 1964, pp. 206–207).
[24] See U.S. Department of State (n.d., p. 27).

The educational problem remains urgent at every level. In 1965, only 34 percent of the 5-14 age group and 25 percent of the 5-19 age group were enrolled in school.[25] Educational wastage remains enormous. In 1966 nearly 85 out of every 100 children did not complete primary school, although enrollment rose in the period 1960-66 at the rate of 6.4 percent a year, twice the population growth rate. Guatemala in 1966 was short of some 22,600 primary school teachers, a formidable challenge to already-strained teacher training efforts. At the secondary level, 93 out of every 100 children were not enrolled in school in 1964, and the dropout rate of those enrolled was almost as great as at the primary level. At university level, the average dropout rate amounted to some 60 percent over the period 1962-67.[26] Adult illiteracy could be reduced to about 37 percent by 1979 only if primary education were expanded sufficiently to give all children six years of schooling before their fifteenth birthday. Without this, the adult illiteracy rate in 1979 would stand at 55.8 percent, a reduction from 1960, but an increase in actual numbers from 1,411,000 in 1960 to 2,039,000.[27] Nearly 80 percent of the illiterates are Indians, who in turn, constitute the majority of the population.[28]

Educational reorganization and innovation are at work: a 15-year planned assault (1965-80) has been launched and the Inter-American Development Bank has poured in money for educational support. Between 1962-70, Guatemalan public expenditures for education have taken a higher proportion of the budget in some years than in Argentina, Brazil and Chile.[29] Given the starting point, however, the prospects for a changed educational status are clearly not immediate.

We turn now to general indicators of the status of education in Latin America as a whole and to a consideration of the major factors affecting the problem of bridging the gap between demand and supply in education.

THE STATUS OF HUMAN RESOURCE DEVELOPMENT IN LATIN AMERICA

Demand and Supply in Latin American Education

A study of Chile and Guatemala reveals in differing degrees the major factors at work generating the modern increase in demand for educational development throughout Latin America. The increased demand for education stems from the stimulus of the Alliance for Progress; the need to meet the increasing educational needs of a rapidly growing population in both urban and the rural areas; the

[25] U.S. Department of State (1970). The figure for the 5-14-year-old group rose to 38.5 percent in 1968.

[26] Inter-American Development Bank (1969, p. 348). The majority of the students enrolled at the two leading universities were studying law. Cf. Schwartz (1970, pp. 240-260).

[27] See U.S. House (1969, pp. 33-34).

[28] See Pan American Union (IA-ECOSOC) (1968a, pp. 53-55).

[29] See Pan American Union (1967, p. 100). From Inter-American Development Bank (1967, 1968a, 1969a, 1970), note the following percentages of total central government expenditures for education in

Years	Guatemala	Argentina	Brazil	Chile
1966	14.5	15.3	7.4	18.3
1967	13.5	17.7	7.2	20.1
1968	17.9	13.8	7.1	10.7
1969	16.5	4.2	8.7	11.8

broadened recognition that improved economic opportunity comes with better education; and the acceptance by all Latin American governments that education is a key determinant of growth. Any continuing shortage of skills would clearly contribute losses in labor and capital productivity in Latin America.[30]

Tables 6.5 and 6.6 supply a hypothetical picture of the educational status of the Latin American labor force in 1965, while Table 6.7 gives some indication of the growth in demand for education during the period 1960-69. Tables 6.5 and 6.6 once again confront us realistically with initial conditions in education, four years after the Charter of Punta del Este. Only 1.4 percent of this total labor force in Latin America had any university training, and nearly half the labor force had a primary education of less than three years. Almost one-fifth of the administrative and managerial group and more than half of the operatives and artisan workers had less than three years of primary school.[31]

Quantifying the status of education in Latin America in relation to labor market and development needs is a highly hypothetical exercise, given the state of the data. Table 6.8 shows some hypothetical projections of expansion requirements in education and in professional and vocational training over the period 1965-80.[32] Another projection assumed a depletion rate of 25 percent over the period 1960-70 of the skilled manpower population (secondary school and university graduates or equivalent) totaling about 22.5 million in 1960) and estimated replacement requirements at 5.6 million. The supply of secondary and higher education graduates produced during the period was estimated at only 4.5 million, and this figure would fall to just 2.2 million if the need for teachers were taken into account.[33] This projection represents an underestimate in comparison with projected needs in Table 6.8, and the table itself is an underestimate for a variety of obvious reasons. Nonetheless, the data supplies some proximate evidence of the magnitude of the problem of bridging the gap between demand and supply in Latin American education to meet immediate development needs.

The Educational Gap: Experience Under the Alliance for Progress

The experience of meeting even the limited goals of the Alliance for Progress confirms the size of the problem and makes it clear that bridging the educational gap is a long-term problem. The Alliance for Progress aimed at eliminating illiteracy and at providing access to at least six years of primary education for each child of school age. The elimination of illiteracy is, of course, dependent on the latter goal because the literacy ratio is improved by the increase in educated 15-year-olds and the death of the aging illiterate population. The population factor in Latin America, however, is such that although school enrollment increased by 6 percent a year in the period 1960-67 and the percentage of children not enrolled

[30] See UNECLA (1968a, p. 42).

[31] Cf. Ducoff (1960).

[32] The projection assumed an expansion of the Latin American population from 236 million to 364 million in the period 1965-80; an increase in the number of children age 5 to 14 from 61 to 93 million; an increase in the population of active age (15–64) from 163 to 212 million; and an increase in the labor force seeking employment from 77 to 120 million. Additional assumptions include a 2.5 percent annual average increase in productivity; a change in average annual productivity per employed person from $1150 to $1700; and an increase in aggregate GNP from $89 billion to $200 billion.

[33] Lourié (1965, p. 33).

TABLE 6.5

Educational Profile of the Labor Force, 1965[a] (In Thousands of Persons)

	Total	Professional and technical	Administrative and managerial	Employees and salesmen	Operatives and artisan workers	Services
University training						
Complete and incomplete	1,060	660	230	170	–	–
Secondary education	8,730	1,500	1,050	3,010	2,700	470
General	6,240	640	930	2,580	1,620	470
Complete	1,490	280	350	860	–	–
Incomplete	4,750	360	580	1,720	1,620	470
Technical	1,770	140	120	430	1,080	–
Teacher training	720	720	–	–	–	–
Primary education	67,096	632	1,039	5,401	51,142	8,882
Three years and over	29,700	370	580	3,000	21,540	4,210
From less than three years to none	37,396	262	459	2,401	29,602	4,672
Total	76,886	2,792	2,319	8,581	53,842	9,352

[a]The figures in this table are estimates with widely varying degrees of approximation and are given solely for illustrative purposes.

Source: UNECLA (1968a).

TABLE 6.6

Educational Profile of the Labor Force, 1965[a] (In Percent)

	Total	Professional and technical	Administrative and managerial	Employees and salesmen	Operatives and artisan workers	Services
University training complete and incomplete	1.4	23.6	9.9	2.0	–	–
Secondary education	11.4	53.7	45.3	35.1	5.0	5.0
General	8.1	22.9	40.1	30.1	3.0	5.0
Complete	1.9	10.0	15.1	10.0	–	–
Incomplete	6.2	12.9	25.0	20.1	3.0	5.0
Technical	2.4	5.0	5.2	5.0	2.0	–
Teacher training	0.9	25.8	–	–	–	–
Primary education	87.2	22.7	44.8	62.9	95.0	95.0
Three years and over	38.6	13.3	25.0	34.9	40.0	45.0
Less than three years or none	48.6	9.4	19.8	28.0	55.0	50.0
Total	100.0	100.0	100.0	100.0	100.0	100.0

[a] The figures in this table are estimates with widely varying degrees of approximation and are given solely for illustrative purposes.

Source: UNECLA (1968a).

TABLE 6.7

Selected Indicators of Educational Progress, 1960–69

	1960	*1969*
Literacy (in percent)	66.8	73 (1970)
Average schooling of population (in years)	2.2	–
Elementary school enrollment (in thousands)	25,239.4	41,817.5
Percent of children of primary age not enrolled	52.2	43.2 (1967)
Secondary school enrollment (in thousands)	3,374.4	8,933.1
Higher education, students matriculated (in thousands)	522.7	1,212.7
Total enrollment in educational system	29,136.7	51,963.3
Percent of total population enrolled in educational services	17 (1965)	20
General secondary school teachers employed (all levels)	193,107	391,252 (1967)
Ratio of number of secondary and higher education teachers per thousand people	6	10 (1967)
Share of public expenditures for education (in percent)	9.3 (1961)	13.3 (1967)
Index of central government expenditures on education (in constant 1966 prices)	100 (1961)	161.8 (1967)
Public and current investment expenditures on education as percent of GNP	3.5	–

Source: Figures for 1967: U.S., Department of State (1969b).
Remaining figures: Inter-American Development Bank (1969a).

declined from 52 to 43 percent, the actual number of children not enrolled in primary schools in 1967 was 740,000 more than in 1960, as a result of population expansion. Primary school enrollment was expected to reach a total of 69 million children by 1970. Table 6.7 makes clear that in 1969 the enrollment was short of this figure by some 27 million. In fact, given a 6 percent average annual increase in primary school enrollment, the total would not reach 69 million until 1979, and enrollment of the entire population of school age is hardly possible before 1986.[34] By 1979 the school age population would have increased to 92 million and 23 million children would still not be enrolled by that date.

In any case, full enrollment of the children of primary school age depends on the rate at which new classrooms can be provided and the rapidity with which new teachers can be trained, as well as a number of other factors. With a student-

[24] U.S. House (1969, pp. 34–35).

TABLE 6.8

Educational Expansion Requirements, 1965–80

	Average number graduating in 1965 (in thousands)	Total to be trained by 1980 (in thousands)	Estimated average annual graduation requirements 1965–80 (in thousands)	Projected annual percentage increase
University level	70	1,800	120	70
Secondary level	370	3,600	500	35
Technical education	140	7,200	480	244
Intermediate level training–primary teachers	70	1,400	90	29
Skilled operatives and artisans		7,000		

Source: Data from UNECLA (1968a).

teacher ratio of 31 children to each teacher, an enrollment of 69 million children by 1970 would have meant increasing the number of teachers to 3.2 million from a total of 1.2 million. This, in turn, would have meant training about 700,000 teachers a year instead of 136,000 a year, the figure for 1967. In fact, the rate of output of trained teachers to solve the enrollment problem by 1970 would have had to be more than 700,000, since one-third of the trained teachers left the profession every year. To accommodate the increased enrollment by 1970 would have also required tripling the number of classrooms—all impossible tasks within a very short period.

It is possible to bridge the gap in skilled manpower through importing foreign personnel, but there are obvious limitations to this alternative. Thus the onus is on the education system to increase the ratio of skilled manpower to meet development needs. We now look at the major deterrents to increasing the absorption and retention ratio (see Table A.36) of the Latin American educational system and to transforming the whole system so that education can contribute more effectively to modernization demands.

MAJOR CONSTRAINTS ON EDUCATIONAL DEVELOPMENT IN LATIN AMERICA

The Force of Tradition

As in Chile and Guatemala, although tradition is undergoing significant transformation, it still constitutes the single most powerful obstacle to educational development in Latin America. Traditional attitudes predetermine the irrelevance of much of Latin American education to modernization needs; the administrative chaos; the constraints on access to primary education; the nonintegration of training at primary and secondary levels with the admission requirements of the universities; the career choices of university graduates; the concentration of educational facilities in the towns; and even the training, attitudes, and status of the teaching profession.

Tradition expectedly is yielding ground only very slowly in Latin America in relation to the immediacy of the needs. Considering that in the eighteenth and nineteenth centuries Latin America was no less well educated than Europe, the current educational gap between Latin America and Europe and Latin America and North America can only be explained in terms of Latin America's greater difficulty in adjusting social values to the values required for rapid industrialization. In Latin America, independence continued to protect the original Hispanic values.[35] The concept of elitism remained dominant; education was to train leaders from the privileged classes for a few chosen traditional professions. In Puerto Rico, the adjustment of education to modern development needs occurred earlier than elsewhere in Latin America because of cross-fertilization with American values. *Arielismo*, the Latin idea of the dominance of spiritual values, came to terms in Puerto Rico with pragmatism and the need for technological change (especially after 1940) without *arielismo* losing its distinctive spiritual force.[36] The land grant college may yet appear in Latin America, but obviously it should have been a distinct part of the education landscape long ago.

The control of education by traditional groups produced initial deficiencies in the administration organization and administration of education which still have to be overcome. In 1963, for instance, national centralized control of curriculum, study programs, supervision, inspection, teaching materials, teacher appointments, and certification of students and teachers was more the rule than the exception. Even in countries like Brazil, Argentina, Mexico, and Venezuela, where authority was ostensibly decentralized to the states and the provinces, national control actually remained.

The result was rigidity emanating from central control and instability at the ministerial level because of the frequency with which ministers were changed. Central control, however, has its Achilles heel. Trained administrators, curriculum specialists, school inspectors, and training institutions were all in short supply. Public funds for education were limited and private funds were not forthcoming. Secondary school education was verbalistic and academic; agricultural and vocational type education was limited. Enrollment in vocational education amounted to only 25 percent of the enrollment at the secondary education level. Teachers in rural areas normally received no training, and those who received training frequently had no intention of teaching at the end of their training. Universities on the whole lacked study programs in preprofessional studies. There was general indifference to adult education. Where private education filled gaps, access to education was as limited as in public higher education.[37] As late as 1968 traditional practices still spelled empty classrooms and idle equipment for many months of the year.[38] Efforts to integrate education plans with development plans are now only at the beginning stages in most Latin American countries.

---

[35] Cf. Tannenbaum (1966, pp. 95–96); UNECLA (1968a, pp. 57–95). See also Duncan and Goodsel (1970, pp. 3–8) and Silvert (1968, pp. 128–142).

[36] Cf. the observation of Prieto (1963, p. 161). Prieto was a former president of the Senate of Venezuela. Latin American schools from the start were to serve the privileged few who could afford to pay for education. "This," in Prieto's view, "created a parasitic intellectual class living at the expense of those who worked on the farms or in the mines. . . . We have remained captives of a literary humanism. When the continent needed expert labor and technicians, we were turning out lawyers to settle suits among landowners, clergymen and poets." See also Mora (n.d.).

[37] See Hauch (1963).

[38] See Oliver (1968).

Counterproductive Education

Traditional education in Latin America has been counterproductive for several major reasons. The curriculum at all levels remained, until recent reorganization efforts, irrelevant to development needs. The desertion rates at primary and high school levels are high, so that in 1965 the average educational level of the Latin American population was fourth grade at most. Technical training was largely ignored at the secondary level, and at university level traditional career choices in medicine, law, and the humanities have been difficult to modify (see Table 6.9). Conventional careers are the traditional means of getting up the social ladder.[39] Obviously, scientific and technological careers must become equally prestigious as alternative career choices, as is happening, for instance, in Brazil, Mexico, Colombia, and Argentina.

Allocation of Resources: The Urban–Rural Dilemma

The task of educational adjustment is complicated by the traditional concentration of educational resources in the urban areas. The central offices of education are in the towns. The major universities, the majority of the secondary and primary schools, the majority of teachers and other support personnel, and the main organs of mass communication are similarly located in the towns. It is true that the rapid increase of the school age population of the towns is in significant measure due to the migration into the cities of the poorly educated parents of the educationally deprived children of the rural areas. In Costa Rica, Nicaragua, and Panama, for instance, the urban school age population because of migration from the rural areas increased in the period 1960–65 by some 33 percent. In Chile, the same group increased some 25 percent. The children who migrate into the towns in such massive numbers, especially those in the critical age group, 12 to 15 years, have usually had only one year of schooling in the rural areas. The city, therefore, with its limited financial resources, constantly faces the job of providing compensatory education for children who have fallen behind, and of

TABLE 6.9

Distribution of University Graduates, by field, 1965

	Percentage of total number of graduates
Medicine	28.1
Humanities	21.2
Law	13.4
Social Sciences	13.3
Engineering	11.3
Natural Sciences	5.6
Architecture and Art	4.3
Agricultural Sciences	2.8
Total number of university graduates	71,000

Source: Inter-American Development Bank (1966, p.36.)

[39]Pan American Union (1967e, p. 165).

providing training in skills for illiterate parents to enable them to survive and contribute to economic advance. There might be some justification then for the allocation of resources in favor of the town.

On the other hand, the alternative argument holds true. A more adequate provision of education facilities in the rural areas could contribute to slowing down the flow of rural children into the towns. Moreover, the educational status of the countryside is far more desperate than that of the towns. In 1963, 40 percent of the children in rural areas in Costa Rica had no access to primary schools going beyond grade 4. The dropout rates in the rural areas of Latin America are far higher than in the towns. In 1961–62, almost half the primary school teachers in the rural areas were untrained.[40] In 1965, 80 percent of the agricultural population of Latin America was untrained. Illiteracy ratios are far higher in the rural areas than in the towns. In Honduras, 62 percent of the rural population was accounted illiterate as against 23 percent of the urban population in 1965. In Ecuador, 45 percent of the rural population were illiterate around 1965 as against 12 percent of the urban population. The illiteracy of rural parents, linguistic separatisms in the countryside, the scattered nature of the population, and the lack of transportation are all traditional obstacles to educational development in the rural areas. Within countries, there continues also an unhappy disequilibrium, as in the case of Brazil, in educational provision and advancement. The eastern and southern parts of Brazil in 1964 had 75 percent of the total primary school enrollment, 82 percent of the enrollment at secondary levels, and 83 percent at university level. The northeast, with 30 percent of the population of the country, had only 16 percent of the enrollment at primary level and 12 percent of the secondary and university enrollment.[41] Changing these traditional situations is far from easy.

Financial Constraints

It is now possible to deal realistically with financial constraints to more rapid development of education in Latin America. Table 6.7 shows the rise of public expenditures for education as a percentage of total central government expenditures in Latin America between 1960 and 1969. These indicators can be compared with those in Table A.35. Obviously there have been significant advances in the Alliance years. Table A.37 shows that all governments in Latin America except Argentina, Brazil, Colombia, the Dominican Republic, and Venezuela by 1968 were devoting more than 15 percent of total central government expenditures to education. Indeed, Bolivia, Costa Rica, El Salvador, Panama, and Peru were spending more than 25 percent.

Given the stringencies of the budgetary situation in Latin America and the competing claims, financial support of education implies nonsupport in other areas, i.e., high opportunity costs. There is inadequate cost information—a factor which in itself hampers educational development—but existing figures cast some useful light on the problem of financing improved and expanded education in Latin America. Table 6.10 indicates the financial implications of meeting educational needs projected in Table 6.8 by 1980. Between 1965 and 1980, the numbers of students enrolled will have doubled but total expenditures will have more

[40] See Pan American Union (1967e, esp. pp. 197–198).
[41] Inter-American Development Bank (1966, p. 121).

TABLE 6.10

Estimates of Resources Allocated to Education, Enrollment, and Unit Costs

	Total expenditures[a]		Current expenditures[a]		Investment and other expenditures[a]		Number of students enrolled[b]		Current annual expenditure per student[c]
	1965	1980	1965	1980	1965	1980	1965	1980	1965
University education	650	1,500	560	1,300	90	200	800	1,300	700
Secondary education	930	3,600	890	3,400	40	200	5,100	9,600	175
General			510	1,100			3,300	4,400	155
Vocational			260	1,800			1,240	4,400	210
Training of primary school teachers			120	500			560	1,200	210
Primary education	1,520	5,409	1,380	4,900	140	500	32,900	70,000	42
Out-of-school and informal educational activities	100	500							
Total	3,200	11,000	2,830	9,600	270	900	38,800	80,900	73

[a] Millions of dollars at 1960 prices.
[b] Thousands.
[c] Dollars.

Source: UNECLA (1968a).

than tripled. This would represent an estimated increase from 3.5 percent to 5.5 percent of the gross domestic product in fifteen years. Yet these calculations probably represent underestimates of the financial requirements up to 1980. In any case, an annual expenditure of $73 per student is still well below the estimated figure of $97 for the United States in the 1950s (see Table A.35). While, therefore, it may be argued that the proportion of expenditures on education as a percentage of the GDP compares well with the United States, for example, the fact is that to catch up educationally with the United States within any specific time period, Latin America would have to spend a far higher proportion of the GDP on education than the United States.

The sources of the increased costs of educational development are easily identifiable. In 1965, it was calculated that Latin America spent about $42 a year per primary school student, $175 per student at the secondary level, and $700 per university student. Increased costs would obviously come from the increased numbers still needing enrollment and the greater number of children stemming from the rapid population growth. Calculations beyond this have to include expenditures for more and better qualified teachers and administrative personnel, better pay for teachers, and increased equipment and other forms of support. In 1965, for instance, 90 percent of the current expenditure was for teachers' salaries and student welfare. Yet these salaries, standing at the low level of $70 per month in 1965, will have to be improved to attract and retain teachers in the profession. The argument has been put forward that teachers at the university level in many countries of Latin America enjoy salaries which are 20 to 25 times the per capita income, while the salaries of their counterparts in the United States are usually only four or five times the per capita income.[42] This is hardly surprising in view of the low per capita income in Latin America and the international market advantages enjoyed by university staff today. Despite the comparison, therefore, university salaries in Latin America will have to improve to attract and retain staffs. Similar considerations apply to educational administrators and technical support personnel.

At the student level, increased enrollments imply a higher rate of expenditures for school supplies, school meals, welfare services, and even increased subsidies for fees since low income parents are not able to meet the costs of schooling.[43] To take a final example, expenditures on educational plant and buildings must unavoidably increase. Between 1960–65, in the face of an annual increase in enrollment of 5.4 percent, 10 percent, and 9.3 percent at primary, secondary, and university levels, most Latin American countries were spending only 5 percent of the public budget on new capital development in education.[44]

Improved education in Latin America spells reformed curricula at all levels and by implication increased costs. These are all visible costs. But concealed costs are rampant throughout the educational system. These include making curricula more relevant to development needs in order to improve the rate of return to investment in education, lowering the dropout rates, and correcting the administrative featherbedding, duplication, and other manifestations of the internal inefficiency of the system. Considering the dropout rates, Louvié

[42] See UNECLA (1968a, p. 248).
[43] See U.N. Department of Economic and Social Affairs (1951, p. 50).
[44] Pan American Union (1967b, pp. 1–87).

calculated that in 1965, 72 percent of the educational budget was used to pay for studies which were never completed, expenditures which yielded only a low return to society.[45]

CONCLUSIONS

From empirical evidence, investment in education contributes more to aggregate output than any other factor of production. In Latin America, educational development remains a severe constraint on economic development. The obstacles to educational development, which we have identified, are, however, not easily removable in the short run. Given the size of the problem, existing levels of expenditure, the budgetary constraints and the alternative costs and the limitations inherent in foreign financial assistance for education, significant changes in education can only come about largely through eradication of the internal inefficiencies of the education system. The traditional stumbling blocks here make bridging the gap between the demand for education and the supply of education to meet development needs a very long-run proposition.[46] This situation in turn contributes its own limitations on the prospects for Latin American economic advance.

We turn in Part II of this book to an evaluation of Latin America's economic performance in the light of the economic status and development ambitions of the region.

[45] Lourié (1965, p. 35).
[46] See UNECLA (1969b, p. 51) and Inter-American Development Bank (1969, p. 161).

THE LATIN AMERICAN ECONOMY:
STATUS, STRUCTURE, AND PERFORMANCE

CHAPTER 7

AN OVERVIEW OF THE
LATIN AMERICAN ECONOMY

In Part I of this book, the view is put forward that the rapid growth of the population of Latin America generates massive pressures for the immediate acceleration of economic development. In turn, however, the acceleration of economic development is obstructed by formidable constraints emanating from the sociocultural milieu of Latin America. We attempted, as far as data and space allow, to convey the quantitative and the qualitative dimensions of these constraints and the extent to which they inhibit the transformation of the economic conditions prevailing at the beginning of the Alliance for Progress.

In Part II of this book, we look at the economic status and structure of Latin America and attempt to measure the performance of the economy and the extent to which it has succeeded in weakening the growth-inhibiting constraints. In assessing the changing economy, we come to terms with the strategic importance of the traditional variables, particularly capital investment, and with the changing relationship between the two key sectors, agriculture and industry. We come to terms, however, with much more than these critical factors, for we arrive at some evaluation of the extent to which endogenous forces in Latin America are or are not succeeding in replacing traditional dependence on exogenous economic stimuli as the sources of growth.

Involved in the internal-external trade-off is the question of Latin American nationalism's effect on the inflow or withdrawal of foreign capital and the consequences for Latin American industrialization ambitions. Latin American nationalism would obviously support the internalizing of the development process, thus weakening or canceling out traditional external dependence. This emotional ambition partly explains Perón's attempts at making Argentina self-sufficient in manufacturing.[1] It also helps to explain Brazilian relations with foreign capital, especially in the period 1947-64; Peruvian relations with foreign firms; the Chileanization of foreign interests under Eduardo Frei, the Christian Democratic president of Chile until 1970, and the more radical measures proposed by his Marxist successor, Allende; and the measures taken earlier by Castro.[2] Any realization of ambitions to replace or to modify radically Latin American dependence on foreign capital is confronted by at least two basic

---

[1] See, for instance, Scobie (1964, esp. pp. 215-237) and Randall (1964a, pp. 123-142).
[2] Cf. Skidmore (1967, pp. 244-302). See also *New York Times* (1970b, p. 39 C). The reader may consult the following for general background: Smith (1966), Matthews (1963, p. 103), Hanson (1967, esp. pp. 163-192), May (1968, esp. pp. 105-119), and Roper (1970, esp. pp. 1-5).

difficulties. First, Latin America cannot readily separate its economy from the international economy nor can traditional economic relationships be modified easily in the short run without serious alternative costs. Second, Latin America cannot mobilize from within the domestic economy all the capital and personnel resources needed for a significant development breakthrough.

In this chapter, we confine ourselves to considering the similarities and differences within the Latin American economy, the structure of the economy, sectoral relations, and the resource status of the economy within the international economic context. We then assess the effect of Latin America's resource and trade position on the development prospects of the region.

SIMILARITY AND DIFFERENCE AMONG LATIN AMERICAN ECONOMIES

We have treated Latin America as a region with basically common economic characteristics, facing a common problem of economic development. We have seen that the rapid population growth cannot be checked in the immediate future despite the necessity for such a check and despite increasing attempts to provide family planning education and support. Since the rapid growth of population tends to negate such gains as do come about from an economy held back by a variety of formidable constraints, the hope for a higher standard of living lies in accelerating the speed at which the economy grows.

Having identified the major constraints to an acceleration of economic development in Part I of this book, we now see that the basic structure of the economy and the differing states of the individual economies add to the problem. For within the basically similar economic pattern in Latin America there are profound differences in detail, making for discrepancies in degree of economic advance and differences in the dilemmas confronting economic development. Uniformity and difference characterize most continents of the world—and Latin America is no exception. But if we are to appreciate the improbability of a short-run solution to Latin American development problems, we must come to terms with these differences for they add to the difficulty of improving economic life for the whole area.

Latin American countries differ widely in area, population size, population growth rate, population density, literacy level, physical structure, commercial strength, and in other respects. Areas range from a giant-sized land like Brazil, the fifth largest country in the world and accounting for 47 percent of the land surface of South America, to an independent country like Barbados with an area of only 166 square miles (see Table 1.1). At the same time, while by 1980, the Brazilian population may exceed 124 million, the population of Barbados would still be under 300,000. We have already noted differences in population growth rates, with Costa Rica leading the world in 1970 while in Argentina and Uruguay the population growth rates are more like those in developed countries. Population densities range from a low of 3 per square kilometer in Guyana to densities of 184 per square kilometer in Haiti and 621 per square kilometer in Barbados. (See Table A.39). Levels of literacy vary, as we have seen, with Haiti at the bottom and Argentina and Barbados at the top. Physical terrain varies from the unreachable heights of the rugged Andes and deserts like the Atacama and parts of Lower California in Mexico, from the practically empty lands of the Paraguayan Chaco to some of the most fertile and flattest plains in the

world like the coastal region of Guyana and the Argentine pampas. Transportation complexes range from sophisticated networks to mule tracks as in
Honduras. Economies range from those at Rostow's traditional stage to the
region around Sao Paulo, one of the world's greatest manufacturing regions.
It is these widely differing levels which have to be reconciled in the development
process. Indeed, it is appropriate to divide Latin America into the advanced
economies and the relatively less advanced economies.

Advanced and Relatively Less Advanced Economies

Three countries, Brazil, Mexico, and Argentina, dominate the regional economy
in terms of land space, total population, and contribution to the gross national
product. These three republics account for two-thirds of the total area of the
21 countries included in Table 1.1, for around two-thirds of the total population,
and for slightly over two-thirds of the total gross national product (see Table 7.1).
If Venezuela, Colombia, Chile, and Peru are included, then seven countries in
Latin America traditionally account for close to 90 percent of the total GNP
(see Table A.40).

The position of these countries, however, becomes modified when we
examine the data on per capita product. Table A.41 shows that Venezuela and
Argentina traditionally lead the way with the highest per capita gross national
product, Venezuela's per capita GNP in 1967 ($911) being over twice the
average for the 18 republics ($429). Chile, Panama, Uruguay and Mexico are
next highest in per capita GNP, but Brazil, Peru, and Colombia are lower down
the scale, yielding place to Costa Rica and Nicaragua.

The data reveal further that some Latin American economies can actually
be characterized as stop-go economies. The per capita GNP of the Dominican
Republic in 1965 was less than it was in 1955 and practically stood still between
1966 and 1968. The per capita income of Uruguay stood at $625 in 1955. It
has never reached that level again. In fact the trend in Uruguay's per capita GNP
is almost seismographic as that of Argentina, despite the leading position of the
latter country. Honduras and Paraguay remained almost at the same per capita
GNP level for almost a decade. In the case of Haiti, the per capita GNP of $70 in

TABLE 7.1

*Contribution of Argentina, Brazil, and Mexico of Total Gross National Product
of Latin America (at 1967 Prices in Millions of U.S. Dollars)*

(1)	Total GNP for 18 republics (2)	Argentina (3)	Brazil (4)	Mexico (5)	Columns 3, 4, and 5 as percentages of column 2 (6)
1950	45,456	9,200	12,560	8,705	67.0
1960	74,637	12,420	22,012	15,734	67.3
1968[a]	108,116	15,650	31,650	25,820	67.6

[a] Preliminary.

Source: U.S. Department of State (1970aa). Column (6) calculated.

1967 represented an unfinished stage in the continuous downward trend of the economy.[3]

The gap between the world-wide GNP and the GNP of Latin America is very wide. Latin America with 11 percent of the world population accounts for only 6 percent of the total GNP of all countries outside of the Soviet bloc. On the other hand, North America, Western Europe, Australia, and New Zealand with 25 percent of the world's population outside of the Soviet bloc (just over twice the population of Latin America), account for 77 percent of the total GNP, or 13 times the contribution of Latin America. Similarly the per capita GNP of North America, Western Europe, Australia, and New Zealand combined stood in 1968 at $2600 (U.S.), nearly six times the average per capita GNP of Latin America and nearly three times the per capita GNP of Venezuela which, as we have seen, has the highest per capita GNP in Latin America.[4]

Sectoral Indicators of the Status of the Economy

In low income countries, the agricultural sector dominates, employing the majority of the economically active labor and contributing the largest share to the gross national product. The agricultural sector is, however, generally the most backward sector of the low income economy. In Latin America, the agricultural sector clearly dominates the economy. As Tables 7.2 and 7.3 show, the majority of the economically active labor force is employed in agriculture and fishing. According to the projections in Table 7.3, the dominance of agriculture as the major employer of the labor force is likely to change only very slightly over the next decade or so.

The relative contributions of agriculture, manufacturing, and other sectors of the economy have been undergoing change. In 1968, for instance, agriculture contributed 19.6 percent to the GDP of Latin America as against 22.0 percent

TABLE 7.2

Estimates of Product and Employment, 1965[a]

	Domestic product (in millions of dollars)	Labor force (in thousands of persons)	Product per employed (in dollars per person)
Agriculture and fishing	19,348	35,499	545
Mining and quarrying	4,279	743	5,760
Manufacturing	20,031	12,048	1,663
Construction	2,869	3,706	777
Basic services	6,731	4,185	1,608
Other services	35,389	20,705	1,709
Total	88,647	76,886	12,062

[a]The figures in this table are estimates with widely varying degrees of approximation and are given solely for illustrative purposes.

Source: UNECLA (1968a).

[3] See International Bank for Reconstruction and Development (1969).
[4] See U.S. Department of State (1969d).

TABLE 7.3

A Hypothetical Projection of Product and Employment, to 1980[a]

	Gross product (in millions of dollars)		Employment (in thousands of persons)		Sectoral composition of the product (in percent)		Employment structure (in percent)	
	1965	1980	1965	1980	1965	1980	1965	1980
Agriculture and fishing	19,348	36,000	35,499	49,300	21.8	18.0	46.2	41.1
Mining and quarrying	4,279	9,000	743	1,000	4.8	4.5	1.0	0.8
Manufacturing	20,031	58,000	12,048	20,000	22.6	29.0	15.7	16.7
Construction	2,869	7,000	3,706	7,200	3.3	3.5	4.8	6.0
Basic services	6,731	21,000	4,185	8,500	7.6	10.5	5.4	7.1
Other services	35,389	69,000	20,705	34,000	39.9	34.5	26.9	28.3
Total	88,647	200,000	76,886	120,000	100.0	100.0	100.0	100.0

[a]The figures in this table are estimates with widely varying degrees of approximation and are given solely for illustrative purposes.

Source: UNECLA (1968a).

in 1960 (see Table 7.4). On the other hand, the figure of 24.9 percent for manufacturing in 1968 indicates that manufacturing was gaining ground. But the percentage share contributed by manufacturing industry during the period 1960-68 exceeded the percentage share contributed by agriculture only in five countries: Venezuela, Argentina, Mexico, Chile, and Uruguay. In four countries, the contribution of agriculture to the GDP between 1960-68 amounted to more than 30 percent; in eight countries it was between 20 and 30 percent; and only in one country, namely Venezuela, did it amount to under 10 percent. Honduras stood highest in the list with 38.4 percent of the GDP being attributed to agriculture and only 15 percent to manufacturing. By comparison, in the United States in the same year, agriculture contributed 3 percent to the gross domestic product while manufacturing contributed 28 percent.[5]

In terms of value of product per person employed, the situation works out expectedly. As Table 7.2 shows, product is lowest in agriculture; manufacturing, basic services, and other services are more than three times as high and mining is more than ten times as high. Where the per capita gross product is comparatively high, there is a high degree of correlation between a low percentage of the labor force in agriculture in comparison with nonagricultural employment, a lower share contributed to the gross product by agriculture in comparison with industry, and a lower average product per worker in agriculture in comparison with industry. In Argentina, for instance, with the second highest per capita GNP in Latin America, 20.5 percent of the labor force were in agriculture in 1965 as against 28 percent in manufacturing. In that year agriculture contributed 17 percent of the gross domestic product as against 33 percent from manufacturing.[6] The average product per worker in agriculture stood at $1230 as against $1800 for industry.[7]

The correlations seem to accord with Engel's law, Fisher's thesis, and the findings of Clark, namely, that with increased income there is a shift in demand from primary to secondary to tertiary industries.[8] Engel's law is clearly

TABLE 7.4

Structure of Gross Domestic Product by Economic Sectors (In Percent)

	1960	1968
Agriculture, forestry, and fishing	22.0	19.6
Mining (including petroleum)	4.6	4.3
Manufacturing industry	22.3	24.9
Construction	3.4	3.5
Electricity, gas, and water	1.4	1.9
Transport and communications	6.3	6.4
Commerce and finance	18.4	19.0
Other services	21.6	20.4
Total	100.0	100.0

Source: CEPAL (1970aa).

[5] U.S. Department of Commerce (1969, p. 836).
[6] See Inter-American Development Bank (1965a, p. 117).
[7] Prebisch (1970b, p. 34).
[8] Ernst Engel, a Prussian statistician, first published in 1895 his findings that as incomes increase, a lower and lower proportion is spent on food and housing. Fisher first pro-

relevant to the development problem. Output must increase across the whole economy if increased incomes generate shifts in demand away from the primary sector. Labor must shift from the primary sector to the industrial sector to generate an improvement in industrial output. At the same time, agricultural labor productivity should increase with the transfer of excess labor from agriculture to industry. To put matters in terms of Fei and Ranis, the reallocation of labor from agriculture to industry, given increased per capita incomes, is essential in order to shift the center of gravity away from primary production and towards industrialization. The percentage of the labor force in each sector supplies some preliminary index of the rapidity with which the reallocation of labor is taking place and the rapidity with which the center of gravity is moving toward industry.[9]

The occupational shifts identified by Fisher and Clark which follow increased per capita income and the changing pattern of demand are thoroughly validated by empirical data drawn from the historical experience of developed countries. In the United States, for instance, agriculture employed 30 percent of the labor force in 1910, but only 8.1 percent in 1960.[10] At the same time, employment shifted away from manufacturing to services to such an extent that by 1962 nearly 60 percent of the labor force was employed in service-producing industries.[11] We may note that per capita GNP in the United States (estimated at capacity output and in 1958 dollars) grew from $1488 in 1910 to $3215 dollars in 1960.[12] The occupational structure of Latin America, however, embodies some peculiar characteristics which limit the parallel with the history of occupational and sector shifts in a developed country like the United States, and it is these characteristics which form an essential part of the development challenge.

In the developed countries, as per capita income increased over time, employment increased more rapidly in the industrial sector than in the agricultural sector. There was also a subsequent shift in employment from industry to the services, as we have seen in the case of the United States. In Latin America, there is a phenomenal flow of labor from the rural areas into the towns. This flow of labor moves not into industrial jobs, but into low-paying jobs in the service industries. It also moves from disguised unemployment in the rural areas into open unemployment in the cities. This is obviously out of accord with the historic pattern of occupational shifts in the United States.

A few indicators illustrate the nature of the problem. Using figures which are somewhat at variance with the figures in Tables 7.2 and 7.3, we see that in the period 1950-65, the labor force in Latin America grew at an annual average

---

pounded (1935) the division of the economy into primary, secondary, and tertiary sectors. Clark's empirical findings supported the Fisher thesis of changes in the share of the contribution of each of the three sectors as the economy advanced. See Ackley (1966, p. 221). See also Kindleberger, (1965, pp. 168-181), Hagen (1968, pp. 42-51), Bruton (1965, pp. 88-95), and Fei and Ranis (1964, pp. 114-115).

[9] See Fei and Ranis (1964, pp. 111-117).

[10] Cohen (1966, p. 47).

[11] See Bloom and Northrup (1965, pp. 22-23). Service-producing industries include the following: transportation and other utilities, trade, finance, insurance and real estate; services and miscellaneous; and federal, state and local government.

[12] See Suits (1970, p. 108).

rate of 2.6 percent; the agricultural labor force grew at a rate of 1.6 percent; and the nonagricultural labor force at a rate of 3.5 percent. We would expect at this stage that employment would increase more rapidly in industry than in the services. The evidence shows the opposite trend. The data in Table 7.5 shows the agricultural labor force as a percentage of the total labor force declined, the percentage of the nonagricultural labor force in the services rose, and that in the industry group fell. This trend is expected to continue, unless reversed. Here is another example of economic events happening out of sequence in Latin America. The population explosion came before the economy had got off the ground. Urbanization came before large-scale industrialization; migration from the rural areas mounted in intensity before the development of modernized agriculture and before the emergence of a sufficient capacity in the industrial sector to provide jobs for the urban labor force, increased by natural causes and by migration from rural areas. The services sector expanded—a normal expectation—but on a scale far greater than would be expected at this stage.

At the same time, the labor force has clung on redundantly in "labor-expelling activities" such as personal services and street-vending.[13] For this group, existence is no more than marginal. They could literally be released with no loss of efficiency, yet the last column in Table 7.2 shows that the average product per worker in the services is higher than in the other sectors. However, this indicator is subject to a good deal of qualification.

The incomes of the redundant labor force are very low, a fact which is an index of the complicated character of the occupational situation in Latin America. We deal with the problems of growth and labor absorption in the next chapter, and with the problem of industrialization in a later chapter. At this point, however, we can review a number of characteristics which modify the significance we attach to occupational shifts and changes in income levels. In Latin America, using the percentage of the labor force in the three sectors to indicate the status of the economy conceals much more than it reveals. On the one hand, in the United States it took 35 years (1855-90) for the proportion of the total labor force in agriculture to drop from 63 percent to 42

TABLE 7.5

Distribution of the Labor Force[a]

	PERCENTAGE OF TOTAL LABOR FORCE		PERCENTAGE OF NONAGRI-CULTURAL LABOR FORCE	
	Agricultural	Nonagricultural	Industrial[b]	Services[c]
1950	50.2	49.8	35.0	65.0
1965	43.1	56.9	31.8	68.2

[a]Excludes Cuba, for lack of data.
[b]Includes industry, construction, and mining.
[c]Includes overt unemployment.
Source: Prebisch (1970b, p. 28).

[13]Prebisch (1970b, p. 29).

percent; in France (1827-1921) it took 94 years. But in Latin America it took only 39 years (1930-69). In the United States and France, when agriculture employed 42 percent of the total labor force, the nonagricultural labor force in industry amounted to 48 percent and 57 percent, respectively. In Latin America, the corresponding figure was only 31 percent.[14]   At the same time, average incomes in Latin America are far lower and income distribution far more inequitable than in developed countries.

Prebisch calculated that "the mere correction of the occupational structure of the labor force" would cause the aggregate product in Latin America to rise 7 percent annually instead of 5.2 percent (as in the period 1960-69) and the average per capita product to rise 3.9 percent instead of 2.5 percent.[15] The low level of income and the inequalities in the distribution of income reflect unexpected economic features peculiar to Latin America. We already know that the agricultural sector in Latin America is in a primitive state. In general, only a very small part of the Latin American labor force has access to modern technology, and where it does, the levels of productivity are high.[16]   The differences in sectoral income in turn reflect differences in technology and productivity. Fundamentally, however, low incomes persist because, among other things, Latin American entrepreneurship, given this situation, has failed to use the advantage of a labor surplus to capitalize the economy and to initiate innovations on a sufficient scale to absorb the surplus labor force.

Let us look briefly at the nature of the opportunities that have not been effectively exploited. We know that, despite the occupational shifts, there is a high degree of redundancy in agriculture, in industry, and in the services. It is estimated that some 40 percent of the economically active population of Latin America or more than 150 million people are affected (see Table 7.6)[17]. It has been suggested that agriculture actually accounts for nearly 50 percent of all unemployment and underemployment in Latin America, affecting some 60 million underemployed Latin Americans and some 18 million Latin Americans who are completely without work. These figures, even though subject to qualification, help to explain why wage levels in both industry and in agriculture are not very high and will not be high for a long time to come. An example of

TABLE 7.6

Estimated Unemployment (as Percentage of Economically Active Population in Each Sector)

	Estimated unemployment
Latin America	40
Industrial group	15.6
Commerce, finance, and other services	32
Agriculture	27.7

Source: CEPAL (1970d).

[14]See Prebisch (1970b, pp. 28, 30).
[15]Prebisch (1970b, pp. 3-4).
[16]See CEPAL (1970c).
[17]CEPAL (1970d).

salaries in manufacturing are the wages paid chemical workers in Brazil (the highest salary in 1965): about $78 *a month*. The equivalent figure in the United States stood at $3 *an hour*.[18] In Brazil, as in most of Latin America, a very small group commands the largest share of the agricultural income. The real average per capita income of the higher income bracket of the agricultural labor force, less than one percent of the agricultural labor force, is estimated at 20 times the average per capita income of 60 percent of the low income rural families.[19] UNECLA calculates that 60 percent of the rural families of Latin America (except in Argentina and Uruguay) earn an average annual income of less than $300. The data suggests that 60 to 70 million Latin Americans do not earn more than $60 a year—obviously a subsistence wage. The labor surplus situation together with other factors makes for the distribution of income in favor of a few people at the top.

It is clear that the excess labor from agriculture must find jobs in the industrial sector, and redundant labor in the services must be reallocated. At least two key requirements are obvious. Economic advance involving an increase of output in all sectors requires a reallocation of the labor force into the industrial sector. The more rapid the reallocation of labor, the more rapid the chances for improved productivity in industry, the services, and agriculture. In turn, however, the readjustment of the labor force depends on the willingness of "the few" to use their surplus resources to capitalize the industrial sector and, through labor-absorbing innovation, to provide jobs for the otherwise redundant labor force.[20] If the few who enjoy surplus incomes are unwilling to channel investment in the required directions, much will depend on the ability and willingness of the government to adopt necessary policies to influence investment. Involved in this is the question of the extent of government intervention. Presumably this is a matter of ideology or a matter of realism, or a mixture of both. Mexico, Venezuela, Puerto Rico, and other Latin countries have clearly put their faith in a mixed enterprise system in their push towards an industrial status.[21] Cuba has adopted a complete command economy with somewhat unspectacular results so far. Chile is now under another ideological mix.

In concluding this section, we note that an analysis of the development status of the Latin American economies cannot be based solely on the proportion of the labor force in agriculture. Mexico and Argentina, for instance, present exceptional situations.[22] In 1965, nearly half the total labor force of Mexico was in agriculture as against 20.5 percent in Argentina. Yet in both countries, around 40 percent of the nonagricultural labor force was in industry and about 60 percent in the services. In Argentina, occupational shifts from agriculture to industry would have less effect than elsewhere in Latin America on pushing up the average product per worker since in Argentinian agriculture, average product per worker stood at $1230, close to the average product per worker in industry ($1800). Yet, although Mexico had a surplus labor force in

[18] Figures taken from Pan American Union, (1969, Table 49).
[19] UNECLA (1969b, p. 328).
[20] Cf. Lewis (1962, pp. 279-303).
[21] See *Newsweek* (1967, pp. 60-66).
[22] The data is taken from Prebisch (1970b, pp. 31-36). See also First National City Bank (1969) and Banco de Mexico (1968).

agriculture and only 20.6 percent of the total labor force in industry as against 32.6 percent for Argentina, the cumulative annual growth rate of the Mexican economy in the period 1950-65 was 6.3 percent, almost twice the rate for Argentina (3.2 percent), and the 3.0 percent growth of the Mexican per capita income more than twice that of Argentina (1.2 percent). During this period, Mexico retained more people in industry than in the services. But even in the services, the annual growth rate of income per economically active person during the period was greater in Mexico (2.7 percent) than in Argentina (0.8 percent). In Argentina itself, the annual rate of growth in agriculture (2.9 percent) was faster than in industry (2.1 percent). As in Mexico and Argentina, data on other Latin American countries reveals exceptions to the generally applicable observations of Fisher and Clark.

TIME HORIZONS

We have emphasized throughout that the population pressures in Latin America and the low quality of life intensify the problem of the time it will take for Latin America to acquire a developed status. It is easy to theorize that every-thing depends on the rapidity with which labor is reallocated and on the invest-ment initiative of the few with surplus income in this patently inequitable income distribution situation. Prebisch suggests that even if the average increase in product per worker in agriculture and industry remains the same as in the past, the mere getting rid of the distortion in the present labor force structure would raise the rate of economic growth to 7 percent by 1980. Beyond that, if the average productivity of the worker were improved, the average rate of economic growth could be raised to 8 percent by 1980 (1970a, pp. 67-80). Prebisch himself recognized that a 7 percent growth target meant "exceptionally hard and unremitting effort" for over two decades. The 8 percent target would not be realizable until 1980, at which date the proportion of the labor force in industry might have recovered to 35 percent of the total labor force, the position at which it stood in 1950 (1970a, p. 79).

Assigning time horizons, however, is a highly speculative exercise. There are too many unknowns. The variables involved are the rates of population growth; the rates of growth of the economically active population; the capacity of the industrial sector to absorb a growing labor force in the towns; the willingness of foreign and local entrepreneurs to invest in labor-absorbing rather than labor-economizing innovations; the effect of labor additions on returns from the industrial sector; the attitudes of government; and other interrelated variables which affect those named. It is obvious, as Fei and Ranis suggest, that the rate of increase of the industrial labor force must be greater than the rate of growth of the population "if a particular labor surplus economy is to meet the criterion of success as characterized by the fact that the center of gravity is shift-ing toward the industrial sector."[23] Their rigorously formulated definition of the critical minimum effort for successful development states that:

[23]Fei and Ranis (1964, p. 121); they continue, "If P is the total labor force and L the industrial labor force, L/P must be increasing overtime, that is $n_{L/P} > 0$."

the rate of industrial capital accumulation n_K must be large enough, the intensity of innovation J high enough, the labor-using bias of innovations B_L strong enough, and the law of diminishing returns to labor E_{LL} weak enough so that their combined effect on the demand for labor exceeds the population growth rate. [24]

To calculate specific time periods over which the desired shifts can be brought about, we have to get behind the truisms of Fei and Ranis. The wide range of unknowns in Latin America stands in the way of accurate calculation. We can only make a general conclusion at this point that the rate of labor reallocation depends: (1) on the rate at which changes come about in the land tenure system and in the obstacles to labor mobility; (2) the rapidity with which the traditional non-wage receivers in Latin America can be transformed into enthusiastic modernizing profit-maximizers; (3) the rapidity with which the technical and managerial capacity of many Latin American governments can be upgraded; and (4) the stability of national attitudes toward foreign capital, even under realistic joint agreements.[25]   All these factors involve an enormous break with the traditional milieu discussed in Part I of this book.

The Mexican experience demonstrates the difficulty of the problem. With a population growing approximately 3.2 percent a year, and with half the population at a cash income level of just over $100 a year, in the period 1964-67 Mexico could provide only 180,000 additional jobs a year instead of a needed 400,000. Yet Mexico poured public capital into the economy, and (outside of mining and public utilities) vigorously attracted private capital, with the result that the annual average growth rate of the GNP was 6.5 percent between 1957 and 1967.[26]

THE EXTERNAL SECTOR

In this section we assess the external status of the economy and the relation between Latin America's foreign trade and its development status and ambitions. We consider briefly the question of the adverse terms of trade, a continuing source of controversy ever since Prebisch, as secretary general of UNECLA, gave expression to the problem of the deterioration of the terms of trade for primary producing countries.[27] Finally, we consider the problems involved in evaluating and developing the potential resources of Latin America and the relevance of any such prospect to the acceleration of economic development in the area.

Importance of the External Sector

The external sector has been blamed in many quarters for all the major, if not all, the economic ills of contemporary Latin America: for enclave developments

[24]Fei and Ranis (1964, pp. 121-122). The Fei and Ranis equation for the critical minimum effort is as follows:

$$n_P < n_L = n_K + \frac{B_L + J}{E_{LL}} \qquad (\text{for } n_w = 0)$$

[25]See also CEPAL (1968b) and Johnson (1968a, pp. 46-47).
[26]*Newsweek* (1967, pp. 60-66).
[27]See UN (1950b).

on the coast; for regional disequilibrium; for noncommunication between sectors of the region; for social, economic, and technological dualism; for continuing external dependence; and for the peripheral status of the Latin American economies in relation to the world economy. The external sector has been associated with colonialism, imperialist exploitation, foreign domination, and similar terms. Whatever the merits or demerits of the image of the external sector, the emotions generated by Latin America's traditional international relations can prevent an objective evaluation of the role of the external sector.

The plain fact is that Europeans, largely the Spanish, Portuguese, British, French, Dutch, and later Americans and others invested in Latin American staple agriculture, minerals, and other primary materials for which there was an export outlet in their more highly developed home countries.[28] In turn, the colonies imported manufactured goods from the metropolitan country. Given the level of development among the pre-Columbian population of Latin America, the alternative of a self-sufficient internal market was impossible and remains impossible today. The colonial economy therefore set the stage for the traditional export orientation of the Latin American economies. This orientation remains conspicuous.

We need not consider, at this point, the controversial aspects of foreign trade. Suffice it to say that without foreign trade, the present economic status of Latin America might well have been even less advanced. It is true, of course, that foreign trade gave rise to enclave areas of industrial concentration on the coast. It was easier to settle on the coast than to live in the Andean Cordillera, or in the cold hostile plains of Patagonia, or the Amazon lowlands. Through foreign trade, the ports emerged as the export outlets for agricultural products and raw materials to Europe and to the United States. They became the centers for the agricultural regions which developed around them and the centers for the resulting transport complex. As major concentrations of population, the ports, became industrial bases and political centers, attracting institutions and infrastructural support of one kind and another, which in turn consolidated their dominance. But the economic concentration on the coast, as we have seen, generated increased isolation from the interior of Latin America, adding to the dimensions of the modern development problem.

The strength of the external sector remains of critical importance to the acceleration of development in Latin America. Foreign earnings determine Latin America's capacity to import the capital and intermediate goods essential for sustaining a desirable rate of industrial development. Any weakening in foreign trade has an adverse effect on the domestic economy.[29] Table 7.7 shows the contribution of merchandise exports to the GDP of Latin America. As the data indicates, this contribution varies from under 10 percent in five countries to over 20 percent in six countries. In two countries, it is over 30 percent. The gains from foreign trade are too well known to need repeating.[30] The point of importance is that foreign trade is the test of a country's capacity to compete at world market standards. A country or a region which cannot survive in international competition cannot survive at a satisfactory level of domestic development.

[28] See, for instance, Stein and Stein (1970).
[29] See Kindleberger (1963, appendix E).
[30] See, for instance, Enke (1963, pp. 444-463).

TABLE 7.7

Contribution of Merchandise Exports to the Gross Domestic Product, 1966

	Percentage of GDP		Percentage of GDP
Mexico	5.4	Peru	15.0
Brazil	6.5	Guatemala	16.2
Colombia	6.9	Bolivia	19.1
Argentina	7.8	Costa Rica	21.2
Haiti	8.5	Nicaragua	22.3
Paraguay	10.4	El Salvador	22.8
Uruguay	11.9	Honduras	25.7
Panama	12.5	Venezuela	30.5
Chile	13.3	Trinidad and Tobago	52.6
Dominican Republic	13.3	Latin America	11.0
Ecuador	14.8		

Source: International Monetary Fund and Agency for International Development, Inter-American Development Bank (1969a, p. 31).

The Nondominant Economy

Despite the fact that the vital importance of foreign trade was recognized by the Alliance for Progress, basic weaknesses have still to be removed. In terms of competitive power to hold, penetrate, and enlarge markets for traditional products or for a changed export mix, Latin America is in what could be called a nondominant status in most respects in the international economy. Latin America is nondominant in terms of its share of the world's total supply or output of mineral resources, power resources, agricultural products, and raw materials. Latin America is nondominant in terms of its share of total world trade. It is obviously nondominant in terms of control over prevailing world prices for its principal exports; it is in almost all essentials a dependent and largely monoproduct economy, continuously caught in the dilemmas of inflation and balance of payments deficits. Latin America remains nondominant in terms of its comparatively low possession of high-talent manpower—the administrators, managers, foremen, technicians, and entrepreneurs needed to transform the economy from a nondominant position to a position of international influence and even control in strategic areas of importance to Latin American economic well-being.

Minerals

Table 7.8 shows the position of mineral production in Latin America in relation to world production. Latin America produces a large share of the world's bauxite and silver, and a significant amount of copper and tin. In terms of known and potential mineral reserves, the status of Latin America is even more significant. Jamaica, Guyana, Surinam, and Brazil, together accounting for three-quarters of the known reserves of the region, have a very significant proportion of world reserves of bauxite. Chile and Peru account for about 30 percent of the world reserves of copper. The iron ore reserves of Venezuela are among the most extensive in the world and iron is of importance or potential importance to Venezuela, Brazil, Peru, Mexico, Chile, Colombia, Bolivia, Surinam, and Guyana. Manganese is of importance to Brazil, Bolivia, Mexico, and Chile; lead to Mexico, Peru, and Argentina; and zinc to Mexico, which has 50 percent of the reserves of Latin America. Minerals account for 79 percent of the total export values in Bolivia, 89.4 percent in Chile, and 51.1 percent in Peru. In general, the production index for minerals (1963=100) increased from 48 in 1950 to 117 in 1968.[31]

If Balassa's forecasts are to be followed, the prospects of developing countries in international trade in bauxite, silver, copper, zinc, and possibly lead do not appear pessimistic over the next decade (1964).

Table 7.8 shows, however, that except for bauxite and iron, Latin America's share of world production has declined in the years 1950-66. The rate of Latin America's production of all minerals has been lower than the world average for the period 1950-68. Indeed, except for Guyana, Jamaica, Bolivia (9 percent), and Chile (6.5 percent), the mineral sector contributes less than 5 percent to the GDP of industrial Latin American countries. The development of mineral production and export in Latin America is complicated by a variety of difficulties. The case of copper illustrates some of the problems.

The Case of Copper

Exploitation under the direction of American companies gave Chilean copper a high degree of international market penetration, particularly in the U.S. market. On the other hand, anticipating significant gains for Latin American exporters of copper during periods of increased prices is a difficult matter. From 1963-64, for instance, the price of electrolytic copper rose by 50 percent on the London Metal Exchange. Nonetheless, the price of electrolytic copper sold by major U.S. producers rose by only 4.6 percent. Chilean copper remained pegged at this price. In 1964, demand threatened to outstrip supply. Added to this, copper workers in the United States and Chile were threatening to strike. The major world producers of copper at this stage removed themselves from the London Metal Exchange and set up a major producers' price. The high level reached in market quotations, however, held little significance for Latin American exporters of copper, since, according to UNECLA, "the bulk of their output is controlled by United States companies and is therefore subject to the price

TABLE 7.8

Mineral Production as a Share of World Production (In Percent)

	Bauxite	Copper	Tin	Lead	Zinc	Silver	Iron
1950	44.1	19.0	19.2	22.3	16.6	38.1	–
1955	47.0	17.9	15.8	18.4	17.4	37.2	7.6
1960	46.2	19.3	16.4	16.8	15.3	36.5	10.1
1965	45.7	17.7	17.0	14.9	12.8	36.5	12.3
1966	45.6	18.2	17.2	14.5	12.3	36.0	12.1

Source: CEPAL (1970aaa).

[31] See CEPAL (1969e).

policy followed by the major producers in that country."[32] Fourteen percent of Chilean copper sells at London market prices, but 86 percent sells at export prices fixed by the major producers. In general, most of Latin America's copper is sold at prices fixed by the major American producers. On the other hand, where copper prices controlled by the major producers, are cushioned from the fluctuations in world prices, as is the case with other primary commodities exported by Latin America.[33]

There is, of course, no guarantee that copper production would expand proportionately to an increase in world demand. For instance, in the period 1948-63, world copper output expanded 84 percent, but Chilean copper production increased only 46 percent; Mexico's copper output remained at a standstill over the period; and Peruvian output rose between 1948-60, then fell. Internal demand for Latin American copper is small because Latin American industry used very little copper.

Under President Frei, copper production became partly Chileanized and major programs were initiated for the substantial expansion of copper production and for refining most of the copper in Chile.[34] Under Allende, further nationalization became inevitable.

Earnings from copper depend on a variety of factors and this makes it difficult to plan for orderly economic advance. Uncertainty, however, is the essential characteristic of international economic life and there is little convincing evidence that any particular ideology can successfully contain economic uncertainty. These observations apply to the changing price of Chilean copper. Externally, copper after 1965 confronted three fixed prices in the United States. On the London Metal Exchange the prices of major producers varied from day to day. Drought and landslides affect supply conditions; government intervention and policies affect prices. For instance, in 1965 with the intervention of the Chilean Government, the prices of copper exports rose from 36 to 38 cents a pound, and in 1966 to 70 cents a pound. In the United States, government policy is directed to holding down the domestic price of copper. Wars increase copper prices; peace may bring them down. Labor problems can cause a rise in copper prices; a slowdown in industrial activity can bring them down. Water and electric power shortages in Chile may cause shortages and push prices up; the acceleration of industrial substitution of other materials for copper may bring prices down.[35]

Figure 7.1 shows the variations in copper prices between 1962-68. Prebischism certainly applies to this somewhat wild price situation during a period

---

[32] UNECLA (1966, p. 257).

[33] For an extended analysis, see also Powelson (1964, pp. 128-138).

[34] El Teniente mine, for instance, came under the partnership of the Chilean government (51 percent of the shares) and Kennecott Copper Corporation; the Exotica Company belongs 75 percent to the Anaconda Company and 25 percent to the Chilean government. The Anaconda Group has the following subsidiaries: The Andes Mining Company, a partnership of the Cerro Corporation (75 percent) and the government of Chile (25 percent), which operates the El Salvador mine and the Potrerillos refinery and smelter; and the Chile Exploration Company (operating the Chuquicamata mine). (See Pan American Union [IA-ECOSOC and CIAP] [1967c, pp. 102–103]).

[35] See Chase Manhattan Bank (1969a, pp. 10-12).

of adverse prices for copper in relation to the prices of manufactured products.[36] Chile, however, produces less than 15 percent of the world's copper. Chile's nondominant position obviously imposes limitations on the country's bargaining strength in copper.

Out of these considerations, a fundamental rule emerges. So long as a country's position is nondominant, it must reduce internal rigidities within its own economy to facilitate the transfer of resources from areas of weaker bargaining power in the international economy to areas where its bargaining power is better. The ability to reallocate could certainly cushion developing countries from the harsh uncertainties of international economic bargaining.

The Composition of Exports

The composition of the exports of Latin America underwent some change over the 1960 decade; manufactures and semimanufactures increased as a percentage of the total value of exports. Foreign earnings, however, traditionally accrue from one group of products, namely foodstuffs and raw materials, which account for over 80 percent of the total value of Latin America's exports. In turn, food and beverages contribute over 40 percent of the export earnings accruing from primary export products. In fact, 16 of the countries listed in Table 7.9 depend on one product for over 40 percent of their export earnings. In three of these countries, a single product accounts for over 70 percent of the export earnings.

In turn, the few products on which Latin American export earnings depend are highly vulnerable to price changes (see Table 7.10) and these price

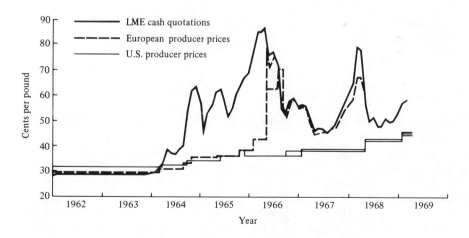

FIGURE 7.1
Disparate Pricing Arrangement in Copper Market
Source: Chase Manhattan Bank (1969a).

[36]Cf. Baer (1969, pp. 203-218), Haberler (1963, pp. 275-307), and Street (1967, pp. 44-62).

TABLE 7.9

Monoproduct Dominance in Export Earnings, 1965-67

	Principal exports as percentages of total exports
19 Latin American republics	petroleum and petroleum products, 25; coffee, 14
Central American Common Market countries	coffee, 34; cotton, 16; bananas, 13
Argentina	wheat and corn, 30; meat and meat products, 24; wool, 8
Bolivia	tin, 62; lead and zinc, 7
Brazil	coffee, 44; cotton, 6
Chile	copper bars, ores and concentrates, 74; iron ore, 9
Colombia	coffee, 62; petroleum, 15
Costa Rica	coffee, 39; bananas, 24
Dominican Republic	sugar, 55; coffee, 14; cocoa, 7
Ecuador	bananas, 54; coffee, 19; cocoa, 11
El Salvador	coffee, 49; cotton, 14
Guatemala	coffee, 43; cotton, 18
Haiti	coffee, 49; bauxite, 10; sugar, 9
Honduras	bananas, 47; coffee, 14; wood, 8
Jamaica	bauxite and alumina, 47; sugar, 21
Mexico	cotton, 17; coffee, 6
Nicaragua	cotton, 42; coffee, 16
Panama	bananas, 51; refined petroleum, 28
Paraguay	meat, 32; lumber, 18; cotton, 6; sugar, 6
Peru	fish and fish products, 27; copper, 23; cotton, 10; sugar, 6
Trinidad and Tobago	petroleum and petroleum products, 79
Uruguay	wool, 47; meat, 27; hides, 9
Venezuela	petroleum and petroleum products, 92; iron ore, 5

Source: U.S. Department of State (1969d).

changes adversely affect the trade gap and the prospects for more rapid economic growth.[37]

A wider range of factors enter into the explanation of fluctuating prices of primary commodities. These include Engel's law; weather conditions affecting output; interruptions in the supply of labor and other factors of production; domestic policies of the government; tariff policies; the state of international competition; the rate of emergence of substitute products; and changes in taste and incomes. Fluctuations in the price of coffee illustrate the effect of some of these variables. Although stockpiling, for instance, has been no more than 5 percent since the International Coffee Agreement, prices declined because

[37] See, for instance, U.S. Senate (1967d, p. 3). The trade gap was defined here as "the difference between the growth of imports (and of debt-service payments) required to achieve a 5 percent development rate and the prospective slower growth of earnings."

TABLE 7.10

Price Indexes of Principal Export Products

	BASE OF 1963 = 100									ANNUAL AVERAGES			Weighting[b]
	1960	1961	1962	1963	1964	1965	1966	1967	1968	1951–55[a]	1956–60[a]	1961–68	
Food, beverages, and tobacco	92	89	87	100	108	100	96	92	90	–	–	95	41.6
Agricultural raw materials	101	101	98	100	105	101	102	95	97	–	–	100	12.1
Metals	107	104	103	100	117	129	152	142	148	–[c]	–	124	12.5
Petroleum and derivatives	105	105	102	100	94	93	91	88	89	99[c]	104[c]	95	33.7
Total for 21 products			97		104	101	101	97	–				100.0

[a]Recalculated on basis of 17 products with base of 1958 = 100.
[b]Calculated according to participation of each product in the value of total exports in 1963.
[c]Crude petroleum.

Source: CEPAL (1970bb).

world consumption grew too slowly.[38] Price ranges and quotas did not stop a steady price decline after 1962. In 1966-67, a bumper crop of coffee intensified a declining trend in world prices.[39] The position of Latin America coffee became weakened by another factor. Between 1948-64, Africa's share of world coffee exports increased from 13.6 percent to 31.3 percent while Brazil's share of the world exports of coffee dropped in the same period from 54.4 percent to 32 percent.[40]

There are similar examples of price declines and of declining rates of participation in world exports in other primary products. Between 1955-57 and 1968, Latin American sugar exports (excluding Cuba) dropped from 55 percent to 47 percent of world exports; cocoa dropped from 28 percent to 19 percent; Venezuelan petroleum dropped from 27 percent to 16 percent, partly as a result of the competitive expansion of Middle East oil exports.[41] The multiplier effect of a fall in coffee prices is readily visible in a country like Colombia where coffee employs one out of every four Colombians of working age and where it is estimated that a drop of one cent in the world price of coffee means a loss to Colombia of $7.5 million of export earnings.[42]

The argument is not that price fluctuation and a declining share of the world export market or of world trade are inevitable secular consequences for Latin American primary exports. The point is that the prices of primary exports have fluctuated while the unit values of manufactured imports have gradually risen (see Tables 7.10 and 7.11). A look at the general picture for 1950-68 shows the rate of growth of Latin American exports during the period was only 3.1 percent, less than half of the rate of growth of world exports. Latin America's share of world exports dropped from 11.2 percent in 1950 to 5.4 percent in 1967.[43]

Latin America's share of its major export market, the United States, even dropped by 10 percent between 1955-57 and 1967-67. Indeed there was a slight over-all decline in Latin America's share in all its principal export markets taken together (United States, the European Common Market, Latin America, itself, eastern Europe, Britain, and Japan). There is evidence, however, on the other side. Between 1961-68, both the volume and value of Latin American exports rose. In the same period, Chile's export values nearly doubled from $506 million (U.S.) to $933 million largely because of a 97 percent increase in copper prices. Panama, Bolivia, Nicaragua, Honduras, Costa Rica, and Guatemala increased their exports at a rate superior to the rate of growth of world exports, estimated at 8.7 percent for the period.[44]

---

[38] The International Coffee Agreement came into effect in 1962. The agreement, among other aims, set out to regulate the supply and demand for coffee to assure consumers of adequate supplies of coffee and producers of markets at fair prices. The agreement also sought to mitigate the effects of "unduly large stocks" and "excessive fluctuations in coffee prices." See UNECLA (1963a, pp. 203-204). See also Pan American Coffee Bureau (1967).

[39] See UNECLA (1969b, pp. 68-70).

[40] UNECLA (1966, pp. 237-242).

[41] See Farley (1971).

[42] See Chase Manhattan Bank (1967d).

[43] See CEPAL (1969b).

[44] See Inter-American Development Bank (1969, pp. 23-27).

Nonetheless, price declines for primary exports as against steady prices for manufactured imports undoubtedly make for adverse terms of trade and for weakening Latin America's capacity to import. Table 7.12 illustrates the interrelations in Colombia for the period 1960-66. At no time in that period did the export-import price ratio reach 100 nor did the capacity to import.[45] The weakening of the capacity to import also has an adverse effect on the rate of growth of the domestic economy. In Colombia, for instance, the value of coffee exports fell in 1965, and the value of total exports also declined. The capacity to import likewise declined. The government imposed a multitude of restrictions to meet the deteriorating balance of payments situation. Imports in 1965 dropped 20 percent below the level of 1964. Particularly critical was the drop in the import of capital and of intermediate goods essential to domestic economic development. Government investment expenditures dropped, and gross fixed investment declined over 8 percent. The rate of growth of the economy between 1964-65 slumped from an average of 6 percent to 3.5 percent. Unemployment increased nearly 3 percent. Increased financing by the Central Bank of Colombia to save further deterioration was not only ineffective; it added to inflationary pressures which, in turn, further affected the domestic capitalization of the economy.[46]

TABLE 7.11

Export-Import Exchange Ratios (1963 = 100)

		UNIT VALUE OF IMPORTS		EXCHANGE RATIO	
	Total unit value of exports	Total	Consumer goods and capital	Total	Consumer goods and capital
1950	111	84	67	132	166
1955	121	99	82	122	148
1960	103	97	91	106	113
1961	103	98	95	105	108
1962	99	100	100	99	99
1963	100	100	100	100	100
1964	106	104	105	102	101
1965	104	105	107	99	97
1966	106	104	110	102	96
1967	103	106	111	97	93
1968	105	107	114	98	92
		AVERAGE OF INDEXES			
1951-55	125	98	79	127	158
1956-60	111	98	88	113	128
1961-68	103	103	105	100	98

Source: CEPAL (1970bb).

[45] See also "Economic Bulletin for Latin America" (1967, pp. 90-106); Pan American Union (IA-ECOSOC and CIAP) (1968a).
[46] See DANE (1967, pp. 70, 775-782); Pan American Union (IA-ECOSOC and CIAP) (1968a, pp. 11, 14, 34, 45).

TABLE 7.12

Colombia: Capacity to Import (1952 = 100)

	Index of quantum of exports	Export-import price ratio	Capacity to import	Index of quantum of imports
1960	115.9	79.8	92.5	1168
1961	109.9	77.7	85.4	1183
1962	122.7	73.1	89.7	1063
1963	120.3	66.2	79.6	1083
1964	124.9	79.7	99.5	1213
1965	118.0	81.5	96.2	919
1966	115.0	64.7	74.5	1274

Source: DANE (Departamento Administrativo Nacional de Estadistica) (1967).

INSTABILITY IN EXPORT EARNINGS: THE SEARCH FOR SOLUTIONS

From the experience in Latin America, we can draw the preliminary conclusion that instability in export earnings and deterioration in the terms of
trade can never be factored from national calculations. The recurrence of
instability is not confined to a particular set of products nor is it confined to
developing countries alone. Careful studies come up with mixed evidence which
disallows dogmatic conclusions about the inevitability of fluctuations in the
price of primary products, or the inevitability of a long-run deterioration in the
terms of trade for less developed countries with a high concentration of
primary exports.[47] On the other hand, it is clear that the classical theory that
international economic relations work out well on the basis of factor endowments, comparative advantages, and specialization does not hold up in the face
of the many political-economic forces affecting modern international trade.
The need to find solutions to the problem of export instability and deterioration in the terms of trade, emerges from the primary-export country's need
to earn sufficient foreign exchange to buy the capital and intermediate goods
required to promote domestic development. Since solutions are not easy to
find, except perhaps in the long run, the weaknesses of the external sector
constitute another critical constraint on more rapid development. As we have
seen, the economy remains largely a prisoner of traditional attitudes and
methods. Because of the limitations in entrepreneurial capacity and the lack
of sufficient development, Latin America cannot mobilize the domestic
resources needed for its transformation. Barring foreign assistance, Latin
America has no alternative but to depend almost totally on the earnings
from foreign trade to secure critically needed capital imports.

Expanding Markets for Exports

We now look at various policies which could be adopted to strengthen the
external sector or to rid the economy of the weaknesses of the external
sector. Latin America can seek to expand exports beyond its traditional
market outlets in the United States. In fact, between 1958-67, while the value

[47] See, for instance, Cohen (1968, pp. 334-343).

of Latin American exports to the United States and Britain practically stood still, the value of the Latin American exports to other areas of the world increased significantly—over three times for Canada, over four and one-half times for the Federal Republic of Germany, over four times for Japan, and nearly double for Communist areas in eastern Europe and Asia.[48] Trading with the last-named areas is full of uncertain political variables so that it is difficult to calculate the future of trade here, but in the other areas, Latin America has the advantage of historical connection. The political variables are known and can be tackled within a different framework of relationships. Here, of course, Latin America faces competition from other developing countries selling primary products; competition from synthetics and substitutes; competition from farmers in the developed countries who produce sugar, cotton, and rice, for example, as in the United States; obstruction from protectionist interests; governmental policies which seek to keep consumer prices low; technological changes economizing on the use of imported raw materials; and other variables.

Trade diversification is another escape route from dependence on a highly concentrated group of primary exports. Indeed, trade diversification is one of the major goals of the Alliance for Progress.[49] There has been some success here in terms of structural changes in favor of manufacturing, in increases in the export of manufactured goods, and in the introduction of new agricultural exports. The changes in diversification, however, do not make the immediate and tremendous difference demanded by present economic conditions. As a result of socioeconomic constraints, anachronistic economic structures still prevail in most of the countries. Between 1960-67, manufactures only increased from 9 percent of the total exports of Latin America to less than 15 percent, although the rate of increase over the period (91 percent) is impressive. There is no reason to expect that in a competitive world Latin American manufactures would escape the variety of factors which inhibit market expansion of primary products in the developed countries. In fact, the deterrents to increasing the manufacturing exports from Latin America might even be greater if we accept the view that the present tariff structures of industrially advanced countries discriminate more severely against processing than appears from the nominal tariff rates.[50] Trade diversification is no guarantee of stable demand or of full employment of resources, and if it is undertaken as a matter of expediency, it may even lead to misallocation of resources and interfere with rational over-all development policies.

Import Restrictions

In Colombia, the recurrent declines in coffee prices over the last decade were followed by import restrictions and strict foreign exchange control. This is a natural policy resort to meet an immediate emergency situation. If the import restrictions shut out inessential goods, there is no harm done to development. But, as we have seen, if they shut out capital and intermediate goods, then the development path can be adversely affected. If the import restrictions are

[48]See U.S. Department of State (1969d, p. 26).
[49]See U.S. House (1969, p. 17).
[50]Streeten (1968).

intended to shut out competitive foreign goods in order to encourage import substitution industries, the results can be mixed. Export prices may increase because higher wage demands follow the higher costs of the products of the substitute industries. Thus export earnings may fall with obvious consequences for economic development. Beside this, the management of import restrictions is a highly complicated matter and a great strain and temptation for weak administrations.

Government Control of Marketing

Governments sometimes use temporary periods of instability as an excuse for nationalizing the marketing of primary and other exports. This may seem plausible, but it can lead to distorting the value of the price signals. The procedure is quite simple. The government pays a stable price for local production whether world prices are high or low. Obviously, when prices are high, the government gets rid of commodity stocks and gains foreign exchange. When prices are low, the producers win out by getting the fixed price from the government, which accumulates stock and loses foreign exchange since it has to sell foreign exchange for local currency to people who want to import. But, as Enke asks, what criteria enter into establishing a "normal world price," and into determining whether the scheme should start in a high or a low world-price year? If the low prices last, the normal price of a marketing board might encourage unjustified production (1963, pp. 469-470). An important point is that government may be a very inefficient salesman for the country's products. Nationalizing marketing does not solve the problem of instability—as Perón discovered in Argentina. The prices Perón paid were so absurdly low, his salesmanship was so bad, and the corruption and wastage were so great that the Argentinian economy simply ceased to grow.[51]

International Commodity Agreements

When primary export earnings are unstable and thus have the potential of damaging the development effort, the international commodity agreement comes prominently into the picture as a policy proposal. The necessity for such agreements is reiterated frequently at international and regional trade conferences. Like the International Coffee Agreement of 1962 and the new International Coffee Agreement of 1968, these agreements generally seek to regulate the output of a particular product, to stabilize prices, to police extraquota trading, and to encourage agricultural diversification.[52] The road to stabilizing prices is paved with good intentions and actually some good things have come about through commodity agreements. The evidence points, in the case of coffee, to some success in moderating short-term fluctuations in prices. There is no guarantee, however, that international commodity agreements could fully solve either short-term or long-run problems.

It would be useful at this point to look at the uncertainties surrounding international commodity agreements. The basic difficulty lies in the fact that commodity agreements cannot easily, if at all, overcome the very complicated and continuing range of self-interest. Hence negotiations are usually long and

[51] See Scobie (1964, pp. 225-227).
[52] See, for instance, Chase Manhattan Bank (1969c, pp. 15-16).

sometimes the gains do not justify the time. If the commodity is homogeneous and substitute-free, if the demand for it is inelastic, and if the producing country is willing and able to control production of the commodity, then we have the basic conditions for an effective commodity agreement.[53] Few commodities would satisfy these criteria. It is difficult to get individual countries to conform to quota limits, since one country may want more money from more exports or may want to secure a power base for rebargaining. It is difficult even with financial incentives to secure diversification since people like to stick to the activities they know about and alternative investment outlets may be difficult to find. Climatic and physical factors may best suit the particular crop from which resources have to shift. It is difficult to control weather conditions, and good weather may mean surplus production—which no one can stop. Stable prices and a quota system may discourage the very diversification that the agreement wants to encourage. Indeed, stable prices may encourage individual farmers to increase rather than decrease their output.

There are those who argue that instability in export earnings has little to do with variations in domestic output, that developed countries suffer just as much from fluctuations in export earnings, so that commodity agreements are useless. Others argue that commodity agreements are simply agreements to conceal a grant-in-aid to primary producing countries since they maintain the price of the commodity above the price which would have been obtained in the free market. This grant-in-aid represents an unfair tax on the consumers of the developed country, and there is no guarantee that the benefits of the concealed grant-in-aid would be evenly distributed in the exporting countries. Others argue that price-supporting agreements would freeze the division of the market where it is and generate discontent and refusal to cooperate on the part of those who can get higher prices; that low-cost producers would receive more assistance than high-cost producers who need assistance most; and that assistance would be distributed without regard to the comparative absorptive capacity of the country for capital and its ability to plan development.[54] There are other arguments that developing countries need more than price stability. They need increased foreign earnings and commodity agreements provide only the former. To sum up, there is obviously no consensus that international commodity agreements are the answer to the problem of instability in export earnings.

Modifying Tariff Barriers

Instability in export earnings is the source of constant pressure for lower tariff barriers or for preferential tariffs for the products of developing countries. Implicit in these pressures is the assumption that, other things being equal, the elimination or reduction of tariffs on the exports of developing countries would lead to an expansion of the market for the products of developing countries. No such assumption can be sustained. There is no guarantee that Latin American exports would be more competitive than exports from other developing countries. There are no guarantees about elasticities of supply or of demand. With regard to politically designed preferences, much depends on the

---

[53]U.S. Senate (1967d, p. 154). See also Killick (1970, pp. 533-538).
[54]Killick (1970, pp. 537-538).

world situation and the political leverage of Latin America as against other regions. There is no economic reason compelling any developed country to give tariff preferences to support budding exports from Latin America or elsewhere. All depends on circumstance. Developing countries must separate concessions based on moral arguments from concessions which would be gained from economic analyses showing mutual profit. Once again, we are in an economic no man's land which produces no realistic short-run solution for the problem of instability in export earnings. Even on the domestic scene, Latin American countries find it difficult to remove tariff barriers to encourage their own intraregional trade. There is no reason why the difficulties should be less when it comes to extraregional relations—even if it is admittedly clear that effective high tariffs imposed on processed raw materials from developing countries force the developing countries to export the raw materials rather than process them for exporting.[55]

International Measures: Compensatory and Supplementary Financing

There are two further measures used to help solve the problem of instability in the export earnings of developing countries. The first is the system of compensatory financing introduced by the International Monetary Fund (IMF) in 1963. Under this scheme, after 1966 a member country, in addition to its regular drawing rights, could, in case of short-term export declines (shortfalls), borrow up to 50 percent of its IMF quota. Money so borrowed was repayable in five years.

Balance of payments difficulties over a protracted period came under the supplementary financing scheme proposed by Britain to the United Nations Conference on Trade and Development (UNCTAD) conference in 1964 and adopted for study by the International Bank of Reconstruction and Development. The supplementary financing scheme aims at providing long-term loans to support countries which have suffered reasonably explicable shortfalls in export earnings. These two schemes, important though they are, represent no more than after-the-fact recognition of the condition. They assist afterwards; they do not solve the basic problem. Devaluation falls under the same consideration. It is a shot in the dark which may or may not work.

Alternative Use of Resources: The Special Case of South America's Economic Frontiers

We deal now with the special case of what the Inter-American Committee on the Alliance for Progress (CIAP) calls the frontiers of South America.[56] CIAP argued in its analysis that the growing technological and industrial competence of South America in combination with new technology and capital from abroad makes possible the economic development of some regions which remained undeveloped because of natural barriers, soil limitations, and endemic disease. These regions acquired significance because of the need (1) to widen the markets for South American products; (2) to win the race between food production and demand; (3) to enable South America to become a food exporter again; (4) to put to work unexploited natural resources to provide chemical fertilizers,

---

[55]U.S. Senate (1968c, p. 362).
[56]Pan American Union (CIAP) (1967h).

minerals, and fuels for the development of the continent; and (5) to expand foreign exchange earnings.

CIAP identified nine major potential unused regions of South America. Going south counterclockwise from the Panama Canal, these were: the Darien Gap; the wet tropical lowlands other than flood plains; the wet tropical lowlands (flood plains); the East Andean Piedmont (upper tropical lowlands); the Campo Cerrado; the Gran Chaco and the Gran Pantanal; the River Plate drainage system; the Rio-Sao Paulo-Buenos Aires axis; and the Guiana complex. Map 7.1 identifies some of the possibilities under active study and implementation. We have already noted the importance of developing some of these areas since they form part of the spatial dimensions of the development problem of Latin America. The development possibilities of the other regions are being pursued and obviously this drive gains momentum as time goes on.

A summary of the development potential of these regions is essential. We have already discussed the development efforts in the Guayana region of Venezuela. The Darien Gap, opened up by the Pan American Highway link, can expand potentialities for cattle raising and other agricultural and forestry development, and possibly pull population away from the over-crowded areas of Panama. The wet tropical lowlands (other than flood plains) of the Amazon and Orinoco basins could become a major source of food and of permanent tree crops like rubber. The wet tropical lowlands are really the flood plains of the Amazon and cover an area of over 25,000 square miles. Again, the development possibilities of this area are being actively explored. The East Andean Piedmont (upper tropical lowlands), an area some 3000 miles in length and 10 to 50 miles in width, contains an estimated 3 million acres of arable land. The region is a good potential source of meat, dairy products, tropical foods, tobacco, tea, and other cash crops. It is already being opened up by the Carretera Marginal de le Silva. The Campo Cerrado, a vast area of some 400 million acres, has considerable agricultural potential. The Gran Chaco and the Gran Pantanal have similar agricultural promise. There is considerable potential for navigational and hydroelectric power development in the River Plate drainage system, while the Rio-Sao Paulo-Buenos Aires axis might constitute in the future of South America a potential metropolitan strip comparable to Chicago or New York.

Several qualifications must be introduced in evaluating the development of the potentialities of these regions as an immediate alternative to dependence on fluctuating export earnings. First, although development seems impossible without a minimum resource base, the possession of enormous potential resources obviously does not guarantee spontaneous economic transformation.[57] Second, the pressure for accelerated development in Latin America is immediate but the prospects for developing the areas we have identified is long term. The obstacles to pushing out the production possibility frontiers through development of the interior include several real factors: (1) the high costs of access and of transporting products to the market; (2) the high costs of populating and settling areas without the facilities and infrastructure of the coastal area; (3) the lack of established information on the interior areas; (4) technological inadequacies interfering with the conquest of the interior; and (5) lack of legal provision or public policy, as well as the possibility of international friction.

[57] Cf. Pepelasis, Mears, and Adelman (1961, pp. 18-45).

○ River basin projects
△ Colonization projects
□ Extractive industries
▨ Health projects

0   300   600
━━━━━━━━━━ Miles
━━━━━━━━━━ Kilometers
0   400   800

MAP 7.1
Actual and Potential Projects in South America
Source: Pan American Union (CIAP) (1967h).

Selected List of Projects, Actual and Potential	Number[a]
A. Argentina	
Colonization	A1
Airport development	A2
Rio Bermejo development project	A3
Rio Dulce project	A4
Eastern Seaboard Megalopolis—Rio to Buenos Aires	A5
B. Bolivia	
Colonization of the Interior	B1
Alto Beni colonization	B2
Okinawan colonies	B3
Lake Titicaca development	B4
Mutun iron ore deposits development	B5
Malaria eradication problem	B6
Hemorrhagic fever control	B7
Riberalta-Guayaremerin road	B8
Feasibility studies	B9
Mineral survey and geology training	B10
Abapo Irrigation project	B11
Carretera Marginal	B12
C. Brazil	
Agrarian reform and frontier development	C-1
Education for rural development	C-2
Agricultural output colony	C-3
Rio Grande do Sul North production road	C-4
Fortaleza-Brasilia highway	C-5
Paranagua-Foz do Iguacu highway	C-6
Rio-Salvador coastal highway	C-7
Belem-Brasilia highway	C-8
Frontier and penetration roads in the state of Pará	C-9
Brasilia-Acre-Peruvian border highway	C-10
Work fronts	C-11
Boa Esperanca dam	C-12
Frontier activities	C-13, 14, 15
Sete Quedas hydroelectric project	C-16
D. Guiana	
Air transport (feasibility study)	D-1
Berbice River harbor	D-2
Penetration roads to the interior	D-3
Savannah soils investigation	D-4
Mineral resources development	D-5
Aerial Geophysical Survey	D-6
Forest industries development study	D-7
Atkinson-Mackenzie road	D-8

[a]See Map 7.1.

E. Colombia
    Potential colonization projects   E1
    Basic resources survey   E2
    Land settlement and improved land use and tenure   E3
    National territories Air Navigation Service (SATENA)   E4
    Mineral resources survey   E5
    Potential feasibility studies   E6
    Prefeasibility and feasibility studies   E7
    Atrato-San Juan waterway   E8
    Colombian-Ecuadorian economic integration of frontier areas   E9

F. Ecuador
    Upano River Valley development   F1
    Arenillas irrigation project   F2
    Consortium highway program   F3
    Penetration roads to Amazon headwaters area   F4
    Development of Guayas river basin   F5

G. Panama-Colombia
    Pan American Highway–Darien Gap   G1
    Isthmian sea level canal   G2

H. Paraguay
    Navigation study of the Paraguay River south of Asunción   H1
    Malaria eradication   H2
    Apipe hydroelectric and navigation project   H3
    Road construction and maintenance training (farm-to-market roads) H4
    Colonization   H5
    U.N. special fund survey of "Triangle" area   H6

I. Peru
    Highways   I1
    Air access to the frontier   I2
    Private sector development   I3
    Colonization in East Andes   I4
    Irrigation development   I5
    Carretera Marginal   I6

J. Uruguay
    Development of the Laguna Merín basin   J1
    El Palmar hydroelectric project   J2

K. Venezuela
    Industrialization of southeast Venezuela   K1
    Agrarian reform program   K2
    Inter-American gas pipeline   K3

Obviously, there are prospects for substantially important changes in the resource base of Latin America. Evaluating these potentialities, however, requires research, surveys, mapping, and other fact-finding exercises. Implementing them will take time. It takes time, apart from other requirements, to mobilize technical personnel, to carry through research, and to mobilize capital, entrepreneurship, and other supportive factors to transform research findings into actual development by private or public action or both.[58]

Given these deterrents, Latin America for the present must continue to depend on its current export structure for foreign earnings. In fact, increasing the traditional export earnings is essential in order to finance the development of the unutilized areas.

THE ESSENCE OF THE PROBLEM

We have dealt at some length with the role of the external sector and the consequences for economic development of instability in export earnings. We do not accept the long-term view of the inevitability of adverse terms of trade or the view that there is something essentially fatal in the exportation of primary products. The case of Norway, for instance, is instructive. According to Balassa's analysis, in 1949 primary activities (agriculture, fishing, forestry and mining) accounted for 42 percent of Norway's commodity production; intermediate products (processed fish, pulp and paper, aluminum, ferroalloys, and fertilizer) for 21 percent, and manufactured goods for 37 percent. By 1966, the share of primary products fell to 24 percent; intermediate products rose to 27 percent; and manufacturing industries to 48 percent.[59] To some extent, New Zealand, Denmark, Japan, and even Australia are examples of this kind of economic shift. We look at another instructive example later in this book—the case of Venezuela.

We do not argue against the expected use of political bargaining power to negotiate for international commodity agreements, for tariff preferences, and for innovations like compensatory or supplementary financing. Nor do we argue against the necessity for expedient tariff protection or devaluation measures. These measures do not, however, necessarily go to the heart of the matter. The essential weaknesses in the export sector stem from a carryover of traditional social values and business and organizational attitudes which are anachronistic in the harsh world of international competition. An underdeveloped country which seeks to conquer the markets of the world entrepreneurially by reducing costs, improving quality, strengthening management and marketing organization, changing the mix of its products, and imaginatively advertising is more likely to escape the recurrence of instability in export earnings than countries which moralize in the face of uncertainty or, worse yet, retreat behind tariff walls to

[58]Cf. Nutter (1957, pp. 51-63). Cf. also Pan American Union (CIAP) (1967h, p. 5): "The answer to these questions must be established region by region and project by project against the background of expanding research and exploration, for, despite the powerful attraction the South American interior has to adventurous minds, there is a great deal we do not know. Investment decisions must be based on the answers to these questions."

[59]Balassa (1970, pp. 28-33).

give inefficiencies even more shelter than before. Smallness of the domestic market is a constraint on investment and development only in those countries where the entrepreneurial vision is small. The markets of the world are there for all who dare to be internationally competitive.[60] There is no other approach which offers a fundamental and straightforward cure for the recurrent problem of export instability.

The continuing weaknesses in the external sector of Latin America, therefore, are a reflection of the constraining values we described in Part I of this book. Only nations which demonstrate superior will and superior ingenuity escape from the weaknesses of existing situations or advance weak situations into positions of greater competitive strength. From this point of view, the weaknesses of the external sector should not be a matter for further international complaint and moralizing, however appealing or justified these resorts may be. These weaknesses continue (whether short term or long term is immaterial) and complaint and moralizing have not changed matters very much. There might be good or bad reasons for this state of affairs so far as the developed countries are concerned. This, too, is immaterial; it is the situation which resists easy change that is relevant. Other countries have accepted realities as given data—hurdles which must be overcome by being better at the gamesmanship demanded for survival in international economic competition. In this sense, therefore, it should be reemphasized that the weaknesses of the external sector reflect the internal weaknesses in the capacity of Latin America to compete as if survival matters.

We turn now to an analysis of the over-all performance of the Latin American economy, particularly during the years of the Alliance for Progress.

[60]Cf. Keesing (1967, pp. 303-320).

CHAPTER 8

THE PROBLEM OF AGRICULTURAL DEVELOPMENT

An accelerated development of the agricultural sector is clearly fundamental to the transformation of the Latin American economy. This is borne out by theory as well as by the evidence we have so far seen. Even a slight excursion into the history of economic thought reveals the continuous importance given to agriculture in major theories of economic growth and development. The physiocrats, for instance, believed that agricultural investment should take priority over investment in industry as a precondition for the fullest possible realization of production possibilities in agriculture as well as in industry.[1] Adam Smith recognized the primary importance of agriculture without denying the importance of other sectors of the economy. Ricardo and Malthus could hardly, of course, expound their own classical views without sharing Adam Smith's outlook. Marx was also concerned about agriculture—in his own distorted way. Friedrich List, the most prominent member of the German historical school, saw agriculture as basic to the economic salvation of tropical developing countries and the only activity to which they could profitably confine themselves—though even for temperate countries, he saw agricultural development as a logical prelude to industrial development.[2]

We have already referred to the place of agriculture in the analysis of Fisher and Clark. Rostow assigns to agriculture three distinct roles "in the transitional process between a traditional society and a successful take-off." First, agriculture must produce more food to meet the needs of a growing population. Second, rising incomes in agriculture can stimulate new modern industrial sectors "essential to the take-off." Third, surplus incomes derived from agriculture can be used to capitalize a modern industrial sector (1960, pp. 22-24). Rostow, of course, is not alone in assigning specific dynamic roles to agriculture in the transition process.[3] W. Arthur Lewis, for instance, in referring to the necessity for poor governments to initiate measures to raise the national income in order to expand their own services, emphasizes that "the crux of the problem is usually a backward system of agriculture" (1969, p. 122).

---

[1] For a critical evaluation of the physiocrats see Hoselitz (1960, esp. pp. 54-60). The physiocrats were an eighteenth-century group of economic thinkers led by the French economist François Quesnay (1694-1774). To the physiocrats, land was the sole source of wealth.

[2] See Brunner (1966, pp. 150-152). See also Baldwin (1966, pp. 20-25) and Bell (1967).

[3] Ruttan (1968, p. 7).

IMPORTANCE OF THE AGRICULTURAL SECTOR

The theoretical underpinnings of the key role of agriculture in the development process need not be detailed further. Previous indicators have already demonstrated its importance in the Latin American economy. Agriculture, for instance, employs a larger proportion of the labor force than any other sector (see Tables 7.2 and 7.3) except in Argentina and Uruguay. These were the only two countries in 1967 (see Table A.43) with less than 20 percent of the economically active population in agriculture. Even so, this is three times the corresponding figure of 6 percent for the United States in that year. Although Table 7.3 shows that the manufacturing sector in 1965 contributed slightly more than the agricultural sector to the gross domestic product of the region as a whole, Table A.38 shows that this occurred in 1967 only in Argentina, Chile, Mexico, and Uruguay. Agricultural exports, as we have seen, are the principal source of foreign earnings in Latin America (Table 7.9) and basically determine Latin America's capacity to import.

The theoretical recognition of the key role of the agricultural sector in economic development is readily supported by the empirical evidence. Stagnation, unemployment, low wages, inequitable income distribution, malnutrition, and general conditions of social despair characterize the rural areas of Latin America.[4] The development of the agricultural sector is therefore fundamental to the transformation of rural life. The rapid growth of the rural population and the evident inability of the manufacturing sector to absorb the rapidly growing urban population, to say nothing of the migrants from the rural areas, make agricultural development essential to provide more jobs in rural areas. Agricultural development is also essential to raise the level of incomes and, under the operation of Engel's law, the level of demand for the products of the manufacturing sector. Agricultural development is needed to provide more food, better food, and cheaper food for the entire population. Agricultural development is critically necessary to maintain and increase the level of foreign earnings so that importation of capital and intermediate goods can be increased in order to promote industrial development. Agricultural development is also a key determinant of the level of government revenues in most countries of Latin America.

But above all, because of the size of the agricultural sector in relation to the whole economy, its rate of growth affects the over-all rate of growth of the whole economy. As Yudelman points out in a 1966 study, agricultural output in the United States grew only at a rate of 2 percent or less over the previous decade. This low rate of increase did not, however, constitute a brake on the growth of the American economy since agriculture contributed less than 5 percent of the gross national product and a one percent change in output amounted to a change of less than .05 percent of GNP. But it is a different matter altogether in a country where agriculture contributes more than 30 percent of the gross domestic product. Given this position, a 3 percent growth rate in agriculture would contribute only 0.9 percent to total growth rate

[4]See, for instance, U.S. Senate (1967e), U.S. Department of Agriculture (1969, pp. 25-26), and UNFAO (1965, p. 5).

while an even 10 percent growth rate in industry, if industry is assumed to contribute 16 percent of the gross domestic product, would contribute only 1.6
percent to the total growth rate.[5] Given then a 10 percent growth rate in
industry, which is high, a 2.5 percent over-all growth rate of the economy
would reflect the effect of the size of the agricultural sector and the effect of
the lower rate of growth in that sector.

Understandably, most Latin American countries have given priority to the
acceleration of the industrial sector. Since the agricultural, the industrial, and
the general growth rates are interdependent, development in Latin America will
remain inhibited by any continuation of economic inertia in the agricultural
sector.

The meeting of the Presidents of America at Punta del Este recognized the
critical importance of modernizing the agricultural sector. Hence their specific
declaration:

*We will modernize the living conditions of our rural populations, raise agri-
cultural productivity in general, and increase food production for the benefit
of both Latin America and the rest of the world. The living conditions of the
rural workers and farmers of Latin America will be transformed to guarantee
their full participation in economic and social progress. For that purpose,
integrated programs of modernization, land settlement, and agrarian reform
will be carried out as the countries require. Similarly, productivity will be
improved and agricultural production diversified. Furthermore, recognizing
that the continent's capacity for food production entails a dual responsibility,
a special effort will be made to produce sufficient food for the growing needs of
their own peoples and to contribute toward feeding the peoples of other
regions.*[6]

However, to transform the agricultural status of Latin America means facing
the formidable traditional constraints which retard agricultural change and
over-all economic advance throughout the continent.

Indicators of Over-all Performance in Agriculture

It would be useful to begin an appreciation of the dilemmas confronting
agricultural development by looking at selected indicators of performance. We
have already indicated that although the statistical data is subject to qualification, it is indicative of trends and relationships.[7]

Table A.44 shows that in the period 1961-69 total agricultural production
increased in every Latin American country except Haiti, Jamaica, and Uruguay.
But because of the rapid population growth, per capita production remained
practically stagnant. Between 1943-63 agricultural production increased by

[5] Yudelman (1966, p. 6).
[6] U.S. Department of State (1967a, p. 12).
[7] See a very useful note on limitations of production data by Thieusenhusen and Brown
in U.S. Senate (1967e, p. 176). Cf. also U.S. House (1969, p. 23): "It is . . . a trivial
view [to] . . . deal only with gross output and not relate it to needs. Yet there is no
simple way to relate production to needs, since country resource endowments are so
varied, and countries can or should import and export widely differing proportions of
their consumption and output."

2.6 percent a year, increasing the per capita production only 0.2 percent a year.[8] Since consumption during the period increased at an annual average rate of 3.7 percent, the gap was closed only by reducing exports and increasing agricultural importation to approximately $450 million.

The period 1953-66 is equally instructive. Using U.N. Food and Agriculture Organization (FAO) and Alliance for Progress minimum growth targets helps to throw further light on the picture. FAO calculated that with a population growth of 2.5 percent a year, a 6 percent yearly rise in national income could result in a rise in the over-all demand for food of 4 to 4.5 percent a year.[9] With a population increase of about 3 percent a year, a 2.5 percent per capita annual increase in product the goal of the Charter of Punta del Este, and an income elasticity of demand of 0.5 percent, as a minimum for the region, food production in Latin America would have to increase by 4.5 to 5 percent a year, if the rest of the economy increased at the same rate. An income elasticity of demand of 0.7 for food would necessitate an increase in food production of 6 percent a year.[10] The original minimum growth target for agriculture of the Alliance for Progress had to be changed, of course, to a new goal of 5 percent: 3 percent to keep up with population growth rate; one percent for a modest improvement in diets to insure 200 more calories per day per person; and one percent for export which would add approximately $1 billion to export earnings.[11]

Between 1953-65, the average annual rate of increase of total agricultural and food production in Latin America was higher than all developing continents, except the Near East, and exceeded that of North America, Western Europe, and Oceania.[12] In per capita agricultural output, Latin America was behind every continent except North America. Despite differences in figures both FAO and the U.S. Department of Agriculture estimates show that in 1955-65 the average annual rate of increase of total and per capita agricultural and food output failed to reach minimum goals, although five countries, namely El Salvador, Nicaragua, Bolivia, Peru, and Venezuela, achieved an average over-all growth rate of more than 5 percent. The picture for the period 1960-61 to 1967-68 introduced no change. Total agricultural production increased at an average rate of 3 percent a year, barely keeping up with the annual increase in population, while total food output, increasing at 4 percent a year, barely exceeded the annual rate of population growth.[13]

[8] UNECLA (1963c, p. 54).

[9] UNFAO (1967, p. 7).

[10] Pan American Union (1967e, p. 41). See also Population Reference Bureau (1968, p. 7): "When the Alliance for Progress was set up in 1961 . . . a modest goal of 2.5 percent annual per capita increase in GNP was set, and an average 6 percent per year rise in agricultural production."

[11] U.S. Department of Agriculture (1967, p. 16).

[12] See Organization for Economic Cooperation and Development (1967, p. 20). Average annual increase in food production (1953-65): Latin America—2.88 percent; developing countinents—2.85 percent; Near East—3.30 percent; Far East—2.85 percent; Africa—2.65 percent. See also UNFAO (1966). The FAO regional index numbers of total agricultural production for 1965 (1952 = 100) are as follows: Latin America—141; North America—118; Western Europe—129; Oceania—135; all the regions of the world—133.

[13] See Inter-American Development Bank (1969a, p. 10). During the period, only Nicaragua, Panama, and Venezuela registered an annual average increase of over 5

Other indicators confirm this somewhat adverse over-all picture of agricultural progress in Latin America. The volume of agricultural exports only increased at a lower rate than the volume of total exports, and the prices of agricultural exports pulled down the over-all index of prices for exports. Latin American imports of agricultural products from outside the region continued at the level of some $600 million a year, a serious matter for a region characteristically suffering from a serious shortage of foreign exchange.[14] Nutritional standards gained ground in some areas but, as we saw in Part I, it was hardly a spectacular change. The domestic price of food skyrocketed in the period 1960-69. The index was nearly six times higher in Argentina in 1969 than in 1960; nearly 30 times higher in São Paulo; over eight times higher in Chile; and nearly 30 times higher in Montevideo, Uruguay.[15] The per capita value of production of the Latin American agricultural work force as a percentage of its U.S. counterpart amounted to only 7 percent in 1967. Only in Argentina, Trinidad and Tobago, and Uruguay did this figure exceed 20 percent.[16] Nowhere did it exceed 25 percent. Agricultural output in the period 1960-69 grew at a slower rate than every other sector of the economy and grew more slowly than the economy as a whole. In 1966, for instance, electricity, gas, and water grew by 10.4 percent, construction by 9.5 percent, manufacturing by 6.3 percent, but agriculture, forestry, and fisheries advanced only 0.5 percent. The over-all rate of growth of the gross domestic product was therefore only 4.1 percent.[17]

An increase in the labor force in agriculture contributes far less to the gross domestic product than is the case with other sectors of the economy.[18] The status of the agricultural sector constantly threatens the whole economy with further deterioration. With the rapid growth of the rural population, the labor redundancy in the rural areas and in the cities, the limited capacity of industry to absorb labor, and the likelihood of even more labor displacement as developing industry pulls new labor from the ranks of the urban unemployed rather than from the agricultural sector, agricultural development offers the only alternative outlet for its own surplus labor. As Theisenhusen and Brown point out, the situation in Latin America is quite different from the structural

---

percent for the period in total agricultural production; and only Mexico, Nicaragua, and Venezuela had an annual average increase in total food production. Only Nicaragua showed a per capita increase of over 2.5 percent in both total agricultural and food output. Here again we see the difficulty of reconciling official figures. *A Review of Alliance for Progress Goals* (U.S. House, 1969, p. 29) lists 16 Latin American countries with a growth of 5 percent or more in total agricultural production, and seven countries with 5 percent or more per capita growth in agricultural production. On page 24 there is, however, a very useful comment on the limitations of using output per worker or yield per unit of land as indicators of agricultural progress in Latin America.

[14] See U.S. Senate (1967e, p. 175). U.S. Department of State (1967d, p. 10). UNECLA (1968b, p. 331) gives a figure of $1,200 million a year.

[15] See Inter-American Statistical Institute (1970).

[16] See Inter-American Development Bank (1969a, p. 5).

[17] UNECLA (1969b, p. 4). Cf. Griffin (1969, p. 60).

[18] See U.S. Department of Agriculture (1969, p. 20).

evolution in Russia, Japan, Western Europe, and the United States, where industrialization was well developed before absorbing labor on a large scale.[19]

Increased employment possibilities in agriculture, however, depend on the rate of increase of agricultural production and on the rate of increase of the product per worker. We identify later some of the major constraints to agricultural development in Latin America. At this point, it is simply necessary to recognize the inseparable relation between agricultural and over-all economic development. Increased incomes in agriculture could mean an increased capacity to capitalize the agricultural and the industrial sectors. Increased incomes could result in increased domestic demand for agricultural products and, following Engel's law, income redistribution in favor of the lower income rural strata could result in increased demand for more and better food. Increased agricultural production, other things being equal, could also tend to lower the cost of industrialization by supplying cheaper food to the urban areas and reducing inflationary pressures.

Prebisch calculates that if Latin America's agricultural production had grown at a faster rate than the actual average annual rate of 3.6 percent for the period 1950-65, with the rise of product per worker remaining at the rate of 2.2 percent, agriculture could have retained labor at an annual rate of more than 1.5 percent. The ability of agriculture to retain labor would also have been increased if the increase in the annual average per capita income of 2.5 percent a year (accompanied by an annual 1.1 percent increase in the demand for food) had been more equitably distributed in favor of the lower income group (1970a, pp. 36-37).

Despite the need, the boundary conditions in the agricultural sector are too severe for any dramatic and permanent improvements in the immediate future. Yet an increasing demand for more food and for better food is inevitable. The total number in the market sector for food may very well double in the period 1965-75. Kriesberg estimated, for instance, that in 1965 (assuming a population of 253 million) 90 million Latin Americans were in the market for all their food needs. But by 1975, assuming a 4 percent rate of over-all growth, the total number could possibly amount to 160 million. With a 6 percent rate of economic growth, the total number in the market for all their food needs could increase to some 183 million.[20] This prospect is serious enough, but the problem of calculation goes beyond this. As Table A.45 indicates, at least 147 million Latin Americans or 44 percent of the projected total population may still be largely outside the market economy in 1975.

Considered another way, UNECLA has calculated that if the over-all consumption of agricultural commodities had to increase by 4.6 percent a year and agricultural production by 4.2 percent a year (with a 3 percent annual increase in per capita income), production would have to expand between 1963-83 by some 130 percent, or 50 percent more than the previous 20-year-period.[21] Yudelman estimated in 1966, on the basis of the limited data available, that total agricultural output would have to increase by about 5 percent a year to meet the

[19] U.S. Senate (1967e, p. 179).
[20] See Kriesberg (1968, pp. 5-7).
[21] UN Economic and Social Council (1963, pp. 54-56).

TABLE 8.1

Average Annual Rates of Change of Agricultural and Food Production[a] (In Percent)

	Average annual rate (1955-56 to 1959-60)	*Average annual rate (1960-61 to 1964-65)*
FAO estimates		
Agricultural output		
Total	3.6	1.6
Per capita	1.2	0.8
Food output		
Total	2.8	2.4
Per capita	0.6	0.0
USDA Estimates		
Agricultural output		
Total		2.0
Per capita		0.2
Food output		
Total		3.8
Per capita		0.6

[a] 1952–53 to 1956–57 = 100.

Source: Inter-American Development Bank (1965a, pp. 84–85).

minimum growth targets set by the Alliance for Progress (1966, pp. 35-38).[22]

Past trends, as shown in Table 8.1, in agriculture, are so bad that a UNECLA study on the prospects for agriculture in Latin America noted:

if income and consumption were to continue to increase at the same rates as in the past fifteen or twenty years and the existing distribution patterns were to be maintained, it would take one hundred years for the low-income half of the population to attain the levels of food consumption of the higher income groups which are by no means very high.[23] Even if annual per capita income grew at 2.5 percent a year, it would still take an estimated 50 years—unless income was drastically redistributed in favor of the low-income groups. Given past trends, unsurprisingly, FAO anticipated that the gap between the Latin American demand for agricultural products and Latin America's supply would not be closed even by 1975. According to FAO calculations, assuming an average annual growth in gross domestic income of 3.9 percent a year in the period 1962-75, agriculture production would possibly increase at 2.8 percent a year, but demand is likely to grow at the rate of 3.1 percent a year. The gap is likely to be slightly larger with a higher annual growth in gross domestic income of 5.8 percent a year between 1962-75. With this rate, demand for all agricultural products would possibly increase at 3.8 percent a year but agricultural production

[22] Yudelman's 5 percent estimate is arrived at as follows: an increase of 2.8 percent to meet population growth; 1.2 percent to meet increased demand following increased incomes; and 1 percent to meet export requirements (to earn foreign exchange and maintain and increase the regional capacity to import for growth and debt-servicing needs).

[23] UNECLA (1968b, p. 357).

would increase at 3.4 percent a year. At even the lower rate of growth, in income of 3.9 percent a year, the gap between agricultural production and demand, estimated at $1.5 billion (U.S.) in 1962, could increase to a minimum of $2.9 billion (U.S.) or even $3.3 billion (U.S.) by 1975.[24]

Production and Productivity

It can be easily seen that the continuation of these unsatisfactory trends in agricultural production would mean the worsening of the poor conditions of life in the rural areas and the increasing of growth-inhibiting constraints to rapid over-all economic advance. A 1966 calculation of UNECLA suggests that with a 4.6 percent annual growth rate in internal demand for agricultural commodities, a 2.5 percent annual increase in exports to countries outside of Latin America, and a 3.3 percent annual decrease in imports, from outside of Latin America, agricultural production must expand by 4.3 percent a year between 1965-80 (see Table A.42).[25]

Although the figures must be treated cautiously, these projections give some useful approximation of the challenge to be met in agricultural production. Agricultural output must increase, but past sources of supply cannot meet the need. In the past, increased agricultural production came from extending the agricultural crop area. Between 1943-63, for instance, 60 percent of the increase in output of 24 staple agricultural commodities came from extending the cultivated area by 38 percent. Only 16 percent came from increased yield.[26] According to a 1966 UNECLA estimate, two-thirds of the increase in production of many crops came from extending the crop area and only about one-third from improved yields.[27]

Because of limitations to bringing more land under cultivation, future increases in agricultural output will depend largely on the rate at which productivity increases. In turn, increases in productivity will be determined by the effect of

---

[24] See Inter-American Development Bank (1967, pp. 28-29). Cf. also UNFAO (1967, p. 8). The UNFAO projections are as follows:

	Growth Rates 1958-63	PROJECTED INCOME GROWTH RATES 1962-75	
		Low (3.9 percent per annum)	High (5.8 percent per annum)
Production			
All agricultural products	2.3	2.8	3.4
Food	2.5	3.0	3.6
Demand			
All agricultural products		3.1	3.8
Food		3.2	3.5

Source: Data from UNFAO, *Agricultural Commodities: Projections for 1975 and 1985,* vol. 1 (Rome 1967), p. 48, as quoted in Inter-American Development Bank (1967, p. 28).

[25] UNECLA (1968b, p. 360).
[26] UN Economic and Social Council (1963, p. 56).
[27] UNECLA (1968b, p. 361).

changes in the input mix, by the effect of technological and organizational changes in agriculture, and by the type of policies adopted to promote improvements in productivity.[28]

It is important to our argument to note the limitations to increasing agricultural output through extending the cultivated area. We saw in the last chapter that there is a feeling that large areas of unused and cultivable land still exist in Latin America. Their extent and quality is being researched. Our argument is that these lands are not immediately available for extending cultivation. The UNECLA calculation in 1966 that there are 50 million hectares lying fallow, plus another 375 million hectares of natural pasture land lending itself to some cultivation, does not invalidate the argument that these lands are not immediately available for the enlargement of the cultivated area. Their suitability for agriculture has to be established. The maintenance of the fallow land might be essential for crop rotation, and the settlement of new and hardly accessible land is a costly business. UNECLA calculates that an investment of some $25,000 million may be necessary to bring 50 million hectares of new land under cultivation between 1965-80 (see Table A.42).

A recent official study claims that new and unsettled lands in Latin America can provide employment for many thousands of new farmers during the coming years.[29] Despite the possibilities, there are many deterrents to immediate utilization. These include (1) the need to discover new techniques; (2) the need for transportation facilities; (3) the high cost, heavy work, and the time entailed to clear the land; (4) the lack of knowledge about the soils or the productivity of the land; (5) the lack of capital and credit; and (6) the over-all evidence of the tremendous difficulties involved in settling and using new lands.[30] With new technology and determination, the apparently improbable could become possible, but it would be foolhardy to anticipate long-run technological achievements. To increase agricultural output through the extension of cultivation, however, in the short run is not a viable alternative to the improving the productivity output per worker or the yield per unit of land.

At this point, it is only possible to generalize about productivity possibilities in Latin America because of the characteristics of existing data and the deficiency of data on productivity trends. Yudelman calculated that productivity per agricultural worker probably rose by 1.75 percent a year in the period 1950-60. If this rate continues, accompanied by an annual increase of the labor force of 1.5 percent a year, output would rise 3.25 percent a year. But productivity would have to rise another 1.75 percent a year to obtain a growth rate of 5 percent a year in agriculture.[31] Similarly, on the assumption that half rather than two-thirds of the increased agricultural output between 1965-75

---

[28] The concept of productivity here follows Fabricant's (1969, pp. 3-4) definition: "When the same resources that were employed in the past now produce more than they did before, we agree that productivity has increased. Obviously, attempts to establish whether and how much productivity is changing take into account the relationship between what comes *out* of production and what goes *into* production, that is, the ratio between *output* and *input*."

[29] U.S. Department of Agriculture (1969, p. 54). A hectare is equal to 2.471 acres.

[30] U.S. Department of Agriculture (1969, pp. 56-60).

[31] Yudelman (1966, p. 41).

must come from enlarged acreage, yields must rise by 2.5 percent a year to meet production targets. This would be a 70 percent rise over the average yields in 1965.[32] UNECLA estimated in 1966 that the seeded area had to be extended by 1.5 percent a year, (25 million hectares) and this in turn meant raising unit yields by 50 percent by 1980, or about 2.8 percent a year, double the previous rate.[33]

We must allow, however, for a considerable degree of uncertainty in the whole picture, though this uncertainty is steadily being eroded as research proceeds and the results are published. Evidence seems to indicate that poor production methods, poor farm management, and low labor productivity and earnings generally go together.[34] To be more specific is difficult. A critical evaluation of the Alliance for Progress over the years 1966-67 concluded that agricultural productivity expressed in terms of output per agricultural worker or per man-year of agricultural labor was not, at that stage, a measurable concept for most of Latin America because of the lack of data on agricultural employment. Venezuela was an exception because figures were available for increases in yield per hectare and productivity per agricultural worker. The Venezuelan figures showed that productivity per hectare grew 2.2 percent a year between 1961-62 and 1965-66 and productivity per economically active person in agriculture grew 6.1 percent a year between 1961-67.[35] Although, however, the aggregate value of agricultural production per economically active person in agriculture increased from $574 in 1961 to $821 in 1967, comparison with the United States, for instance, shows a wide gap in productivity per worker in agriculture. In 1967, the per capita value of production of the agricultural work force in Venezuela was only 11.7 percent that of its counterpart in the United States.[36]

These reservations are equally applicable to the interpretation of rates of increase in agricultural yield per hectare. On the one hand, FAO found in its analysis of yields for five crops in each of 18 Latin American countries between 1962-66, that yields had increased in 60 cases out of the 90 crop-country combinations. On the other hand, yields varied a great deal from crop to crop, from year to year, from country to country, and conditions were so different that firm conclusions about trends is an elusive proposition. In Mexico, for instance, crop yields increased by 4.5 percent during the period 1962-65. Table 8.2 shows the relative change in yields for the six most important crops since 1955. The rise in wheat yields is clearly outstanding. The increase in yields for these crops is a result of a combination of factors which are relevant and significant in assessing yield prospects elsewhere in Latin America. These factors include the expansion of the irrigated area, significant increases in the rise of fertilizers, improved seeds, insecticides, research support, the Mexican government price support program, and vital contributory initiatives since 1943 from the Rockefeller Foundation.[37] In fact, by 1960-62, average wheat yields in Mexico surpassed those of the United States.[38]

[32] Ibid., p. 45.
[33] UNECLA (1968a, p. 361).
[34] See U.S. Department of Agriculture (1969, pp. 23-25).
[35] U.S. House (1969, pp. 23-25).
[36] See Inter-American Development Bank (1969a, p. 5).
[37] See U.S. House (1967, p. 158).
[38] Yudelman (1966, p. 45).

TABLE 8.2

Mexico: Relative Change in Crop Yields Since 1955 for the Six Most Important Crops

	Index Numbers (1955 = 100)	
	1961	*1965*
Corn	119	130
Cotton	118	145
Wheat	158	249
Sugar cane	101	110
Beans	119	114
Coffee	98	112

Source: U.S. House (1967), p. 158.

These persistently upward trends in yield do not typify all crops and all of Latin America. Between 1952-66, for instance, cereals, roots and tubers, pulses, oilseeds, cotton fiber, and tobacco increased by only 1.6 percent a year, while the cultivated area increased by 3.3 percent a year.[39] Latin American yields generally remained far below those of North America and Europe, and below world averages. Though Mexican wheat yields trebled and cotton yields doubled between 1948-52 and 1964-65, staple products like maize and rice yields improved only slightly.[40] Similarly, Mexican meat, milk, and wool yields are generally low, but poultry production and fishing have a good production record. Much research is still needed to allow clearer interpretation of trends. In fact, a review of the agricultural record during the period 1961-68 supported the conclusion that if Latin American countries are grouped according to rates of growth of production, per capita production, and productivity, the three always would have "little in common."[41]

CONCLUSIONS

As theory suggests, the development of the agricultural sector is critically important to the acceleration of economic development in Latin America. The development of agriculture, however, must take place simultaneously with development in the other sectors of the economy, particularly the industrial sector. Latin America is critically dependent on agricultural development for increased food supply, foreign earnings, an increased capacity to import, improvement in living conditions, increased job absorption and income levels, and for the creation of a mass market for agricultural commodities and domestic industrial goods. The data on agricultural production and productivity are still defective. But generally speaking, per capita output as well as output per worker and yield per acre continue to be low in comparison with world standards and in relation to needs. There are limitations to the immediate expansion of agricultural production through enlarging the cultivated area. The only viable alternative is to increase output per worker and yields per hectare. In turn, the improvement of productivity and agricultural advance in general

[39]UNECLA (1968a, p. 316).
[40]*Ibid.,* p. 317.
[41]U.S. House (1969, p. 26).

depends on a changed input-output relationship, major technological advances, and on an immediate transformation of the institutional setting of agriculture in Latin America. In the next chapter, we deal with the institutional setting and the problem of agrarian reform. We then review the major general conditions for agricultural progress in the region, in terms of assembled evidence.

CHAPTER 9

LAND TENURE, AGRARIAN REFORM,
AND AGRICULTURAL PRODUCTIVITY

AGRARIAN REFORM AND ECONOMIC EFFICIENCY

Because of the concentration of landownership in Latin America, agrarian reform is widely regarded as an essential precondition for the transformation of the agricultural sector. No question perhaps in Latin America evokes more political passion than the question of land tenure and agrarian reform. A group of U.N. experts noted long ago in a famous basic document that, given extreme landownership concentration and the disincentive-effects of a weak bargaining position on the tenant farmer or farm market, land reform was an urgent prerequisite to agricultural progress.[1] The key importance of the issue is reflected in the declaration of the Alliance for Progress that it was the purpose of the Alliance:

to encourage, in accordance with the characteristics of each country, programs of comprehensive agrarian reform leading to the effective transformation, where required, of unjust structures and systems of land tenure and use, with a view to replacing latifundia *and dwarf holdings by an equitable system of land tenure so that, with the help of timely and adequate credit, technical assistance and facilities for the marketing and distribution of products, the land will become for the man who works it the basis of his economic stability, the foundation of his increasing welfare, and the guarantee of his freedom and dignity.*[2]

In 1967, the American chiefs of state meeting once again at Punta del Este called upon CIAP to give "due attention to agrarian reform programs in those countries which considered these programs an important basis for their agricultural progress and economic and social development."[3]

The relation between agrarian reform and increased agricultural productivity is, however, neither simple nor direct. On the one hand, the principle of equity is invoked to support the demand that the large estates, the *latifundias*, be broken up to allow the widest possible diffusion of landownership. The moral basis of this claim receives support from the clear record of low productivity, inefficient utilization of the factors of production, and monopolistic power which traditionally distinguishes the latifundist system. On the other hand, redistribution of the land does not necessarily guarantee a solution, much less an immediate one, to the problem of economic backwardness in agriculture.

---

[1] See U.N. Department of Economic Affairs (1951, p. 21). See also Millikan and Hapgood (1967, pp. 91–107).
[2] U.S. House (1966, pp. 102–102).
[3] Pan American Union (1967g, p. 16).

171

This is not arguing against the moral justification for land reform. It is simply taking note of the fact that agricultural inefficiency distinguishes not only the *latifundia* but every other form of land holding in Latin America except for the foreign commercial plantation. The matter goes further. Redistribution of land-ownership, with every man getting an equal share of the land, assuming that sufficient land is available for all, could cut across basic requirements for better economic performance. Certain agricultural exercises, for instance, can only be profitably pursued under large-scale economic operation. In this case, equity would immediately conflict with the requirements for efficiency. Of course, in other cases, operating on a large scale may not be necessary for profit maximization, depending on the requirements for the particular activity. But the production of sugar cane, cereal, and cattle, for instance, normally requires large areas of land if the operation is to be efficient.[4] Simple blanket reform, that is, a sudden breaking up of the large estates, has to take into account a large number of considerations in the interests of maintaining and improving economic performance in agriculture. In some cases, variations in the character of the land are such that it does not lend itself to fragmentation into holdings of 10 to 20 hectares. In these cases, protection of the land from overcropping is the big requirement and simply breaking up the large land holdings could have results which run counter to sound economic land use and conservation practices.[5] Again, in some cases, large areas of land have to be kept idle, maintained as pasture or forest because the land is too sandy, too rough, or too poor for crops. In this case the land is being put to its best use.[6] Land reform can also have an ironic result if the large estates are broken up into innumerable small holdings only to increase the productive limitations characterizing small holdings in much of Latin America.[7]

In fact, the problem may get worse before it gets better. For while equity may require that landownership be redistributed, increasing unit yields in agriculture may require the expansion of mechanization. This, in turn, introduces the dilemma in that yields may go up but labor redundancy may increase because there are no alternative sources of employment. UNECLA may suggest that preference be given to those methods of introducing modern techniques which raise productivity by increasing land yields "rather than by making investments designed to economize on manpower."[8] The difficulties here involve not only coming up with technological research data on which to base these techniques but of also accepting the sacrifice of growth now to save the alternative cost of increased labor redundancy, despite the urgent need for increased agricultural production.

These considerations accentuate the economic aspects to be taken into account in implementing any policy of general redistribution of landownership, if productivity is to be accelerated. For although there are a few cases (outside of the commercial plantation) of efficient agricultural operation under large-scale landownership, the traditional feudal attitudes of the landed oligarchy and the

---

[4] See U.S. Department of Agriculture (1969, p. 69).

[5] *Ibid.*, p. 68.

[6] *Ibid.*, p. 69.

[7] *Ibid.*, p. 70.

[8] UN Economic and Social Council (1963, p. 58). See also Prebisch (1970i, pp. 85–88). Cf. U.S. Senate (1967e, p. 186): "The emphasis should be on increasing production at low cost through yield-increasing technology along with maximum employment and unemployment security. It is not yet clear that this combination can be achieved on any one type of farm."

demonstrable waste and inefficiency in agriculture make general agrarian reform an unavoidable precondition to the modernizing of agriculture. The large traditional landowner acquires his wealth not because he is entrepreneurial, but because in most cases his monopoly of land, his political and social power, and his monoponistic position vis-à-vis the excess supply of labor allow him, even as an absentee landowner, to arrogate to himself the greatest possible share of the agricultural output. Imposing a tax on the land, for instance, would not guarantee desirable change because the political power of the traditional landowner prevents any such tax imposition and makes it possible for him to avoid any such tax payment.

As we have said, agricultural inefficiency characterizes not only the large landowner but every form of landholding in Latin America except the foreign commercial plantation. Even the foreign plantation introduces inhibitions to agricultural development. Castro's ideological alternative, as we argue later, supplies no evidence that a solution has been found to the problem of land tenure. Agrarian reform must, therefore, in the light of the social situation and economic requirements in Latin America, be broadened to embrace a search for a form of land tenure which is consistent with equity and at the same time with economic efficiency.[9] In this sense, two acres and a cow, or individually owned family units of 10 hectares of irrigated land (which Chile aimed to provide under the Agrarian Reform Law of July 16, 1967) may satisfy the principle of equity but not necessarily the criterion of efficiency, taking into consideration different crops, soil conditions, factor availabilities, and production scale requirements.[10] Again, if agrarian reform aims at producing agricultural commodities for the ex-market, competitive international standards of efficiency must be taken into account if foreign earning levels are to be maintained and increased. The need to adjust to international standards of competitive efficiency may cut across the passionate desire for the equity of each man or family owning the same size piece of land.

We now review briefly the forms of landholding in Latin America before turning to case studies of organization, management, and economic performance under each type, and considering some general conditions for improved economic performance in Latin American agriculture.

FARMHOLDING: THE INSTITUTIONAL PICTURE

Farms in Latin America can be conventionally classified as (1) the large multifamily farm, (2) the medium-size family farm, (3) the family farm, and (4) the *minifundia*, which cannot support a family. The large multifamily farm (the *latifundia* or hacienda) employs more than a dozen people and sometimes well over 100. Medium-size multifamily farms employ from four to a dozen people, while the family farm employs two to four people, usually members of the family. The *minifundia* employs less than two people.

[9]We are thinking here simply of least-cost combinations of inputs to produce given outputs. We have already argued that for some kinds of production, least-cost production is impossible except under large-scale operation.

[10]See Pan American Union (1967a, pp. 120–138). See also Baerwald (1969, pp. 95–96). Cf. U.S. Senate (1967e, p. 186): "It would probably be a mistake . . . for any country to adopt a uniform ceiling on landownership applicable to all farms."

The *microfinca* is an even smaller holding, a miniscule plot of land such as those under cultivation in Guatemala. Here, according to the 1950 agricultural census, 308,073 small farms equivalent to 88 percent of the total number of farms accounted for only 14 percent of the cultivated land area. In the Guatemalan highlands, 75,000 three-quarter-acre farm holdings supported some 300,000 people.[11]

The classification used by Thiesenhusen and Brown immediately casts light on the qualitative differences between the various types of farm holdings. They group Latin American farm holdings into progressively managed large farms and plantations; traditionally managed large farms; existing small farms; and new peasant farms created by land reform.[12] The progressively managed large farms concentrate on feeding the cities and on providing export earnings. The traditionally managed large farms are, of course, the *latifundias* or the haciendas. The existing small farms are run by self-employed farmers. The new peasant farms, created out of the *latifundia*, are larger than the *minifundia* but in many respects similar.

While the classifications above are extremely useful, for our considerations we divide landownership in Latin America into six principal types: the hacienda, the *minifundia*, the *ayllu* and *communidad* systems, the *ejido*, and the commercial plantation system. The picture is not complete, however, unless we take into account the landless who, together with the farm holders, complete for the rural areas what Barraclough calls "the interest groups" in agricultural policy and land reform.[13] A recent study has broken the landless into five groups.[14] First, there are the crop-share tenants who use their own equipment but pay the landowner for the use of the land with an agreed share of the crops. Second, there are the cash renters who pay the landowner in cash for the use of the land. Third, there are the permanently or semipermanently attached labor force on the *latifundia* who, in return for low wages, a small share of the crops, and residential rights, traditionally carry out farming activities under the detailed supervision of the landowner or his representative. This group is called a variety of names in different areas of Latin America, such as *yanacones, huasapungueros, colonos*, or *inquilinos*. Fourth, lower down the scale of security, are the regular or permanent farm laborers ranging from the skilled, like tractor operators, who get better wages, to the unskilled. This group is employed for a larger number of days, though at the same low wage levels as the fifth group of landless, namely the

[11] See Inter-American Development Bank (1965a, p. 362). Approximately 74,000 farms (21.3 percent of the total number of farms and 0.8 percent of the total farm land) had a total area in 1950 of 70,424 acres. See Lockley (1963–1964, p. 50).

[12] See U.S. Senate (1967e, pp. 184–187). See also U.S. Department of Agriculture (1969, pp. 22–23).

[13] Barraclough (1970, pp. 906–907). Barraclough's interest groups covered (1) large landowners plus commercial, banking, and bureaucratic groups, (2) low-income small producers and the landless, and (3) urban consumers, manufacturers, and employers of rural migrants.

[14] U.S. Department of Agriculture (1969, pp. 16–17). See also Griffin (1969, pp. 50, 81–85). The variety of names describing the landless laborers who work under various types of conditions and obligations differ from country to country and can be multiplied according to the nature of their rights and obligations. For instance, *huesipungero, arrimado*, and *yanapero* apply to Ecuador; *bracero* to Peru; *inquilino, afuerino*, and *mediero* to Chile, and so on. *Peones* and *campesinos* are alternative all-inclusive terms.

itinerant farm laborers, a group with no legal protection who work under the most ad hoc and insecure agreements with the landowner or his representative. In 1967, 60 percent of all farm laborers were landless in Brazil, 48 percent in Chile, 35 percent in Ecuador, and 25 percent in Guatemala.[15]

Agricultural Development Objectives Restated

The Alliance for Progress, as we have seen, set out to establish "an equitable system of land tenure." We have noted, however, that equity is not necessarily consistent with the goal of improving the efficiency of agriculture. Efficiency in Latin America requires that output be maximized; that the costs of production be competitively reduced; and that welfare be improved through fair distribution of the returns, through increasing possibilities for the employment of large numbers of the population in agriculture, and through widening the participation of all those involved in agricultural production. These objectives are not all reconcilable.

It is important to understand the emotional background. The traditional political, social, and economic role of the large landowner has been such that there can be no stemming the demand for expropriation and break-up of the large estates. There is little evidence that the *hacendado* can change. Tannenbaum, for instance, is firm in his judgment that the hacienda cannot escape or meet the challenge of economic, political, and social change and that the hacienda lacks any built-in device which would allow a reform of the system and at the same time enable the hacienda "to transform itself" and "survive and adjust to the present" (1966, p. 91).

The problem of agricultural development, however, would not be solved with the disappearance of the hacienda. As UNECLA recognized bluntly, land distribution is "far from being enough."[16] Though the hacienda can meet neither the demand for equity nor the demand for efficiency, the alternative forms of landholding also do not meet these criteria. It is important to recognize that all forms of landownership in Latin America have imposed limitations on agricultural development and that if the *hacendado* and his traditional attitudes disappear, economic experience of the effect of land distribution may very well bring about, as in Mexico, changes in policies toward the larger estate which are consistent with economic requirements for increased productivity.[17] The hostility toward the *hacendado* is so great and the range of circumstances is so complex from country to country that predicting any particular form of tenure or any kind of institutional mix is tantamount to underestimating the complexity involved.[18]

---

[15] U.S. House (1969, p. 30).
[16] UN Economic and Social Council (1963, p. 60).
[17] Cf. Lewis (1969, pp. 123–124).
[18] Cf., for instance, Griffin (1969, p. 82):

> The essential ingredient in any program of development and social transformation is a fundamental change in agrarian institutions. The expropriation and redistribution of land and the organization of a mixed system of producer cooperatives, family holdings and state farms should be the basis for all subsequent action in this field.

The Hacienda

The hacienda carries various names in Latin America—*estancia* (Argentina, Uruguay, southern Brazil), *fundo* (Chile), *fazenda* (most of Brazil), *latifundia*, and so on. Whatever the name, the hacienda provides the nominal umbrella for the same unique cultural phenomenon. It dominates the landholding patterns of Latin America. The hacienda system mirrors the unchanging Latin America resistance to the evolutionary and revolutionary demands for political, social, and economic modernization. The hacienda is, in dynamic terms, well-nigh stationary in Latin America, the backward world of the Americas. In the hacienda system reside inflexible hierarchical arrangements; traditional patron–peon relationships; and the caste system and social rigidity. But contemporary Latin America demands an open society through which its entrepreneurial genius, whatever the social origin, may rise. The hacienda system supports the dead aspects of regionalism and the negative virtues of isolation, *caudillismo* and *caciquismo*. The world of the hacienda is practically a dead world, extending its depressing influence to the world around it. The hacienda could almost be forgotten were it not for the fact that it constitutes a barrier to be overcome if rising expectations are to be satisfied and the stagnation of the Latin American countryside ended without unhelpful violence. Practically the only movement on the hacienda beyond the historically embedded routines is movement out. The hacienda exports its cultural backwardness to the cities, for the landless peon leaves it for the town when and if he can. The values around which this cultural phenomenon coheres interfere even with the emergence of values essential to manufacturing management. Agrarian-based *personalismo*, *dignidad*, and *individualismo*, secure and continuously recognized and fostered within the rigidly static world of the hacienda, yield with difficulty to the impersonal, driving, delegating values which must typify the modern manufacturing manager.

The approximate statistical dimensions of the hacienda are easily set out. In 1950, about 1.5 percent of the individual farm holdings of Latin America exceeded 15,000 hectares. In turn, these holdings accounted for approximately 50 percent of all agricultural land in Latin America.[19] In Uruguay in 1966 there were 3860 farm units over 1000 hectares, accounting for less than 5 percent of the total number of farm units in the country, but for over 58 percent of the total farm area (see Table 9.1). On the other hand, 23,453 farm holdings, ranging from 1 to 9 hectares, accounted for around 30 percent of the total farm units, but for less than 1 percent of the total farm area, and were considered too small for economic exploitation. In Argentina, the discrepancy is even more graphic. In 1960, out of a total of 457,173 farms, 11,459 farms or 2.6 percent of the total number of farm units between 2500 and 10,000 hectares and over accounted for 59.8 percent of the total farm area. If farm units between 1000 and 2500 hectares are included, 5.9 percent of the number of farm units accounted for 74.5 percent of the total area utilized. On the other hand, the farm units of 5 hectares or less, totaling 15.7 percent of the total number of farm units, accounted for 0.1 percent of the total farm area.[20]

Brazilian land distribution patterns are no different. In 1960 farm units of

[19] UN (1951, pp. 10–11).

[20] See Pan American Union (1968b, p. 16). Other figures on land distribution in this chapter are also from this source, unless otherwise noted.

TABLE 9.1

Uruguay: Land Distribution, 1966

Size of holdings in hectares	Number of holdings		Area in hectares	
1–4	11,035	13.9%	30,000	0.2%
5–9	12,418	15.7	84,000	0.5
10–19	12,563	15.9	174,000	1.1
20–49	13,848	17.5	433,000	2.6
50–99	8,299	10.5	585,000	3.5
100–199	6,880	8.7	969,000	5.9
200–499	6,808	8.6	2,148,000	13.0
500–999	3,476	4.4	2,458,000	14.9
1,000–2,499	2,654	3.4	4,124,000	24.9
2,500–4,999	898	1.1	3,049,000	18.4
5,000–9,999	260	0.3	1,717,000	10.4
10,000 and over	54	0.1	763,000	4.6
Total	79,193	100.0%	16,534,000	100.0%

Source: Pan American Union (1968b, p. 23).

over 10,000 hectares amounted to less than 0.1 percent of the total number of farm units and accounted for 15.6 percent of the farm land. Farms above 1000 hectares accounted for less than 1 percent of the total number of farms, but made up 44.2 percent of the total farm area in Brazil. At the other end of the scale, farms under 10 hectares amounted in 1960 to 44.8 percent of the number of farm units, but accounted for only 2.4 percent of the total area of farm land. In Chile, the holdings of 1000 hectares or more accounted for 1.3 percent of the farm units in 1965, but represented 72.7 percent of the total area of farm land. Farm units between one and 4.9 hectares accounted for 48.8 percent of the holdings but for less than 1 percent of the total area of farm land.

In Bolivia, the agrarian structure sparked the revolution in 1952. Its agrarian structure makes Bolivia a publicly proclaimed target for Castroite designs. In 1950, official figures indicated that farms of under 5 hectares amounted to 59.3 percent of the farm holdings and accounted for less than 0.2 percent of the total arable land. Farm units, however, of 1000 hectares or more, amounting to 6.3 percent of all holdings, accounted for 91.9 percent of all arable land.

The anachronistic pattern repeats itself in Colombia, in Peru, in Ecuador, in Paraguay, and in Central America. The 1960 agricultural and livestock census showed that 0.7 percent of the holdings of Colombia were 500 hectares or more, and accounted for 40.5 percent of the total cultivated area, while 62.5 percent of the holdings were less than 5 hectares and amounted to only 4.5 percent of the total cultivated area. In Peru, the holdings under one hectare, according to the 1961 census, amounted to 36.8 percent of all holdings but only to 0.7 percent of the total farm area; holdings of over 2500 acres amounted to 0.1 percent of the total farm area. In fact, in Peru in 1961 the holdings over 1000 hectares amounted to only 0.2 percent of all farm holdings but accounted for 69.2 percent of the total farm area. Table A.46 gives an indication of land distribution in Central America. The statistics, on the whole, actually underestimate the degree of concentration of landownership in Latin America since one property owner may own several large properties, and be counted as an owner in each case.[21]

Though the hacienda system is rooted in history and has been hallowed by over 400 years of tradition, it has never been without examples of virulent protest.[22] The *hacendado* traditionally enjoys innumerable advantages which would constitute an effective incentive to any rational agricultural producer. Taxes on real estate, for instance, are low or nonexistent or easily evaded, thanks to the political power of the *hacendado*.[23] The *hacendado* enjoys easier access to and preferential terms for public and commercial credit in comparison with the small and medium-size landowner.[24] The hacienda traditionally occupies the best situated and most fertile acreage and continues to arrogate these pieces whenever new land is opened up.[25] The hacienda is normally given privilege within the domestic market either through tariffs, quotas on imported products, special tax rebates, export subsidies of one kind or another, or privileges in regard to import duties. Wealth accrues to the *hacendado* anyway since, in most cases, the value of land steadily goes up while property taxes stay down. The extent of his landed property and the fertility of the soil, as well as his immediate command of imports, give him the scope to experiment with new farming techniques and to introduce a variety of innovations which could maximize output, reduce costs competitively, and improve the welfare of his employees. Nothing of the kind usually happens. The *hacendado* does not pursue economically efficient methods of production for the market in order to increase profits. The hacienda system is, not, by and large, distinguished by first-rate management, commercial drive, research, or the pursuit of cost-reducing innovations. The *hacendado* is a captain of power in a society kept static under his influence or with his support. We do not say that the *hacendado* is completely to blame for the stultifying traditional position of Latin American agriculture; we will see later that there are additional reasons for the critical situation in agriculture. But the *hacendado* is a key contributor and his position and power are powerful deterrents to the essential and rapid structural change needed for improving productivity in the sector.

The large estate practically runs itself. It is handed down from father to son and the *hacendado* is generally an absentee.[26] In 1959, most of the large landowners in Chile with farms of 200 hectares and over were absentees.[27] A 1966

---

[21] See Smith (1969, p. 259).

[22] For a detailed historical background, see any good general text book on Latin American history or politics, such as Bailey and Nasatir (1960), Fagg (1963), Burnett and Johnson (1968), or Smith (1965).

[23] See UNECLA (1968b, p. 338); U.S. Senate (1967e, p. 283).

[24] See U.S. House (1967, p. 64).

[25] See U.S. Senate (1967e, pp. 252–253).

[26] See the evidence of Professor Marvin R. Brown in U.S. Senate (1967e, p. 275). Gruning (1969, pp. 21–46) reports that Colombian latifundists who bought or rented land after 1964 regard land as a productive resource and tend to be entrepreneurial. The majority of the Colombian latifundists, from Grunig's evidence, espouse traditional values, regard land as an inheritance, do not weigh costs and returns, and are not profit-maximizers. Although they could double or triple their returns by changing from livestock to crops, they remain content with a sufficient income for conspicuous consumption (housing, exclusive clubs, schools for their children, leisure, real estate, and so forth).

[27] See Inter-American Development Bank (1965a, p. 127).

official report on agricultural development in Latin America describes the owner of large landholdings in Chile generally as "an urban dweller engaged in financial, industrial, or commercial activities."[28] He is interested in the land because it is a source of prestige, power, and position in the upper class, and a hedge against inflation. He wants a limited and protected market, but he has no particular interest in improving agricultural productivity. Generally the *hacendado* is untrained in farm management. His hired farm manager and the rest of his employees are equally untrained and they do not have any authority to make even the slightest change in traditional routines.

The land remains innocent of scientific farming and land is wasted. Large areas are underutilized land and use patterns remain unchanged from decade to decade. The 1954 agricultural census of Ecuador showed that while 85.2 percent of the total area of farm holdings under 5 hectares were cultivated or in pasture, the corresponding figure for farm holdings of 500 hectares and over (accounting for 45.1 percent of the total farm area) was only 16.1 percent.[29] The larger the land holding, the more extensive the method of cultivation and the more wasteful the use of the land devoted year after year mainly to export crops. Rotation of hectares would be an unusual feature. Large areas remain fallow on the large estate, not because of scientific routines but simply because the land is left idle. Despite his monopolistic share of the agricultural product, the large landowner does not generally reinvest his share of the agricultural income in methods of improved production and productivity. He prefers to invest in industry or use his income in conspicuous consumption.[30] Government price controls, as in the case of Chile on meat and milk products, vegetables, and other basically necessary foodstuffs, have admittedly been no incentive to agricultural production, but they could also have been a stimulus to the agricultural producer to cut costs. Since inertia has characterized the economic behavior of the *hacendado* for centuries, there is little reason to believe that a reversal of the terms of trade in favor of the existing group of *hacendados* would have caused any significant reversal of the flow of investment from industry and conspicuous consumption to agriculture.[31]

The majority of the *hacendados* are tradition-minded people who have failed to pioneer. They have not been entrepreneurial risk-takers. Despite their control over a labor surplus, they have failed to use it to advantage. Wages remain low; the labor force is factored out of economic decision-making and has no bargaining power for an improved share of the agricultural income; and agricultural productivity does not improve.

Poverty and insecurity characterize the labor force and therefore constitute an obvious deterrent to worker productivity. In Chile, the *inquilino* works throughout the year for a small wage in cash and in kind, in return for the right to pasture animals and grow food for the family on a small plot of land. He often ends up wageless because of indebtedness to the landlord.[32] In addition, the

---

[28] U.S. House (1967, p. 58). See also U.S. Department of Agriculture (1969, p. 17).

[29] See Inter-American Development Bank (1965a, p. 315).

[30] See UNECLA (1968b, p. 339). See also Grunig (1969, pp. 45–46).

[31] Cf. the argument by Professor Marvin R. Brown in U.S. Senate (1967e, p. 279). See also U.S. House (1967, pp. 61–62) and U.S. Department of Agriculture (1969, p. 93).

[32] See Inter-American Development Bank (1962a, p. 209; 1965, p. 221).

inquilino at peak seasons may be required to recruit *afuerinos*, agricultural employees who are really migratory workers without a fixed occupation, home base, or contract securities. One quarter of the labor force in agriculture may be made up of *afuerinos*, who have no land rights and are only part-timers, coming in at planting and harvest time. There are also the *medieros* or sharecroppers, who normally under verbal contracts are given the right to use a piece of land in return for working for the landlord and turning over a share of the produce to the landlord. Under the *mederia* system, the sharecropper may also be required to provide part of the capital for working the land. Some 20 to 35 percent of the cultivated area in the central zone of Chile falls under this system. Lastly, there are laborers who work under verbal contracts in return for certain privileges (*regalias*) and volunteers recruited by the *inquilinos*. It is clear that under these conditions, the low level of productivity can only be changed by changes in leadership and in basic conditions for the labor force.[33]

The evidence does not support any optimistic view that the hacienda system can reform itself, but the problem of meeting the goals of equity and efficiency do not end with modification of the institutional hegemony of the hacienda. An examination of the other forms of land tenure in Latin America reveals the immense range of additional difficulties confronting goals for agricultural development.

The Minifundia *and the* Ayllu *System*

Minifundism coexists with latifundism almost everywhere in Latin America. Indeed, the aggressive expansion of the latifundist domain combines with the rapid expansion of the population to generate an even more rapid multiplication of minifundist holdings. In Brazil, for instance, farm units of less than 10 hectares increased between 1950-60 from 34.5 percent of the total number of farm units to 44.8 percent. But as a percentage of the total area of farm land, farm units under 10 hectares increased from 1.3 percent in 1950 only to 2.2 percent in 1960.[34] In fact, the average size of the small farms dropped from 4.3 hectares in 1950 to 3.9 hectares in 1960.[35] The *minifundia* spread to the new lands which were opened up because most of the new land was also taken over by the hacienda. Because the hacienda also spread out to the new lands, very limited areas were left for new people, and the rest of the land had to be subdivided—hence *minifundia*. With no hacienda in new lands, probably there would have been no *minifundia* development. In Guatemala, the increase in small holdings between 1950 and 1960 could not absorb the increased families.[36] Table 9.2 shows the similar dominance of the *minifundia* in the Dominican Republic. Over 88 percent of the farms are under 7 hectares and amount to less than 24 percent of the total farm area.

The *minifundia* are intensively cultivated, but the minifundist alternative cannot solve the problem of increasing productivity or improving the

---

[33]Schmid (1968, pp. 33–34), suggests that, with higher wages and better living conditions, the Guatemalan farm worker should be capable of higher labor productivity. He found the actual earnings per family in migratory agricultural work, however, averaged $0.75 per day on coffee farms, $0.86 on sugar cane farms, and $1.18 per day on cotton farms.

[34]Inter-American Development Bank (1965a, p. 183).

[35]See Smith (1969, p. 50).

[36]*Ibid.*

TABLE 9.2

Dominican Republic: Land Distribution, 1960

Size of holdings in hectares	Number of holdings		Area in hectares	
Less than 0.3	65,600	14.7%	10,000	0.4%
0.3–0.6	60,501	13.5	26,000	1.1
0.6–0.9	72,100	16.1	49,000	2.2
0.9–1.3	34,400	7.7	34,000	1.5
1.3–1.9	57,700	12.9	81,000	3.6
1.9–2.5	32,480	7.3	65,000	2.9
2.5–3.1	22,070	4.9	58,000	2.6
3.1–4.7	37,570	8.4	135,000	6.0
4.7–6.3	13,351	3.0	70,000	3.1
6.3–18.9	35,634	7.9	338,000	15.0
18.9–31.4	7,624	1.7	171,000	7.6
31.4–62.9	4,735	1.1	195,000	8.6
62.9–188.7	2,450	0.6	240,000	10.6
188.7–314.5	418	0.1	103,000	4.6
314.5–628.9	258	0.1	121,000	5.4
628.9–1,572.3	136	0.0	190,000	8.4
1,572.3 and over	71	0.0	371,000	16.4
Total	447,098	100.0%	2,258,000	100.0%

Source: Pan American Union (1968b, p. 22).

opportunities for employment. Breaking up the large estates into miniscule operations may meet the problem of equity but not satisfy the need for efficiency. There are entrepreneurial elements among the *minifundia*, but this is more the exception than the rule.[37] We can go around in circles and say that with help matters will improve. Certainly, supporting the small farmer is vital. Although the land is used intensively in contrast to the wastage of land on the hacienda, yields are low. The minifundist needs credit and technological help of one kind and another. He needs more bargaining power against the *hacendado*, and in some places unions and cooperative action are being fostered. But essentially the volume of production and the capacity to absorb more labor are limited by the scale of the minifundist operation. The minifundist can cultivate labor intensive crops like potatoes, vegetables, fruits. He has little land left for pasture or forage crops. The scale of operation is too small for beef cattle or sheep, or for maize, wheat, cotton or cereal, which need large-scale production along with machinery.

In Colombia, for instance, 75 percent of the 1.3 million farms in 1966 were less than 10 hectares and the average size of the farms under 10 hectares (25 acres) was only 0.5 acre. These farms produced most of Colombia's coffee, the chief source for the country's foreign exchange, in addition to a significant output of potatoes, small grains, corn, yuca, *platano*, vegetables, and fruits. Yields are, however, low, and in most cases the small farm is hardly able to produce a surplus above the subsistence needs of the family. To maintain themselves, the families have to sell a considerable amount of the output they really need to maintain a minimum level of nutrition. They cannot buy fertilizers or other

[37] See, for instance, Grunig (1969, pp. 3–24).

production inputs. They cannot absorb more labor and they cannot contribute very much more to the national output. Size is a boundary condition to any significant contribution to total output; size is a boundary condition to labor absorption. Size is also a boundary condition to mechanization. It is calculated that in Colombia commercial farms practicing mechanized agriculture require a minimum of 75 to 100 acres of planted cropland.[38] The minifundist is only able to live at near-starvation levels if he devotes his full time to his plot of land; alternatively he has to supplement his income by working for the *hacendado* or in the near-by towns. Universal minifundism would therefore put severe limits on productivity possibilities.

The same limitations are true of the *ayllu* system, institutionalized from pre-Incan times and still existing among Peruvian Indians. Under this system, long before the political organization of the Incas, the inhabitants of the Peruvian Andes lived in groups called *ayllus*. Under the *ayllu* system, land and work were divided proportionately under a regime of communal use and distribution of wealth.[39] The *ayllu* tradition persists, historically significant but economically inefficient.

INDEPENDENT PEASANT PROPRIETORSHIP: HAITI

Land ownership in Haiti contrasts with the disposition of land under the latifundist system: the percentage share of farm holdings and total farm area is in favor of the small man (see Table 9.3). According to the 1950 census, holdings under 6 hectares account for 93 percent of the total number of farm holdings and 73 percent of the total cultivated land area of this republic.

But peasant proprietorship as an alternative form of land tenure to the hacienda does not guarantee the improved productivity required for Latin American agriculture, though it may provide equity. Despite the dominance of the peasant landholder, agricultural productivity in Haiti is perhaps lower than anywhere

TABLE 9.3

Haiti: Land Distribution, 1950 (In Percentages)

Department	Less than 0.55 hectares	0.65 to 1.3 hectares	1.3 to 2.6 hectares	2.6 to 3.9 hectares	3.9 to 6.5 hectares	More than 6.5 hectares
North	11.0	24.9	33.7	14.9	9.5	4.9
Northwest	14.8	26.5	28.9	13.5	9.9	6.4
Artiobonite	12.2	22.1	31.5	16.2	11.5	6.5
West	18.7	23.8	28.5	13.5	9.7	5.3
Average of four departments	12.3	23.8	32.1	15.3	10.5	6.0

Source: Censo General 1950, Institut Haitien de Statistique, quoted in Pan American Union (1967f, p. 93).

[38] See U.S. House (1967, p. 81). Cf. U.S. Department of Agriculture (1969, p. 70):

Land distribution is conceived of as a means of benefitting the minifundista. However, the redistribution would be of little benefit to him and none to the community if the reform did not actually increase his land but merely increased the number of minifundistas.

[39] See Llosa (1960).

else in Latin America. Agriculture is extremely important in Haiti. It employs some 80 percent of the country's active population (see Table A.43) and contributes 45 percent of the gross national product, 95 percent of the foreign exchange earnings, and most of the revenues of government through taxation of agricultural exports. Despite the wide spread of landownership, agriculture is deteriorating (see Table A.44) and the state of the island falls more and more into disrepair.

It is obvious the government should adopt policies to counteract soil erosion, establish marketing facilities, build up infrastructure, and devote much more than 9 percent of the public budget to agriculture (as against 43 percent for military expenditures). Marketing suffers greatly from lack of transportation; the condition of the roads allows only two major forms of transportation, mules or the human back. The government could assist in breaking the stranglehold of speculators on the internal market and on export commodities. Four firms control 75 percent of the coffee exports and of the internal market in textiles and edible oils. One firm controls the export of meat and another 75 percent of the operations involved in the export of sugar. The state monopolizes the distribution of various necessities, loading them with taxes which are passed on to the consumer in inflated prices. Agriculture in Haiti needs extension officers and trained administrative personnel. This checklist of possible areas of government support can be justified by the fact that 90 percent of Haiti's coffee production comes from 140,000 farms of less than 2.5 hectares each. And the list could be extended.[40]

Increasing output and productivity per acre or per agricultural worker in Haiti is subject to constraints from many directions—soil erosion, the high degree of illiteracy, the incapacity of the farmer to use any but primitive techniques, the negative effects of the marketing system on incentive, and the constraints imposed by the small size of the plots. Land per capita in Haiti is more limited than anywhere else in Latin America except Trinidad and Tobago (see Table A.8) and is likely to get worse, given the growth of the rural population in Haiti (Table A.5). The rural population of 3.7 million occupies an area of 1.5 million hectares of farm land, only 370,000 of which are arable. The rest is rugged territory subject to soil erosion. The plots are too small for economic farming and continuous fragmentation is characteristic because of the overcrowding of the plots by too many people increasing too rapidly over too small an area. Rural incomes are low—less than 70 cents a day for millions. The capacity of the land holdings to absorb labor is obviously very low, also. Disguised unemployment is estimated at well over 50 percent of the rural labor force.[41] From the evidence of Haiti it could be said that independent peasant proprietorship of land does not satisfy the requirements for increased agricultural productivity in Latin America.

In terms of our criteria, let us now evaluate the *ejido* as an alternative to the hacienda.

[40] See Pan American Union (CIAP) (1967f, p. 93). See also Mintz (1962, pp. 786–799).
[41] Cf. U.S. Department of Agriculture (1969, p. 70):

> Farms too small for adequate return are the evil that the reform would set out to cure. However, political directors of a reform are under very strong pressure to benefit as many persons as possible and this policy would result in many small farms rather than a smaller number of medium-sized ones.

THE MEXICAN ALTERNATIVE: THE EJIDO

The Mexican Revolution of 1910, intellectually, if somewhat unwittingly, sparked by the Mexican aristocrat and intellectual Francisco Madero ended the presidency of Porfirio Díaz (1876-1910), broke up the power of the hacienda (though not without further struggle), and made possible the institution of the *ejido* as the peculiar Mexican innovation in land tenure.[42] At the time of the revolution, the degree of land concentration in Mexico was perhaps higher than anywhere else in Latin America and the level of wages and general social condition of the *campesino* were equally desperate. Over 96 percent of the Mexican population was landless.[43]

The Mexican land reform movement therefore constituted one of the most remarkable land reform movements in history. The *ejido* was sanctioned under the famous Article 27 of the Constitution of 1917, which introduced the new legal theory that the ownership of property was compatible with socially harmonious use. Under the *ejido* system, land tenure rights are vested by the state in a village; in turn the village or *ejido* community vests the right to ownership of a piece of land in each villager. This plot of land may not be sold; it may not be mortgaged; it may not be taken over by a large estate owner. The individual villager, should he and his family cease to work the land, stands to lose his plot of land, under the law. The *ejido* community is in principle both self-governing and democratic.

Although the individually owned *ejido*, operated under communal control, stands out as the most prominent feature of agrarian innovation in Mexico, the new changes created another type of *ejido*, the cooperative *ejido*. This is larger than the individually owned *ejido* and is worked communally. Organization, production, the sharing of the product, and every other aspect of the operation are subject to communal decision-making. As Navarro points out, agrarian legislation from the beginning was almost preferentially concerned with the individual small holder as against the communal holders of *ejidos* and, in fact, Article 27 aimed at breaking up the haciendas to create small holdings.[44]

As a result of the revolution, land distribution became the continuous obligation of every president of Mexico. Between 1915 and August 31, 1967, a total of 147.7 million acres of Mexican territory was distributed to 2.6 million farmers. The area covered by the program was 163.2 million acres, and the amount distributed between 1915 and 1967 amounted to just over 25 percent of the total area of Mexico.[45] Figures differ a great deal but they are indicative of the continuity and vigor of the process.[46] During the Alliance years, 17.5 million acres were distributed between 1961-64 to over 120,437 farmers, and between Sept., 1964, and Aug., 1965, 39.6 million acres were distributed to 301,364 farmers.[47]

---

[42] For a brief review, see Huizer (1969) and Navarro (1969, pp. 206-229).

[43] See Flores (1967, p. 117).

[44] Navarro (1969, p. 215).

[45] Inter-American Development Bank (1967, p. 214).

[46] Inter-American Development Bank (1962a, p. 328), gives the following data on average annual distribution: 1950-58—500,000 hectares; 1958-59—1.2 million; 1959-60—2 million; 1960-61—3.5 million. For the period 1915-58, see estimates in Flores (1967) in comparison with estimates in Mexican Presidential Reports in Huizer (1969, p. 141).

[47] Inter-American Development Bank (1967, p. 214; 1969a, p. 393).

The pace of land distribution expectedly varied in relation to the commitment of the president to agrarian reform and other circumstances. Carranza, for instance, the first president under the constitution of 1917, was a reluctant agrarian reformer. He distributed a maximum of 200,000 hectares during his regime (1915-20).[48] Obregón was more committed and distribution in his regime (1920-24) totaled 1.5 million hectares.[49] Calles (1924-28) established a banking system to give advice and financial support and distributed over 3 million hectares.[50] The outstanding contributor, in terms of implementing the intentions of the agrarian reform, was Lázaro Cárdenas (1934-40). In his regime, some 3 million hectares were annually reclassified as *ejidos*.[51] Cárdenas not only redistributed; he innovated.[52] Figures for subsequent years show that between 1940-58 only 500,000 hectares were distributed annually, increasing thereafter under the presidencies of Mateos (1958-64) and his successor, Ordaz. In 1960, there were 1,523,796 *ejidatarios* in possession of land, and *ejido* holdings represented 55.9 percent of all holdings and 43.4 percent of all arable land.[53]

The land reform movement has been persistent, if not spectacular, for over 55 years. Evaluation of the Mexican experience in terms of equity and efficiency in agriculture is complicated because of the web of events involved in the evolution of the land tenure system in Mexico and the differing physical and climatic conditions of Mexico which affect production and productivity.[54] So far as equity is concerned, agrarian reform put an end to the system of peonage and instituted new and viable relations between various groups of agricultural producers in Mexico. The *ejido* system ended the worst excesses of the pre-1910 land-tenure situation. The productive capacities of individual farmers found outlets and feudal constraints to labor mobility were eradicated. In terms of the effect of the revolution on economic performance in agriculture, criticisms of earlier years do not constitute fair comment. The period after the revolution was a time of extraordinary disequilibrium and search for adjustment. Labor moved to the towns in search of jobs or tried to adjust to the agricultural institutions. Capital fled from agriculture in the midst of dismal prophesies about the economic future of Mexico. Vernon calls the period 1910-20 the "lost years of Mexico."[55] But the years after the revolution were years of determination and constructive innovation on the part of Mexican government. The revolution did not end in 1940, the year which marks the end of Cárdenas's monumental

---

[48] See Cumberland (1968, p. 296). See also Huizer (1969, p. 141). Flores gives 172,997 hectares; Mexican Presidential Reports 224,393 hectares. Raymond Vernon (1963, p. 67) suggests that in dealing with a variety of "sources of dissidence and opposition" (local generals, labor leaders, foreign oil companies, local politicians, the Church, peasant groups, etc.) Carranza may have had "little room for maneuver."

[49] Flores gives a figure of 1,556,983 hectares; Presidential Reports, 1,677,057; Cumberland (1968, p. 296), approximately 1,750,000 hectares.

[50] Flores, 3,045,802; Presidential Reports, 3,195,028. See Cumberland (1968, p. 297).

[51] Inter-American Development Bank (1962a, p. 328).

[52] See Vernon (1963, pp. 73-74).

[53] See U.S. House (1967, p. 155).

[54] Cf. U.S. House (1967, p. 155). Even classifying holdings as large, medium or small on the basis of total area of arable land is difficult because of the variation in moisture conditions. The data on irrigation and adequacy of rainfall by size of farm is inadequate.

[55] Vernon (1963, p. 79).

contribution to the land distribution commitment of the revolution. The commitment to the revolution has been continuous. No president of Mexico dares to renege on this, and each president has made his own unique contribution to agrarian reform in terms of land distribution, infrastructure, credit, or other institutional advances. Because of this visible commitment to the revolution, some degree of stability was established because it became clear that a return to the days of Porfirio Díaz was impossible. This was a tremendous psychic gain, with immense potential advantages for the release of the productive and organizational genius of the Mexican people.[56]

Vernon notes that agricultural production recovered in the 1930s, with irrigation and access to credit gradually increasing in the period 1926-40.[57] The Mexican economist Urquidi notes, however, that until 1940, agricultural output barely increased 1.5 to 2 percent a year.[58] Between 1940-55, crop production increased at an average rate of 6.3 percent a year, one of the highest rates in the world. In 1956-60, this rate dropped to 3 percent. Between 1960-61 and 1967-68, agricultural production in Mexico advanced at an average rate of 4.7 percent a year, faster than anywhere else in Latin America, except Venezuela. During the same period, food production grew 5.7 percent a year.[59] Crop yields increased from an average of 2.5 percent a year in the years 1940-62 to 4.5 percent a year in the period 1962-65. During the Alliance years, employment in agriculture actually increased. Between 1961-67 it rose from 6.3 million to 7.2 million, while productivity per worker rose by 10.8 percent.[60] In fact, by 1965 Mexico had become practically self-sufficient in food, importing less than 2 percent of its food and even becoming an important exporter of agricultural products. Corn and wheat are outstanding examples of products of which Mexico has a surplus for export.[61]

The determined support by the government of the objectives of the revolution is the basic factor behind these remarkable results. The increase in production and the rise in productivity and employment were accompanied by tremendous increases in fertilizer input, research, better seeds, expansion of irrigation and transport systems, financial support, educational improvement, and continuous institutionalization and innovation.[62]

The problem of increasing production, productivity, and employment in agriculture in Mexico is still far from solved. Historical dilemmas still continue. Though improved, economic performance on the *ejidos* in general is still below

---

[56]The reader may with advantage read Glade and Anderson (1963). In the author's view, this is one of the most enlightened and perceptive appreciations of the course of events in Mexico, which happily ignores the unhelpful categorizing of "good economists" (North Americans) and "bad economists" (Latin Americans).

[57]Vernon (1963, pp. 82-83).

[58]Urquidi (1967, p. 181).

[59]See Inter-American Development Bank (1969, pp. 10, 380) and U.S. House (1967, pp. 156, 158).

[60]Inter-American Development Bank (1968, p. 218).

[61]U.S. House (1967, p. 163).

[62]*Ibid.*, pp. 154-164. See also Singer (1969, pp. 55-66) and Inter-American Development Bank (1961-69).

performance on the private holdings.[63] The *ejidos* were expected to perform miracles in agricultural production—to meet domestic food requirements as well as maintain if not improve export levels to strengthen the foreign exchange position in both directions. But by 1940, it was clear that productivity was in trouble in the *ejido*. The reasons for this poor performance constitute some of the most profitable sources of real experience. The contributors to low productivity included lack of managerial experience, illiteracy, overpopulation on the *ejidos*, irrigation deficiencies, credit and marketing inadequacies, and lack of a general preparedness for this fundamental transformation. The larger *ejidos* (the collective type) were better off, but of course they are in the minority.[64]

Reality, therefore, forced protection of the large private farm property. In the Land Law of 1949, various devices were used to insure large private holdings against expropriation and at the same time insure the minimum scale of operation appropriate for profitable output.[65] By 1962, productivity and income levels were still low in the *ejidos* for a variety of traditional reasons—lack of irrigation facilities; excessive subdivision of the land and uneconomic farm sizes; low technical levels of cultivation and livestock protection; and shortage of credit for the *ejidatarios*, among others. At the end of the 1960s, agriculture remained divided into two groups: a commercial sector comprising less than 15 percent of the farmers of Mexico but producing over 75 percent of the crop sales of the country; and a large body of small farmers, a significant proportion of whom were not even integrated in the domestic market economy.[66] At this point, the government had to come to terms with the fact that land for distribution was reaching its limits.[67]

Despite the remarkable changes we have identified, the per capita value of the production of the agricultural work force in Mexico in 1967 was only 5.8 percent of its U.S. counterpart.[68] Except for Bolivia and Brazil, this ratio was lower than anywhere else in Latin America. Because of continuing low incomes, a rural population growth of 1.6 percent a year, an unemployment ratio estimated at about 30 percent of the agricultural labor force, and serious limits to the quality of life as well as to the capacity of agriculture to absorb more labor, the rural labor force continued to migrate to the towns.[69] It was becoming

[63]Thiesenhusen and Brown in U.S. Senate (1967e, p. 191) comment: "There is no clear indication of any significant difference in crop yields between *ejidos* and private farms over 12.5 acres, when all commodities are aggregated." A Chase Manhattan Bank report on Mexico (1968, pp. 2–9) notes, however, that the productivity of Mexcian agricultural workers was only about one-fifth that of workers employed in industry and the services. Hence agriculture, which employed more than half of Mexico's economically active labor force, accounted for only one-sixth of the country's GNP.

[64]See Fulton (1968, pp. 2–9).

[65]See Cline (1963, pp. 214–215).

[66]See Inter-American Development Bank (1968, p. 219). The 1960 agricultural census showed that 72.8 percent of the holdings were still under 10 hectares and accounted for 1.2 percent of the cultivated land, while 1.6 percent of the holdings were 1000 hectares and above and accounted for 78.4 of the cultivated land. See Pan American Union (1968b, p. 20).

[67]Inter-American Development Bank (1969a, p. 392).

[68]*Ibid.*, p. 5.

[69]Chase Manhattan Bank (1968, p. 19).

increasingly clear in official circles that many peasants had to stop being peasants and take jobs in industry.[70]

From the fact that Mexico, despite its determination, has not solved the agricultural problem after six decades, we can judge the dimensions of the problem in the rest of Latin America. Fortunately, Mexico took no chances. While protecting the dominance of Mexican norms, the government also protected the private sector, a sector dominated and led by Mexicans who after 60 years of unwavering Mexican nationalism understand both the necessity and the boundary conditions for their entrepreneurship.

The revealed difficulties of transforming traditional agriculture in Mexico underline the naïveté of the proclamation that Cuba has solved the problem of agricultural production and productivity as well as satisfied equity simply by the adoption of a new political ideology. This seems to be the implication, for instance, in the following observation:

The mere removal of the imperialist yoke enabled revolutionary Cuba to put into immediate cultivation vast areas of fertile land previously neglected or misused by absentee landowners.... The adoption of a centrally planned economy is enabling Cuba to go further, to lay the groundwork of a balanced, healthy, cultivated and eventually rich society. That is the lesson of Cuba for underdeveloped countries—that without a social revolution there is no possibility of going beyond the introduction of largely ineffectual reforms. The experience of the Soviet Union and of China proved it before; now Cuba has proved it again. The Latin American countries may not have learned the lesson from distant Russia and China, but it will be driven home to them by the example of neighboring Cuba.[71]

In 1960, when Huberman's comments were made, Castro had just come to power. An analysis of agrarian change in Cuba reveals the limitations of the plantation system as an alternative to the hacienda in terms of equity and efficiency. But the analysis reveals, too, that the Cuban alternative has not, after ten years or more, generated the economic miracle implied by the comment above. In other words, the search for an alternative land tenure system for Latin America is still incomplete.

We turn now to an evaluation of agrarian change in Cuba.

THE IDEOLOGICAL TRAP: THE CUBAN ALTERNATIVE

On January 1, 1959, the island of Cuba acquired a new leader, a new ideology, and a new promise, among others, to implement a revolutionary program of agrarian reform. One dictator, Fulgencia Batista, had fled; a new one came in. Batista, like Díaz of Mexico, was completely indifferent to land reform; Castro, on the other hand, verbally went beyond Cárdenas in giving expression to land reform as a priority. The principal object of attack in Castro's case was the foreign commercial plantation. The redistribution of land was the sine qua non to implement ideals of equity, which were interpreted to spell out a spontaneous upsurge in farm productivity. On May 17, 1959, Castro set up the National Institute of Agrarian Reform (INRA), with him-

---

[70] Kanner (1968, p. 210).
[71] Huberman (1963, p. 56).

self as president, to carry through the long-promised agrarian reform. A realistic appreciation of Castroite actions in this area is impossible without some historical background.

The United States assumed military control of Cuba in 1898, after the American declaration of war on Spain in the same year. In the years 1899–1903 Cuba remained under American military control. In 1903 Cubans assumed the governance of the island, but not before the signing of the Platt Amendment. This amendment supplied a legally permissible basis for American intervention in Cuban affairs, should this step be considered essential to the defence of American economic interests. In return Cuba secured an increased share of the American market, through favorable tariff reductions up to 20 percent on Cuban sugar and other exports. The United States secured even more favorable reciprocal concessions ranging from 20 to 40 percent, and the Platt Amendment of course reinforced the protection for and advantages of American investment in Cuba. Cuban sugar came to dominate the American domestic market and American investment controlled the Cuban sugar industry. Cuba became the leading producer of sugar in the world, controlling sugar prices in the same way that Brazil controls coffee prices. [72]

Between 1903 and 1934, Cuba developed the most modern sugar industry in the world, as the consequence of more than $1 billion in American capital poured into the island. The Platt Amendment was repealed in 1934, at the urging of U.S. diplomat Sumner Welles and after violent protests against the regime of the Cuban president, General Machado. The dominance of sugar in the Cuban agriculture, however, continued unaffected.

The events which complicated the Cuban situation before the Castro takeover had already taken root. These events included noneconomic ones like American intervention in Cuban affairs under the Platt Amendment, the dictatorship of Batista, and the economic and social situation emerging from plantation agriculture and dependence on a single product. America sent troops to secure order and protect U.S. property in Cuba in 1906 and 1912 and again in 1917. Under the 1903 treaty, the United States retained Guantánamo Bay and Bahia Hondo as leased military bases—through the latter was handed back in 1912. Batista ruled Cuba between 1932–40 with the aid of some seven servile presidents and after an intervening period of 12 years, under Cuban presidents Grau San Martín and Carlos Prió Socarrás, returned again as dictator by way of a military coup. The Batista regime developed into an ugly dictatorship. On January 1, 1959, Batista fled, after being defeated by Castro forces and deserted by the general body of the population.

The Economic Status of Cuba in 1959

Economic conditions in Cuba reveal frustration in the midst of wealth. The

[72] For critical evaluations of Cuban economic issues as they evolved particularly in relation to U.S. capital, the following books, among many others, may be referred to: Bernstein (1966, see his reading list); Smith (1966; an excellent reference reading list on Cuba); Boorstein (1968); Smith (1965); Huberman and Sweezy (1968); Seers (1964); Higgins (1968, pp. 790–817, for a summary case study of the Cuban economy); Silvert (1968, esp. pp. 228–256); Blanshard (1947, esp. pp. 304–309); Stark (1963, esp. pp. 110–121); and Hanson (1949).

frustration stems basically on the one hand from the potentialities of Cuba and on the other hand from the realities. Cuba is a large island of 44,218 square miles with a population (in 1967) of 8,033,000.[73] One quarter of the surface is mountainous, the rest constituting of largely flat fertile land. The lay of the land invites mechanization. In 1959, the Cuban economic position looked very favorable in comparison with the rest of Latin America. The per capita income stood at $516 (U.S.), the fourth highest in Latin America after Argentina ($799 U.S.), Venezuela ($644.50 U.S.), and Uruguay ($560.90 U.S.).[74] Cuba with 3.3 percent of the population of Latin America enjoyed a higher per capita than Mexico ($415.40 U.S.) with 17 percent of the population of the region and Brazil ($374.60 U.S.) with 34.4 percent of the population of the region.

In 1960 Cuba had a 7.1 percent share of the aggregate value of all Latin American exports, fifth after Venezuela (29.3 percent), Brazil (14.7 percent), Argentina (12.5 percent), and Mexico (8.8 percent). In terms of staple commodity exports, Latin America supplied 48.70 percent of the world exports of sugar in 1958–60, but Cuba contributed 73.1 percent of the Latin American exports of sugar. Cuba's death rate of 6.5 per 1000 inhabitants was the lowest in the Americas (including the United States which stood at 9.5) and one of the lowest in the world around 1960. The growth rate of the population stood at 2.1 percent a year for the period 1955–60, the lowest in Latin America except Uruguay (1.3 percent a year) and Argentina (1.8 percent a year). It was certainly lower than the average of 2.9 percent for Latin America. At the same time, real income grew in 1959–60 at an annual average rate of 3.2 percent.

Affluence and Poverty

In 1959 Cuba had one of the best managerial elites in Latin America; a high level of infrastructural strength; a monopoly of the best sugar market in the world, namely, the United States; a capital city with an immense tourist pull just across a 90-mile stretch of water from the best tourist market in the world; potentialities for mineral development; an excellent climate; and promising preconditions for a take-off. There were, however, basic entrenched drags. These were the dependence on one crop; landlessness; unemployment and underemployment; and conditions bordering on or of actual social despair, particularly in the countryside.

The sugar plantation system, wherever it exists, is a source of controversy. It has been so historically in the Caribbean.[75] Sugar yields are greater with large-scale cultivation under the plantation system than under any smaller land-holding unit of cultivation.[76] To choose sugar, however, is to choose a fate in terms of the land that must be acquired and held for the profitable exercise of the sugar

[73] International Bank for Reconstruction and Development (1969).
[74] UNECLA (1963, p. 122).
[75] See Farley (1956, 1958, pp. 194–199); Williams (1944); Ragatz (1963).
[76] Cf. UN (1951, p. 22):

It is generally believed that the division of the plantations into small farms would be likely to reduce the area planted to sugar-cane, which would reduce the demand for labor and also the volume of agricultural production. So far as plantation crops other than sugar are concerned, the difference in yield between large and small farms is not great enough to outweigh the social advantages which would be gained by resettlement on smaller farms. So far as sugar is concerned, the division of plantations under present conditions would probably result in a decline in yields.

business. On the other hand, to choose sugar is to choose inevitable political and social concern, if not hostility and violence. Economic necessities are one thing; social sentiment another. This was exactly the dilemma in Cuba. Because of the advantages of the Platt Amendment, the security and incentives of the world's most coveted sugar market, and the flat, fertile, well-watered land inviting easy mechanization and low transport costs, some 60 percent of U.S. investment and knowhow in Cuba went into sugar. It was inevitable that when the world's most aggressive entrepreneurial class—the American businessman—entered the sugar business of Cuba, that business would acquire an efficiency which made the social dilemma even more painful in a society still unaccustomed to the exacting demands of competitive business in the United States.

The concentration of land in a few hands—traditional before the U.S. occupation in 1898—was accelerated through the activities of the few dominant sugar corporations. In 1934, one corporation alone owned 771,025 acres of land; a second corporation 520,600 acres; and a third 280,760 acres. Between 1899 and 1934 locally owned farms declined from 60,711 to 38,105. By 1939, some 75 percent of the sugar business was in U.S. hands, over five times the extent of foreign control since the beginning of the twentieth century. The agricultural census of 1946 showed that the farms between 0.4 and 24.9 hectares, a total of 111,278 farms or 69.6 percent of the holdings, accounted for an area of 1,021,900 hectares, or only 11.2 percent of the land area. On the other hand, the farms of 1000 hectares or more—a total of 894 farms or 0.5 percent of the landholdings— accounted for an area of 3,261,100 hectares or 36.9 percent of the land area. By 1959, 28 of the largest sugar producers owned or controlled over one-fifth of the territory of Cuba, half of which was used and half kept in reserve.

It was sugar dominance all the way. Sugar accounted for one-fifth of Cuba's GNP; over 40 percent of Cuba's total farm income; 76.9 percent of the value of total exports; 50 percent of the population in agriculture; over 200,000 landless families; nearly half a million unemployed; and a rate of seasonal and disguised unemployment unbelievable to those accustomed to this phenomenon in sugar islands like St. Kitts and St. Lucia in the Caribbean.[77]

The accompanying social conditions are easily spelled out. In 1960, 45.4 percent of the Cuban population was rural. Thus nearly half the population was caught in the sorry backlash of the sugar vortex. Cuba was an economic dependent of the United States and, in turn, Cubans were *colonos*, sub-*colonos*, tenant farmers, and squatters dependent on the sugar industry. Ten years earlier, 44.8 percent of the total number of occupied dwellings were without piped water inside or outside, but the proportion without such provision in the rural areas amounted to 85.6 percent. In the rural areas 55.2 percent of occupied dwellings were without any kind of flush toilets, private or common. In 1960 in Cuba men could expect to live for 50.7 years as against 66.4 years in the United States. Other comparisons around 1960 are interesting (see table, p. 192).[78]

Agrarian Reform Under a Command Ideology

Clearly, this was a difficult situation in terms of basic requirements. Operations in sugar, to be profitable, had to be on a large-plantation basis. But the rural

[77]The number of unemployed appeared to vary between an average of 350,000 to 400,000 a year, about 16 percent of the labor force. See UNECLA (1963, p. 266).
[78]See UNECLA (1963, pp. 132–137).

	Cuba	United States
Doctors per 10,000 inhabitants	9.7	13.4
Hospital beds per 1000 inhabitants	2.3	9.1
Percentage of illiterates in the population of 15 years and over		
Total	22	3
Rural	40	5
Percentage of persons enrolled in		
Primary schools (5–14 age group)	49	88
Secondary schools (15–19 age group)	–	60
Higher education per 100,000 persons	–	1511
Newspaper circulation per 1000 persons	70	347
Government expenditures in education		
In dollars per capita	18	97
As a percentage of Gross National Product	–	4.6

conditions of poverty, illiteracy, landlessness, and joblessness in Cuba were intolerable. Puerto Rico, annexed by the United States in 1898, the year of the military occupation of Cuba, followed its democratic leader Luis Múñoz Marin to a reconciliation of sugar plantation and peasant interests.[79] Castro in 1959 espoused a different set of original values. A command economy was set up, and the whole Cuban economy fell under state control through a series of new institutions, under leadership which shared the ideological presuppositions of Castro.

The command institutional complex includes a council of ministers; a central planning agency (JUCEPLAN) modeled after the Soviet COSPLAN; a number of subordinate provincial and local planning committees; and the executive ministries and other official agencies responsible for executing the details of the plan as recommended by JUCEPLAN and approved and directed by the council of ministers. In the field of agriculture, the National Institute of Agrarian Reform *(Instituto Nacional de la Reforma Agraria—INRA)* controls the implementation of over-all plans for development in agriculture.[80] Castro heads both JUCEPLAN and INRA.

INRA came into existence with the enactment of Cuba's first land reform act on May 17, 1959. The intentions of the act included several major objectives: elimination of dependence on a one-crop system; facilitating and increasing the growing of new crops to supply new industries with raw materials, meet local food demand, and save foreign exchange; improving the standard of living in the rural areas and expanding the domestic market; ending the insecurity and ineffi-

[79] For a brief account see UN (1951, p. 23).

[80] See UNECLA (1963c, p. 259):

the country's wealth and means of production have been nationalized and most of the latter have become the property of the State. This in turn has entailed modifying the organization of the public sector in order to fit it for direct management of the various production, trade and services units, and a system of planning and centralised direction of economic activity has been established. . . . Cuba's economic organization implies the coordination of all sectors of productive activity and their subordination to the overall and specific objectives established in the plans sanctioned by the Government.

ciency of sharecropping, tenant farming, squatting, and absentee landlordism; ending in inequitable land distribution as shown in the 1946 census; ending wastage of land in cattle raising, and so on.[81] The principle of social justice was invoked to support the law and large landholding was condemned as uneconomical, thus justifying the replacement of extensive cultivation by intensive cultivation under cooperative production "which brings with it the advantages of large scale production."[82] Once again, the principle of equity was invoked as if agrarian reform spelled a spontaneous upgrading of agricultural productivity.

The Agrarian Reform Law determined that land distribution should be as follows:

1. The maximum area of land which could be owned by any one person was not to exceed 30 *caballerías*. Large landholding was forbidden and any land held beyond the legal limits was subject to expropriation.
2. State lands as well as privately owned lands occupied by farmers who were *colonos*, sub-*colonos*, *colonos* growing sugar cane, sub-*colonos* growing sugar cane, sharecroppers, or tenants were to be first in the order of priority for expropriation.
3. Corporations were forbidden to operate sugar plantations unless all their stocks were registered and held by Cuban citizens who were not owners or officers of sugar-manufacturing companies.
4. Only Cuban citizens could own rural property.[83]

The law provided for a "vital minimum for a peasant family of five," two *caballerías* of fertile land, without irrigation, far from urban centers, growing only crops of medium economic yield. This vital minimum was the yardstick to be used by INRA for determining any other vital minimum. Owners of smaller parcels of land were to be given land up to this limit provided it was available and that it was to be personally cultivated. The order of priority for redistribution was also laid down, priority groups being: farmers dispossessed of land which they were cultivating; farmers working in the area where land was being distributed and who held land less than the vital minimum; farmers from elsewhere in the same situation; agricultural workers and others who could prove their case. And of course veterans and families of Castro supporters had first preference in the awards of land.

It might be mentioned that agricultural production was frozen under three state-authorized organizations: a public sector comprising sugar cane cooperatives; people's farms and farms under direct state management; and a private sector comprising small holders and owners of farms with an area of more than 67.1 hectares (five *caballerías*). In addition, Cuba was divided into a number of administrative zones corresponding to the political and administrative subdivisions of the island. In turn, the management of the agricultural sector was frozen under the centralized control of the General Administration for the People's Farms *(Administración General de las Granjas del Pueblo)* and the General Administration for Sugarcane Cooperatives *(Administración General de Cooperativas Cañeras)*. Under a second land reform act in 1963, the command organization was then nuclearized, if this term may be used, into Basic Agricultural Production Groupings *(Agrupaciones Básicas de Producción Agropecuaria)*, each consisting of

[81]Summarized from Smith (1965, pp. 145–149).
[82]*Ibid.*, p. 148.
[83]*Ibid.*, pp. 149–152. A *caballería* equals 33.5 acres.

a number of farms. Each group and each farm within the group was then put into a position of financial dependence—the ultimate controlling device.[84]

Productivity Under State Control

Reportedly, equity through redistribution was put into effect by a series of measures which included land reform, increased expenditures on housing, education, social services, and infrastructure.[85] Reportedly too, under the first land reform act, approximately 100,000 tenants, sharecroppers and squatters (*precaristas*) got land of their own and also the right to receive fully the profits of their farming activity. Clearly, however, the independence of the new landholder could only be tenuous in the light of the command structure under which all agricultural activity was controlled. Further, land redistribution could hardly be as far-reaching as originally promised because the state extended its own control of the farm land, taking over the major share of the agricultural assets of the country. These assets included the large estates as well as the installations owned by foreign sugar companies. In 1959, the state owned some 40 percent of all the farm land in Cuba. By 1963, the state owned more than 60 percent of all the farm land, and this, of course, included the best farm lands of Cuba. In 1963, all rural estates of more than 67.1 hectares were nationalized. In 1961 the state owned some 40 percent of the sugar cane plantation land (about 550,000 hectares); in 1963, the state controlled some 70 percent (886,000 hectares approximately). Similarly, the state increased its ownership of cattle herds from 27 percent to some 60 percent.[86] By the end of the decade, only very small farms remained in private hands.[87]

We need not examine this case study in every detail. It is enough to indicate that such evidence as is available indicates that the ideological alternative imposed in Cuba gave rise neither to equity nor to the immediately promised increases in production or productivity. By 1967, the over-all average growth rate of the Cuban economy declined 0.8 percent, between 1961 and 1967. The per capita GNP had by then fallen to $330 (U.S.).[88] Total and per capita agricultural production generally declined after 1961. Sugar production also declined, the 1969 crop being less than 6 million tons. Cuba thus failed to reach the target of 10 million tons set for 1970.[89] Constant complaints of apathy and low productivity continued.

There were, of course, a number of contributor factors. Externally, there was the change in trade relations with the United States and the substitution of a dependent and unilaterally dictated relationship with the Soviet Union, China,

---

[84] See UNECLA (1963, p. 265). See also Mesa-Lago (1970).

[85] For further details, see UNECLA (1963a, esp. pp. 266–267). For a first-hand report on the subversion of morale in Cuba, despite these reported "incentive" activities, see Kanner (1968, pp. 210–211).

[86] UNECLA (1963a, p. 265).

[87] Chase Manhattan Bank (1969, p. 17).

[88] International Bank for Reconstruction and Development *Rates* (1969).

[89] See Castro (1968, p. 4): "And, of course, we state and repeat that we will inexorably reach our goal of ten million tons in 1970! [Applause] There will be more than enough cane, thanks to the enormous effort that we are now making to reach that goal." In turn, of course, Cuba's dependence on the Soviet Union as a sugar market reduces her bargaining power, her foreign earnings, and her prospects for rapid industrialization.

and other centrally planned economies. Internally, there was the flight of Cuba's managerial class; the flight of capital; the lack of spare parts; the uncertainties of the authoritarian system now under new leadership and a new ideology; the haste of the state farm sector to prove its ideological correctness; the passivity of the private sector comprised of owners of more than 67.1 hectares (5 caballerías) which in turn amounted to 30 percent of the arable land; and the unresponsiveness of labor to moral incentives.

Enough time has passed to prove that this ideological alternative to the plantation system did not usher in a spontaneous millennium of agricultural efficiency. The landowner, transformed into a *colono* in the pre-Castro days by the driving efficiency of the plantation system and the ruthless indifference of Batista, became under the dogmatic authoritarianism of Castroism not an independent landowner in the real sense of the term, but a landless *colono* directly controlled by a totalitarian state and a victim of Castro's betrayal of reformist democracy.

ESSENTIAL CONDITIONS FOR IMPROVING AGRICULTURAL PRODUCTIVITY

We have found so far no system of land tenure which offers an immediate solution to the problems of satisfying equity and development needs in agriculture. Our concern ends at identification of the issues involved. Satisfactory alternatives to the hacienda may emerge but, whatever these alternatives, certain general conditions are essential for the improvement of agricultural yield in Latin America. These general conditions include the upgrading quantitatively and qualitatively of trained manpower in agriculture and of general enthusiasm for agriculture; the spread of entrepreneurial attitudes into the business of agriculture; the availability and deployment of capital and technology in agriculture; the development of research, planning, and organizational know-how in agriculture; the attitudes and action of the state; and the success with which population growth can be restrained on the one hand and industry expand on the other to absorb redundant manpower from the agricultural sector.

Upgrading Manpower Skills

Latin America has a very low ratio of agricultural specialists to farm people. The United States has more than 15 for every 1000 farmers, but Brazil would have to quadruple the number of farm experts to achieve a ratio of one technician per 1000 farmers. FAO calculated that Latin America had only 21,000 university graduates in agriculture, 590 in forestry, and 9000 in veterinary science—a figure far below the requirements of modernization in agriculture. Latin American countries were graduating 1500 agriculturists a year which hardly covered annual losses in the profession due to death, disability, or change in profession.[90]

Panama in 1967 had 200 extension agents for a rural population of 500,000.[91] (See Table A.47) The prestige of agricultural sciences, as we have seen, fights an uphill battle against classical tradition and abstract training needs to be reinforced by field work, by case studies, and by experiment beyond the laboratories of the ivory tower. Agricultural colleges are increasing in number, but salaries for agricultural specialists are low and field support poor in most countries. The rate of

[90] U.S. Department of Agriculture (1967, p. 3).
[91] U.S. House (1967, p. 11). See also U.S. Department of Agriculture (1967, p. 3).

migration to other jobs and other countries is thus extremely high. The matter goes further. Sometimes the government does not have jobs for its own graduates and, in a few cases, the training is of such low order that it may not even be counted as upgrading individual skills. In the private sector, except for the foreign plantation, farm management is poor in Latin America. Increasing the number of trained farm managers is obviously essential. But any increase in agricultural technicians and trained farm managers must be accompanied by inducements to entrepreneurs to invest in agriculture and by mass education of the farm population. Modernizing agriculture so that the rural agriculture labor force will play a full participant role is impossible without effective mass education.

Technological Inputs

Increases in trained personnel and improved education however are not sufficient to change conditions. Significant improvements in production and productivity require increased inputs of fertilizers, seeds, machinery, irrigation, electrification, and transport. These factors are all interrelated. The extent to which fertilizers are used has come to be regarded as one of the most important indicators of technical progress in agriculture on the basis of the FAO conclusion that "the use of fertilizers . . . has the greatest single effect on productivity per hectares and per men employed."[92] The use of fertilizers is increasing throughout Latin America and yields have improved wherever these increases have taken place. Mexico is an outstanding instance. One estimate suggests that with increased use of fertilizers, productivity in Latin American agriculture could be increased 50 to 100 percent.

The increased use of fertilizers, however, requires the removal of a number of key obstacles. These include ignorance of profitable farming techniques and the high cost of fertilizers in relation to the price of the product. In turn, the high cost of fertilizers reflects the import duties imposed on fertilizers in many parts of Latin America, the high cost of transporting fertilizers over long distances, the charges imposed by the middleman, the high cost of locally produced fertilizers in many places where import substitution has taken place, and the difficulty of getting credit for the purchase of fertilizers.[93] A comparison of North America and Latin America shows that while the United States and Canada use an annual average of 94 pounds of fertilizer per head, the per capita figure for Latin America is only 8.9 pounds.[94] Obviously, the use of fertilizers has to be correlated with the use of seeds, crop diversification, and with other devices for increased productivity.

Mechanization may or may not add to agricultural output. Blanket statements should be avoided. Certainly mechanization can contribute to increased production when uneconomic small farms are grouped together, but indiscriminate substitution of machinery for labor ignores the need for increased employment. Research is obviously essential to discover forms of intermediate technology which increase production and at the same time increase employment. We should note here that the prices of farm equipment in Latin America are much too high for the smaller farm groups.

[92] UNECLA (1968b, p. 318).
[93] See, for instance, U.S. Department of Agriculture (1969, pp. 95–99).
[94] U.S. House (1967, p. 11).

It is clear that the improvement of transport, the development of hydroelectric power, the expansion of the use of electricity in the rural areas, and the extension of irrigation are all necessary for the improvement of production and productivity in Latin America. Innumerable case studies reveal glaring needs in these areas.

Agricultural Credit

Agricultural credit is essential to agricultural development in Latin America. The building of permanent and effective credit institutions was one of the goals of the Alliance for Progress. Credit, if effectively institutionalized, effectively managed, and effectively supported by advisory personnel and training, can bring about the ultimate self-help aimed at. The large landowner has little difficulty about credit. He has immediate security and therefore ready access to credit. The small landowner and the medium-size landowner are normally not in this fortunate position in Latin America.

Agricultural credit programs have been established throughout Latin America.[95] Special institutions have been created in some countries; in other countries, the commercial and national banks have been drawn into the system, constituting a profound change in traditional commercial banking relationships. The results of credit administration and provision in Latin America have been mixed. In Paraguay, for instance, the system of supervised credit was still defective in 1966 and technical assistance was lacking. Small farmers on the whole lacked credit on the one hand, and on the other loan recovery was unsatisfactory and funds inadequate.[96] In El Salvador, credit service for farmers was fragmented under six institutions and credit resources concentrated on traditional export agriculture and on a few large farmers.[97]

In Mexico, despite the high degree of organization of the farm credit program, there were still difficulties to be ironed out in 1966. The AID Alliance for Progress loans program (ALPRO) for instance did not develop smoothly. The main reasons included (1) the farmers' unwillingness to change farming techniques and to mortgage their holdings, and difficulties with regard to their titles; (2) overcautiousness in selecting borrowers; (3) the exaggeration of estimated risks in lending money to *campesinos*; (4) shortages in the number of supervisory personnel and subject matter specialists; (5) the limited experience of private bankers and of farmers in financial management and relations with each other; and (6) the fact that *ejido* lands cannot legally be mortgaged as security for private commercial loans. These are all major problems to be resolved, but solving them takes time.

Research and Planning

Research is another essential prerequisite for increasing agricultural productivity. Research activity has been expanding in Latin America, but considerable progress still remains to be made.

In 1961, for instance, the U.S. government research budget worked out at

[95] For further details, see for instance: U.S. House (1967) and U.S. Agricultural Credit Technicians (1966).
[96] U.S. Department of Agriculture (1966, p. 22).
[97] U.S. House (1967, p. 225) and U.S. Agricultural Credit Technicians (1966, p. 10).

$45.90 per farmer. The total government research budget for Mexico in 1962 worked out to be 35 cents per farmer.[98] The effect of research on wheat yields in Mexico supplies ample evidence that research pays off. Acreage production of wheat in the northern regions of Mexico is now equal to the acreage production on the best farms in the United States, thanks to research. Yet in 1943 Mexico was importing half its wheat. In 1944, the Mexican government and the Rockefeller Foundation initiated a joint research program at Chapingo, Mexico, to develop new high-yielding wheat varieties to make Mexico self-sufficient. In 1948, the new varieties of wheat were planted with the new seeds. By 1956, Mexico was not only self-sufficient in wheat, but had become a consistent exporter of wheat. Research also paid off for the Mexican farmer. In 1944, the Mexican farmer averaged 11.5 bushels of wheat per acre; the average now is 34 bushels of wheat, three times the average of a generation ago.[99]

Significant research efforts have developed at agricultural research centers like Chapingo, Mexico; the National University at La Molina in Peru; the Agricultural College at Palmira in the Cauca valley of Colombia; the ICA center of the Sabana Bogotá of Colombia; the former Imperial College of Tropical Agriculture in Trinidad and Tobago, now part of the University of the West Indies. Tropical studies are being undertaken at places like Tabasco, Mexico; Turrialba, Costa Rica; Matao and Campinas, Brazil; Santa Cruz and Riberalta, Bolivia; and Merida, Venezuela. International organizations have been increasing the flow of research information. These bodies include: FAO, AID, CIAP, IDB, IMF, IBRD (International Bank for Reconstruction and Development), the Rockefeller, Carnegie, and Ford foundations, the U.S. Department of Agriculture (USDA), and other North American and European government and private research agencies.

But there are still critical areas where breakthroughs in research must be registered as a precondition for needed productivity breakthroughs.[100]

The Role of the State

The state in Latin America has the responsibility of supplying the incentive to private initiative and of safeguarding the public's interests while integrating these goals with the need for improved economic performance in agriculture.[101]

Government's critical role includes: (1) the encouragement of research; (2) the communication of research findings and the encouraging of their application; (3) the support of agricultural education, training, and extension courses; (4) the furthering of modernizing techniques and the encouraging of action to

---

[98]U.S. Department of Agriculture (1967, p. 3). If private research expenditures are taken into account, the U.S. figure works out to be $75 per farmer. Most developing countries spend less than $1 per farmer.

[99]See U.S. Department of Agriculture (1967, p. 3); and (1967aa, p. 7).

[100]See U.S. House (1967) for a summarized account. See also UNFAO (1965) and Wright and Bennema (1965).

[101]Cf. Chamberlain (1965, p. 209):

There are, of course, some public services which cannot be disaggregated to the local level. These must be carried on by the central government directly. . . . In the case of such activities, public and private objectives can be brought closer together by what may be termed the "priva-tising" of public objectives—the contracting with private enterprise for their development and operation. There is seldom any reason why the government need carry on such activities itself, even if its initiative is required to set them in motion.

offset the inevitable consequences of mechanization; (5) the provision of infra-structure and price supports where these are essential; (6) help in rationalizing and lowering the costs of marketing; and (7) modifying tariff barriers or at least working to reduce manufacturing costs in inefficient, tariff-protected local indus-try, to eliminate discouragingly high prices. The role of government is so critical that continuing inertia on the part of government could inhibit any agricultural improvement.[102]

As late as 1966, however, many Latin American governments had no specific sectoral plan for agricultural development. In other cases, agricultural develop-ment occupied a minor place in over-all plans for development. Brazil, for instance, with under 10 percent of the farm area under cultivation in 1966, concentrated until recently on industry and practically ignored agriculture. Up to 1967, Brazil had developed no comprehensive sectoral plan for agricultural development. This situation has changed somewhat with the initiation of a 10-year development plan for the period 1967-76.[103] Colombia, too, in 1967 had no comprehensive sectoral plan for agriculture, although AID and USDA had been invited to assist in preparing such a plan. The Dominican Republic was in a similar position. The government of Honduras included agricultural development in its National Plan for Economic and Social Development 1965-69, but reportedly remained indif-ferent to supplying incentives to expand the agricultural and forestry potential of the country. Agriculture had top priority in Paraguay's development plan, but there was no sectoral plan for agriculture—although some independent studies existed.

In many countries of Latin America, agriculture does not enjoy a place of priority in the public budgetary allocations. Every country in Latin America, ex-cept Costa Rica, Mexico, Panama, and the Dominican Republic, allocated a larger share of the budget to defense than to agriculture—at least during the period 1961-67. Uruguay, for instance, allocated 1.6 percent of the public budget in 1967 to agriculture but 12.9 percent to defense; Paraguay devoted 20 percent to defense but only 8.1 percent to agriculture.[104] From 1963-67, defense expend-itures for Latin American countries averaged 12.3 percent of the budget; agricul-tural allocations averaged 5 percent. The 1968 allocations for agriculture show a slight improvement: probably half the countries in Latin America were spending

[102]Cf. Reid (1966, p. 211):

> Agricultural administrations, services, and institutions are not being strengthened with the speed required to enable more capital to be used effectively. Most of the developing countries are now in a position to command the facilities necessary to meet reasonable requirements for the training of skilled manpower and for the improvement of their administrative structures. Why, then, are they not taking fuller advantage of these oppor-tunities? One reason could be the resistance of interests within the agricultural sector which are vested in the status quo. In other cases, the answer lies largely in the inability or reluctance of governments to provide sufficient recurrent budgetary funds for the employment of all the necessary skilled manpower that they have available or could obtain. One way toward overcoming this problem of agricultural development would be for such institutions as the World Bank and the International Monetary Fund, in their assistance to countries in economic planning, to emphasize more strongly the need for allocating current funds for agriculture in national budgets.

[103]See U.S. House (1967, p. 44).
[104]U.S. House (1969, tables B, C, F, pp. 64–66).

10 percent of the public budget on agriculture. Traditional priorities were clearly difficult to shift.[105]

The areas in which governments can take the initiative on behalf of agriculture are innumerable. Many Latin American governments have come to terms with their responsibilities to agriculture very late in the day. Farm price policies and marketing efficiencies are obviously critical incentives to agricultural productivity. Yet in many countries, governmental policy is either lacking or lacking in effectiveness. A cursory examination of the state of affairs in these two areas reveals drawbacks even in "advanced" Latin American countries as late as 1967.[106]

1. Argentina, for instance, had only scattered data on the agricultural marketing structure and no coherent official policy to deal with problems of spoilage and defects in distribution and processing.
2. Bolivia was no better off and retail prices in Bolivia were higher than in the United States. No reliable data existed on farm profits, marketing risks, input costs, even on storage adequacy and spoilage rates which are very high.
3. Brazil had no overall studies on the spread between farm prices and consumer prices; on farmers' net earnings; on marketing risks; on input costs; and on distributing and processing (including roads, rural electrification, cooperatives and so on).
4. In Colombia, no firm analysis existed of farm profits nor were there any firm farm records. No firm studies existed of marketing risks and only scattered studies of input-output relations. Government did have a policy of price supports especially for food staples and price ceilings for other goods. But there were no studies to give a background for decision-making. Farm-to-market road studies did not exist, and political expediency rather than research findings determined road construction decisions.
5. In Honduras, data was so deficient that guess-estimates were the only possibility.
6. Even in advanced Mexico, only very limited data existed on the agricultural marketing structure.
7. Nicaragua had only limited, hardly usable data, about farm profits. Marketing risks were very high. There was then no commercial refrigerated storage. Roads were limited; distribution was traditional and costly.[107]

The transformation of the agricultural sector is impossible without increased investment and increased investment depends on government's evaluation of the importance of the agricultural sector and on the policies pursued to secure an increased flow of investment into agriculture. This is a formidable matter. FAO estimated, for instance, that agriculture in Latin America needed an investment of $2.5 billion to $3 billion a year to achieve a growth rate of 4 to 5 percent a year. In the period 1961–67, however, investment in agriculture from all sources, foreign and domestic, averaged only $500,000 a year.[108]

CONCLUSIONS

We have seen that although it is still possible to increase production in agriculture by an expansion of acreage, the eventual alternative is to increase yields per acre

[105] See U.S. Department of State (1970aa).
[106] See U.S. House (1967).
[107] For a more detailed study, see Pan American Union (CIAP) (1967a).
[108] See U.S. House (1967, pp. 15–20). Cf. Yudelman (1966, p. 81) and UNECLA (1968b, pp. 366–369).

and output per worker. The traditional land tenure system, however, not only transgresses equity but militates against the possibility of increasing agricultural productivity. The hacienda is the principal target of hostility since it is regarded as the key stumbling block to equity and efficiency in agriculture. The hacienda cannot reform itself. It clearly must go. The breaking up of the hacienda system is traditionally the principal object of agrarian reform. This is, however, too simple a view, though understandable against the historic background. Analysis shows that every alternative form of land tenure in Latin America falls short of satisfying the criteria of equity and efficiency. Agrarian reform, therefore, applies to every form of land tenure. Latin America is still in search of a land tenure system which meets both criteria. In fact, reform in the interests of improving economic performance in agriculture involves much more than land distribution or redistribution. Reform must take into account a large number of general factors which affect performance in the sector, including the role of the state.

The prevailing drawbacks in agriculture as late as 1967 and the rapid growth rate of the rural population do not allow much optimism about a short run improvement in the status of agriculture. The high level of underemployment and unemployment in agriculture and the rate of population growth do not allow much optimism that the labor absorption capacity in agriculture will improve significantly, even in Mexico. Although we have said that research on intermediate technology, which results in both increased productivity and increased employment, is important, it is more than likely that the modernization of agriculture would mean less employment.

We must come to the conclusion that the conditions of the countryside thrust upon government a basic task of spreading the locus of industrial activity. Industrial activity in Latin America is, as we have seen, largely urban-based. Industrial activity is not expanding rapidly enough to absorb the population needing and seeking work in the towns, a population which includes the refugees from the cultural backwardness of the countryside. Historical and contemporary advantages are likely to continue to play their part in consolidating the town as the locus of factory activity. Despite these inherently rigid factors, it is clearly a part of the requirements of the Latin American situation that economic development be deployed also to the countryside. Governments have an obligation to use means to accelerate factory location in the countryside. This requires decentralization of incentives and regional determination of incentives to attract and retain private entrepreneurship wherever there are profitable prospects for industrial activity. This has already happened in Puerto Rico and it is already happening in Mexico where industrial parks are increasingly being located in the countryside, creating new jobs and generating a new standard of living.[109]

[109] See *Newsweek* (1967, p. 65). See also Klaasen (1967).

PART III

INDUSTRIALIZATION, CAPITAL FORMATION, AND
ECONOMIC INTEGRATION IN LATIN AMERICA

CHAPTER 10

THE CHALLENGE OF INDUSTRIALIZATION

At this point the necessity for more rapid industrialization in Latin America becomes clear. In this chapter, we review briefly the evolution of industrialization in Latin America, the rationale for accelerating industrialization, and the policies being pursued to support more rapid industrial development. We evaluate the extent to which these policies have succeeded and then consider the major dilemmas which will confront industrial development in Latin America for some time to come. Despite some impressive achievements, the evidence does not indicate that removing the remaining obstacles to more rapid industrial development in Latin America is a short-run prospect.

THE EVOLUTION OF INDUSTRIALIZATION

With the institution of the Alliance for Progress, industrialization, *ad hoc* and accidental in its origins, became a planned national and continental determination. The Charter of Punta del Este expressed the new determination in the following declaration on industrialization:

The American Republics agree to work toward the achievement of the following fundamental goals in the present decade. . . . to accelerate the process of national industrialization so as to increase the productivity of the economy as a whole, taking full advantage of the talents and energies of both the private and public sectors, utilizing the natural resources of the country, and providing productive and remunerative employment for unemployed or part-time workers. Within this process of industrialization, special attention should be given to the establishment and development of capital goods industries. [1]

Industrialization was not new in Latin America. As far back as 1883, Chile established a Society for the Development of Manufacturing Industry (*Sociedad de Fomento Fabril*) and in 1897 protectionist statutes were instituted. During this period, Chile was producing agricultural equipment, transport material, and some kinds of steam-driven machinery. [2] There were scattered bits of industrialization in Peru around 1896 and also the National Association of Industries (*Sociedad Nacional de Industrias*). Cuba, as mentioned earlier, became a large-scale sugar manufacturer, particularly after the Platt Amendment of 1903. Mexico began making steel in 1901, and at the same time its textile industry, with some 700,000 spindles and over 20,000 looms, provided jobs for about

---

[1] See U.S. House (1966, p. 102).
[2] UN (1966, p. 8).

30,000 employees. Uruguay had a packing plant industry at that time, as well as large-scale tanneries, textile mills, and manufacturing industries. By 1910 Argentina was able to satisfy one-third of its domestic demand for farm machinery. Five years later it had 40,200 industrial establishments employing 323,000 industrial workers. Long before the depression of the 1930s, the Rio-São Paulo axis was a great center of industrial activity.[3] By the time of the Charter of Punta del Este, what was new in Latin America, apart from the adoption of industrialization as a deliberate policy, was the intensity of the demand for industrialization.

The process and progress of industrialization in Latin America expectedly differs in detail from country to country, but three common features emerge. First, what developed prior to World War I was primarily cottage industry. Isolated industries financed by foreign interests, with production geared to export markets, did appear in or near urban locations here and there. But the majority of local factories were engaged in simple acts of transforming local raw materials, and their activities bore little dynamic relation to the local economy. In 1914, for instance, in an advanced country like Argentina, less than 10 percent of the industrial labor force was engaged in producing finished capital goods.[4] Industrialization at this stage was no more than a side effect of foreign investment aided by urban concentration, which offered an internal market outlet in addition to the foreign market outlets in particular cases, and by immigration which brought an increasing nucleus of entrepreneurial talent.

Second, in the period 1915–46, industrial development advanced under the stimulus of measures adopted by Latin American governments to protect internal income in the face of the crises brought on by two world wars and the intervening depression. These measures consisted principally of import restrictions and controls, an increase in the exchange rates, and the purchasing or financing of surplus output. They were designed, as a UNECLA study noted, to cushion the economies of Latin America against the adverse effect of these external shocks, but they served also to accelerate internal industrial development.[5]

The crises which affected the external trade structure forced a reallocation of resources in favor of domestic industrialization through tariff protection and import substitution. World War I thus served as an unexpected stimulus to Latin American industrialization. When imports of manufactured goods were cut off, the only alternative was the enforced replacement of imported manufactures by local production. Not all Latin American countries, of course, were in a position to respond to the external disequilibrium in this way. In Brazil, however, the contraction of external sources of supply stimulated internal industrial development to the extent that by 1920 it had a total of 309,000 employees in industrial establishments and an industrial output valued at 282

[3] See Jaguaribe (1968, pp. 130–139), for a summary of the development of manufacturing industry in Brazil in the early nineteenth century. See also Baer (1965, esp. pp. 12–34) and UN (1955, pp. 127–140).

[4] UN (1955, p. 127). UNECLA (1964, p. 1) grouped the industries which emerged as *residentiary* industries (textiles, footwear, clothing, furniture, etc.): "traditional, low productivity industries. . . . insufficient to impart to the domestic economy a vigorous growth of its own." See also Scobie (1964, pp. 177–179) for a summary of the status of industrialization in Argentina in 1914 and at the end of World War I.

[5] See UNECLA (1964, p. 2).

million cruzeiros gross.[6] It should be noted that the industrial labor force in 1920 accounted for only 13 percent of the total labor force.[7] Of that industrial labor force 73 percent was in finished consumer goods, 17 percent in other finished goods, and the rest in intermediate materials.[8]

During the depression years, particularly the years in the 1930s, the "change in data," as Alexandre Kafka termed the new external shock for Latin America (1963, p. 11), resulted in a further acceleration of internal industrialization in Latin America. The prices of primary products fell and exports earnings went so low that Latin America's capacity to import dropped some 50 percent in the period 1914-45.[9] The protection of domestic industry, the acceleration of local domestic industrial development through import substitution, and the pursuit of self-sufficiency became inevitable results. Protectionist policies in the face of price declines for traditional primary exports made investment in industry obviously more profitable than investment in the primary sector. In Chile, for instance, the number of factory employees increased over 33 percent between 1928-37, although the population grew only 6 percent; earnings from secondary industry increased by some 50 percent; textile, paper, glass, and cement industries became firmly established; and the contribution of the industrial sector to net national product came to exceed that of agriculture. The character and pace of the structural shifts differed from country to country, but Table 10.1 is indicative of some of the changes in production patterns.

The stimulus supplied to industrialization in various Latin American countries was even greater in the period of World War II. The difficulties of importing goods were greater than during World War I and the war lasted longer. But Latin America by this time had accumulated experience in using protectionism to stimulate substitute domestic manufacturing in crises of this kind. Brazil, for instance, supplies evidence of the shift in importance of agriculture and industry. In the years 1925-29, the index of agricultural production was 42.8 percent higher than the index of industrial production. For the period 1945-49, however, the index of industrial production was 33.7 percent higher than that of agriculture. Indeed, from 1925-29 to 1945-49, agricultural production increased 55.8 percent, but industrial production increased 197.5 percent.[10] Table 10.1 gives some indication of the expansion of industry in four Latin American countries during World War II.

The experience of using protectionist devices to counteract the shock of external crises led to the emergence in the late 1950s of the third feature which characterizes the evolution of industrial development in Latin America. This was

[6]See UN (1955, pp. 135, 136). Baer (1965, pp. 16-17) notes that 5936 new industrial establishments were set up between 1914-19, the value of industrial production increasing in real terms by 150 to 160 percent during the period.
[7]Baer (1965, p. 18).
[8]UN (1955, p. 138). Finished consumer goods included food, textiles, tobacco, furniture, jewelry and plate, musical instruments, toys and leather. Other finished goods included stone clay, metal and engineering implements, tools and instruments, vehicles and boats, rubber boots, and plastic goods. Intermediate materials included wood, paper, chemicals, leather and certain other semifinished materials. See also Poppino (1968, pp. 203-204).
[9]UNECLA (1964, p. 2). For a detailed survey of industrial development during the period 1919-49, see UN (1951).
[10]UN (1951, p. 204).

TABLE 10.1

Selected Indicators of Progress in Industrialization in Argentina, Brazil, Chile, and Mexico, 1915–47

	Argentina			Brazil			Chile			Mexico		
	1915	1938	1947	1915	1938	1947	1915	1938	1947	1915	1938	1947
Number of industrial establishments (in thousands)	40.2	44.3	83.9	13.0[a]	41.0	78.4[b]	4.3	19.0	—	48.1[c]	12.8	30.5[d]
Employment in industrial establishments (in thousands)	323	1,001	1,921	309[a]	835	128.3[b]	45	120	176	317[c]	270	440[d]
Net industrial production (millions of the natural currency at current prices)	643	1,006	6,992	—	6,957	49,235[b]	—	663[c]	3,802	508[c]	889	5,169
Motive power in manufacturing industry (installed power in units of a thousand horsepower)	634	698	1,271	—	—	—	—	—	—	—	—	—
Average net per capita output of manufactured goods (in current U.S. dollars)	84	24	105	—	9	52	—	18[c]	93	14[c]	8	38

[a] 1920. [b] 1951. [c] 1928. [d] 1944.

Source: UN (1955).

the general incorporation of these measures and instruments into officially adopted policies for the promotion of industrial and general economic development in most of Latin America. These policies emerged largely out of the common experience of protecting internal incomes and filling the demand gap under the conditions of uncertainty introduced by war and depression.[11] As a key Latin American official pointed out some time later, it is not always easy to separate from the variety of provisions constituting general economic policy those which are "specifically appropriate to industrial policy as such."[12] Industrial policy, however, generally came to include four types of "actions, measures, and objectives": (1) measures to protect domestic industry against foreign competition; (2) general measures to regulate and stimulate industry; (3) direct government promotion of industrial development; and (4) government provision for technical assistance to industry as well as measures "to facilitate the transfer of technology."[13] This industrial policy generally aimed at supplying incentives for the development of manufacturing activity, at stimulating particular types of industrial development, and at improving the efficiency and productivity of existing enterprises.[14] We appraise the effectiveness of these measures later in this chapter.

By the time of the Charter of Punta del Este, the change of data and the change in policy emphasis to meet the change of data had in turn induced basic shifts in the production structure of the major Latin American economies. Outward-looking policies had largely surrendered to the inward-looking drives after industrialization. By 1950, industrial not agricultural production dominated in terms of total value and percentage contribution to the gross domestic product. In that year, agricultural output was valued at $8603 million and manufacturing output at $10,155 million.[15] Indeed, agriculture employed 57.9 percent of the labor force but contributed only 25.8 percent of the gross product while the manufacturing industry and construction, with only 16.6 percent of the labor force, contributed 25.9 percent of the gross product. The product per worker in manufacturing and construction was estimated at $1078 (at 1950 prices) as against $308 in agriculture.

At the same time, the production of capital goods registered the strongest industrial acceleration. Chile, for instance, was producing steel in appreciable quantities in 1951 and 1952. The basic iron and steel industry was spreading to Argentina, Colombia, and Peru. Brazil and Mexico were increasing their capacity

---

[11] See Scitovsky (1969, pp. 34–35):

> The desire for economic self-sufficiency was a natural reaction to these experiences, and import substitution—industrialization behind a wall of protection—was the simplest and most obvious policy with which to implement this desire. Some countries even drifted into such a policy unwittingly.

> See also Macario (1964, p. 63): "Originally dictated by external factors, industrialization became, especially under the pressure of vested interests, a fundamental objective of the economic policy of the governments concerned."

[12] Reynoso (1969, p. 9). Reynoso spoke as Mexican Undersecretary of Industry and Commerce.

[13] Ibid., p. 9.

[14] Ibid., pp. 9–10.

[15] See UN (1953, p. 24). See also UNECLA (1963e, vol. 1, pp. 32, 33; vol. 2, pp. 17, 19, 20, 21).

and volume in this area. The expansion of this basic industry in turn generated the development of secondary mechanical industries and equipment factories.[16] Tables 7.3, 7.4, and Table A.38 all show that the manufacturing sector continued to outdistance the agricultural sector in total value of the sectoral product and in percentage of contribution to the gross domestic product.

Long before the 1960s, however, the Latin American demand for industrialization had become both an economic and emotional compulsion. It is difficult to separate one compulsion from the other, for they are practically indivisible, and will remain so for a long time to come. Hirschmann observes that "not long ago, industrialization ranked high among the policy prescriptions which were expected to lead Latin America and other underdeveloped areas out of their state of economic, social and political backwardness" (1969, p. 237). This is an understatement. The demand for industrialization has come to be fed by a nationalism which requires industrialization as an escape route from the inertia and feudal constraints of the agricultural sector and a cushion against the adverse effects of war and depression. The push for industrialization came to symbolize a revolt against colonial status, with primary production and external economic dependence as its symbols. The demand for industrialization expresses the Latin American determination to bridge the gap between underdevelopment and the economic status of a developed nation, in fact, nothing less than national equality with the developed nations. With the emotional drive behind industrialization, the tension springing from any frustration of this effort is likely to be of more than ordinary significance.[17]

General indicators of industrial growth in Latin America show substantial achievement, as we have seen. Table 7.4 shows that by 1968 manufacturing activity accounted for one fourth of the value of the gross domestic product— a larger share than agriculture, forestry, and fishing. The index of manufacturing production increased by some 40 percent in the period 1963–68 in 11 Latin American countries.[18] After electricity and construction, manufacturing, which grew at an average rate of 5.4 percent in the years 1961–68, for instance, was the most rapidly growing sector.[19] The figures for Argentina, with industry contributing over 35 percent of the value of the gross domestic product, make it appear more industrialized than the United States (31 percent) and Japan (28 percent).[20] The evidence of industrial transformation in Mexico is impressive. Industry grew at 8 percent a year in the period 1948–69. In the 1950s, Mexico made such a complete transition from the manufacture of consumer goods to the production of intermediate and basic goods that in the years 1960–68, pig iron production increased from 660,000 to 2 million tons; steel production from 1.5 million to 3.3 million tons; cement from 3.1 million tons to 6 million tons. Capital investment in the total of 136,000 industrial establishments in

[16] See UN (1953, pp. 179–181). See also Hanson (1951, pp. 137–139).

[17] Cf., for instance, Simonsen (1963, pp. 137–142). See also Nehemkis (1966, esp. pp. 167–182).

[18] See U.S. Department of State (1970aa, p. 12). Selected indexes for 1968 (1963 = 100); 11 Latin American Republics–138; Argentina–139; Brazil–134; Chile–117; El Salvador– 179; Guatemala–114; Mexico–159; Peru–141; Uruguay–102 (1967); Venezuela–131 (1967).

[19] Inter-American Development Bank (1969a, p. 13).

[20] *Ibid.,* pp. 15–17.

1965 amounted to some $8 billion.[21] Despite this overt evidence of substantial achievements in industrialization, a closer analysis of the results of the industrialization policies reveals equally substantial limitations to the acceleration of industrialization in Latin America.

The problems still confronting Latin American industrialization in no way invalidate the choice of industrialization for the development breakthrough which Latin America requires. The necessity for industrialization is clearly supported by all the evidence we have marshaled. The rescue operations of the Latin American governments in the face of the foreign trade crises were essential. But so long as the obstacles and difficulties confronting industrialization remain, they restrict the transformation of agriculture even while they restrict the prospects for general economic advance. We now turn to an identification of the major problems emerging from the policies of protectionism and import substitution.

INDUSTRIALIZATION: POLICIES, PROBLEMS, AND PROSPECTS

We have stressed the evolutionary character of the industrialization process in Latin America. Although the process was accelerated at the end of World War II, we must realize that this acceleration of manufacturing was hardly a planned, deliberate, and consistent process, nor were all features of the process common to all Latin American countries. Import-substituting industrialization, for instance, was indirectly stimulated by measures taken to protect the domestic economy against external disequilibrium. The major instruments of protectionism commonly consisted of tariffs, multiple exchange rates, and quantitative controls, but they varied in importance, emphasis, and detail from time to time and from country to country. For instance, the protective tariff largely dominant before the 1930s had to be reinforced by exchange controls in the 1930s to counteract the serious effect of the depression on the supply of foreign exchange. In turn, exchange controls were reinforced during the years of World War II and after by the use of direct quantitative controls.

It is true that direct government promotion of industry added massive impetus to the speeding up of industrialization. But in Mexico, for instance, Reynoso notes that despite the general belief that the government's support of industrialization began in 1947, the industrialization process began in the second quarter of the nineteenth century, encouraged by all Mexican governments "and, with greater intensity, by those of the post revolutionary period."[22] Substantial and direct government promotion of the process of industrialization in Latin America, particularly after World War II, in other words, has been only part of the whole picture.

GOVERNMENT PROMOTION OF INDUSTRIAL DEVELOPMENT: THE CASE OF MEXICO

A few indications of the range of direct and indirect state initiatives to accelerate industrialization supply some perspective on the evolution of industrial policy.

[21] Reynoso (1969, p. 16).
[22] Ibid., p. 12. See also UN (1966, p. 175).

The case of Mexico, for instance, is instructive. Although in many respects, the values inspiring Mexico's economic advances are unique, they nonetheless cast light on the industrial aspirations of Latin America which are part of the whole spectrum of political and social transformation which Latin America wants to achieve.

The industrial transformation of Mexico should be viewed as part and parcel of a total effort to mexicanize the national economy, with the public sector taking the leadership in stimulating and enforcing judicious subordination of all private economic activity—local and foreign, industrial and nonindustrial—to Mexican national sensitivities. In a sense, the Revolution thrust the government into the center of the stage as the key agent of economic change. The remarkable acceleration of industrial progress which Mexico achieved during World War II became possible not only because of the opportunities of the war but also because of economic innovations in Mexico before the war.[23] Apart from its peculiar restructuring of land ownership patterns in Mexico, the Mexican government brought the banking system under domestic control, poured an immense amount of money into infrastructure and public works, and supplied so much support and encouragement to Mexican entrepreneurs that by 1940 the private sector had more or less learned to coexist and cooperate with the public sector.[24] The state, as proclaimed in the first Six Year Plan and in the second Six Year Plan (1941–46), is expected to exercise an a priori rule in the regulation of economic conditions. In fact, the state assumes decisive authority in directing the national economy.[25]

The Mexican government backed industrial promotion with increased intensity during 1941–46 in at least four principal ways:

1. through the enactment of specific laws encouraging the development of new or essential manufacturing industries through exemption from or reduction of import duties or other taxes
2. through the institution of specialized credit agencies to grant credit for industrial development
3. through direct government action in specialized commissions
4. through international action in specific areas.

By decree of December 30, 1939, the Mexican government granted a five-year exemption from several taxes to new industries, at the same time disallowing these exemptions to industries which might compete with already-established industries. The Law of Manufacturing Industries enacted on April 21, 1941 (*Ley de Industrias de Transformación*) broadened the range of these benefits. By August, 1944, over 285 enterprises had been created under the new law in the following industrial fields among others: fibers, metallurgy and manufactured metal goods, construction materials, vehicles, ships, clothing, food products, wood products, chemicals and pharmaceuticals, and paper and pulp.

On December 31, 1945, Mexico passed a law for the development of manufacturing industries (*Ley de Fomento de Industrias de Transformación*). Under this law, new and necessary industries were redefined and specific conditions

---

[23] See, for instance, Glade and Anderson (1963, pp. 19–20).
[24] See, for instance, Vernon (1963, pp. 96–97).
[25] See UN, Department of Economic Affairs (1947, p. 3). Cf. Wionczek (1963, pp. 150–182); Kolbeck (1967, pp. 177–214); and UN (1950, esp. pp. 155–159).

set out under which they could earn exemption from or reduction of import duties as well as other taxes. In order of priority to Mexico's industrial development, new and necessary industries fell into three categories, and tax concessions varied with the order of importance. In the first category were industries considered basic to the industrial development of Mexico. These industries enjoyed tax exemptions and tax reductions for 10 years. The second category included industries with some but not fundamental importance. These industries enjoyed tax advantages for seven years. In the third category were industries which enjoyed tax advantages for five years. New and necessary industries were distinguished from basic and fundamental industries, the latter enjoying even greater concessions.[26] The exemption from or reduction of import duties on construction materials, machinery, equipment, spare parts, and tools required for domestic manufacturing rested upon another condition, namely, that these items be unobtainable or inadequately produced in Mexico.

At the same time, public power was used to accelerate the mexicanization of the money market under the Bank of Mexico by means of banking legislation and the solving of two critical problems. These problems were the supplying of credit to manufacturing activities which needed substantial sums of money and which were not attracting private initiative and the creation of a national stock market to attract private savings into investment and public bonds and thus support the industrialization efforts of the country. Once again, these developments must be viewed in an evolutionary light. Set up in 1925, as the central bank of Mexico, the Bank of Mexico (*Banco de México, S.A.*) became the sole bank of issue in Mexico, with full power to coordinate and regulate the banking and financial system of the country through measures which dealt with the control of liquidation, the regulation of the liabilities of the banking system, and the channeling of the funds of the banking system. The Bank of Mexico was able to play an increasingly critical role in the promotion of Mexico's economic development because of the control it enjoyed over the wide range of credit institutions which Mexico created to meet development needs. By law, all credit institutions—whether national, privately owned or agencies and branches of foreign banks—were required to subscribe to the shares of the Bank of Mexico. The general law for credit institutions enacted on May 3, 1941, distinguished between institutions engaged in purely commercial operations and those engaged in capital investments, and provided legal regulation of their activities accordingly. By 1944, an estimated 136 credit and auxiliary institutions were under the legal control of the Bank of Mexico.[27]

Among the most important of the new specialized credit institutions ushered in by law were the *financieras*, which came into existence to promote development through the channeling of local and national capital into long-term investment. Their establishment therefore symbolized an expansion of public power into the control of the long-term capital investment market of Mexico—traditionally a foreign enclave. One year after legally approving the establishment

---

[26] See Reynoso (1969, p. 13).

[27] These included the following national credit institutions created for specialized credit: *Banco Nacional de Credito Agricola*; *Banco Nacional de Credito Ejidal*; *Banco de Fomento Cooperativo*; *Banco Nacional Hipotecario y de Obras Publicas*; *Banco Nacional de Comercio Exterior*; *Nacional Financiera, S.A.* See UN (1947, p. 7).

of private *financieras*, the government created the National Financial Society (*Nacional Financiera, S.A.*) by decree of December 27, 1933. It was given supervisory and regulatory power over national security and long-term credit markets, as well as power to promote investment capital for every kind of enterprise at any stage, to support Mexican finance and investment companies, to supervise and direct the functioning of stock exchanges, and to act as a finance and investment company, a savings bank, and an advisory body to various levels of government in all financial matters. Under a 1940 law, *Nacional Financiera, S.A.*, was given power to financially support enterprises concerned with production which found it difficult to attract private capital and to create a national stock market which could guide private savings into investment in public bonds and other bonds essential to accelerating Mexico's industrialization.

By the end of the war years, *Nacional Financiera, S.A.*, had invested directly or through bond acquisition in the following industries, among others: cement, cinema, coal, electrical appliances (*Industria Eléctrica de México*). fertilizers (*Guanos y Fertilizantes, S.A.*), hydroelectric power (*Cia, Hidro-electrica de Chapala*), paper (*Compañia Industrial de Atentique, S.A.*), rayon (*Celanese y Viscosa Mexicana*), and steel (*Altos Hornos de México*), In the years 1941-46 the bank had supplied over 400 million pesos in credit to a variety of Mexican private entrepreneurs active in producing artificial fibers, canned goods, cement, movies, glass, coal, fertilizers, electrolytic copper, electrical appliances, gasoline, paper, steel, highway equipment, sugar, hydroelectricity, railroad equipment, electric generators, and so on.

After the war Mexico's industrialization drives intensified. Under the leadership of the public sector, despite changes in detail, there was an obvious continuity in the instruments used to accelerate internal industrial development. In 1954, for instance, Mexico passed a law for the development of new and necessary industries (*Ley de Fomento de Industrias Nuevas y Necessarias*) which is still of importance and force. Under the new law, the granting of incentives to industry became subject to such considerations as the quantity of raw materials to be utilized by the new industries, the technological investment and research status of the industry, employment prospects, the contribution of the industry to the domestic market and to the export of manufactures, and the social significance of the industry. A greater degree of selectivity in industrial support emerged with the new law.

By 1959 the import permit became, according to Mexican evidence, the most important instrument for the protection of industry.[28] From the enabling act of Article 28 of the Mexican constitution the government derived its power to prohibit imports to be sold in Mexico under conditions of unfair competition and to restrict other imports and exports according to the economic needs of the country. The control of imports and import permits not only protects existing industry but encourages the establishment of new industries which meet the nation's requirements. Factors taken into account include the location of the industries according to prejudged national advantages, increased use of domestic output for the manufacture of finished products, and the extent and character of foreign participation in certain enterprises and the use of natural resources. The domestic manufacture of certain imported goods is permitted only when

[28] Reynoso (1969, p. 13). See also Macario (1964, p. 67).

the manufacture of these goods is shown to be economically feasible. After 1962, the import permit began to be one of the most effective instruments to secure and to accelerate the integration of domestic Mexican industry.

To summarize: to safeguard the country against external imposed disorganization, the role of government had to be different from nineteenth-century laissez faire expectations and also from expectations in the United States where private entrepreneurial decision-making dominates. In almost every area, the government influences, if not controls, development in the nonindustrial as well as the industrial sectors. It insures that private entrepreneurship—whether local or foreign—works harmoniously within the framework of Mexican national values as spelled out by the Revolution. Mexico rejected all development which cut across these national values. At the same time, the public sector has demonstrated such national self-discipline that its actions were geared to support, bolster, and encourage both Mexican and foreign private enterprise, provided these were prepared to work harmoniously within the national values. To insure this, as well as to accelerate domestic manufacturing development in accordance with national needs, credit and capital were brought under public control and influence through the measures we have described. To attribute Mexico's spectacular economic development to the role of the Bank of Mexico, *Nacional Financiera, S.A.*, and the effect of import controls would be inaccurate. The effectiveness of these institutions and devices must be related to a whole mass of interrelated factors for which the government was directly or indirectly responsible. Among these factors are the development of technical training, developments at all levels of education, the continuing vigor of institutional innovation in the public and private sectors, the maintenance of nondogmatic attitudes to local as to foreign private capital, the pursuit of political mobility, and pragmatic monetary and fiscal policies.[29]

We have indicated earlier the impressive gains in the structural transformation of the Mexican economy. Table 10.2 shows the decisive key position occupied by the Mexican government by 1962. In addition, the government held a controlling interest in several other industries and exercised almost complete authority in banking and finance, consumer distribution, and other areas.[30] In 1960s,

[29] See, for instance, Bank of Mexico (1967, pp. 60–66) and Inter-American Development Bank (1961, sections on Mexico).

[30] Government-controlled industries included Mexico's only railroad car manufacturing plant; the second largest automobile and truck assembly plant; two of the largest textile mills; Mexico's only newsprint manufacturing plant; a large sugar mill; the largest electrical products manufacturing concern; a meat packing plant, a shipbuilding concern, and a warehouse business. See Brandenburg (1962, p. 10). There are of course immense differences in the operational role of the state in Latin America. In some Latin American countries, public industrial activity appears overwhelmingly dominant in some sectors. For example, CVF sugar mills account for 40 percent of Venezuela's production. In Columbia public industrial activity accounts for 100 percent of the production of caustic soda, 60 percent of petroleum refining and 40 percent of fertilizers. In Brazil it accounts for some 85 percent of the petroleum refining and 45 percent of the production of steel ingots. In Argentina it accounts for 60 percent of the production of steel ingots. In other sectors, public industrial activity is very small. In Argentina it accounts for only 4 percent of the production of motor vehicles and in Brazil in the same field it accounts for one percent. In actual fact, taking the whole sector into account, public industrial enterprises amount to only a small share of the total industrial production and in Brazil only 6.3 percent. See UN (1966, pp. 174–175).

TABLE 10.2

Mexico: Nonprivately Owned Sectors of the Economy, 1962

	Percentage owned by the state
Communications and transportation	
Telegraph	100
Railroads	97
Municipal railways	92
Maritime transportation (by tonnage)	70
Docks and other port facilities	90
International commercial aviation (owned domestically, according to projects pending)	65
Newsprint manufacture by paper mills in which state owns majority equity	100
Newsprint distribution	100
Motion picture distribution and exhibition	80
Motion picture production (financing)	35
Basic industries	
Electric power (installed capacity)	85
Electric power (sales to public)	96
Petroleum exploration (ownership of sells, natural gas reserves, oil lines and gas lines)	97
Petroleum refining	96
Petrochemicals (percent of total investments)	70
Iron and steel production (by mills in which the state enjoys majority control)	60
Other indicators	
Private investment as percent of total investment, 1950	61.1
Private investment as percent of total investment, 1961	55.0
Percentage of total national investment directly attributable to foreign capital, 1951	13
Percentage of total national investment directly attributable to foreign capital, 1961	23

Source: Brandenburg (1962, pp. 9-11).

Mexican manufacturing expanded at an average rate of 8.8 percent a year, one of the highest rates in the world. Public policy can be credited for this remarkable achievement, for governmental policy showed innovative flexibility all through the 1960s. The government continued to control imports, credit, and key productive activities, and the government continued to invest in electric power generation, irrigation, and road construction. All of these activities were supportive of speeding up manufacturing development. In addition, the government initiated policies to upgrade domestic efficiency through quality control, better management practices, and the maintaining of intermediate and raw materials at steady prices.[31]

[31] See Inter-American Development Bank (1969a, p. 381). The reader may wish to compare the experience of Mexico with that of Brazil. See Baer (1965). See also Furtado (1970, esp. pp. 113-199).

Despite the vigor of Mexico's inward-looking policies to promote internal industrialization under protectionist devices, there are still formidable constraints to the transforming of the economy at the speed required to meet the country's needs. The problems which remain to be resolved are predictable.

IMPORT-SUBSTITUTING INDUSTRIALIZATION UNDER PROTECTIONISM

Generalizations can be dangerous, but we must now attempt a summary of the obstacles to industrialization resulting from a policy of import-substituting industrialization, not only in Mexico but throughout Latin America. Hirschman declared that, in the last few years in Latin America, "considerable disenchantment . . . has set in" with industrialization which "ranked high among the policy prescriptions" as the "particular solution of the development problem" (1969, p. 237).[32] Hirschman's penetrating and constructive views, of course, are based on hindsight; and the term *disenchantment* may give an ambiguous impression which can distort perspectives.

In the first instance, it must be recognized that Latin America cannot retreat from the path of industrialization and that Latin America will hardly retreat from protectionism in the near future. Industrialization is not an alternative path to economic salvation in Latin America; it is the essential escape route backed both by emotional compulsion and economic rationality. This credo is succinctly expressed, for instance, in Urquidi's observation that "industrialization as such does not need to be justified today; it is the only means of attaining a permanent rise in the standard of living."[33] Second, with its emotional revulsion against a colonial status, its frequent exposure to economic shocks, the revealed weakness of its international bargaining power as a primary producer, and the conflict between the operation of foreign capital and the region's ambition to build an independent and viable internal economy, Latin America has had no choice but that of protectionism and the use of public power to influence decision-making. Third, to judge Latin America's import-substituting industrialization efforts by standards which attribute theoretical advantages to free trade as against protectionism constitute an empty exercise.[34] Free trade has always been as much a myth as laissez faire. Latin America could pursue no other economic course but that of industrializing through protectionism. It is hardly likely that protectionism will be abandoned readily in the near future because one fundamental condition is not likely to change in the near future. That condition is the continuing dependence of Latin America on primary products for foreign exchange and its continued dependence on foreign imports. Table 7.9 illustrates the first point. Tables 7.10 and 7.11 reveal the continuation of Latin America's weak export-import price exchange ratio. We may note that in the period 1914–45 Latin America's capacity to import, after falling by some 50 percent following the decline in export earnings, did not recover to the pre-1914 level.[35] But since internal demand remained the same and there was a foreign exchange shortage, the gap could be filled only by stimulating domestic

[32] For a broad critical survey of protectionist policies in developing countries including Latin America, see Maddison (1970, esp. 63–90).
[33] Urquidi (1967, p. 173).
[34] Cf. Myint (1971, pp. 147–173).
[35] UNECLA (1964, p. 2).

production. This situation still prevails. Under these circumstances, rational consideration of the disadvantages of free trade was an irrelevant exercise.

Finally, an industrial revolution takes time. It is an adjustment experience which is sometimes beyond the comprehension of homogeneous or new societies like Western Europe and the United States where a separate export sector does not even exist because the economy provides at one and the same time for internal and external needs, and where foreign capital is marginal to the needs of the economy. In fact, Alexander calmly rationalizes the defects of the import-substituting process. With protection and import substitution, a readymade market is there. Profits are easy, and costs and inefficiency are irrelevant since consumers have no choice but to buy domestic goods. Agricultural development can be ignored, since high profits can easily be made within the existing market. Only when the import-substituting strategy reaches a point of exhaustion must matters change and markets be expanded to continue the process of development and growth.[36] The point of importance is not disenchantment with the industrialization process but Latin America's recognition of the dilemmas and costs thrown up by protectionism and its determination to devise and follow through on solutions to the revealed problems. Abandonment of industrialization is out of the question as is abandonment of protectionism, except within the framework of an integrated Latin American market. We now identify some of the major problems created by the policies of import-substituting industrialization under protectionism.

We have argued that import-substituting industrialization was an unavoidable choice. In fact, UNECLA legitimately creating a principle of the circumstances under which "externally geared development" must give place, as in Latin America, to "internally geared development" observed:

When it is impossible to maintain or to accelerate the previous growth rate of traditional exports, recourse is had to import substitution—chiefly industrial items—in an attempt to counteract these disparities, and thus begins the internally-geared development of the Latin American countries.[37]

Import substitution achieved a remarkable position for Latin America, namely, one of the lowest import coefficients in the world (the ratio between imports and the total domestic product). In 1929, imports for Latin America as a whole accounted for 20 to 25 percent of the total domestic product.[38] In 1945–49, the import coefficient stood at 13.1 percent. In 1960 it dropped to 10.8 percent.[39] In 1964 it dropped again, to 9.4 percent.[40] Brazil, with an import coefficient of 3.6, had the lowest import coefficient in Latin America.

The significance of import coefficients is, however, subject to a good deal of

---

[36] See Alexander (1968, pp. 297–308).

[37] UNECLA (1963e, p. 104).

[38] UN (1966, p. 21).

[39] UNECLA (1963d, vol. 1, p. 24).

[40] Pan American Union (IA–ECOSOC)(1967i, p. 22). Cf. UNECLA (1963d, vol. 1, p. 28):

indices . . . assessing the share of imports of consumer goods in total consumption, of capital goods and building materials in fixed investment and of imports of fuels, raw materials and intermediate goods in the domestic product . . . roughly correspond to what are usually called import coefficients.

qualification. A low import coefficient is not always an index of significant advance in the industrialization effort and growth in total product—although it may be so in some countries. In Argentina, for instance, imports amounted to 6.2 percent of the gross domestic product in 1960, but the GDP grew only 2.3 percent and the manufacturing sector only 2.9 percent. The pattern of correlation varies so much from country to country that the reduction of the import coefficient cannot be listed as a firm achievement for industrialization under protectionism.

The progressive lowering of import ratios in Latin America changed the composition of Latin American imports, but it did not necessarily end the degree of dependence on foreign imports nor did import substitution necessarily save on scarce foreign exchange. There is strong evidence that import substitution may have reached its limits and even that an upturn in imports may be necessary to revive or give added dynamism to the industrialization drive. What the United Nations called "the stage of easy substitution" has now practically passed in Latin America.[41] The easy substitution stage involved extensive substitution for imports of consumer goods and to a lesser extent for imports of capital goods. In the years 1949–59, for instance, the proportion of consumer goods as a percentage of total imports dropped from 22.0 percent to 20.3 percent (see Table A.49). An even greater decline occurred in the case of capital goods. On the other hand, the proportion went up for fuels and for intermediate goods.

By 1960, many Latin American countries were approaching self-sufficiency in the area of manufactured consumer goods (see Table 10.3). But the intermediate and capital goods sector still remained a difficult challenge for import substitution breakthroughs. The foodstuffs, beverage, and tobacco industries accounted in 1960 for some 37 percent of total manufacturing production in Venezuela, some 20 percent in Argentina, 20 percent in Brazil, and 35 percent in Colombia. Despite this uniformly high participation of the foodstuffs, beverage, and tobacco industries in the production of manufactured goods, the import component of supplies for these industries was almost uniformly low. On the other hand, the import component of supplies of capital goods remained uniformly high. In Brazil and Argentina, where the domestic production of capital goods amounted to some 70 and 60 percent, respectively, of the total supply of these goods, the import component of supplies amounted to the relatively high figures of 40.4 and 23.7 percent. Contrastingly, in Chile and in Peru, where domestic production of capital goods amounted to some 30 percent and 10 percent respectively of total production, the import content of the total supply of capital goods in 1960 was still very high—amounting to 73 percent and 88.3 percent respectively.

Import substitution does not guarantee any lessening of dependence on the external sector. The development of one industry necessarily generates new interindustry requirements, particularly in terms of intermediate products. This in turn generates new import requirements and leads to an elevation, not a lessening, of import coefficients. In fact, a comparison of Table 10.3 and and Table 10.4 shows that in Latin America, manufacturing production was fastest in precisely those industries where the import component was highest.

[41] UNECLA (1963d, vol. 4, p. 105).

TABLE 10.3

Import Component of Manufactured Goods, 1960 (In percent)

	Argentina	Brazil	Chile	Colombia	Mexico	Peru	Venezuela
Import component of total supply of							
Manufactured goods	6.8	8.5	16.4	15.8	16.6	18.4	26.8
Consumer goods	1.4	2.1	5.1	2.8	5.0	7.8	n.a.
Intermediate goods	8.2	7.1	19.0	12.2	12.3	14.1	n.a.
Capital goods	23.7	40.4	73.0	82.4	70.2	88.3	n.a.
Import component of total goods produced in sectors of							
Foodstuffs, beverages and tobacco	0.1	1.0	6.4	1.5	1.9	5.3	10.2
Textiles	2.1	0.1	4.4	4.4	3.9	5.8	28.7
Clothing and shoes	—	—	1.1	0.6	2.0	5.6	6.3
Lumber and wooden furniture	6.6	—	0.6	2.1	2.1	3.2	9.1
Paper and paper products	14.7	12.6	14.3	31.2	13.1	21.2	31.3
Consumer goods	—	—	—	5.0	—	—	a
Intermediate goods	16.1	13.7	19.0	38.4	14.6	23.3	—
Capital goods	—	—	—	73.1	—	—	—
Publishing and printing materials	0.4	2.7	8.8	—	4.1	2.7	7.9
Leather	—	—	3.6	—	16.4	—	12.5
Rubber	7.7	—	12.1	6.9	4.3	7.9	17.5
Chemical products, petroleum, and coal, total	7.0	14.4	33.6	19.0	17.6	23.7	13.2
Consumer goods	4.7	10.6	23.9	3.8	8.9	22.6	a
Intermediate goods	8.6	17.5	45.0	22.8	24.2	24.1	a
Capital goods	—	—	14.3	73.1	—	—	—
Nonmetallic minerals	1.6	1.1	7.3	5.1	4.4	4.5	18.0
Metals and metal products, total	15.9	19.0	49.0	44.0	37.9	51.4	76.4
Consumer goods	4.8	2.7	17.7	20.8	16.8	38.5	83.0
Intermediate goods	11.7	6.2	12.6	8.1	5.0	12.8	44.7
Capital goods	24.5	41.0	81.8	84.8	70.0	91.1	96.7
Other industries	2.9	6.2	5.7	15.0	31.8	17.4	76.6

a No data available.

Source: Pan American Union (IA-ECOSOC) (1967), Table C-4.

TABLE 10.4

Quantum Indexes of Manufacturing Production (1963 = 100)

	1960	1961	1962	1963	1964	1965	1966
Food, beverages, and tobacco	87	90	96	100	104	108	117
Textiles	97	100	99	100	110	110	111
Clothing and footwear	98	101	100	100	114	116	123
Paper and paper products	80	89	93	100	110	117	127
Leather	122	114	108	100	109	116	119
Rubber	87	94	100	100	113	122	137
Chemicals, petroleum, and coal products	78	89	96	100	112	119	128
Non-metallic mineral products	92	96	100	100	111	116	125
Basic metals	83	88	92	100	116	120	132
Metal products, machinery, and transport equipment	89	103	104	100	116	123	135
Total	88	94	98	100	111	116	124

Source: CEPAL (1969a).

On the other hand, though it is urgent that Latin America pursue industrialization, the intermediate and capital goods stage is particularly difficult to establish for a variety of reasons. For one thing, there is bound to be a certain lag in transferring resources to intermediate and capital goods industries from consumer goods industries, the traditional outlet for import substitution activities. Overconcentration in consumer goods industries is not easily changed. But more than this, the development of intermediate and capital goods industries would demand far greater resources in terms of capital, entrepreneurial capacities, and manpower skills, and a market far wider than the limited market of the several individual countries of Latin America.[42] In Latin America these boundary conditions cannot readily be overcome.

The root of the shortcomings of import-substituting industrialization in Latin America lies in the *ad hoc*, indiscriminate, and disorderly beginnings and development of the process under protectionism. Import-substituting industrialization in Latin America frequently worked out to be a case of promoting internal industrialization at any cost. Although the situation is changing, the legacy of past policy persists. Protection in Latin America, because of this disorderly

[42] Brazil offered an exceptionally favorable situation for industrialization precisely because of the size and structure of the domestic market. But as UNECLA (1964aa, p. 57) notes: "The items that currently make up the major part of Brazil's imports and include categories suitable for substitution are capital goods. These are, however, products of consequential demand which does not itself justify substitution. Where will the demand come from to warrant such substitution?"

process, is not established at any uniform levels. It may range from zero to over 300 percent.[43] Tariffs remain uniformly high in many countries, unrelated to any clearly conceived development priorities, and more geared to revenue mobilization than to speeding up development. Together with other restrictions, tariffs aid the perpetuation of high production costs; competitive inefficiency; inflation pressures; regional imbalance and urban concentration; severe maldistribution of income; biases against export; administration and retardation of progress towards Latin American economic integration, sometimes without compensatory savings in foreign exchange. While all this is explicable in historical terms, and though corrections are being made with varying degrees of vigor, these impediments delay the speed of the over-all development of Latin America and therefore delay the resolution of social tensions.

The evidence is overwhelming that, with few exceptions, the incidence of import duties and charges is an invitation to administrative chaos, corruption, or delay. The new Industrial Development Law enacted in Guatemala in 1959 to replace the earlier law of 1947 is typical of Latin American intentions. The law, in an attempt to stimulate the manufacture of a wider variety of products in larger quantities, raised duties by 20 percent or more on a list of items produced in the country and on luxury items. It provided for tax and import duty exemptions for new industries and for existing industries planning expansion of production.[44] Macario, however, noted that, in actual operation, most if not all Latin American imports, including raw materials and capital goods, were dutiable, that in most cases the duties were exceptionally high in comparison with duties for similar products on the European Economic Community tariff schedule, and that, paradoxically, duties were highest on all imports which competed with Latin America's traditional exports and where protection was presumably least necessary.[45] High duties on raw materials, intermediate products, and capital goods obviously rob protectionism of rationality and indeed reduce the effects of protection.[46]

Indiscriminate policies bolstered high costs and great inefficiencies. In many cases, the more inefficient the industry and the lower it stood in the scale of manufacturing development priorities, the more protection it received. In Mexico, for instance, traditional policies protected industries which produced high-priced products. These high prices in turn limited domestic demand and factored out the products from international competition.[47] Because of these traditional policies, obsolete industrial plants survived and it was difficult to scrap these obsolete structures because of the effect on employment.

High costs and high prices perpetuated by traditional protectionist policies isolated the lower income group from the benefits of industrialization; discouraged individual enterprises from adjusting to economies of scale; and isolated much Latin American industry from the wider world of international competition. Because of protection, high prices, and high profits, there was either too

[43] Statement by Eugenio Heireman, president of the Chilean Manufacturers Association, in Inter-American Development Bank (1969b, p. 73).
[44] Bank of Guatemala (n.d., p. 24). See also Bank of the Republic (Colombia) (n.d., pp. 65–75) for a detailing of taxation incentives in Colombia for national and foreign investors.
[45] Macario (1964, pp. 74–78).
[46] *Ibid.*, p. 77.
[47] Reynoso (1969, p. 18).

much competition, which generated wastage of scarce resources without gain through the reduction of product prices, or too little competition, which fostered the entrenchment of inefficient monopolies.[48] It is important to note that monopolies are not always bad. Monopolies are sometimes essential for efficiency in some industrial activities, but the protectionism resulting in monopolies in Latin America is not likely to have encouraged maximum efficiency.[49]

Indiscriminate protectionism encouraged even further urbanization, further geographical concentration of industry, and further regional disparities and sectoral imbalances—problems which we have already discussed. The policies pursued frequently ignored agricultural development in favor of industrial development. The undercapitalization of agriculture in turn contributed to lower agricultural production, high food prices, and inflationary pressures. It also helped to accelerate migration from the rural areas into the cities, to increase urban unemployment, and, of course, to support terms of trade favoring industry rather than the rural sector. New industry tends to concentrate where industry already exists because of external economic advantages and because that is where the market is. Supporting the establishment of new industry where industry already exists only leads to the freezing of industrial concentration and further regional disparities. At the end of the 1960s, Mexico, for instance, was still confronted by the problem of geographical concentration; 50 percent of the value of Mexico's industrial production was concentrated in the Federal District and only 3 percent in 11 federal subdivisions.[50]

Paradoxically, because of the traditional protectionist policies pursued, Latin America remains rigidly dependent on a few critical imports vital to the maintenance of the import-substituting industries, while, on the other hand, discouraging exports, the earnings from which are essential to the accumulation of vital foreign exchange, often without any significant saving in foreign exchange. Latin America's exports suffered because protection afforded higher profits in the domestic market, while many Latin American products were priced out of the world market. A circular problem confronted Latin America. Because the fastest-growing industries were precisely those in which the import content was highest, Latin America had to increase its production of capital and intermediate goods for export to maximize its capacity to secure imports essential for accelerating import substitution in the intermediate and capital goods area.[51]

In foreign exchange, the disorderly import-substituting policies ushered in only unprofitable results in many cases. One estimate, for instance, showed that in the production of tractors, Argentina used $7 of domestic resources to save one dollar of foreign exchange. The figures in Table 10.5 show graphically the

[48] See Scitovsky (1969, p. 42).

[49] See comment in UNECLA (1964aa, pp. 9–10). But cf. UNECLA (1963, vol. 1, p. 72):

In the shelter of high tariff barriers and other import restrictions or prohibitions, anti-competitive practices, if not virtually monopolistic combines, have become widespread. Well-equipped establishments operate alongside others where costs are high, in a sort of tacit mutual benefit society, the latter safe-guarding their marginal existence and the former reaping the big profits that accrue from the cost differential.

[50] See Reynoso (1969, p. 19). See also UNECLA (1964aa, pp. 52–53). Cf. Newsweek (1967, pp. 60–66).

[51] For further discussion, see Pan American Union (1963d, p. 31) and Inter-American Development Bank (1963a, p. 3). Pan American Union (IA-ECOSOC) (1967i, pp. 88–92).

TABLE 10.5

Average Effective Rates of Protection (In Percentages)

	All Manu- facturing	Consumer goods	Intermediate goods	Capital goods
Argentina	246.0	220.0	315.0	194.0
Brazil	118.0	160.0	89.0	100.0
Mexico	32.6	34.0	27.6	34.7
Japan	29.5	50.5	29.2	22.0
United Kingdom	27.8	40.4	28.7	23.0
United States	20.0	25.9	23.1	13.9
European economic community	18.6	30.9	20.0	15.0
Sweden	12.5	23.9	13.0	12.1

Source: Scitovsky (1969, p. 38).

percentage excess of the value of domestic resources used over the value of foreign exchange saved. Argentina is obviously an extreme case among the countries listed. Argentina paid on average 246 percent more for domestic resources than it would have paid had the imports been supplies by a foreign firm which was not restricted by a protectionist policy.[52]

The protectionist policies pursued inevitably resulted in the use of the authority of the state to modify the workings of the price mechanism and the establishment of a government bureaucracy to administer regulations. A brief indication of the difficulties which emerged will suffice. Overvalued exchange rates, for example, led to excessive importation and inefficient use of scarce resources. We have seen that government engaged in direct promotion of domestic industry. But public institutionalization for industrial promotion, despite remarkable achievements in many countries, involves inevitable problems—problems of instability in political leadership and sudden changes in direction; problems of coordination and consultation between central planning agencies, sectoral planning agencies, and regional planning agencies, and between the public and private sectors of the economy; problems emerging from informational inadequacies and shortages of trained personnel; problems of follow-up, auditing, and budgetary relationships.

In an earlier chapter we attempted to set out the dimensions of the problem of manpower absorption in Latin America. Given the rate of growth of the population, the intensity of the rural exodus, and the occupational distortions characterizing the distribution of the labor force, Latin Americans expected that accelerated industrialization would solve the problem of manpower absorption. Industrialization, however, has not fulfilled this hope. Indeed, as it is, Latin America confronts an essentially agonizing choice in industrial advance— between increasing output ("the efficiency criteria") and increasing employment ("the employment criteria"). The maximizing of output and the maximizing of employment do not necessarily go together. Manufacturing has not been able to absorb the growing labor force. In Brazil, for instance, evidence indicates that

[52] See Scitovsky (1969, pp. 37–38) and Macario (1964, p. 81).

almost all the increase in urban labor—some 1.5 to 2 million persons a year—ended up in the urban services sector where low productivity, low income, and high levels of open and disguised unemployment prevail.[53]

In fact the situation may get worse. Modern manufacturing in Latin America has tended to be less and less labor intensive, and therefore less and less effective in absorbing manpower. A number of factors tend to push matters in this direction, among them import substitution and protection, which enlarges and consolidates the market for domestic manufactures; importation from advanced countries of machinery developed for the larger demands of developed countries; the actual characteristics of markets for industrial goods and for construction; and the drive toward higher and higher productivity to meet emergency development needs. The development of capital intensive industry has tended to emerge more and more as a response to the rise in labor costs resulting from legally imposed social benefits for workers, or as a response to existent or anticipated trade union pressures or labor uncertainties. In many cases, capital intensive industry is encouraged because there is such a shortage of skilled labor that the only choice is intensified technological concentration. Certainly, the employment criterion gets a better chance with the more backward artisan subsector and the traditional industries of Latin America. But the productivity criterion does not.

CONCLUSIONS

The object of this chapter has not been to generate pessimism about the prospects for industrialization in Latin America. Accelerated industrialization is essential to accelerated economic development in Latin America. We have seen, however, that the evolution of import-substituting industrialization has left Latin America with problems which may not be resolved readily in the short run. Undoubtedly, as Reynoso points out for Mexico, the dilemmas have been recognized and new policies are being promulgated to modify the biases against export and competition and toward high cost and inefficiency, which were generated by traditional protectionist policies.[54] Once again, there is firm grasp of reality in this area of Latin American endeavor. Despite population pressures and the urgent demand for social solutions, the dilemmas confronting industrialization must be solved. But Latin American nationalism is mobilizing new initiatives to modify systematically the biases unavoidably thrown up by traditional protectionist policies—policies which were, however, essential to safeguarding the Latin American economy against the consequences of unexpected external shocks. We deal next with the question of mobilizing financial resources to meet the industrialization and general development needs of Latin America.

[53] See CEPAL (1968b). See also UNECLA (1964aa, vol. 1, pp. 53–54) and Reynoso (1969, pp. 19–20).
[54] The Mexican government, for instance, is attempting to improve the productivity and efficiency of existing industries. New import authorizations are being granted for a period of not more than five years provided that the price of the domestic product not exceed 25 percent of the international price. Obsolete and inefficient industry is losing government support. Government is encouraging; processing industries as well as small rural, farm, livestock, and fishing industries to increase worker incomes as well as provide more jobs. Excessive protectionism is being reduced and the Mexican government is fully supporting efforts for the speeding up of Latin American economic integration. See also UN (1966, pp. 227–272).

CHAPTER 11

CAPITAL FORMATION, THE MOBILIZING OF DOMESTIC RESOURCES, AND EXTERNAL FINANCING

CAPITAL FORMATION AND DEVELOPMENT

In this chapter, we concentrate on the problem of capital formation in Latin America. Arguments as to whether capital formation takes first place or not as a determinant of growth (or Griffin's reservations (1969, p. 117) that the use of the famous Harrod-Domar model, with its emphasis on capital inputs generating increased incomes and in turn making possible more capital formation, can be "misleading") do not invalidate the fact that capital formation is essential for development.[1] Griffin argues that the problem of countries like "Spanish America . . . is not so much 'growth' as it is development." Growth can take place, it is true, without development, but there can be no development without growth and capital formation is a key determinant of the rate of growth of the economy.

The general relationships are well established. The rate of capital formation depends upon the rate of investment and the capital–output ratio. In turn, the rate of investment is dependent on the rate of domestic savings and on the rate of supply of foreign investment.[2] It is clear, however, from our earlier analysis of socioeconomic variables in Latin America, that capital formation is not sufficient condition for economic development. But it is a necessary condition.

The Charter of Punta del Este recognized capital mobilization as a vital priority along with the other major goals of the Alliance for Progress. Participating Latin American countries agreed to incorporate self-help efforts toward "more effective, rational and equitable mobilization and use of financial resources through the reform of tax structures." The participating countries also recognized the necessity to "obtain sufficient external financial assistance . . . in order to supplement domestic capital formation and reinforce their import

---

[1]See, for instance, Kindleberger (1965, pp. 83–103).

[2]The general relationships can be expressed in the following formulas:

Capital formation equals proportion of national income which is invested;

Domestic savings equals personal or household savings plus business saving plus government savings (that is, equals government revenues for development or total tax revenue minus government recurrent expenditures);

Savings-income ratio equals savings as a proportion of the gross domestic product;

Capital-output ratio equals amount of investment needed to increase national output by one unit;

Rate of growth of the economy equals savings ratio over capital output ratio.

For an explanation of these relationships, see Tinbergen and Boss (1962, pp. 15–31) and UN (1960, pp. 8–18).

capacity."[3] If Prebisch (1970, p. 123) is to be followed, one of the purposes of accelerating domestic capital formation in Latin America is to remove the need for external financial assistance by raising the coefficient of domestic investment resources to cover over time the whole of the investment required. But on the evidence presented by Prebisch, the Latin American economy at the end of the 1960 decade was still not saving enough to accelerate economic development as rapidly as needed.

In this chapter, we examine indicative trends and problems related to the financing of economic development in Latin America. First, we review various estimates of investment requirements for Latin American development and attempt to form a general picture of the rate and patterns of capital formation. Second, we review trends in the performance of the public sector in the mobilization and use of resources for development. Third, we summarize the trends in external financing and conclude with a brief assessment of the problems to be resolved in the interest of more effective mobilization and use of resources.

Estimating Investment Needs

Generalizations about the critical role of capital in economic development are easy because the general evidence is there. Quantifying the rate of capital formation, however, is an elusive task in Latin America. Gross fixed capital is usually taken into account, and working capital more or less ignored—a common error of government planners in developing countries, as Enke (1963, p. 212) points out. There is incomplete data on changes in stocks, especially in the field of manufacturing, and incomplete data on fixed capital stock by sectors. This, of course, makes for an incomplete picture of the total economy. There is incomplete data on the marginal productivity of investment in Latin America, making it difficult to evaluate the effects of price changes and other factors on changes in capital formation and to assess accurately the relations between changes in capital formation and changes in the rate of economic growth.[4] Apart from the implications for further research, the valid point here is that it takes time to resolve these uncertainties, and as long as they exist, they are stumbling blocks to calculations for accelerating economic development in Latin America.

There are, of course, any number of uncertainties which make for difficulty in estimating desired levels of investment in relation to desired rates of economic growth. Correlations between investment coefficients and the rates of growth of the domestic product, therefore, are not easy to establish.[5] Argentina enjoyed a

---

[3]See U.S. House (1966, pp. 95, 104, 105). In support of well-conceived programs, the Latin American countries were to obtain over the next 10 years (1961–71) at least $20 billion capital from external sources, largely from public funds and largely for the relatively less developed countries. See also Pan American Union (1967g, pp. 17–18).

[4]See Carranza (1967, p. 121).

[5]Cf. U.S. House (1969, p. 55). Predictions of the productivity of investment or the adequacy of its level to produce a desired growth rate, based on comparisons with current or recent rates of investment and growth, may not work out for several reasons. After the gestation period, for instance, costs may turn out to be more than anticipated. New facilities may have produced more but old facilities may have produced less. Anticipated market demand may fail. Private decisions to invest are affected by a very wide range of variables—confidence about profits and opportunities, managerial know-how. Political factors can also affect productivity.

high rate of capital formation for the periods 1951-54 and 1955-59, but the gross domestic product between 1948-49 and 1959-60 grew at an annual average rate of only 1.3 percent.[6] Yet in Venezuela, which also had a high ratio of capital formation in relation to the gross domestic product, the gross domestic product for the same period grew at an annual average rate of 7.3 percent. Peru, with a ratio of capital formation to gross domestic product much higher than that of Argentina and, between 1955-59, almost as high as in Venezuela, had an average annual domestic product growth rate of only around 3.4 percent. Obviously, it is not easy to arrive at consistent generalizations about the relations between capital formation and economic growth rates in individual Latin American countries or in Latin America as a whole.

Nor is there necessarily any clear correlation between the structure of gross capital formation and the rate of economic growth. The data for 10 countries for the periods 1951-54 and 1955-59 shows that in most of these countries construction dominated the pattern of investment of gross fixed capital formation.[7]

The factors above explain the differences in estimates of the investment needs of Latin America and indicate why these estimates can only be conjectural. Nonetheless, these estimates are useful indicators of the dimensions of the problem. An estimate made in 1954, for instance, put Latin America's investment needs at $7.25 billion a year in order to maintain a 2 percent growth rate in living levels. This was $1.3 billion more than Latin America's total investment in 1953.[8] Felipe Herrera (1960, p. 20) speaking in 1960 as president of the Inter-American Development Bank, calculated that if Latin America was to make "satisfactory" progress in the future, it was essential that gross investment be increased from about 15 percent of the gross national product to some 20 percent. This increase was equivalent to some $3 billion a year. According to CEPAL, the rate of growth of Latin America during the next decade ought to advance at a rate of more than 6 percent a year, if not 7 percent. This meant that the coefficient of investment to the gross product had to increase from 16 percent to 25 percent.[9] The U.N. *Economic Survey of Latin America* (1966, p. 11) suggested that if Latin America were to achieve a growth rate of around 6 percent a year, the capital formation coefficient would have to be above 20 percent "and probably as high as 22 percent." According to a UNECLA report (1963, p. 48) three years earlier, Latin America, in order to achieve a growth rate of 3 percent would have to raise the coefficient of gross investment to 20.5 percent, and to achieve a growth rate of 4 percent, the coefficient would have to be raised to 23 percent.[10] One of the latest estimates conjectures that

[6]Gross capital formation as a percentage of gross domestic product (at current prices) for the periods 1951-54 and 1955-59, respectively, are as follows: Argentina—18.8, 19.7; Venezuela—28.1, 24.9; Peru—23.9, 23. See Carranza (1967, p. 123).

[7]Carranza (1967, p. 12).

[8]Stark (1961, p. 202).

[9]CEPAL (1968a).

[10]Cf., U.S. Department of State (1967d, p. 13):

In 1967, for example, Brazil's gross national product is expected to increase about 6 percent. Yet prevailing conditions—annual population growth of about 3 percent, explosive expansion of urban populations overwhelming to authorities who must cope with it, vast shortcomings in housing and education, technical backwardness in most areas—dictate annual growth of about 8 percent merely to maintain the present state of employment and minimal individual advancement. For Brazil to reach that goal requires increasing its investment ratio, now approximately 15 percent of the gross national product, to an estimated 23 percent.

Latin America will have to raise the total investment coefficient to 26.8 percent in 1980 if the region is to achieve a growth rate of 8 percent a year by that date.[11]

Even allowing for data deficiencies (which are being corrected through active research), these conjectural estimates of the investment needs of Latin America allow for some evaluation of Latin American performance, achievement, and prospects in the area of capital mobilization.[12] Using the relation of investment to the GNP as the standard measure, gross investment averaged around 18.8 percent of GNP for the period 1960-69 (see Table 11.1). It was about the same for the period 1950-60.[13]

Investment Trends

Except for 1963, gross investment in dollar terms—by any of the calculations—has increased every year between 1960-69. The position in 1963, striking because in that year the ratio of gross investment to gross domestic product dropped from 19.2 percent (1960) to 17.4 percent, again spotlighted the weight carried by the major countries in Latin America. The decline of the investment coefficient in Latin America for that year reflected the decline of investment coefficients in Argentina and Brazil following stabilization efforts and reduced credit availability and government spending.[14] Again, except for a few individual years, the over-all ratio of investment to the gross national product has exhibited no decisive upward strength for the last two decades. In no year during the Alliance decade did the ratio of investment to the gross product exceed 20 percent for the region as a whole, although individual countries like Colombia, Costa Rica, Mexico, Panama, Nicaragua, Peru, Trinidad and Tobago, and Venezuela did do so in particular years.[15] In fact, in individual countries, the trends in the rate of capital formation

TABLE 11.1

Gross National Product and Investment 18 Latin American Republics[a] (1968 prices)

	Investment as percent of GNP		Investment as percent of GNP
1960	19.2	1965	18.7
1961	19.1	1966	18.7
1962	18.2	1967	18.4
1963	17.4	1968	19.4
1964	18.7	1969[b]	19.7

[a] Excludes Haiti.
[b] Preliminary.
N.B.: Data are unadjusted for inequalities in purchasing power among countries.

Source: U.S., Department of State (1971).

[11] Prebisch (1970, p. 109).
[12] Cf. Sheahan (1968, p. 101): "Some of the best Colombian economists are inclined to doubt that higher investment is necessary, because of the evidence that the country has a great deal of idle capacity."
[13] See U.S. Department of State (1967e).
[14] See U.S. House (1969, p. 56); and UNECLA (1963, pp. 25-28).
[15] See Inter-American Development Bank (1969a, p. 64). Trinidad and Tobago (24.2 percent), Peru (20.5 percent), Mexico (20.2 percent) exceeded the 20 percent average for the period 1961-68.

were both highly inconsistent and highly unstable. On the basis of past trends, predictions for the future become difficult.

Trends in savings are equally inconsistent. For the period 1961–68, over 90 percent of Latin America's gross total investment came from internal Latin American resources, the savings investment gap being closed by foreign resources. A report submitted to the Committee on Foreign Relations of the U.S. Senate in 1967 suggested, on the basis of U.N. figures, that Latin America between 1961–66 had invested $91 billion of its own resources in development, while the U.S. contribution amounted to $6.5 billion.[16] In fact, except for Venezuela, Latin America's contribution to total gross investment from its own savings reached 98 percent in 1965.[17] Between 1961–65, external contributions averaged only about 5 percent of gross investment.[18] Nonetheless, savings trends were as erratic and as inconsistent as rates of capital formation, giving no firm basis for future calculations.

The rate of savings for the period 1961–68 averaged 17.2 percent of the gross domestic product for the region as a whole, which was lower than the rate of investment. In addition, there were tremendous variations between individual countries. In Venezuela, the average was over 20 percent; in Argentina, Brazil, Colombia, Mexico, Peru, and Trinidad and Tobago it was over 15 percent. In Haiti it was less than 1 percent.[19] There were similar variations in the ratio of savings to investment (the savings gap). Savings in Argentina, Brazil, Mexico, Uruguay and Venezuela, for instance, provided from 90 to 100 percent of gross domestic investment for the period 1961–68. Savings in Haiti provided only 16 percent. In some cases the level of savings exceeded the level of investment, while in other cases the level of savings declined despite efforts to raise it.[20]

The ground is no firmer if we try to establish correlations between investment rates and the rate of growth of the economy. The evidence is mixed, confirming our earlier observation that while increased capital formation is an essential condition for speeding up the rate of economic growth, it is not a sufficient condition for development. A few illustrations of the mixed results will suffice. In the period 1961–68, for example, gross investment as a percentage of the gross domestic product averaged over 20 percent in Peru, Mexico, and Trinidad and Tobago. In these countries the per capita product for 1961–69 exceeded the Alliance for Progress minimum goal of 2.5 percent. But Argentina, which had an average gross investment ratio of over 19 percent for 1961–68, failed to achieve the minimum per capita goal of the Alliance. In Uruguay, which had a low gross investment ratio of 13.1 percent for 1961–68, the gross domestic product declined over the period at an annual average rate of 0.4 percent a year. On the other hand, in Bolivia the gross investment ratio was 15.4 percent for 1961–68, but the gross domestic product grew at a rate of 5.7 percent a year, higher than

---

[16]U.S. Senate (1967a, pp. 16–17, 43–50, 52–54, 67). The $6.5 billion included AID, SPRF, Food for Peace, the Export-Import Bank, and other economic programs—in other words, U.S. government assistance through these agencies. However, it did not include private investment by U.S. companies in Latin America.

[17]Pan American Union (1967b, p. 1–45).

[18]U.S. Senate (1967a, p. 44).

[19]See Inter-American Development Bank (1969a, p. 65).

[20]*Ibid.*, pp. 62–63.

that of Mexico or Peru. A conclusion can clearly be reached at this point: accelerating development in Latin America requires the simultaneous raising of the gross investment ratio together with the removal of factors which inhibit the productivity of capital in every country of the region.

Estimates provided by Prebisch indicate the size and the implications of the problem (see Tables 11.2 and 11.3). If Latin America is to achieve an 8 percent annual growth rate of the economy by 1980, the domestic component of gross investment must grow from 14.5 percent of the gross domestic product in 1966–68 to 24.6 percent in 1990 and a vital inflow of foreign capital must be maintained to allow the total gross investment coefficient to increase from 18.3 percent for 1966–68 to 26.5 percent by 1990. Even though average per capita product will probably more than double by 1990, consumption will have to be sacrificed in favor of investment.

The necessities of the situation underline the key role to be played by the state in determining and executing policies appropriate for meeting the financial needs of development. Fiscal policies must be pursued which restrict consumption, redistribute income, encourage or compel savings through a variety of incentives and disincentives, and at the same time foster the most productive use of investment resources. This is not necessarily inconsistent with the encouragement of national private enterprise or with the articulation of foreign capital into the scheme of desired national development objectives.

TABLE 11.2

Total Gross Investment Coefficient, Share of Domestic Resources, and Gross Inflow of Foreign Capital (In Percentages of Product)

	Domestic resources[a]	Gross inflow of foreign capital	Total gross investment
1966–68	14.5	3.8	18.3
1980	24.0	2.5	26.5
1990	24.6	1.9	26.5

[a] Includes the additional domestic savings effort required to meet the implications of an 8 percent growth rate.

Source: Latin American Institute for Economic and Social Planning, quoted in Prebisch (1970b, p.110).

TABLE 11.3

Per Capita Product and Percentages Assigned to Consumption and Investment[a]

	Average per capita product (dollars)	PERCENTAGE ASSIGNED TO		PERCENTAGE GROWTH RATE 1966–68		
		Consumption	Investment	Consumption	Investment	Total
1966–68	400	85	15	–	–	–
1980	630	75	25	2.6	7.5	3.6
1990	1,030	75	25	3.6	6.2	4.2

[a] Excludes outflows of financial resources abroad.

Source: Latin America Institute for Economic and Social Planning, quoted in Prebisch (1970b, p. 110).

We turn now to a consideration of the major trends in government's revenue performance and expenditure patterns in order to discover any significant relationships between government's financial performance and desired changes in the Latin American economy.

The Public Sector: Revenue Trends

That government in developing countries must play a key role in the process of capital formation is now a well-established principle.[21] Apart from conventional reasons, Latin American governments must increase their own revenues if only because past evidence shows that external financing is not only highly conservative in its choice of investment outlets but also highly unreliable. For the period 1956-60, for instance, foreign investment contributed only 8 percent to the gross capital formation of the region, or around 12 to 15 percent if loans and credits from official national and international sources are included. Some 70 percent of the foreign direct investment came from the United States. Almost half of this investment was in petroleum, nearly a quarter in manufacturing, and most of the rest in trade, mining, and smelting.[22] By 1967, U.S. investment in Europe was much larger than in Latin America, a reversal of the position in 1960.[23]

Under the Charter of Punta del Este, participating Latin American countries agreed that their "national development programs should incorporate self-help efforts directed to more effective, rational, and equitable mobilization and use of financial resources through the reform of tax structures, including fair and adequate taxation of large incomes and real estate, and the strict application of measures to improve fiscal administration."[24] From the evidence of the Alliance years, it is difficult to predict the rate at which these ideals will be fulfilled. Once again, there are complex deterrents to be overcome. Before considering these, let us look at revenue performance.

In absolute terms, total current government revenues for the region increased between 1961-68 at a rate of 5.7 percent a year, compared with a 4.9 percent annual average growth rate in the gross domestic product. Tax collections accounted for approximately 85 percent of the total current revenues and the rate of growth of tax collections was also superior to the rate of growth of the gross domestic product.[25] However, the picture changes if we apply conventional standards to the evaluation of revenue performance during these years. Lewis, for instance, states that effective contribution to the promotion of economic development requires that government's current revenue should amount to some 17 to 19 percent of the gross domestic product.[26] By that criterion, central government revenues averaged just over 13.1 percent for the period 1961-68.[27]

---

[21] See Heller's famous article, "Fiscal Policies for Underdeveloped Economies" (1968, p. 452); see also Rostow (1960, pp. 24–25) and Prebisch (1970b, pp. 187–188).

[22] See UN (1961, pp. 14–15; 1965, p. 215).

[23] See U.S. Department of Commerce (1968, p. 21).

[24] U.S. Senate (1966, p. 105). For detailed studies, see Pan American Union (1965) and Inter-American Development Bank (n.d.).

[25] Inter-American Development Bank (1969a, p. 68).

[26] See Jamaican Ministry of Development & Welfare (n.d., p. 31).

[27] U.S. House (1969, p. 61).

In Chile, tax as a percentage of the gross domestic product increased from 16.4 percent in 1961 to 20.5 percent in 1967. In Venezuela, the tax ratio averaged over 20 percent of the gross domestic product for the period 1961-67. In 10 out of 18 Latin American countries, however, the ratio was less than 10 percent, making the tax ratio for the 18 countries barely more than 11.5 percent for the period.[28] In comparison with developed countries, the tax ratio in Latin America ranks low.[29]

There have been some significant efforts to upgrade the quality of the tax systems in Latin America in the interests of increasing revenue collections, of equity, and of making the tax system more appropriately related to economic development needs.[30] It is not, therefore, a question of whether action is being taken. It is a question of the speed with which the necessary reforms can be effectively enforced. The initial deterrents yield ground slowly. The tax administration and collection machinery remains defective. The tax structure remains traditionally regressive in many countries. Fluctuations in export prices still make for uncertainties in total revenues collected, and in some countries there are still too many taxes, while tax evasion is widespread.[31]

There are other dilemmas to be resolved—dilemmas which retard the speed of economic advance. Under the Alliance for Progress objectives, equity in income distribution and increased tax ratios go together. The bottom 50 percent of the population cannot reduce their consumption further. Increased tax burdens will therefore fall on the upper 5 percent and on the middle groups. Yet these are also the groups which save most. Apart from this, the top 5 percent enjoy political power and their resistance cannot be discounted in a politically unreformed Latin America. Latin America also faces a dilemma common to most developing countries. Tax policies in a world of competitive concession-making to attract foreign capital have to take into account the effect of increased taxes on the inflow of foreign capital, if this inflow is essential.

Because of these boundary conditions, the last decade has shown only slow changes in the tax ratios and in correcting the inequities in income. Property taxes tend to increase, but very slowly. The ratio of income taxes to total government current revenues also increased slowly between 1961-68. In fact, while the ratio increased from 35.2 percent to 45.6 percent in Mexico and from 40.6 percent to 47.6 percent in Venezuela, the ratio declined in such countries as Argentina, Brazil, Haiti, the Dominican Republic, Peru, and others. Indirect taxes in 1968 accounted for over 70 percent of total central government current revenues in at least nine countries of Latin America—reaching a maximum of over 83 percent in Uruguay—and amounted to nearly 50 percent of total Latin American government tax revenue.[32]

---

[28] *Ibid.*, p. 62.

[29] See Lotz and Morss (1967, p. 479). The tax ratio of the United States is put at 26.2 percent; France at 37.7 percent; Sweden at 37.2 percent; Canada at 27.7 percent; Israel at 26.4 percent; Australia at 23.6 percent.

[30] See for instance, Pan American Union (1967) and Sommerfield (1966). UNECLA (1969b, pp. 103-105).

[31] Cf. Pan American Union (1966, p. 27): "Nuestra sistema tributario es sumamente complejo por el numero excesivo de impuesto, tasas, aportes, etc."

[32] See Inter-American Development Bank (1969a, p. 74) and Pan American Union (1967b, pp. 1-65). Cf. the observations on income distribution in Latin America in U.N. (1967aa, pp. 49-50):

It is difficult to estimate the effect of varying tax levels, and structure, and development with the existing data. Accurate figures are essential if tax policies are to conform with development objectives. We can only make a cautious conclusion at this point—that accurately predicting the progress of capital mobilization under the state is not possible at the present time and may not be for some time to come.

The Public Sector: Expenditure Trends

Under the Charter of the Alliance for Progress, participating Latin American countries agreed that development programs should include the adaptation of budget expenditures to development needs.[33] We have already asserted that government in Latin America must contribute directly to the acceleration of capital formation. To do so, public policy, as in the case of tax revenues, must overcome a number of severe constraints. Once again, however, predictions for the future cannot be based on past experience.

Between 1961-67 public expenditures, for instance, did increase for the region as a whole by some 44 percent—if Argentina and Brazil are included. But the rates of increase expectedly differed in different countries. Expenditures declined for Argentina, Brazil, the Dominican Republic, Haiti, and Uruguay but increased by over 178 percent in Mexico between 1961-65, by 174.6 percent in Peru, and by 146 percent and 142 percent, respectively, in Nicaragua and Costa Rica. Because of these declines, however, the increase in total central government expenditures averaged only 13 percent between 1961-67.[34] Detailed interpretation of trends vary from country to country, but some significant general observations are possible.

If we use Heller's criterion that, generally speaking, government expenditures in low income countries average about 12 percent of the gross national product (1962, p. 453), Latin America appears to be doing well. But although expenditures increased, the ratio of government expenditures to the gross product dropped from about 17 percent in 1961 to about 15 percent in 1967. Total government expenditures increased less than the rate of increase in total domestic revenues so that the traditional budget deficits for the region as a whole declined slightly from 2.3 percent of the gross domestic product in 1961 to under 1 percent in 1967.[35] On the other hand, public capital outlay as a percentage of central

---

As in Argentina, the tax system seems to have done little to redistribute income, because of the predominance of indirect taxation, generally non-discriminatory, which can often be passed on to the final consumer. The proportion of indirect taxation in total tax revenue rose from 66.6 percent in 1950 to 72.8 percent in 1960. In the same year, 23.7 percent of the revenue from direct taxation was derived from taxes on labor, and the proportion would be more than 60 percent, if social security contributions are included. These and other features of the tax system, together with the greater margin for tax evasion in less visible categories of income other than wages and salaries, account for the rapid progressiveness of the taxes on those income brackets which in 1962 ranged from 250,000 to 1.2 million *cruzeiros* and the weakening of the rates in the higher brackets. In the same year, surveys conducted in different cities revealed the regressive effects of income tax and social security contributions: in the state capitals, the middle groups (250,000 to 800,000 *cruzeiros*) suffered a reduction in available income, while the position of the higher income groups was strengthened and the same applied to the cities in the interior.

[33] U.S. House (1966, p. 105).
[34] See U.S. Department of State (1968b, pp. 60–64).
[35] See U.S. Department of State (1968b, pp. 60–64).

budgetary expenditures increased from 26.4 percent of the total budgets in 1961 to 30.9 percent in 1967.[36] Nonetheless, as a ratio of the gross domestic product, net government capital expenditures fell slightly between 1961–67, from 4.2 percent to 4.1 percent.[37]

The pressure for increasing current capital public expenditures is obviously continuous—to meet the needs of population growth and urbanization and urban unemployment, and to enable the government to expand the provision of economic and social infrastructure. Increased recurrent expenditures may mean reduced capital expenditures and the slowing down of capital formation. Increased public capital expenditures may mean reduced current expenditures. Yet increasing current expenditures may be necessary to support an expansion of public capital investment. In any case, increased expenditures are dependent on increasing tax revenues, and the boundary conditions to expenditures are set by the taxable capacity of the region, the rate of general development, and the possibility of filling the gap in capital and recurrent requirements through external financing. In the attempt to accelerate capital formation, budgetary management faces many-sided uncertainties. Included in these uncertainties are the principles and values of the moment which determine priorities in budgetary allocations.

We illustrate some of these points from Latin American experience over the last decade. Current expenditures, for instance, rise with the salary increases of the evergrowing number of government personnel needed for expanding government services or swollen by widespread featherbedding practices. Increased recurrent expenditures obviously weaken the government's ability to invest in physical infrastructure. Featherbedding apart, Latin American public salaries are low and improvement in salary levels is unavoidable. In 1965, in at least six Latin American countries, salaries as a proportion of current expenditures stood at over 60 percent; in seven others, salaries represented between 50 and 60 percent; in two others, salaries were between 40 and 50 percent; and in two others, salaries were more than 30 percent of current expenditures.[38] In the Dominican Republic, salaries represented 43.4 percent of all current expenditures in 1970.[39] Transfers to autonomous public agencies, accounting for some 50 percent of current expenditures in Guatemala and Haiti, for example, adversely affect capital formation. Some of these agencies are inefficient and those which are efficient are disallowed from charging more reasonable user rates.[40] Defense expenditures continued to secure more than twice the budgetary allocation for agriculture for the region as a whole.[41] In Colombia, government's capital expenditures increased more than two and one-half times between 1964–68. The increase might have been

[36] U.S. House (1969, p. 63).
[37] See Inter-American Development Bank (1969, p. 73).
[38] See Pan American Union (1967b, pp. 1–72).
[39] Banco Central de la Republica Dominicana (1970, p. 92).
[40] See Pan American Union (1967e, p. 95) and Prebisch (1970b, p. 128). See also Inter-American Development Bank (1967, p. 16). For a discussion of basic principles and long standing dilemmas, see Political Quarterly (1950), Boskey (1959), and Riggs (1956, pp. 70–80).
[41] Share of central government expenditures for the region as a whole is as follows: 1961—defense, 11.5 percent; agriculture, 3.6 percent; 1968—defense, 12.4 percent, agriculture, 4.8 percent. See U.S. House (1969, p. 63) and U.S. Department of State (1969, p. 54). See also U.S. Senate (1967) and U.S. Senate (1968).

greater if defense expenditures had not almost doubled during the same period.[42]

At this point, we reiterate that neither the rate of government capital forma-tion nor the size of government's capital outlay is a sufficient condition for speed-ing up the rate of development. In Chile, taxes as a proportion of GNP grew from twice the ratio for Mexico in 1961 to over three times in 1967. Similarly, capital outlay in Chile as a percentage of central government expenditures was 27.2 per-cent in 1961 as against 25.4 percent in Mexico, and 32.2 percent in 1967 com-pared with 24.5 percent in Mexico. Yet the Mexican economy advanced during the period at an average rate of 6.7 percent a year, while Chile's economy ad-vanced just over 5 percent a year. Clearly, other counterproductive factors must be taken into account.

EXTERNAL FINANCING

Like most developing countries, Latin America would prefer to meet domestic capital requirements from its own internal resources. This would at least permit internal economic decision-making without considering any boundary conditions laid down by the metropolitan head offices of international conglomerates or by foreign central governments.[43] The Charter of Punta del Este set no specific tar-get date for Latin America to attain self-sufficiency in meeting its own domestic capital requirements. It stated, however, that:

The economic and social development of Latin America will require a large amount of additional public and private financial assistance on the part of the capital exporting countries, including the members of the Development Assist-ance Group and international lending agencies.[44]

Prebisch, on the other hand, while recognizing that continued inflow of external assistance was critical for the desired rate of domestic capital formation, conjec-tured that Latin America might become self-sufficient enough to meet its domes-tic investment needs by 1990. This conjecture presupposed, among other condi-tions (see Tables 11.2, 11.3), that the investment coefficient in Latin America would rise to about 26.5 percent by the 1980s and that industrial countries would contribute, as the U.N. recommended, at least 1 percent of their gross product to finance resources to be transferred to developing countries. It was assumed further that Latin America would continue to retain at least 15 percent of these transferred sums, increasing to a total of $4,100 million by 1980: that debt service payments and unfavorable terms of trade trends could be favorably modified; and that Latin America would at the same time improve its own sav-ings capacity.

As we have repeatedly asserted, every developing nation has to believe that the conditions for economic survival will be fulfilled sooner or later. Optimism is a more natural choice than thoughts of economic disappearance. In Latin Amer-ica, nationalism will always generate self-confidence. With the pressures of popu-lation and the necessity for a transformation of the socioeconomic milieu, the question of contemporary importance is always the rapidity with which the

---

[42] See U.S. Department of State (1970aa, p. 9).
[43] This is the heart of the argument in Furtado (1970, pp. 17–89). See also U.S. House (1966, p. 106).
[44] Prebisch (1970b, pp. 224, 149).

TABLE 11.4

Economic Assistance to Latin America by International Agencies and Bilateral Donors (commitments in millions of U.S. dollars)

Fiscal Year	IDB[a] (OC and FSO)	IBRD[b]	IDA[c]	U.N. agencies	OECD (DAC)[d]	IFC[e]	EEC[f]	Total
1961	66	131	27	39	86	3	4	356
1962	138	408	30	39	156	8	5	784
1963	184	123	11	42	205	10	7	582
1964	124	256	12	43	195	7	10	647
1965	238	208	19	55	231	10	9	770
1966	366	375	8	74	207	24	10	1,064
1967	445	271	2	48	189	12	7	974
1968	408	376	9	48[g]	200[g]	17	7[g]	1,065
1969[g]	495	550	10	48	200	22	7	1,332

[a] Inter-American Development Bank, administering the Fund for Special Operations and the Ordinary Capital Fund.
[b] International Bank for Reconstruction and Development (the World Bank).
[c] International Development Association.
[d] Organization for Economic Cooperation and Development (Development Assistance Committee). DAC countries are Australia, Austria, Belgium, Canada, Denmark, France, West Germany, Switzerland, Italy, Japan, the Netherlands, Norway, Great Britain, and the United States.
[e] International Finance Corporation, affiliate of World Bank.
[f] European Economic Community.
[g] Estimated.

Source: U.S. Department of State (1969c, p.17).

transformation can take place. By 1980 or 2000 the position can become worse. In setting a time limit and spelling out the conditions for Latin America's reaching a position of nondependence on external investment resources, Prebisch has produced more definite criteria for evaluating the possibilities of reaching a position which agrees with Latin American nationalist aspirations.

The Flow of Foreign Public Capital to Latin America

For Latin America to attain a position of self-sufficiency in meeting its domestic investment needs requires a fundamental reversal in the experience of Latin America even over the decade of the 1960s. Table 11.4 and Table 11.5 showing the flow of international and U.S. public assistance to Latin America, reveal no strong or stable trends. International assistance reflects the fluctuations in the flow of U.S. economic assistance—a flow which is in turn affected by the vagaries of international political and economic relations, as well as by changes in domestic economic problems and priorities of the lending countries. Table 11.5 shows clearly that grants have been declining while loans, which add to the repayment burdens, have been increasing. The ratio of service costs on foreign public debt to the value of goods and service exports in Latin America rose from 13 percent in 1961 to 14.6 percent in 1968.[45] In fact, in Argentina, Brazil, and Mexico the

[45] See Inter-American Development Bank (1969a, pp. 91–97). See also International Bank for Reconstruction and Development (1968, p. 53).

TABLE 11.5

Economic Assistance to Latin America from Official U.S. Sources (Commitments in Millions of U.S. Dollars)

Fiscal Year	AID[a]			EX – IM Bank[b]	Food for Freedom	SPTF[c]	Other, economic[d]	Total
	Loans	Grants	Total					
1961	144	110	254	450	146	–	2	852
1962	358	120	478	63	128	226	120	1,015
1963	394	148	552	65	167	127	79	980
1964	511	92	613	168	297	42	83	1,193
1965	399	128	532	153	104	101	284	1,164
1966	505	132	647	134	188	24	288	1,271
1967	466	90	556	497	70	5	274	1,402
1968	414	82	496	301	228	5	329	1,359
1969[e]	248	78	326	289	137	2	326	1,080

[a] Agency for International Development (net commitments as of November, 1969).
[b] Export – Import Bank.
[c] Social Progress Trust Fund, administered for the United States by the Inter-American Development Bank (IDB).
[d] Includes Peace Corps, grants for the construction of the Inter-American Highway, and U.S. cash contributions for IDB.
[e] Preliminary figures.

Source: AID Statistical Research Division, quoted in U.S., Department of State (1969c, p.16).

ratio was well over 20 percent. Latin America's external public debt doubled during the period and short-term indebtedness increased. Sixty percent of the external debt in 1968 had a maturity of 10 years or less, compared with a ratio of 52 percent in 1961. Economic performance within Latin American countries did not in the majority of cases increase their ability to meet the increasing burdens of loan repayment. Loan repayments under these conditions certainly involves the alternative cost of weakening the rate of capital formation.

The limitations from which Latin America must escape in order to strengthen the rate of capital formation do not end here. Conforming to the suggestion that developed countries transfer 1 percent of their gross national product to developing countries in order to support domestic capital formation efforts is only a moral obligation. Few countries agreed to this U.N. goal, and it was simply not achieved in the 1960s. In fact, the ratio declined from 0.96 percent of GNP in 1961 to 0.77 percent in 1968. Latin America's share of these international transfers also declined—from 26.4 percent in 1956–59 to about 15 percent in 1964–67. Whether Latin America will receive more or less of these international transfers and whether developed countries will agree to transfer 1 percent of their GNP depends not only on a sense of moral obligation, but also on Latin America's comparative political and economic bargaining power in a world of complex and changeable international relationships. In order to increase its bargaining strength Latin America will have to substantially upgrade its domestic development efforts. And if we follow Nurske's realism that the rich preferably do business with the rich, it is bargaining power vis-à-vis the United States which matters.[46] The OECD countries, like the rest of the world, are caught up with their own domestic economic problems and are not likely to be a major alternative source of public or even private capital. Although bilateral economic assistance from the United States to Latin America declined from 63.9 percent of total external assistance to Latin America in 1961 to 34.2 percent in 1969 while economic assistance from international organizations rose from 20.4 percent to 44.7 percent, it is financial contributions from the United States that still constitute the major source of finance for these international organizations and determine the terms and conditions which prevail.[47]

Loans are not easy or cheap. International and U.S. lending agencies are governed by rules and institutionalized procedures not easy to change. Much depends on the character and weight of external and internal pressures. The World Bank Group, for instance, justifies its existence on the grounds that the commercial banking system must satisfy the massive need for development capital in nations which must borrow at the "soft loan" window because the commercial banking system cannot perform the vital function of financing needed infrastructure.[48] The World Bank Group, operating in Latin America as well as in all less developed countries, includes the International Bank for Reconstruction and Development (IBRD) itself, the International Finance Corporation (IFC), and the International Development Association (IDA). The IBRD, founded in 1944, "the only thing of its kind" as George Woods, the former president of the World Bank group put it, the IFC founded in 1956, and the IDA founded in 1960 all subscribe to the same purposes and have the same prerequisites, but with differing ranges of flexibility.[49] Their basic common purpose is subscription to the economic growth of the member countries of the Bank. The three major prerequisites of the World Bank Group for the successful execution of a project are "satisfactory studies of the proposed project; an organization or institution capable of constructing or administering the project; and policies which are consistent with, and conducive to, the realization of the objectives of the project."[50]

The loans of the IBRD proper are usually long term, at more or less conventional rates of interest, for projects of high priority. IDA lends to the poorest countries—those which cannot really afford to borrow money and service loans on conventional terms. The third affiliate, the IFC, operates exclusively in the private sector, lending money to private business without government guarantees; investing in share capital; and underwriting placements and offerings of securities by new and expanding enterprises.

The 1968 IBRD–IDA annual report shows, for instance, that 48 percent of the total commitments of the IFC for the period 1956–65 went to Latin Amer-

---

[46]See Nurkse (1955, p. 21): "Because of their low level of productivity and hence of real purchasing power, the backward agricultural countries play, as is well known, a minor part in world trade; by and large, the advanced countries are each others' best customers."

[47]See U.S. Department of State (1969b, p. 53).

[48]Rockefeller (1967). See also International Bank for Reconstruction and Development (1968).

[49]See International Bank for Reconstruction and Development (1966–67).

[50]Schmidt (1966).

ica. Despite this degree of benefit and despite the World Bank's recognition of differing circumstances among potential borrowers, loans from the World Bank Group—like all loans from the public sector—have been rising in cost, adding to the burden of Latin American debt servicing and debt redemption, and with adverse consequences for domestic capital formation. The interest charges of the World Bank Group are directly affected by interest levels and monetary and fiscal policies in the United States. For instance, the rate of interest on IBRD credits to Latin America stood at 5.75 percent between 1960–62, declined to 5.5 percent in 1963–64, then rose to 6 percent in 1966, and 6.5 percent in 1967, largely because of the higher rates IBRD had to pay on its own bonds.[51] Similarly, the rate of interest charged by the Inter-American Development Bank (IDS) to the private sector in Latin America as well as its commission increased to 7.75 percent. Agency for International Development (AID) loans cost 5.5 percent in 1960, dropped to .75 percent in 1963, and rose again to one percent for the grace period and 2.5 percent for the amortization period. The rate of interest charged by the Export-Import Bank (EXIMBANK) has risen 0.5 percent since 1966. The vagaries in interest rates as well as in calculations of loan possibilities obviously affect conjectures as to the degree of external support likely for domestic capital formation in Latin America.

United States official lending agencies fall even more directly under methods and procedures conforming to the business and administrative practices of the United States.

Modification of these procedures normally proves to be somewhat difficult, since any country is conservative about its successful internally tested procedures and governments are sensitive to public accountability. The Export-Import Bank, for instance, created in 1934 to aid the promotion of exchange of goods between the United States and foreign countries, became an independent federal government agency under the Export-Import Bank Act of 1941. The capital of the bank is supplied by the U.S. Treasury and additional resources can be borrowed from the Treasury up to an over-all ceiling of $6 billion. The President of the United States appoints the five members of its board of directors.[52]

The Inter-American Development Bank, the bank of the Alliance for Progress, from the beginning of its operation on October 1, 1960, inevitably fell under some United States influenced regulation for U.S. membership in the bank was authorized on August 7, 1959, and initial U.S. appropriations were provided for by law a month later. The bank finances only specific projects, though it has powers to make loans to local development banks which can in turn finance local businesses. Like the World Bank Group, the Inter-American Development Bank, administers a Fund for Special Operations. This fund is really the soft loan

[51] See UNECLA (1969b, pp. 4–5). These interest rates are of course far higher than recommended by the Commission on International Development (1969, p. 164): "the terms of official development assistance loans should henceforth provide for interest of no more than 2 percent, a maturity of between 25 and 40 years, and a grace period of from 7 to 10 years." These rates are also higher than the recommendations proposed to the DAC countries. See Organization for Economic Cooperation and Development (1969, pp. 269–270).

[52] See UN, Economic and Social Council (1963aa, pp. 54–58). EXIMBANK exercises three main functions: (1) granting export credits mainly in the medium-term field to supplement short-term facilities granted by private banks, (2) supplying medium-term export credit insurance, and (3) making medium- and long-term loans to public and private foreign purchasers of U.S. goods and services.

window of the bank, carrying on functions similar to those of the IDA in relation to the IBRD—making loans in special circumstances such as to countries with a balance of payments problem preventing servicing in hard currency, or countries with special situations. The bank, under a trust agreement with the U.S. government, was given on June 19, 1961, powers of administration over the Social Progress Trust Fund (SPTF), which was given the responsibility

to provide capital resources and technical assistance on flexible terms and conditions. . . . in accordance with appropriate and selective criteria in the light of the resources available, to support the efforts of the Latin American countries that are prepared to initiate or expand effective institutional improvements or to adopt measures to employ efficiently their own resources with a view to achieving greater social progress and more balanced economic growth.[33]

The United States is the major financial contributor to these key lending institutions. In 1967, for instance, the resources of the Fund for Special Operations were raised from $1.1 to $2.3 billion, the U.S. increase in contribution amounting to $900 million (U.S.) as against $300 million for Latin America. The rate of public investment flowing into Latin America to support its internal capital formation efforts and the terms and conditions on which it is lent will depend on the operational limits imposed in the United States, the efficiency with which these inflows are utilized in Latin America, and the rapidity with which mutual accommodation can be arrived at where terms and conditions are regarded as inappropriate.[54]

Foreign Private Investment

An understanding of the uncertainties of domestic investment resources, as well as of the flow of public international capital, makes it clear that foreign private capital is essential to strengthen the rate of capital formation in Latin America. Calculating the amount of private capital needed over the next decade would be

---

[53]See U.S. House (1966, p. 156). Under Article I of the Agreement establishing the IDB, its functions were defined as follows:

1. to promote the investment of public and private capital for development purposes;
2. to utilize its own capital, funds raised by it in financial markets, and other available resources, for financing the development of the member countries, giving priority to those loans and guarantees that will contribute most effectively to their economic growth;
3. to encourage private investment in projects, enterprises, and activities contributing to economic development and to supplement private investment when private capital is not available on reasonable terms and conditions;
4. to cooperate with the member countries to orient their development policies toward a better utilization of their resources, in a manner consistent with the objectives of making their economies more complementary and of fostering the orderly growth of their foreign trade; and
5. to provide technical assistance for the preparation, financing, and implementation of development plans and projects, including the study of priorities and the formulation of specific project proposals.

As part of its purpose and function the bank was mandated to cooperate "as far as possible" with national and international institutions and with private sources supplying investment capital.

[54]U.S. Senate (1968b) gives the reader some idea of the detailed scrutiny to which official expenditures of these agencies are subject.

difficult, although planned advance of the economy would require more detailed information on how much capital is needed to fill the gap between domestic capital resources and anticipations of external capital flows. Even if these needs, could be assessed, uncertainties about the size and continuity of the flow of foreign private capital would still be a major factor in future planning.

At first glance, the evidence of past experience of private capital flowing into Latin America would support optimism for the future. Direct foreign investment did increase by over 67 percent between 1961–68.[55] On the other hand, a listing of the advantages of having foreign private investment in Latin America makes Latin America's dependence on foreign private capital seem an inevitable continuum. The recitation of these advantages for the year 1957 is typical. In that year, the total assets of U.S. companies in Latin America (excluding finance and insurance companies) amounted to $11,030 million. U.S. companies in Latin America exported over $3 billion worth of goods, the equivalent of one third of the sales export all Latin America. In addition, goods produced by U.S. companies and sold in the local Latin American market registered a total sales value of well over $4 billion. These companies paid out well over $6 billion in Latin America for wages and salaries, income taxes, other taxes, and purchases of local materials and other services. The taxes paid by these companies for 1957 amounted to over one-fifth of all taxes received by Latin American governments. There was more than this. U.S. companies spent approximately $1.7 billion for property, plant and equipment, and $900 million for additions to inventories and other assets. Of this amount, $1 billion came from U.S. sources, $700 million from retained earnings, $400 million from depreciation charges, and $400 million from local capital. These companies also employed nearly one million people, 98 percent of them Latin Americans.[56]

Added to all this are the taken-for-granted, concomitant benefits of the American business presence. These include the self-evident ingredients of American business drives—new goods and services, new managerial approaches, new technologies, investment in research, new marketing approaches, new methods of training, advertising, and economizing, new business forms—plus the communication of the spirit of American business that there are always new and profitable opportunities to be grasped or to be created.[57] These arguments are updated routinely from year to year.[58]

Despite these massive representations, it will not be possible to assess, for

---

[55] See UN (1965, pp. 138–139). Direct investment is defined as a transfer of capital in favor of private firms established abroad; "thus those remitting the capital control the enterprises concerned." In view, however, of the awkward problems raised by this definition, the document referred to adopted the IMF definitions. Under the IMF definitions, "new direct investment comprises capital contributions of all kinds, as well as reinvestment of profits in enterprises controlled from abroad and in associated enterprises, whether these operations are undertaken by controlling groups of non-residents or by other non-residents who are shareholders in the enterprises concerned." See also UN (1961, esp. pp. 1–2, 9–10).

[56] See Committee for Economic Development (CED) (n.d., p. 40). See also U.S. Department of Commerce (1960).

[57] Cf. Moore (1962, pp. 39–40).

[58] Cf., for instance, Roper (1970, pp. 4, 16).

TABLE 11.6

U.S. Private Direct Investments in Latin America (Book Value in Millions of Dollars)

Total 19 republics	1961	1967	1968	1969
All industries	8,236	10,265	11,033	11,667
Mining and smelting	1,103	1,277	1,410	1,346
Petroleum	3,254	2,903	3,014	3,079
Manufacturing	1,684	3,305	3,711	4,077
Public utilities	681	621	628	620
Trade	775	1,207	1,251	1,308
Other industries	739	952	1,019	1,237

Source: U.S. Department of State (1971).

some time to come, the effect of old and new controversies about the role and power of private foreign capital in Latin America on possible inflows of foreign private capital into Latin America. In the first place, although foreign private capital appears to enjoy a minor share of total investment in Latin America, in fact it traditionally confines itself to the few key strategic areas of the economy which happen also to be the most politically sensitive areas of the economy. U.S. private direct investments amounted to only 2.6 percent of the total investment in Latin America for the years 1962-68.[59] But, as Table 11.6 shows, over 70 percent of that private investment was in petroleum, mining and smelting, and manufacturing. The potential for public reactions is far greater than the smaller public utilities investment figures indicate. The pressure to subordinate private foreign corporate power to national sovereignty in Latin America is continuous for political and economic reasons. It is linked to the outflow of profits, the nonarticulation of foreign investments with national development goals,[60] or to the presence of foreign private capital in key areas of the economy. Yet these are often the very areas requiring vast amounts of social overhead capitalization.

Again, too, historical memories and attitudes persist. It is difficult to assess these variables, and to anticipate their eruption or effect on foreign private capital inflows. History may not repeat itself, but historical fears recur. Private enterprise investment has had a long history in Latin America. There have been abuses (and areas of continuing abuse) in the course of that history and Latin American memories are long. The past may today be unrecognizable in some areas because of reforms in the manner and method of private enterprise operation, but there is an unconscious lag in distinguishing between what is and what was.

Moreover, it may be extremely difficult to break the opposition of the local business groups opposed to modernization, for unreformed local business is usually entrenched politically and socially, and is protected by tariffs and by the built-in acceptance that the fortunes of the business are veritably the fortunes of the nation.[61] The local unreformed business enjoys the potential to rally a criti-

---

[59] U.S. Department of State (1969b, p. 46).

[60] See, for instance, *New York Times* (1971a, p. 1; 1971b, p. 1).

[61] Cf. Oxley (1968, p. 13): "Absentee landlords, for example, are representatives of private enterprise. Their interest may be tied to the preservation of tradition. The owner of a

cal degree of local sentiment. This sentiment finds reinforcement from the past, for during wars and depressions, it was the local business which came to the rescue and kept things alive—despite the cost to the consumer, the nonrestoration of competitive standards once the crisis was over, and the growth of monopolies and quasi monopolies which these circumstances ushered in. The local unreformed business groups also come in on the side of those who, like Furtado, argue for the dominance of investment decision-making at the Latin American national level in the interests of national self-respect and orderly development strategies.

Continuity in the inflow of foreign private capital into Latin America enjoys no a priori guarantee from some of the evidence of the 1960s. Capital has alternative outlets. As we have argued, private capital flows into Latin America will be determined by the comparative returns to capital in relation to risks, by the internal development achieved by Latin America, and by the degree of comparative bargaining power mobilized by Latin America. As it was, for example, the Alliance years witnessed significant changes in the flow of U.S. private direct investment into Latin America in comparison with other areas of the world. U.S. private direct investment in Latin America steadily increased between 1960–67. Indeed, just as the U.S. contribution dominated financial flows the world over—providing some 50 percent of the recorded financial flows for 1967—U.S. contributions dominated Latin America, representing some 80 percent of private foreign direct investment.[62] At the end of 1960, one-fifth of U.S. direct investment was in Europe, but the European total was 20 percent less than in Latin America and 40 percent less than in Canada.

By 1967, relationships had changed dramatically. U.S. direct investments had risen by then to $59.3 billion (U.S.), the book value of nearly double the amount at the beginning of the decade. The pattern of economic development and the technical proficiencies of U.S. businesses, however, made Europe the favorite area for direct investment, and made manufacturing the favorite type of investment. By the end of 1967, therefore, direct investment in Europe rose to 30 percent of all private direct investments abroad, and the European total became 30 percent larger than investment in Latin America and nearly equal to that in Canada.[63] The yield on manufacturing investment in Europe was "considerably above" that of Canada and Latin America, and the yield in Asia (thanks to Japan) and Africa (thanks to South Africa) was higher than in Europe.[64] Latin America had therefore lost ground, comparatively speaking.

It is possible to add to the list of variables involved in forecasting future inflows of private foreign capital into Latin America. The complex of uncertainties indicated so far, however, are enough to indicate the difficulties of estimating

---

well-established business, contrary to his best interests, may be straining to avoid change." UN (1961, pp. 2, 5). U.S. Senate (1960a, pp. 356–357).

[62] See Organization for Economic Cooperation and Development (1968, p. 26).

[63] U.S. Department of Commerce (1968a, p. 21).

[64] *Ibid.*, p. 26. There was some compensation, however, in the increased flow between 1961 and 1966 of private direct capital investment from Canada, Japan, and the OECD countries—and indeed of public capital.

the rate and size of foreign private capital needed for strengthening the rate of capital formation and actually fulfilling expectations.

Domestic Private Investment

It can be safely predicted that there will be no retreat from Latin American determination to assert the national right to regulate the power of foreign corporations operating within the countries concerned. The adjustment will probably be more Mexican than Cuban. While the adjustment process goes on, uncertainties in the inflow of public and private foreign capital may certainly not be reduced. These predictably drawn-out periods of anxiety impose at least two new responsibilities on Latin American private business: first, to invest more in Latin America and build up an atmosphere of confidence for local and foreign capital; and second, to modernize and adjust to standards of international competitive efficiency. These two advances are essential to strengthen the subscription of the national private sector to a more rapid rate of capital formation.

The inevitable controversies over foreign private corporate power and penetration tend to conceal a central point: the local Latin American businessman is the real advertiser of the climate for business and investment. How he succeeds can encourage or decisively discourage all investment. His adapting his own plans to national development interests may have a linkage effect in inducing foreign-related interests to do the same. Basically, the local Latin American business group can cooperate creatively with the national government to bring about the changes in climate which encourage savings and entrepreneurial endeavors.

Once again, however, any such transformation will take time and the rate of the transformation cannot be readily predicted. There are hopeful indications. There is evidence that the much-publicized flight of Latin American capital from Latin America is exaggerated.[65] There is further evidence of the emergence of a new class of modern businessman in Latin America who reinvest a substantial share of their income.[66] The Antiguoians of Colombia enjoy international standing for their skill as entrepreneurs.[67]

Yet severe initial boundary conditions have still to be overcome if the Latin American private business sector is to contribute more effectively to the internal capital formation needs of Latin America. The unincorporated one-man and family business is still far too characteristic. Local stock markets are either nonexistent or underdeveloped, and their development continues to be dampened in turn by the traditional reluctance of the family business to raise money in the stock market. Family businesses frequently prefer to remain the surviving bastions of insiders at the cost of denying themselves the financial advantages of mobilized capital from unrelated public shareholders. The commercial banks, on their side,

---

[65] Cf. Humphrey (1963, p. 18): "We have heard about the flight of capital from Caracas, Rio de Janeiro, and elsewhere to Swiss banks . . . The flight of local capital has to some extent abated and the greater problem now is how to entice back the capital that has already left the country." See also U.S. Senate (1967a, pp. 54–55).

[66] *Ibid.*, p. 18 (Humphrey).

[67] Committee for Economic Development (n.d., p. 45), UNECLA (1967b, p. 91), and Brandenburg (1964, p. 30).

continue in many instances to supply credit support under the traditional influence of long-standing personal ties (though there are changes here, and the new government credit institutions are introducing a widening of credit availability beyond the traditionally privileged groups[68]).

The private Latin American businessman, like his counterpart in the United States, Britain, or any other developed country, engages in self-financing his business, but he does this to a much smaller extent than his U.S. or European counterpart. Again, since incorporation is more the exception than the rule, ploughing money back into the business could amount to no more than a rather fickle decision between personal consumption needs and objective investment requirements. More than this, the large range of built-in deterrents which tend to limit the contribution of the foreign firm to domestic capital formation also exercise the same limiting effect on the Latin American firm. These deterrents include the frequent lack of communication between governments and domestic private enterprise in the formulation of development plans, and discouraging taxation of business profits, contradictory and repeated changes in public policy in a number of critical fields—tax laws, social reform, export and import regulations, credit policies, monetary policies, and remedies against inflation, and other areas. But beyond this, protectionism has all too often cushioned the local firm against any departure from traditionally inefficient pathways.

Yet a strengthening of the capacity of the Latin American private sector to contribute to a faster rate of capital formation is critically urgent. Since nationalism will allow no retreat from the Latin American determination to subordinate the decision-making of foreign corporations to national boundary conditions, the Latin American private sector must be strengthened for at least two reasons. First, local private investors may more spontaneously make decisions consonant with national development objectives. Second, foreign capital attracted to Latin America may find entrée into Latin America increasingly difficult except through partnership with Latin Americans who are given a majority interest in these joint ventures. This necessity is already being recognized.[69] This development accords with the principle we have established that a country may not be regarded as developed if the private entrepreneurs who are nationals are not decisively dominant in all private investment decision-making in their own countries.[70]

Changes are taking place in the directions we indicate, but the rate of change cannot be predicted with any high degree of certainty.

[68]Cf. Ostos (1962, p. 31):

First, it will be noted that an organized, systematic, and fluid supply of common shares in sizable volume is lacking. One reason for this is that a substantial share of important companies belongs to closed groups which have no interest or obligation in spreading their shares among many holders . . . as a result of this situation, most important transactions of common stock are consummated privately among industrial or financial groups . . . there is a lack of systematic and frequent information on the financial position of the companies whose stocks are listed on the exchange.

Ostos was speaking at the time as the executive director, Inter-American Development Bank and deputy director, Nacional Financiera, S.A., Mexico.

[69]See Roper (1970, pp. 17–20).

[70]See Farley (1971, p. 265). See also Prebisch (Aug. 1 and 16, 1969).

CONCLUSIONS

Straightforward conclusions can now be drawn. Accelerating the rate of capital formation, though not a total answer, is an essential condition for Latin American development. The lack of quantified estimates is a serious deterrent to any accurate calculation of the contributions which might be made through domestic efforts and of the size of the gap which might be filled by foreign capital inflows. But even against highly conjectural but reasonable capital formation targets, the past experience of Latin America and the variables which affect capital mobilization allow no firm prediction that capital formation and growth rate targets can be fulfilled in an orderly and continuous manner within the foreseeable future.

The rate of capital mobilization may, however, be stimulated by the progress of economic integration in Latin America. We now turn to a consideration of the evolution of economic integration in Latin America and the problems and prospects for development under a Latin American Common Market.

CHAPTER 12

LATIN AMERICAN ECONOMIC INTEGRATION: THE INSTITUTIONALIZATION OF AN IDEA

INTEGRATION FOR DEVELOPMENT AND SURVIVAL

Despite difficulties and uncertainties, Latin America had some real triumphs during the Alliance decade. Venezuela began to diversify and in the process of diversification initiated the conquest of a rich but isolated interior. Mexico, despite occasional anxieties, initiated a broad path of remarkable progress. Institutionalization for development spread in many countries, and so did a sense of managerial realism. The Alliance for Progress was, at the least, a symbol of a significant hemispheric attack on poverty and of an increase in the dimensions of Latin American cooperation. The will to accelerate and internalize development intensified in many Latin American countries. During the years 1960–69, the gross national product of Latin America increased in value from just over $74 billion (U.S.) to over $116 billion (U.S.). As a sectoral contribution to the gross product, manufacturing at the end of the 1960s was contributing, as we have seen, 24.1 percent, while agriculture contributed 20.4 percent.

These indicators of progress are, however, highly illusory. The evidence we have marshaled shows that the average increase of product per inhabitant in Latin America was far lower than the average for developed countries and developing countries as a whole. The cause of this disastrous difference was the demographic explosion in Latin America—the basic source of the continuing emergency situation in Latin America. Over the period, even Latin America's share of the gross product of the world declined. In Latin America itself, the poor became poorer and the rich richer. The poorer half of the population received little more than 13 percent of the total income, while the upper 5 percent received more than 31 percent.[1] The external sector for the period could be characterized by one word *instability*. World trade showed an extraordinary expansion, but the Latin American share regressed. In the last 20 years, Latin America's share of world exports has declined by more than 50 percent. During a period in which world exports were increasing at an average rate of 7 percent, the average annual increase in Latin American exports was just over 3 percent, a rate of growth not even good enough to meet Latin America's input requirements for economic development.[2]

Even if idealism were disregarded, realism necessitates the integration of the economies of Latin America. Economic integration gives Latin America an obvious chance to modify significantly the increasingly peripheral position which the region occupies in the world economy. Since the prospect of slowing the

[1] See CEPAL (1969c).
[2] CEPAL (1969b).

248

rate of population growth and increasing the rate of economic development for the continent as a whole seems highly uncertain without more intense continent-wide cooperation, the fact that a Latin American Common Market may not be substantially in operation by 1985, as planned, increases anxieties over the future of Latin America. Simon Bolívar's dream of an integrated Latin America still remains vital to the region's economic survival.[3]

We have seen the circular complexity of the web of variables in which Latin American economic growth is caught. Clearly Latin American development would have a better chance if only the demographic explosion could be detonated. This is, however, wishful thinking at the present time, even in the face of courageous family-planning drives. The rural population floods the towns; urbanization advances more rapidly than the rate at which manufacturing expansion can provide employment. The improvement of agriculture can only mean technological substitution and increased labor redundancy; industrial growth has meant the same thing. Externally, the terms of trade deteriorate for one reason and another, impairing Latin America's capacity to import basic capital and intermediate goods for planned industrialization. Internally, savings are limited, incomes inequitably distributed, and enterprise monopolistic, inefficient, and traditionally supported by discriminating import protection which adds to cost push inflationary pressures. Import substitution has reached its limits and social rigidities, reinforced by an irrelevant education system, inhibit the emergence of potential Henry Fords.[4] The absorptive capacity remains triumphantly inelastic and capital is hesitant in the face of the rapid changes affecting the climate for capital investment.[5]

Given these circumstances, the formation of a continental common market must be viewed as a necessary step to speed up economic development and avoid the quiet mounting of mass misery or a retreat into further economic marginality so far as the world economy is concerned—sterile alternatives which Latin America dare not embrace.[6]

We now trace the evolution of the idea of economic integration in Latin America. We assess the progress and problems of the Latin American Free Trade Association (LAFTA), the Central American Common Market (CACM), the Caribbean Free Trade Agreement (CARIFTA) and the Andean Common Market

---

[3]Cf. Herrera (1966, p. 24):

The warning of Bolívar contained in the circular in which he invited the Governments of the newborn Latin American republics to the Congress of Panama in 1824 is as pertinent today as it was delivered 142 years ago: "If Your Excellency be not moved to adhere to it, I foresee immense delays and harm at a time when the motion of the world puts everything in haste, and may do so to our detriment."

For a general theory of customs unions, the reader might profitably consult Vanek (1962, pp. 345–386) and Griffin (1969, pp. 225–241).

[4]There were exceptions, of course, but the situation is bad in relation to the needs. For additionally helpful perspective on this question of individual entrepreneurship, see, for instance, articles by Frank Safford, Howard F. Cline, Frederick B. Pike, J. Fred Rippy, and Jack Pfeiffer in Hanke (1967, pp. 113–154).

[5]See UN, Conference on Trade and Development (1968, esp. pp. 1–31, particularly relevant to the Latin American situation).

[6]Cf. UNECLA (1959, p. 1): "the common market project has become an essential factor in aiding the Latin American economy to escape from the stagnation into which it has been forced by circumstances."

(ANCOM), and then attempt an evaluation of the future of economic integration. Despite the theoretical advantages of economic integration, an empirical examination of the Latin American situation reveals that the road to integration will be, as it has always been, a long, hard, and hesitant one.

The Charter of Punta del Este

The idea of economic integration for Latin America appears here and there in the earlier history of Latin America. References to economic integration were sparked vaguely by Bolívar's dream and by occasional Pan American get-togethers. Trade and communication, for instance, were items on the agenda of the first International Conference of American States, held in Washington from October, 1889, to April, 1890. In Central America, there was not only sentiment; as far back as 1823 Central American countries brought into effect a Confederation of Central American States. In 1948, the means to strengthen the inter-American system as well as to promote inter-American economic cooperation were the principal agenda items of the Ninth International Conference of American States held in Bogota, Colombia.

The serious promotion of the idea of economic integration, however, emerged during and after World War II.[7] In 1948, Colombia, Ecuador, Panama, and Venezuela agreed under the Quito Charter to establish a free trade area. Nothing materialized. Between 1940-54, Argentina attempted on several occasions to initiate integrated regional arrangements among the southern countries of Latin America. Again, nothing substantial emerged. Numerous attempts were also made to rationalize problems emerging from different payment systems and the transfer of balance under bilateral agreements. Meanwhile, the value of total imports in intraregional trade among 10 countries of Latin America amounted to $610 million in 1958. Increasing imbalances in intraregional transactions in turn gave rise to more bilateral trade and payments treaties between Latin American countries to facilitate transfer of balances and promote multilateral compensation within the area. In 1958, for instance, Argentina and Uruguay, and Brazil and Chile, entered into agreements of this kind.[8]

During the 1950s, two significant and practical steps were taken, one at the begininng of the decade, the other at the end. In both cases, the United Nations Economic Commission for Latin America (UNECLA) played a central supportive role. In the first case, the Central American representatives at the yearly meeting of UNECLA in June, 1951, requested the setting up of a Central American Economic Cooperation Committee to study the problems of economic union. The first meeting of the committee took place in 1952.[9] In the second case, after various official conferences on the promotion of regional trade, customs unification, and even the setting up of a common market, a working group on the Latin American Regional Market was set up. This group, comprised of UNECLA experts, began to work in early 1958, and its second session was held in February, 1959. The work of the first group culminated in the establish-

[7]See U.S. Senate (1960a, pp. 428–429, 464–467), Urquidi (1964), and Dell (1966).
[8]UN (1958, pp. 54–55).
[9]See Chase Manhattan Bank (1962, pp. 1–9). See also Committee for Economic Development (CED) (1964, pp. 116–123) for a chronology of the economic integration of Costa Rica, El Salvador, Guatemala, Honduras, and Nicaragua.

ment of a Central American Common Market (CACM) and the General Treaty on Central American Economic Integration, signed in December, 1960, by El Salvador, Guatemala, Honduras, and Nicaragua, and by Costa Rica in 1962. The work of the second group culminated in the establishment of the Latin American Free Trade Association (LAFTA) as provided for under the Treaty of Montevideo, signed in February, 1960, by Argentina, Brazil, Chile, Mexico, Peru, and Uruguay. Bolivia, Paraguay, Colombia, Ecuador, and Venezuela joined later.[10] The merger of these two groups—CACM and LAFTA—constituted the genesis of a continent-wide Latin American Common Market (LACM).

The economic circumstances of Latin America at the end of the 1950s illuminate the references to Latin American economic integration in the Charter of the Alliance for Progress in 1961 and in the subsequent declaration of the presidents of America in 1967. If in the larger international setting, the establishment of the European Common Market in 1957 is regarded as a relevant influence on Latin American efforts at this time, it is sometimes argued that there were essential differences between the European and the Latin American situations.[11] This argument is, however, difficult to sustain.

Europe was devastated by war and menaced by Communism. The European economies are more or less at the same level. Europe did enjoy a complex of preexisting commercial ties. Europe has, as a whole, a more or less stable price structure. Europe is geographically contiguous. The principle of economic integration is, in both Latin America and Europe, not an alternative but an inescapable necessity. Latin America also suffered war damage from being cut off from export markets. Latin America is under Castroite and other ideological and

[10]See UN (1967, pp. 15–16) for a brief survey. See also Cale (1969). The reader should note that a good deal of parallel work was going on at the same time (1955–59). Getting down to a practical program for setting up a Latin American regional market owes its genesis to a resolution of the sixth session of UNECLA in Bogota, Colombia, August–September, 1955, under which a Trade Committee was set up, with an ECLA secretariat. While this ECLA secretariat of the Trade Committee initiated several studies of Inter-American Trade and of multilateral payments in Latin America, the Trade Committee itself set up a second working group—namely, a *Central Banks Working Group* to make recommendations to the Trade Committee on the possibility of setting up a multilateral payments system for Latin America. This group met April–May, 1957, and again in November–December, 1958. A third group—the *Working Group on the Latin American Regional Market*—was directly appointed by the executive secretary of the ECLA (as mentioned in the text). This group, under Galo Plaza, ex-President of Ecuador, and comprised of prominent Latin American economists, government officials, and ex-government officials, formulated recommendations to the Trade Committee on the possibility of setting up a Latin American Common Market. The meeting of the ECLA in Panama City in May, 1959, then approved the appointment of high level *Experts Working Group*, the experts being named by each member government of ECLA, to present on the basis of the findings of the last two groups a draft for agreement by the Latin American governments. The OAS also considered Latin American economic integration at its Economic Conference in Buenos Aires in 1957—the matter having been studied by the Inter-American Economic and Social Council of the OAS. Indeed, in this period, the idea of a Western Hemisphere common market was also being thought about and was actually discussed by the Committee of Twenty-one Presidential Representatives. But these last efforts yielded place to the ECLA working groups.

[11]See Chase Manhattan Bank (1967, pp. 10–11).

physical pressures. Because the Latin American countries differ very widely in economic status and are without traditional commercial ties; because they are geographically isolated and are at varying stages of price stability, Latin America has an even more compelling need to come to terms with the idea of a common market. It can hardly be argued that an equivalent "emotional stimulus" for "closer cooperation" is lacking in Latin America in comparison with Europe.[12]

Disregarding the emotional background, the plain fact was that at the end of the 1950s Latin America's economic situation made economic integration just as essential as in Western Europe. Latin America could not maintain the average annual rates of increase reached in the decade 1945-55 of 2.7 percent in the case of the per capita product and 3.3 percent in the case of per capita income. For in the period 1955-58, these figures fell to 1.1 percent for the per capita product and 0.5 percent for the per capita income. Deterioration in the terms of trade; a continuing high rate of population growth; limitations on the policy of substitution and the increase in costs; an excessively low share of intraregional trade in the total import coefficient; the balkanization, overprotection, and undercompetitiveness of Latin America markets, which throttled the economy and prevented the building up of competitive capital goods export industries, left Latin America at the end of the decade with one clear choice: to build an economically integrated structure.

The Charter of Punta del Este represented a turning point in hemispheric relations. Chapter V, Title III of that charter, "Economic Integration of Latin America," represented the institutionalization of an idea from which there was no rational turning back. The Charter of Punta del Este embodies this recognition in these words:

The American Republics consider that the broadening of present national markets in Latin America is essential to accelerate the process of economic development in the hemisphere. It is also an appropriate means for obtaining greater productivity through specialized and complementary industrial production which will, in turn, facilitate the attainment of greater social benefits for the inhabitants of the various regions of Latin America. The broadening of markets will also make possible the better use of resources under the Alliance for Progress.[13]

The republics recognized the Treaty of Montevideo as well as the General Treaty on Central American Economic Integration as "appropriate instruments for the attainment of these objectives." They recognized further that integration would accelerate specialization and complementary production: that "special, fair and equitable treatment" must be accorded to countries "at a relatively less advanced stage of economic development"; and that integration would strengthen the bargaining power of Latin countries against "the unfavorable treatment accorded to their foreign trade in world markets." Supporting economic integration was to be a decisive criterion in the application of the resources of the Alliance for Progress; in the provision of additional financial resources; in the determination of national institutions for channeling funds; in developing and coordinating transport and communications systems in Latin America; in coordinating national plans or engaging in joint planning efforts; in promoting, the development of national Latin American enterprises; and in facilitating the active participation of the private sector.

[12]*Ibid.*
[13]U.S. House (1966, pp. 109-110).

In all this, "in order to facilitate economic integration in Latin America," it was recognized as advisable that effective relationships be established between LAFTA and the group of countries belonging to CACM "as well as between either of these groups and other Latin American countries." Seven years after these two groups were formed, the faith in economic integration—at least in declaratory terms—was still strong. On April 14, 1967, at Punta del Este, Uruguay, it was resolved that Latin America would create progressively, beginning in 1970, a Latin American Common Market "which shall be substantially in operation in a period of no more than fifteen years." Indeed, the Charter of Punta del Este subscribed vigorously to Latin American economic integration and industrial development. "Economic integration," it was stated under "Principles, Objectives, and Goals," "is a collective instrument for accelerating Latin American development and should constitute one of the policy goals of each of the countries of the region."[14] These goals secured maximum support from the United States.

The Contemporary Arguments for a Latin American Common Market

The arguments in favor of creating a Latin American Common Market at the end of the 1960s involved no basic change in principle. There was certainly, however, a basic change in the intensity with which these arguments were put forward. Powerful Latin American economists stated bluntly in 1965:

Latin America is failing to face resolutely a course of events which is jeopardizing the pace and the very meaning of its economic and social development and shaking its political life to its foundations. Never before have we seen such a population explosion; nor has the legitimate desire of our people for a better life been so strikingly expressed. . . . If we remain disunited, we shall not be able, in our desire to reap the full benefits of contemporary technology, to meet such requirements, among them the need for great economic bases: 95 percent of the industrial output of the more advanced countries is produced within large markets. . . . Our countries, nevertheless, attempt to develop in an area arbitrarily divided into numerous watertight compartments with very little inter-communication.[15]

The proposals advanced by Prebisch and his colleagues emphasized that isolated economic activity on the part of Latin American countries in a world

---

[14] U.S. Department of State (1967a, pp. 12 and 14–17). See also Inter-American Development Bank (1968, esp. pp. 1–2).

[15] Inter-American Development Bank (1965b). The four economists who drafted this statement in reply to a letter dated January 6, 1965, from Eduardo Frei, then president of Chile, were (1) Raul Prebisch, then director-general of the Latin American Institute for Economic and Social Planning; (2) Jose Antonio Mayobre, then executive director of UNECLA; (3) Felipe Herrera, then president of the Inter-American Development Bank; and (4) Carlos Sanz de Santamaria, chairman of the Inter-American Committee on the Alliance for Progress. Herrera (1966, p. 4) distinguishes between the terms *integration* and *common market* as follows:

In practice, the term "integration" has generally been used to refer to a broad range of methods and initiatives for economic cooperation in Latin America. . . . We understand by "common market" an association by a group of nations coordinating their activities in terms of common objectives of economic development and social welfare . . . the establishment of mutually acceptable guidelines on trade policy; the orientation of investment policies and the coordination of monetary, fiscal, social, transportation and agricultural policies. Within the trade system, a common market presupposes a single economic area or space characterized by the substantial elimination of internal tariff barriers

of vast economic blocs deprived Latin America of international bargaining power and reduced the region's chances of using technology effectively and overcoming patterns of development originating in the nineteenth century. The advanced countries had attained an extraordinary opulence. The markets for the primary products of Latin America, however, were "shrinking and closing, without new ones being offered" for Latin American manufactures. This imbalance in foreign trade was a "serious brake" on economic development in many countries and reduced international financial resources for Latin American development. The Common Market, far from being incompatible with national development, contributed to the promotion of vigorous national development.

The core of the problem, however, in Latin America was the need to mobilize considerable capital to expedite economic development in the face of serious tension and the inadequate dynamism in the Latin American economy to absorb human potential. Yet capital was being wasted because of the lack of a great economic base. The four Latin American economists pointed out that Latin America's "industrializing in watertight compartments" militated against the large-scale operation which modern technology required, and against the division of labor and the possibilities of economic viability. Indeed, with a rational integration program, UNECLA and Inter-American Development Bank secretariats, as well as the Latin American Institute of Economic and Social Planning, calculated that "of the probable increase in output of some 15 million tons of iron and steel by 1975, savings of some $3700 million could be made as regards the investments required if each producing country continued making, by itself, all the items for its own consumption." The annual savings in direct production costs would thus be more than $400 million by 1975 —"a considerable proportion of the total steel cost by that date."[16]

Industrializing in watertight compartments was inimical to the expansion of competition, and thus to the proper utilization of capital and the reduction of costs. On the other hand, a simple market with close communication, it was argued, would spur sectoral complementarity or integration agreements, "especially in the major import-substitution industries."[17] To a significant extent, products now imported by Latin America "would be replaced by others of

---

between associated countries and by a common external tariff. As a corollary, a common market also presupposes that people, services and capital will be able to move freely within the integrated economic area. Moreover, for the purpose of implementing such measures, which assume common multinational and even supranational policies, a common market system implies the existence of community organs and institutions empowered to attain those goals. These institutions must be supplemented by a common legal system for the area where joint action is to be taken, as well as by proper coordination of prevailing legislation, to enable the community to function.

[16] Herrera (1966, p. 4). The reader might wish to refer also to Inter-American Development Bank (1963).

[17] Herrera (1965, p. 11), noted that in 1965 Latin America had only 8 percent of the world's railroad network and 3.2 percent of the all-weather road system. Maritime transportation was no better. Adequate port facilities were lacking and the fleet was not suited to carry the actual needs of intraregional trade. Hardly 6 percent of the cargo entering or leaving the region was transported in Latin American flagships which got only 11 percent of the area's freight charges. For this reason, over the last few years, the annual balance of payments deficit of the 19 Latin American republics on account of freight, insurance, and other similar items totaled some $700 million.

Latin American origin in intra-regional trade." More than this, increased competition among Latin American countries within a single economic area would, it was suggested, encourage modernization and readjustment of existing industries.

Any such reduction in costs would, of course, have consequences at the international level. Latin America's persistent tendency to external disequilibrium required, in addition to import substitution, that Latin America export an increasing quantity of industrial goods to the major developed countries. The lowering of manufacturing costs in Latin America was therefore imperative. In turn, Latin America would be enabled to import more larger quantities of the capital and intermediate goods which would, for a long time, be essential to its industrialization efforts. Even to take advantage of preferences, it was necessary to cut production costs in Latin America through the spur of competition.

These arguments clearly echoed the earlier recognition in the Charter of Punta del Este that integration was not an alternative but an essential road for Latin America. The Agency for International Development in an excerpt from its program presentation to the United States Congress outlining the president's foreign aid request for the fiscal year 1969 observed equally firmly:

. . . . the stagnation of exports poses a serious obstacle to future growth and development prospects in Latin America. . . . so long as the region is so heavily dependent on world price trends of a small group of export commodities, Latin American exports will remain vulnerable, and economies will be subject to fluctuations in exchange earnings which will lead to periodic trade and exchange restrictions detrimental to growth. The urgency becomes starkly apparent for programs to help diversify further the production and export of agricultural and industrial goods, and further, to facilitate economic integration to develop and expand markets.[18]

THE PROGRESS OF ECONOMIC INTEGRATION

The Latin American Free Trade Association

An appreciation of the progress of LAFTA emerges from a consideration of the terms and expectations of the treaty under which six Latin American governments—with five others joining later—agreed to establish a free trade area and to institute the Latin American Free Trade Association. It is noteworthy that the treaty embodied the determination of the original signatories "to persevere in their efforts to establish, gradually and progressively, a Latin American common market."

Under Article 2, the free trade area was to be brought into full operation within "not more than twelve (12) years" from the date of the treaty. During that time, the LAFTA countries expected to eliminate gradually "such duties, charges and restrictions as may be applied to imports of goods originating in the territory of any Contracting Party." To achieve this aim, the contracting parties agreed to enter into negotiations from time to time to draw up national schedules of products, the duties on which were to be reduced at not less than 8 percent a year and a common schedule of products on which the contracting parties

[18]U.S. Department of State (1968a, pp. 3-4).

agreed "to eliminate duties, charges, and other restrictions completely, so far as intra-Area trade is concerned." The common schedule consisted of products which constituted not less than 15 percent of the aggregate value of the trade among the contracting parties during the first three-year period; 50 percent during the second three-year period; 75 percent during the third three-year period; and "substantially all of such trade" during the fourth three-year period.

The treaty provided for remedial measures where concessions resulted in "significant and persistent disadvantages" in trade patterns. It also provided for reconciling "import and export regimes" to "ensure fair competitive conditions among the Contracting Parties" and encouraged the negotiation of mutual agreements on complementarity by industrial sectors. The most-favored-nation treatment was to be extended to all parties—except in the case of border trade. On the other hand, where imports from within the free trade area had serious repercussions "on specific productive activities of vital importance to the national economy," the country so suffering could impose "non-discriminatory restrictions" on these imports. If these measures were prolonged for more than a year, a conference would determine the issue. In the area of agriculture, the contracting parties were allowed to limit imports and to equalize the prices between the imported and the domestic product. At the same time, the contracting parties agreed to make an attempt to expand through agreements intra-area trade in agricultural commodities "to cover deficits in domestic production." Provision was made, under Article 32, for countries at a relatively less advanced stage of economic development to adopt appropriate temporary measures to promote specific productive activities, to correct an unfavorable balance of payments, to protect domestic output, to encourage new activities, and to promote or support special technical assistance programs.

The LAFTA countries from the beginning occupied a significant position in the Latin American economy. In 1958, the signatories had a total population of over 137 million people, a gross national product of between $40,000 million and $45,000 million and a foreign trade of $8500 million.[19] The LAFTA countries therefore constituted a significant market. The LAFTA treaty countries in 1960 accounted for more than 60 percent of the Latin American production of coffee and tobacco; for over 70 percent of Latin American coal production; for over 80 percent of the production of grains, root crops, pulses, and cotton; and for over 90 percent of the production of copper, lead, and zinc. The production of the LAFTA countries was significant not only in Latin American terms but in world terms.

With regard to manufacturing, according to UNECLA estimates, the LAFTA countries accounted for all of Latin America's output of manufactured motor vehicles, wood pulp, newsprint, practically all its primary steel products, and a large share of the output of food products, textiles, durable consumer goods, chemicals, machinery and transport equipment.[20] LAFTA countries in 1957 accounted for some 77 percent of the installed generating capacity of Latin America and 51 percent of the foreign trade. By 1966, with the entry of Bolivia and Venezuela into LAFTA, the dominance of the LAFTA

[19] UN (1961, p. 2).
[20] See UN (1961, table 2, p. 3).

countries became even more overwhelming. Even without Venezuela, LAFTA accounted in 1966 for 70.6 percent of the inter-Latin American exports as against 58 percent in 1960, and 78.2 percent of inter-Latin American imports in 1966.[21]

Intra-zonal trade within LAFTA countries expanded more rapidly between 1961–69 than LAFTA's global trade volume and more than doubled in value during the decade. (See Tables 12.1 and 12.2.) A total of nearly 11,000 national list tariff concessions and nine complementation agreements had been negotiated, over the period 1961–69.[22]

Institutionally, there were a number of gains. In 1965, for instance, the central banks of the contracting parties in LAFTA inaugurated a system of reciprocal credits and multilateral clearing every two months to reduce the effects of the dollar shortage on their mutual trade. This agreement was further strengthened in October, 1969, by a new multilateral credit arrangement.

Despite the achievements we have identified, problems accumulated and the differences generated by these problems retarded somewhat the development of LAFTA. The problems are typical of obstacles to almost all attempts to promote economic integration. Given the need however to accelerate economic development in Latin America, within some specific time horizon, we are once again confronted with a situation in which prediction is highly conjectural because it is impossible to predict the rate at which these problems would be resolved if they are resolved at all. In theory they must be resolved. In fact

TABLE 12.1

Intra-LAFTA Trade, 1961–69

	EXPORTS		IMPORTS	
	Value, FOB[a] (in millions of dollars)	Index[c]	Value, CIF[b] (in millions of dollars)	Index[c]
1961	489.2	100	588.3	100
1962	547.0	112	643.4	109
1963	583.4	119	706.7	120
1964	716.3	146	841.9	143
1965	842.2	172	985.9	168
1966	875.8	179	987.3	168
1967	851.7	174	995.6	169
1968	1,000.4	204	1,074.3	182
1969	1,146.9	234	1,284.6	218

[a] Free on board.
[b] Cost insurance and freight.
[c] Based on 1961 = 100.
N.B.: Includes those products traded under concessions and not.

Source: Latin American Free Trade Association (LAFTA) (September 1970).

[21] UNECLA (1969b, p. 25).
[22] U.S. Department of State (1969c, p. 4).

TABLE 12.2

Global Trade Volume of LAFTA, 1961-69

	EXPORTS		IMPORTS	
	Value, FOB[a] (in millions of dollars)	Index[c]	Value, CIF[b] (in millions of dollars)	Index[c]
1961	7,279.4	100	7,329.9	100
1962	7,715.7	106	7,371.3	101
1963	8,178.1	112	7,040.1	96
1964	8,110.8	111	7,366.5	100
1965	9,382.4	129	7,604.3	104
1966	9,919.3	136	8,339.5	114
1967	9,990.6	137	8,653.1	118
1968	10,326.2	142	9,629.7	131
1969	11,400.7	157	10,573.3	144

[a] Free on board.
[b] Cost insurance and freight.
[c] Based on 1961 = 100.

Source: Latin American Free Trade Association (LAFTA) (December 1970).

their resolution comes slowly and uncertainly, although there is a regional faith that they will be ultimately resolved. A brief indication of the major problems will be sufficient at this point. LAFTA really concentrated on removing tariff barriers among its member countries of LAFTA, and by 1967 regional tariffs had been reduced to about 50 percent of the level applicable to non-regional exports. Even so, by 1966 tariff concessions had been made on less than half the tariff items and most of these concessions were put through largely within the first three years of LAFTA and on items not produced by the country making the concessions. LAFTA negotiators began to find it increasingly difficult to reach agreements on tariff concessions on products within the common schedule,[23] as well as to negotiate national schedules.[24] These difficulties reflected a complicated variety of factors standing in the way of faster accommodation. For one thing, the treaty of Montevideo allowed a very high degree of selectivity in the negotiation process. LAFTA was not interpreted as enjoying a supranational status, which would have been an impossible situation, anyway. For instance, countries were allowed negotiated withdrawal of products appearing in the national schedule.

[23] See for instance UN (1968, pp. 8-9). Cf. Cardenas (1968, p. 372). Of 9400 concessions negotiated within LAFTA up to 1966, 23 percent related to agricultural products, 7 percent to products of extractive industries, less than one percent to other products, the rest (some 70 percent) related to manufacturing. Of these, chemicals accounted for 23.7 percent, engineering and electrical equipment 22.2 percent, iron and steel 10.1 percent. Intraregional trade rose 100 percent between 1962-67. Between 1962-65, trade in primary products increased at an average rate of 3.5 percent and exports of manufactures at an average rate of about 20 percent. The three most industrialized countries of LAFTA contributed some 80 percent of total interregional trade.

[24] See Cale (1969, p. 14).

Concessions to encourage border trade were not subject to the most-favored-nation treatment, nor were other members of LAFTA mandated to reduce duties on the same product to the same extent as any other member, if at all. While concessions made on products included in the common schedule could not be modified, no country was obliged to reduce any duty or charges on these products until the end of the 12-year period. In the case of the national schedule, there was no obligation to make concessions beyond the items already being imported among the member countries of LAFTA. Under special provisions made for agriculture, a member country could limit agricultural importation to just the amount needed to meet shortfalls in domestic production and to equalize domestic and external prices.[25] In 1968 the less developed countries pressed to have this limit removed, but this move was unsuccessful.

Differences developed over the allocation of foreign investment, which the less developed countries alleged was being attracted to the more developed countries. The question of a common investment policy keeping out foreign investment from a number of key areas, such as petroleum, petrochemicals, electric power, and transportation had to be postponed for consideration.[26] No agreement could be reached on programmed or automatic tariff reductions.[27] Vested interests continued to resist advances towards a single economic market, securing the political backing of traditionally entrenched and protected commercial interests who could exploit national sentiment to support their case just as in 1961 when a UNECLA-OAS consultant group reported:

The problem of most direct concern to the majority of domestic industrialists in the countries which signed the Montevideo Treaty . . . is the fear that protection enjoyed by their industries will be prejudiced by the development of the broader markets envisaged by the Free-Trade Area.[28]

Galo Plaza, secretary general of the Organization of American States, in an address to the Eighth Florida World Trade Conference, argued that economic nationalism was "perhaps the most dynamic force at work in Latin America today." This nationalism was, in his view, "quite different from the old style isolationism and hatred of foreigners." He stated:

For many Latin Americans the measure of worth of foreign investment is precisely what it does for the economic and social development of their country. Under the new nationalism, only the foreign firm which is able to contribute to economic progress and help promote healthy social change is wanted.[29]

At the level of concrete action, however, matters had not moved as fast as Plaza would have wished. In his study of the obstacles still standing in the way of the automobile industry under the Montevideo Treaty, Baranson was blunt: ". . . vested interests . . . contribute to national sentiment opposed to foreign ownership, despite the fact that international corporations could play

---

[25]*Ibid.*, pp. 3–5.
[26]*Ibid.*, pp. 12, 13.
[27]See Prebisch (1970b, p. 165).
[28]UN (1961, p. 5).
[29]Pan American Union (1969aa, p. 1).

a most helpful role in rationalizing production and marketing in the LAFTA region" (1968, pp. 25-29).[30]

Baranson's study of obstacles to the economic integration of the automobile industry in the LAFTA is an illuminating example of continuing problems. A larger integrated market would allow the automotive industry to enjoy wider economies of scale—increasing production, reducing costs, and enabling the industry to reduce prices and thus increase demand. Production could be concentrated and efficiency improved. In LAFTA countries, however, automotive production is split among eight countries, 82 percent of the production being concentrated in Brazil, Argentina, and Mexico, and 18 percent in five other countries. In 1967, 67 firms were producing some 200 basic models of cars and trucks and there were over 10,000 component and parts manufacturers. This was, according to Baranson, 10 times more than the region could support economically. Baranson reckoned that for minimum production costs, the market for a single basic vehicle type ought to be about 240,000 units. In the largest member country of LAFTA, demand at best stood at 225,000 vehicles in 1967 and there were 10 firms manufacturing some 40 different models and makes of cars and trucks. In turn, the proliferation of the manufacture of parts and components and the atomization of markets has resulted in Latin American manufacturing costs being well above the world average. A light truck made in Mexico costs 58 percent more than an imported model. The average cost of locally manufactured parts were even higher, standing at approximately 119 percent more than imports.[31] Since 1961, no automotive products have been placed on the national or common lists for tariff reductions. Instead, as in Argentina, Chile, and Mexico in 1965, bilateral agreements were signed "permitting parts manufactured in one country to qualify as national content for another." Not only did this cut across the spirit and objectives of LAFTA, but production costs actually increased. Indeed, even under bilateral agreements, exchange was very limited because of exchange rate difficulties, mutual suspicion, and competitive fears.

Since the wide-ranging differences we have identified could not be readily settled, the number of concessions, which in 1962 had risen to a total of 5050 fell to 800 in 1963. Excluding the new members, Venezuela and

[30] On the other hand, cf. Herrera (1966, p. 15):
In our hemisphere, it is a fully established fact in recent decades that private enterprises operate alongside public enterprises; that planning concepts function side by side with free initiative; and that foreign investment, increasingly directed toward industry, is accompanied by the gradual consolidation of the local entrepreneurial class. . . . One of the characteristics that most clearly differentiates Latin America from other developing areas is the presence of an indigenous industrial class which has, in many of our countries, developed under the protection of the State in the form of tariffs, exchange controls, credits and other public inducements. This class must be promoted to a more dynamic role so that it can avail itself of the opportunities that a common market can offer. Consequently, it would be an historic error to indiscriminately dismantle a protective system which, despite all its defects, has served as a long range factor of self-assertion for important social groups in Latin America. On the other hand, in the present effort to modernize our structures, our countries are seeking . . . to promote more harmonious and efficient relations between the public and private sectors.

[31] Baranson (1968, p. 27) also supplies the following data: In Brazil, a domestically manufactured light truck cost 80 percent more than an imported truck; in Argentina 145 percent more, and vehicle components 210 percent more.

Bolivia, they dropped to only 360 in 1967.[32] There was a slight rise, but only to 526 in 1969.[33] Agreement could not be reached on the second stage of the common list, scheduled to be completed by November 30, 1967. By April, 1969, not more than eight complementation agreements had been signed. Indeed, in December, 1969, LAFTA members adopted the Caracas Protocol as a mandatory protocol to the Montevideo treaty. But though it initiated the new strategy of promoting a series of in-depth studies and giving time to the member countries to revise their treaty compromises and review future guidelines, the protocol really insured that the formation of the free trade area would have to be postponed from 1974 to 1980.[34]

Once again, we are confronted with the difficulties imposed by realism on theoretical conjectures. The comments of Carlos Quintana, secretary-general of UNECLA, probably represent an earthy acceptance of the status of regional integration policy at this stage. He observed:

Since the integration process is not going ahead as rapidly as is required, an analysis must be made, in the light of present experience, of the nature of the obstacles which would hamper it, particularly of the reasons for and the extent of the resistance it arouses. An analysis must also be made of the new sub-regional integration agreements and the role which should be played by other instruments connected with regional development programs, river basins, transport and communications, and multinational enterprises. On the basis of this diagnosis and other technical research, a regional integration policy must be framed which would lead to the attainment of the common market objectives and targets established by the Heads of State at Punta del Este. . . . These studies are intended, naturally, to provide information and concrete bases for governments to examine their policies in terms of the conditions prevailing in each country.[35]

The Central American Common Market

The Central American Common Market, unlike LAFTA, had behind it a long history of attempts among the Central American countries to forge political union among themselves. It was also created after far more thorough preparation. When the Central American Economic Cooperation Committee met in 1952, trade among themselves amounted to only 5 percent of the total trade in Central American countries. The largest market for industrial goods amounted to less than 3 million people while the total possible market at the time—if the markets were integrated—should have amounted to 10 million people.[36] The prospective advantages of the larger market became a basic factor in the drive towards integration. When the General Treaty on Central American Economic Integration was signed in 1960, ushering in CACM, in contrast to LAFTA, it

[32] See Cale (1969, p. 14).

[33] See U.S. Department of State (1969b, p. 4).

[34] See LAFTA (July, September, December 1970). The indepth studies covered nine main fields: coordination of commercial policies; industrial development; agricultural development; financial, monetary, and fiscal coordination; common policies toward third countries; international groups of countries and organizations; infrastructure coordination; social legislation; and institutional changes.

[35] Quintana (1969, p. 22).

[36] See Crow (1966, pp. 58–66).

had been preceded by numerous preparatory investigations and studies of basic data.

These studies resulted in the setting up in 1954 of the Central American Institute of Public Administration in Costa Rica and in 1956 of the Central American Institute for Industrial Research and Technology in Guatemala, as well as the adoption of the Uniform Central American Customs Nomenclature (NAUCA). In June, 1958, the CACM countries signed the Multilateral Treaty of Central American Free Trade and Economic Integration and the Agreement on the Regime for Central American Integration Industries. The first treaty became effective in June, 1959, and the second in September, 1963. Together they provided for the setting up of a free trade area and a customs union within 10 years, the immediate elimination of customs duties on 200 commodities, the elimination of export subsidies, the promotion of regional industries, and the expansion of the list of commodities freed from customs duties by earlier agreements. Under these two treaties, new institutions were created, namely, a Central American Trade Commission and a Central American Industrial Integration Commission. The Central American Industrial Integration Commission had the responsibility of identifying and designating "integration" industries requiring a regional rather than the local market. The products of these industries would be exempt from duties within the borders of the CACM. The same products, if produced in Central American countries other than the CACM countries, would be dutiable for a 10-year period, over which the duties were to be progressively eliminated. There was some inhibition, however, built into the process in that these concessions within and without the CACM had to come under separate protocol for each integration industry product.

The next stage was the setting up of a common external tariff—in a more thorough manner than in earlier agreements. In September, 1959, the Central American Agreement on Equalization of Import Duties and Charges was signed. External duties on 272 tariff items were immediately equalized, and provision made for the addition of other items over a period of two to five years. The equalization of these tariffs was to be consistent with the economic development and integration objectives of five Central American countries.

There was disagreement over some aspects of the integration program but the whole program was rescued when in February, 1960, Guatemala, Honduras, and El Salvador signed the Tripartite Treaty for Economic Association, which immediately speeded up integration measures. Under this treaty, immediate free trade status was given to all except 56 natural and manufactured products originating within the three countries. Trade in these commodities was to be free of tariff within five years. A common external tariff was to be established within five years and with this a common customs administration. The treaty abandoned the regional industry concept in the case of integration industries, substituting for this the setting up of a development and assistance fund to accelerate economic integration and development.

The Tripartite Treaty threatened a serious split between the three signatories on the one hand and Costa Rica and Nicaragua on the other. Reconciliation took place with the signing in December, 1960, of the General Treaty on Central American Economic Integration (GTEI), which became the basic instrument for Central American economic integration. Four nations signed this agreement, and provision was made for Costa Rica's accession later on. The General Treaty proposed the establishment of a Central American Common Market (CACM) within a period of five years, eliminating from tariff restrictions all products not mentioned in the special annex to the treaty. Products mentioned in the annex were immediately exempted for free trade, but were made subject to annual tariff negotiations. The integration industries agreement of 1958 was incorporated into the General Treaty—with the stipulation that the first plants must be in operation in six months.

Several other important developments resulted from the General Treaty. All goods emanating in the member countries were subject to no greater restrictions than the domestic products of any particular member country. Fiscal and other legal incentives for investment were made uniform within the CACM countries. Three new administrative institutions were set up to carry out the terms of the treaty: a Central American economic council; an executive council; and a permanent secretariat. The economic council, comprised of the ministers of national economy of the signatory countries, was made responsible for policy-making. The executive council, comprised of delegates and alternates of the member countries, was made responsible for carrying out policy as determined. The permanent secretariat, under a secretary-general appointed for a three-year term by the economic council, served both the economic council and the executive council.

Events moved rapidly thereafter. In May, 1961, the Central American Bank for Economic Integration (CABEI) came into effective operation (see Figure 12.1).[37] In July of the same year, the Central American Clearing House agreement was signed by the five banks and began its operations in October. In July, 1962, the five countries signed the agreement on uniform tax incentives to industrial development. By January, 1964, a general secretariat for Central American tourism integration was set up; the next month a CACM monetary council; and by May, 1964, approval was given for a single common outer tariff schedule for 95 percent of all products. In 1966, the CACM countries set a definite date for a single common outer tariff for all products.

The progress demonstrated by the CACM countries has been impressive. Internal CACM trade was worth $260 million in 1968, 10 times the level of the first year, 1961. Trading in that year (1968) reached its highest level with a 22 percent increase in value over the 1967 figure of $213 million.[38] Indeed trade grew at an average rate of 32 percent a year after the establishment of CACM. Industrial growth after 1962 expanded 11 percent a year. Trade in manufactured goods represented 85 percent of the expansion of intra-Central American trade, double the proportion in 1960.[39] Between 1960–66 intraregional

[37] In November, 1963, CABEI got a loan of $10 million from the U.S. government to support middle class housing and $2.5 million to support specific technical and economic studies relevant to the development of CACM general economic integration. The next month, the Inter-American Development Bank granted CABEI credits totaling $2.9 million to promote higher education on a regional basis. A Central American integration fund administered by CABEI was subsequently set up to push particularly public section investment of a regional character. This fund is jointly subscribed to by the United States and Central America, and started with an initial subscription of $42 million.

[38] Pan American Union (April 7, 1969). See also UNECLA (1966aa).

[39] Cardenas (1968, p. 320).

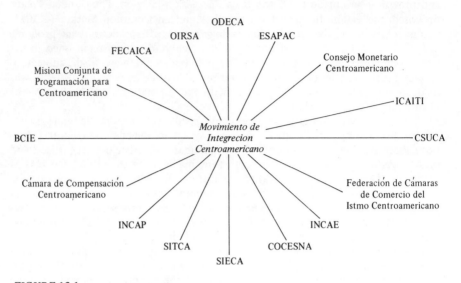

FIGURE 12.1
Principal Regional Organizations Advancing Economic and Social Development and Integration in Central America
Source: Pan American Union (1966b).

(OIRSA)   Organismo Internacional de Sanidad Agropecuaria; San Salvador, El Salvador

(FECAICA)   Federacion de Camaras y Asociaciones Industriales de Centro America, San Jose, Costa Rica

(MISION CONJUNTA de PROGRAMACION PARA CENTROAMERICANO) a/c SIECA, Guatemala, Guatemala

(BCIE)   Banco Centroamericano de Integracion Economica, Apartado Postal 772, Tegucigalpa, Honduras

(CAMARA de COMPENSACION CENTROAMERICANO)   Edificia del Banco Central, Tegucigalpa, Honduras

(INCAP)   Instituto de Nutricion de Centro America y Panama, Guatemala, Guatemala

(SITCA)   Secretaria de Integracion Turistica Centro-Americano, Managua, Nicaragua

(ODECA)   Organizacion de Estados, Centroamericanos, San Salvador, El Salvador

(SIECA)   Secretaria Permanente del Tratado General de Integracion Economica, Centroamericano, Guatemala, Guatemala

(ESAPAC)   Escuela Superior de Administracion Publica en America Central, San Jose, Costa Rica

(CONSEJO MONETARIO CENTROAMERICANO)   Banco de Guatemala, Guatemala

(ICAITI)   Instituto Centroamericano de Investigacion de Tecnologia Industrial, Guatemala, Guatemala

(CSUCA)   Consejo Superior Universitario Centroamericano, Universidad de Costa Rica, San Jose, Costa Rica

(FEDERACION de CAMARAS de COMERCIO del ISTMO CENTROAMERICANO) San Salvador, El Salvador

(INCAE)   Instituto Centroamericano de Administracion de Empresas, Managua, Nicaragua

(COCESNA)   Corporacion Centroamericano de Servicios de Navegacion Aerea

trade in manufactured goods increased over 600 percent to an estimated $125 million.[40] By the end of 1966, 95 percent of the items under NAUCA tariff restrictions had become tariff-free in trade within the CACM. In the period 1960–66, imports originating in the CACM rose from 6 percent of all the area's imports to 18 percent. The gross national product of CACM countries rose by over 40 percent at constant 1966 prices and the increase in the growth rate averaged nearly 6 percent, actually reaching 7.1 percent in 1965. Other indicators of progress were noted at the meeting of the presidents of the CACM countries with the president of the United States on July 6, 1968, in El Salvador. In seven years investment had increased 65 percent, 4000 miles of roads had been opened up for new marketing and expenditures for education had increased 50 percent.

As already pointed out, industrial growth, a particular objective of the CACM effort, had made promising strides. Industrialization within the CACM began to move beyond the traditional industries. The textile industries grew and improved because of the stimulus of a wider and freer market, and intermediate and more complex industries, like chemicals, metal products, petroleum refining, rubber, and nonmetallic products also emerged.

In every basic area of development, there was visible evidence of achievement within the CACM group. We have already referred to the building up of special financial institutions with the strategic support of IDB and, of course, the United States, and to a lesser extent of other developed nations. In monetary policies and payments arrangements, the CACM countries clearly took a remarkable lead in adopting a common monetary unit, establishing a clearing house for intraregional payments, and adopting measures for a more effective monetary union. In contrast to some LAFTA countries, the Central American countries in the CACM have enjoyed a remarkable monetary stability.

The record of progress is similarly significant in basic fields like agriculture, communications, transportation, power, education, health, and housing. Broad vigorous efforts are being made to implement the goals of the CACM treaty and those of the Alliance for Progress. On July 6, 1968, the presidents of Central America and the president of the United States jointly pledged to "perfect the Central American Common Market by removing barriers to trade, and by seeking expanded economic opportunities with other countries and markets."[41] Faith in the future was backed by the confidence which external capital showed in CACM advances in the limited period we are examining. Direct foreign investment flows into the CACM increased from less than $20 million a year in 1960 to more than $60 million a year. American investment reached a total of over $400 million (see Table 12.3).

Despite these achievements, the emergence or continuation of considerable barriers to smooth progress make predictions for the future difficult. Every member country, for instance, in the CACM was still after seven years largely dependent upon a single primary product and the prospects for the prices of primary

[40] See Chase Manhattan Bank (1969, p. 13): Indicators of CACM progress between 1960 and 1968 include (1) an increase in intraregional trade from $33 million to about $260 million, the share of such imports being raised from 6 percent to more than 20 percent, (2) a 13-fold growth of trade in manufactured goods to an estimated total of $140 million, and (3) a 5.2 percent annual rate of economic growth, pushing per capita incomes from $257 to $300.

[41] U.S. Department of State (1968, p. 5).

TABLE 12.3

Economic Assistance to Central America and Panama 1962–66 (In Millions of Dollars)

	United States	Inter-American Development Bank[a]	World Bank	Total
Guatemala	40.7	39.6	0	80.3
El Salvador	66.5	32.2	23.5	122.2
Nicaragua	56.1	50.4	10.6	117.1
Costa Rica	60.7	35.8	22.6	119.1
Honduras	35.8	37.7	14.7	88.2
Panama	77.1	33.8	4.0	114.9
Total	336.9[b]	229.5	75.4	641.8

[a] In early 1967, IDB granted CABEI two loans of $15 million for regional infrastructure. One loan was for $3.5 million from Canadian resources. Previous IDB loans and grants to CABEI totaled $17.4 million. In 1966, Spain provided a loan of $11 million and Mexico $6 million for regional development.
[b] Excludes $82.5 million provided for regional Central America and Panama projects through AID's office for Central America and Panama (ROCAP) based in Guatemala.

Source: U.S. Department of State (n.d.).

products remained uncertain. In the crop year 1966–67, the output of cotton and coffee fell and coffee prices dropped by 11 cents, in turn causing a drop of more than 6 percent in the total value of 1967 Central American exports to the rest of the world.[42] In the area of agricultural exports within the CACM, Nicaragua and El Salvador were being left behind. On the other hand, Nicaragua and Honduras were in regional trade accounts trouble with the rest of the CACM countries because of increased imports of manufactured goods from the more industrialized members as against their slow gains from their largely agricultural exports. The CACM countries themselves were in potential trouble with the outside world because their common external tariff had to be raised much

Central America, 1967

Foreign Trade	Costa Rica	El Salvador	Guatemala	Honduras	Nicaragua	Panama
Balance (in millions of U.S. dollars)	−40	−28	0	+10	−44	−167
Main export (percentage of total)	Coffee 44	Coffee 51	Coffee 49	Bananas 39	Cotton 44	Bananas 45

Source: U.S. Department of State (1968, p.20).

[42] In Nicaragua the total value of cotton exports in 1967 was 15 percent less than in 1965. In Guatemala, because of a drop in coffee prices and cotton exports, total value of exports to the rest of the world fell 22 percent in 1967.

higher than the former national import duties to protect CACM manufacturers—and CACM manufactures had a much higher price tag than imported equivalents.[43]

The location of integration industries remained an unsettled source of conflict, Nicaragua and Honduras claiming preference, while locational advantages really lay on the side of the more industrially developed CACM members. Overall economic policies needed further coordination and local entrepreneurs were still not responding vigorously to the challenge of an enlarged market. Government deficits were mounting for the CACM countries largely because of the loss of revenue from import duties, the deficits more than doubling from $50.4 million in 1961 to $105.4 million in 1967. The tax base remained too narrow, the tax levels too low, and tax reform too slow to bridge the gap.[44] With foreign ex-

Income Tax Collections as a Percentage of GNP, 1967

Costa Rica	10.6
El Salvador	9.6
Nicaragua	9.7
Honduras	10.0
Guatemala	7.2

Source: SPTF: Eighth Annual Report, 1968.

change earnings down, in 1967, for instance, capital formation declined, gross investment growing by less than 6 percent as against 7.5 percent in 1966 and 10 percent in 1965. This was largely owing to a fall in private investment in building and some decline in investments in cotton, although investment in manufacturing continued to be dynamic. Public investment fell in 1967 in El Salvador and Nicaragua, influencing a general decline in Central America. Taxes, as we noted, could not save the day. The sum total of deterrents in turn were reflected in the slowing down of the general growth rate of the CACM block. The percentage increase in total gross national product of the CACM group dropped from 6.1 percent in 1965 to 4.7 percent in 1966 and 4.2 percent in 1967.[45]

Growth Rate of Total Production

	1960–66	1967	1968[a]
Costa Rica	6.4	7.7	8.1
El Salvador	6.5	3.9	3.7
Guatemala	5.2	4.0	5.1
Honduras	5.5	5.3	6.4
Nicaragua	7.6	4.1	4.5

[a] Estimated.

Source: CEPAL (1969d).

[43] See Chase Manhattan Bank (1968, p. 14).
[44] See U.S. Department of State (1968b, p. 60).
[45] The percentage change in GNP per capita was as follows: 1965, 2.6 percent; 1966, 1.2 percent; 1967, 0.8 percent.

Other constraints also remained unresolved during the period. Half the population, for instance, of the CACM countries is outside the money market—a total of some 6 million people. Many regionally created institutions remained underfinanced because of reluctant or overcautious central governments. The free movement of labor was not achieved by the end of the decade. Understandably, protectionist business sentiment yielded reluctantly, if at all, to common policies for promoting industrial development. But even with full integration, the CACM market, with only some 5.2 percent of the GNP of Latin America and 5.6 percent of the population, would still be small. Hence, the future advantage of a merger of the CACM into a Latin American Common Market. The creation of the LACM, according to the official timetable, will not come until 1985. In the international field, as in the rest of Latin America, LAFTA supplies the dominant share of Latin America's total exports. Comparisons between LAFTA exports to CACM and CACM exports to LAFTA show that over the period 1961-68, the former grew by 366.7 percent while the latter declined by 40 percent.[46] In 1969 a new variable developed. The war between Honduras and El Salvador, the two poorest members of the CACM in terms of per capita GNP, reduced intra-CACM trade to a standstill. It is difficult to anticipate the consequences of this conflict and its possible effect on CACM development and on economic integration ambitions in general in Latin America.

We now turn to the more recently established efforts—CARIFTA and ANCOM.

Two other major integration efforts in the Americas are ANCOM and CARIFTA. CARIFTA emerged from the Caribbean Free Trade Agreement signed on May 1, 1968. The Andean Common Market officially came into being on May 26, 1969, with the signing in Bogotá of the Andean Treaty.

The Andean Common Market

ANCOM comprises five Andean countries: Bolivia, Chile, Colombia, Peru, and Ecuador. It is an officially approved regional integration within LAFTA, instituted to achieve liberalization and other development hopes at a faster rate than was possible with LAFTA. The major goals of ANCOM are almost exactly the goals set for intensive study by LAFTA under the Caracas Protocol. The treaty also aspired to enable ANCOM members to bargain more effectively with the larger countries within LAFTA like Argentina, Brazil, and Mexico. The treaty provides for the adoption of a common external tariff in 12 years; a minimum common tariff in five years; automatic and linear tariff reductions within seven years; ending nontariff barriers; joint industrial programming; and preferential treatment for Bolivia and Ecuador.[47]

The first notable result of this effort to found an Andean Common Market was the agreement to establish an Andean Development Corporation (*Corporación Andina de Fomento*) with a capitalization of $100 million. The corporation is empowered to give technical and financial support to multinational projects and approved complementation projects, and to provide appropriate machinery for coordination.

The acceleration of economic integration in Latin America may very well be

[46] See Inter-American Development Bank (1969a, p. 48).

[47] See Cale (1969, p. 16). There are marked differences between the treatment of Bolivia and Ecuador and that of Venezuela, an original member of the Andean group.

strengthened by the example of an ANCOM complementation agreement with unique sectoral emphasis for Latin America. That complementation agreement is the Draft Complementation Agreement on Petrochemical Products (*Projecto de Complementación sobre Productors de la Industria Petroquímica*), specifically designed within the framework of the Treaty of Montevideo to promote an integrated petrochemical industry which, incidentally, in principle overcomes the basic limitations to large-scale industrial production in Latin America.[48]

The Draft Complementation Agreement aims at promoting a balanced development of the petrochemical industry through building and expanding plants for the manufacture of primary, intermediate and final petrochemical products. Plants are to be of optimum size to take advantage of the economies of scale emanating from a larger market, and are to allow for expansion for greater specialization. Account has been taken of the differing levels of development of the countries comprising ANCOM, in order to narrow the gap between the less developed and the more developed countries. The agreement aims at an industry capable of competing in the world markets. Questions of the location of the plants are determined by economic rather than by narrower national criteria. The treatment of foreign capital is standardized among all contracting parties and the double-taxation inhibition is voided for capital originating in one ANCOM country but invested in another. Internal tariffs are to be completely removed within ANCOM by December 1, 1973, and a common external tariff set up. Decisions to remove internal customs barriers are irrevocable. Provision was made for the accession of LAFTA into the agreement and for the institution of an administrative council to supervise the implementation of the agreement, to evaluate its results, and to make recommendations for new products and new investment possibilities, and to negotiate with international lending agencies for new financial support.[49] ANCOM, however, began its official life with differences to be resolved between its member countries and Venezuela, and with a variety of reservations to be ironed out within the ANCOM group.

The Caribbean Free Trade Agreement

The member countries of CARIFTA are the Republic of Guyana, Trinidad and Tobago, Barbados, the states associated with the United Kingdom (Antigua, Dominica, Grenada, St. Kitts-Nevis-Anguilla, St. Lucia, St. Vincent), and Jamaica. Like the Central American countries, the Commonwealth Caribbean countries have had a long history of unification, deunification, and separatism—the process repeating itself in various forms. In 1958, the most far-reaching of these historical attempts came into being with the creation of the Federation of the West Indies, comprising all the British Caribbean territories except Guyana and British Honduras. The Federation, ushered in with lavish cultural extravaganza, faded out in 1962, but not without a "golden handshake"—magnanimous compensation for erstwhile federal legislators and public servants. In 1965, there was a limited revival of economic cooperation when Guyana, Barbados, and Antigua,

---

[48]Cf. Herrera (1965, pp. 18–31). Noteworthy efforts in basic areas include the progress made in the iron and steel industry under the Latin American Iron and Steel Institute (ILAFA); UNECLA studies of the possibilities for supplementation and specialization agreements in the ehemical industry; and FAO-UNECLA-IBD studies of integration possibilities in the production of fertilizers and pesticides.

[49]See Cardenas (1968, pp. 371–372).

through the personal friendship of the political leaders of these three territories, signed a free trade agreement. On July 1, 1968, cooperation broadened out with the founding of CARIFTA.

Once again both sentiment and economic realism stood behind the new agreement. The islands are among the most densely peopled countries in the world (see Table 12.4). Barbados houses over 1500 people per square mile. Beyond the coast, Guyana is an empty land but potentially rich. Sugar dominates as the employer of labor and, except for Guyana, Trinidad, and Jamaica, sugar dominates as the major export earner. In Guyana, it is bauxite and sugar; in Trinidad, petroleum and sugar; in Jamaica, bauxite and sugar. Those who seek jobs can no longer migrate at will to Britain. A change in British immigration policies removed this outlet. Immigration to Canada and to the United States is limited, though U.S. laws have become liberal enough to make it by comparison the most welcoming country in the world for West Indians and others. Even if historical connection is ignored, federation appeared to be a necessity—an inescapable path to the solution of the problems of the Commonwealth Caribbean. For, in the islands, only the lucky have jobs, as the New York Times noted for Jamaica.[51] This is also true in Guyana, but there are the potentialities and the elbow room, and in the Caribbean it has a viable market. It was Guyana, the nonmember of the 1958–62 federation, which determinedly took the lead, under Prime Minister Forbes Burnham, to initiate CARIFTA. In the face of the new and more complex political situations and with past memories still fresh, it is too early to predict the future of CARIFTA, except to say that any retreat from CARIFTA would only add another complex dimension to the future of the Caribbean.

THE FUTURE OF ECONOMIC INTEGRATION

Despite the inevitable difficulties encountered in the evolution of LAFTA and the CACM, the Presidents of America reaffirmed at Punta del Este on April 14,

TABLE 12.4

CARIFTA: Population and GNP, 1968

	Population (in thousands)	GNP per capita (in U.S. dollars)
Jamaica	1,839	460
Trinidad and Tobago	995	630
Barbados	245	400
St. Lucia	106	190
Grenada	99	230
St. Vincent	89	230
Dominica	68	230
Antigua	60	300
St. Kitts–Nevis–Anguilla	58	260
Guyana	662	300

Source: International Bank for Reconstruction and Development (n.d.).

---

[50]Ed. Kanner, New York Times (1968, p. 212). See also Martin (1970, pp. 37–41).

1967, their determination to push the advance of Latin American economic integration through the institution of a Latin American Common Market:

It is necessary to adopt all measures that will lead to the completion of Latin American integration, above all those that will bring about, in the shortest time possible, monetary stability and the elimination of all restrictions, including administrative, financial, and exchange restrictions, that obstruct the trade of the products of the area.[51]

To achieve these ends, in 1970 it was agreed that a Latin American Common Market should be created, to be substantially in operation by 1985. The Latin American Common Market would be based on the improvements to the two existing integration systems. In turn, LAFTA and CACM would initiate simultaneously a process of convergence by stages of cooperation, closer ties, and integration, "taking into account the interest of the Latin American countries not yet associated with these systems, in order to provide their access to one of them." Latin American countries outside of LAFTA and CACM were to be encouraged to join the existing integration systems.

To implement these decisions, the presidents of the Americas agreed to implement a number of basic measures. The measures included accelerating the process of converting LAFTA into a common market by putting into effect between 1970–85 a system of programmed elimination of duties and all other nontariff restrictions and by a system of tariff harmonization to create progressively a common external tariff at levels which would promote efficiency and productivity, as well as expansion of trade. Simultaneously, economic policies and instruments were to be coordinated and national laws which were required by integration harmonized. Sectoral agreements for industrial complementation were to be promoted and the participation of the less developed countries encouraged. Similarly, temporary subregional agreements were to be accelerated, provision being made to reduce tariffs in the subregions and harmonize treatment toward third nations "more rapidly than in the general agreements, in keeping with the objectives of regional integration."

The interests of the relatively economically less developed countries were to be taken into account, as under the Treaty of Montevideo, at all stages of the progress of integration toward the Common Market. To insure balanced regional development, the relatively less economically developed countries were to be given "the greatest possible advantages," and their potential interests were to be safeguarded in several other respects. Special measures were designed to locate in LAFTA countries industries intended for the larger market and to facilitate the access of the products of the less developed countries into LAFTA markets. These countries were also to be entitled to participatory and special preferential rights in all subregional agreements of interest to them.

The presidents also committed themselves to undertake the improvement of the customs union and the setting up of a Central American monetary union; to complete the regional network of infrastructure; to promote a common foreign trade policy; to improve the common market in agricultural products and to implement a joint coordinated policy; to accelerate the process of the free movement of manpower and capital within the area; and to harmonize

---

[51] U.S. Department of State (1967, p. 14).

basic legislation required for economic integration. Once again, the interests of the relatively less economically developed countries were to be taken specially into account. Economic complementation was to be encouraged among CACM members and between CACM countries, Mexico, Panama, and neighboring Caribbean countries and LAFTA.

These determinations were reinforced by the commitment of the presidents not to establish new restrictions on trade among Latin American countries "except in special cases, such as those arising from equalization of tariffs and other instruments of trade policy, as well as from the need to assure the initiation or expansion of certain productive activities in countries of relatively less economic development."[52] Studies leading to the rationalization of trade policies and to the possibility of more complementation agreements were to be conducted.

These laudable determinations can be significantly reinforced if predictions of the future are accurate. By the year 2000, for instance, Latin America should have a market of some $600 billion—equivalent to that of the United States and twice the size of the European Common Market. This estimate assumes a population of at least 600 million people with an average personal income of $1000.[53] The declarations and affirmations at Punta del Este amount to a realistic identification of the obstacles which must be overcome in national development and in the process of integrating the Latin American economies if common market prospects are to be realized. These obstacles include the uncertainties of the external sector; the deficiencies in the Latin American production and distribution structure. the need for capital; the narrowness of the national markets; the relative technological backwardness of the area, and a number of noneconomic variables.[54]

It is obvious that success for a Latin American Common Market would require the setting up of clearly defined objectives clearly communicated to all people; clearly defined quantitative targets to be implemented within a clearly defined time period; irrevocable decisions on already agreed-to tariff eliminations; common market institutions with clearly defined powers and enough support to carry through policy decisions and agreements. National development plans must be clearly harmonized into plans for integration across the whole area, and regional policies clearly formulated to identify and promote integrative projects including the training of manpower. Across-the-board sensitivity to the problems of the economically less developed members of the common market is essential, as well as understanding of the role of international capital investment, of the state, and of the fact that the backward monopolizing local firm sheltered by tariff walls cannot continue to extract high selling prices without disastrous consequences for competitive intraregional international trade. Integration policies

---

[52] *Ibid.*, p. 16.

[53] CEPAL (1969a).

[54] Herrera (1966, pp. 8–9) pointed out in 1966 that only 10 percent of the economically active population of Latin America was employed in enterprises with relatively high technological levels. Generally speaking these were foreign enterprises. The productivity of its labor force reflected the technological backwardness of Latin America. The average productive capacity of a Latin American worker was barely 15 to 30 percent that of a worker in a country where science and technology were intensively applied to raise productivity.

must prevent manufacturing firms from producing the same product in too many places for undersized markets at too high a cost. Success depends on a grasp of the fact that securing the expanding foothold for manufacturing exports that Latin America needs is a matter of hard competition.

Latin America must come to terms with the realities of international competitive competence, and understand that reminders of moral obligations, and appeals to equity, friendship, and other sensibilities can only have limited results. The common market idea is an innovation which could enable Latin America to escape from the trap of poverty. The success of the idea is a matter of Latin American leadership. The resident creative genius is there to do it. Despite the details, the emergence of a common market for all Latin America is fundamentally a matter of politics and the political will of Latin American leadership in favor of the common market.

Political Factors: Necessities and Road Blocks

A significant indicator of political differences occurred at the beginning of the work of the joint coordinating committee of LAFTA–CACM, which was empowered to bring about a merger between the two groups. The committee met first in October, 1968, and agreed on a work program. An immediate problem stemmed from the fact that LAFTA has an item-by-item system of tariff reduction, unlike the automatic system proposed for the LACM. This called for a meeting of the foreign ministers of LAFTA, but they were unable to reach agreement after several months of discussion. A meeting scheduled for early 1969 had to be postponed and indeed was not rescheduled.

A common market implies the political determination to accept a wide-ranging complex of common supranational institutions and innovations. These supranational developments may certainly include a supranational political council; an executive committee to implement policy decisions; a parliament representing public opinion; a court of justice to determine conflicts; an economic and social council; a cultural and technological council; and a whole complex of subordinate advisory bodies. Other developments would certainly involve a common trade policy; free movement of goods and of persons across borders; a regional investment policy; a policy for long-term financing; common policies for foreign investment and for private investment, whether local or foreign; common financial and monetary policies; the coordination of social policies; common policies for education, science and technology, and professional training.[55] Within the region, these necessities were certainly exemplified by the now defunct Federation of the West Indies. Developments of this kind are inevitably emerging under LAFTA, CACM, CARIFTA, and ANCOM.

The supranational institutions and policies involved in the creation of a common market represent, however, compromises all along the line. By definition, each party to the common market is an independent government surrendering some of its economic sovereignty for the common good. The success of institutionalization and innovation for an effective common market depends, first, on the balance of sentiment for and sentiment against the implementation of unavoidable common advances and, second, on the administrative competence which can be mobilized to put policy into effect. Success involves the recon-

[55] See Herrera (1966, pp. 19–22).

ciliation of separate nationalist existences and the merger of separate nationalist outlooks into a common philosophy, a common development ideology, and a stable yet creative pattern of advance. How rapidly this kind of transformation can come about is difficult to determine. Zea goes to the heart of the difficulty:

To provide for mental as well as political liberation was the ideal of Sarmiento and Alberdi in Argentina; Bilboa and Lastarrio in Chile; Montalvo in Ecuador; José María Luis Mora in Mexico; Eduardo Ferreira Franca in Brazil; Varela and José de la Lus y Caballero in Cuba and Andrés Bello in Venezuela. Having given the people their political independence, or, at least, having put them on the way toward it these leaders had to formulate a philosophy, not necessarily of metaphysical scope, but one which was practical and designed to handle the most immediate problems. And this was not all. As politicians, they found themselves in a position to advance solutions to these problems, or to create systems which would facilitate their proposals. They also had to educate those who would, in the future, take over the direction of their countries. In addition they were occasionally forced to leave their desks and enter into active defense of rights and liberties being threatened either from without or from within. There was neither the time nor the place to work out completely new philosophical systems. Dependence on schools and academies was an impossibility. Their philosophy sprang from the urgency of the circumstances conceived in public life, on the battle field, in exile or in prison. Patterns and ideas borrowed from the European model were modified to give rise to a philosophy whose true value can now be gauged from the perspective afforded by modern day historicism.[56]

The immense and varied pressures continuously surrounding Latin American leadership throughout the postindependence history of the Latin American republics cannot be ignored. Philosophic disaggregation, far more than in Europe and North America, characterized not only whole countries, but geographical sections of the same country, groups within the same section, and individuals within the same groups. There is a Latin America, but this fact does not imply a coherent philosophical uniformity across the whole continent. The extent, therefore, to which sentiment has coalesced for development and the emergence of a development ideology is, under the circumstances, a modern-day miracle.

It is difficult to judge how deep-rooted, spontaneous, widespread, and persistent the new development ideology will prove to be. If the development ideology proves to be all these things, we could forecast comparatively smooth sailing for a Latin American Common Market. But the subordination of sentiment to more rapid political push behind common economic advance may be too revolutionary an overthrow of traditional Latin American individualism.

A few examples will suffice to spotlight the type of obstacles that spring from uncoalesced sentiment. Argentina, Bolivia, Brazil, Paraguay, and Uruguay had to postpone their meeting, scheduled for January, 1969, to draft a treaty to set up more formal institutions for the development of the River Plate basin. There were several difficulties in the way. Argentina and Uruguay are in conflict over territorial rights in the River Plate. There is veiled hostility between Brazil and Argentina over Brazil's plans for hydroelectric development in the Brazilian section of the Paraná. Brazil and Paraguay are in dispute over alleged Brazilian settlement in northern Paraguay.[57] Agreements on the Andean Common Market

[56] Zea (1968, p. 4). See also U.S. Senate (1960, pp. 62–69).
[57] See *Latin America* (1969a, pp. 5–6).

were constantly postponed because of the powerful opposition of Venezuela's private sector and the reservations of the Chilean, Peruvian, and Ecuadorean private sectors. It took courage for Caldera, the new president of Venezuela, to rule firmly in favor of Andean integration, but it is too early to assess the political consequences for him.[58]

Narrow nationalist interest delayed the advance of CACM agreements in early 1969. Disputes in that period within the CACM bloc involved such matters as the division of the budgetary support for the Organization of Central American States (ODECA) and political squabbles over the appointment and national origin of appointees to major CACM institutions like ODECA and CABEI. Other problems involved the establishment and powers of a Central American court to settle disputes on integration matters. the taking of unilateral action against the free movement of goods (such as El Salvador's suspension of imported cigarettes from Guatemala in February, 1969, and upon being ruled out by the CACM secretariat imposing a tax on cigarettes regardless of origin within the CACM); the banning of Costa Rican rice imports by El Salvador; the suspension by El Salvador and Guatemala of the 30 percent tax on imports of raw materials and containers for industry under the industrial development law; and the rejection by Costa Ricans of the San Jose protocol for settling the problem of recurrent deficits on current accounts within CACM—a protocol agreed to at the time of President Johnson's visit to Central America.[59] In the Caribbean, separatist and individualist sentiment began to impose a strain on CARIFTA in early 1969.[60] The disputes centered on the location and support for the regional development bank; on conflicts in citrus interests in Jamaica and the Associated States; on the adoption of the Trinidad-owned British West Indian Airways as the carrier for the whole region and on BWIA prices; on support for the University of the West Indies; and on British armed intervention in Anguilla.[61] Issues of this kind can be resolved only if there is overwhelming sentiment for economic integration; otherwise the divisions can become intractable deterrents.

Some Limitations on Economic Administration

There are road blocks in the path of an effective common market. Even if overwhelming sentiment for a common market always wins the day for compromise and advance, there are still other hurdles. Managing a common market introduces new dimensions for economic management in Latin America; yet even without a common market, administrative limitations in Latin America are severe even in the carrying through of traditional administrative functions. The severities are even greater in terms of the dynamic character of administration for development. Development planning involves conception, administration, implementation, and evaluation of development activities—a continuous process. The common market falls into this framework. Decisions are made at the political level. Better decisions are, of course, made with better technical help and advice. But the effective carrying through of these decisions is a matter

[58] See *Latin America* (1969c, pp. 121–122).
[59] See *Latin America* (1969b, pp. 65–66). See also the Chase Manhattan Bank (1969, pp. 13–14).
[60] See *Latin America* (1969d, p. 63).
[61] See *Latin America* (1969e, p. 106).

of public administration. The role of the state is fundamental to the process of consensus and the achievement of cohesion, if the process of decision-making is to enjoy necessary legitimacy.

The new dynamic role of the state, nationally and supranationally in the LACM, and the relation between the public and private sector heighten the distinction between traditional administration and development administration. In 1965, a seminar to evaluate the progress of administration for development in Latin America put forward the view that administration for development distinguished itself from traditional administration in two basic respects: the conceptional scope of the problems to be dealt with, which in turn derive from a change in the role of the state; and the technical problems confronting public administration in its adjustment to the new role of the state. The new demands on the state have shifted its role from simply maintaining social equilibrium and political order to orienting, stimulating, and promoting indispensable reforms. This has conferred upon public administration new dimensions and new qualities. In contrast to traditional concerns with current problems, development administration concerns itself with the new technical problems.[62] In Central America, for instance, as Sedwitz points out, new administrative concepts were emerging as a result of new demands emanating from Central American economic integration. Yet, according to Sedwitz, despite the adoption of new methods and concepts of adminisdration, matters had not reached a stage in Venezuela, Chile, and Colombia, for example, where it was recognized that to overcome the "management gap" meant automatically overcoming the development gap.[63] Perhaps Sedwitz overstates the case, since significant recognition of the critical importance of administration at public and private levels obtained at the end of the decade in all Latin American countries.[64] The deficiencies identified are, however, of such range and magnitude that they underline the urgency of administrative capacity and administrative organization to match the present pressing need to accelerate economic integration.

Finally, effective progress toward a Latin American common market would require widespread popular participation as well as stable political and administrative patterns. These remain, however, dilemma-ridden areas in much of Latin America.[65]

[62] Pan American Union (1967d, p. 2).

[63] Sedwitz (1968, p. 32).

[64] See, for instance, Pan American Union (1965), Pan American Union (1968e), Pan American Union (1966aa), and U.S. Department of Labor (1963).

[65] Cf. U.S. Senate (1967b, 1967c, 1968d).

PART IV

THE ECONOMICS OF REALISM
AND THE POLITICAL VARIABLE

CHAPTER 13

THE ECONOMICS OF REALISM:
A CASE STUDY OF ECONOMIC CHANGE IN VENEZUELA

Our investigation of Latin America has highlighted the anxious race between demography and development within a context of geographic isolation and social separatism, human deprivation and emerging hope. Monocultural dependence and uncertain external markets; fickle growth rates and agricultural stagnation; a schism between town and country; isolated successes in the industrialization drive and a stubborn lag in employment and income equity; increasing public expenditures and defective tax systems; unstable price levels and conflicting approaches to the solutions; the ardent vision of an integrated economic community and a plethora of divisive deterrents along with a severe economic management gap are all ingredients of the Latin American economic situation. The actors on the stage are the Latin Americans, confronted and burdened with awesome problems which must be solved in a hurry.

REALITY AT THE END OF A DECADE

The whole continent south of the Rio Grande belongs to the world of the poor. The incipient ideology is development; the new gospel is self-help; the new reassertion is unity in the interest of Latin America "to strengthen democratic institutions, to raise the standard of living of their peoples and to assure their increased participation in the development process, creating for these purposes suitable conditions in the political, economic and social as well as labor fields."[1] A new hemispheric neighborliness hesitantly evolves, bringing with it through the Alliance for Progress the massive support of all Americans. To keep faith high, a "new action" program was proclaimed in 1967 by the presidents of the Latin American republics, meeting at the original site of the signing of the Charter of Punta del Este, six years after President Kennedy's electrifying proclamation. The new action program was couched in positively evocative terms:[2]

"Latin America will create a Common Market."
"We will lay the physical foundations for Latin American economic integration through multinational projects."
"We will join the efforts to increase substantially Latin American foreign trade earnings."
"We will harness science and technology for the service of our people."
"Latin America will eliminate unnecessary military expenditures."

[1] Pan American Union (1967g, p. 1).
[2] *Ibid.*, pp. 2–5.

This attempt to rekindle the national will came none too soon. For 10 years after the launching of the Alliance, the Latin American economy was still distinguished by an insufficient dynamic. The total product was growing slowly and irregularly. Extreme inequality of incomes still prevailed. Growth was still concentrated in a few relatively modern areas—enclaves, as it were, in the midst of the other sectors. These few modern enclaves accounted for half of the total product but employed only 15 percent of the active population of Latin America. The rest of the population was still predominantly engaged in activities of low productivity or existing at subsistence or below subsistence level. all the way down to actual unemployment. The tension continues. Throughout the period, as we have emphasized, the economy generally failed to achieve the minimum rate of per capita growth set by the Charter of Punta del Este.

We have already pointed out that the increase in per capita income as a long-run feature of the economy is only a limited part of the objectives of development in Latin America. The reader should refer back to the objectives for development we have already identified. Criteria inevitably lead to the search for a model, and it is customary to project Puerto Rico into the center of the economic stage. There are, of course, subtleties in the Puerto Rican situation, particularly its constitutional relation with the United States, which evoke reservations in the mind of the Latin American as in the mind of many North Americans. Many of these reservations emerge from unfamiliarity with the evolution of Puerto Rico under its most noteworthy governor, Luis Múñoz Marin.[3] Puerto Rico, however, despite the value of its economic experience, is not alone as a reference point for Latin America. The new momentum of development is shared, in varying degree, by all the Latin American nations. Indeed, despite differences in the various Latin American economies, it is possible to single out in every country desirable large or small innovations of relevance to development in the next country.

We concentrate here on analyzing and evaluating the economic transformation of Venezuela during the period 1958-70.

VENEZUELA

The Economic Transformation

In 1958 Venezuela enjoyed the highest per capita gross national product in Latin America: around $732 (in 1968 prices).[4] The economic structure and socioeconomic characteristics of Venezuela were, however, typical of most Latin American countries at that time except Mexico. Until the overthrow of the dictator Pérez Jiménez on January 22, 1958, after 10 years of absolute power, and the election of Betancourt as president in December, 1968, Venezuela had experienced almost continuous turbulence, rioting, revolution, and ruthless dictatorship.[5] When oil was discovered early in the nineteenth century,

---

[3] See Farley (1967).

[4] See U.S. Department of State (1968b).

[5] See, for instance, Bailey and Nasatir (1960, pp. 451–456, 665–674) and Alexander (1964, pp. 17–21, 37–50). In the period 1810–88, there were 42 revolutions (excluding riots and minor coups), 7 dictators, and 11 constitutions, see Bailey and Nasatir (1960, p. 451). One of the few breaks was the period 1945–48 when *Acción Democrática* (AD) came into power and Betancourt served as president. Even then AD came into power through a military coup and its power in 1948 was ended by a military coup, see Alexander (1964, pp. 22–36).

Venezuela became comparatively affluent, but like most Latin American countries, it was extraordinarily dependent on this one product. Petroleum exports and petroleum investment gave basic dynamism to the Venezuelan economy, contributing to a rapid expansion of exports and to an estimated annual growth in the gross national product of well over 8 percent a year between 1950-58.[6] On the other hand, extreme dependence on petroleum made the economy immediately vulnerable to any exogenous changes affecting petroleum. In fact, Venezuelan's share of world petroleum exports had been consistently declining before 1958. This declining trend continued and falling prices for petroleum exports immediately after 1958 intensified the crises confronting the new regime. The pattern of dependence was typical. The petroleum industry in 1960 accounted for over 96 percent of the export earnings of Venezuela, some 25 percent of the gross national product, and 60.5 percent of the ordinary revenues of the central government. Some 69 percent of all national income tax revenues was derived from the petroleum sector.[7]

Agriculture (which employed some 35 percent of the labor force) did advance between 1950-58 at the fairly high rate of 5.7 percent a year.[8] But agricultural advance in 1958 had yet to overcome the customary constraints imposed by latifundism and low levels of technical efficiency. In 1956, 80.6 percent of the total number of landowners owned farms less than 3 hectares in size, and only 3 percent of the agricultural land area, while 1.7 percent of the total number of farm owners owned farms of over 100 hectares, or 74.5 percent of the agricultural lands. Approximately 75 percent of the farmers were absentees. Between 1950-58, Venezuela had to import over 600 million bolivars ($1.00 U.S. = Bs. 3.35 in 1962) worth of food annually to feed a population growing at 3.6 percent a year. There was the typical inequity in income distribution between groups and between the city and the rural areas. According to estimates in 1957, 45 percent of all income recipients received 9 percent of the national income, while 12 percent of all the population received 50 percent of all income. Average per capita income was 10 times greater in Caracas than in the rural areas.[9] In 1958, the rural population of Venezuela—equivalent to one-third of the total population of Venezuela—had an average income of only 800 bolivars.[10]

The cities obviously benefited most from the affluence generated through the extraordinary development of the petroleum industry in the previous decade.

[6]UNECLA (1963a, p. 20). The high growth rate of the economy was largely a consequence of the expansion of exports, particularly petroleum exports; but it also resulted from the increase in the purchasing power of Venezuelan exports of goods and of the tourist trade; the increase in net foreign investment and external financing; and the maintenance of a high coefficient of gross investment. The immediate factors which stimulated the expansion of petroleum exports and earnings in the period 1950–57 were of course the Korean War and the Suez Canal crisis. Prices were steady for Venezuelan oil since demand was high and concession-making intensified in Venezuela. Between 1952-57, "return values" (the total amounts used by the oil companies to finance their production costs and pay their taxes) more than doubled, and public expenditures also rose in Venezuela. As a result of all the movement in the variables the per capita gross national product expanded rapidly.

[7]See Inter-American Development Bank (1963b, p. 285) and Venezuela, Central Office of Coordination and Planning (n.d., pp. 1–5).

[8]UNECLA (1964, p. 116).

[9]Inter-American Development Bank (1963b, p. 284).

[10]See Gonzalez (1962, p. 2).

Under Pérez Jiménez, Caracas became a city of spectacular building projects, but in terms of opportunity costs these projects were tantamount to an astounding waste of financial resources.[11] The low levels of rural existence, the concentration of construction and wealth in the towns, and the mirage of better job chances caused the rural population to pour into the towns. The metropolitan area of Caracas accounted for 17.6 percent of the total population of Venezuela in 1961 as against 13.8 percent in 1950. Within that time the population of Maracaibo, Venezuela's second biggest city, increased by 78.6 percent.[12]

At the end of the dictatorship of Pérez Jiménez in 1958 the new government was confronted by the problems of a country with a deformed economy and a poverty-stricken population. Petroleum dominated the exports and foreign manufactured products dominated the imports. Ignorance and misery were embedded in the social order: 40 percent of the people could neither read nor write and 50 percent of the houses were really huts with palm roofs, mud floors, and no sanitary services at all. Open unemployment in Venezuela amounted to an estimated 10.2 percent. Despite its dominance, petroleum could provide jobs for only 2 percent of the active population.[13] Between 1950-58, as we have pointed out, the Venezuelan economy did maintain the high growth rate of over 8 percent, but the economic and social characteristics we have spotlighted demonstrate the limitations of a high growth as an index of development.

In terms, however, of that conventional, but limited, indicator of economic development—per capita GNP—Venezuela in 1969 with an estimated per capita GNP (in 1968 prices) of $948 (U.S.) still retained the lead over the rest of Latin America, excluding Puerto Rico.[14] Escape from the monoproduct dominance of petroleum was still far from complete. Petroleum and petroleum products accounted for over 93 percent of export earnings and some 75 percent of government revenues. With just under 22 percent of the gross national product, petroleum still contributed a greater share than any other sector.[15] Venezuela is, after the United States, the U.S.S.R., and Libya, the largest producer of crude petroleum. In 1969 the daily output in Venezuela amounted to some 3.59 million barrels a day. Income from the petroleum sector continues to finance most of the industrial and social development of Venezuela and underwrites the aim of the Venezuelan government to diversify the economy and escape from monoproduct dependence. It gives the Venezuelan economy its basic dynamism, and fluctuations in export earnings from the petroleum influence fluctuations in the evolution of the Venezuelan economy.

Between 1958-70, there were significant shifts in the economic structure and socioeconomic characteristics of Venezuela. By the end of 1967, Venezuela could boast of a number of specific achievements indicative of these changes. An official report commented:

Venezuela's bolivar has become one of the world's hardest currencies, a reflection of booming economy, sound fiscal policy, and a stable, dynamic government.

[11] See Alexander (1964, p. 45).
[12] Inter-American Development Bank (1965a, p. 576).
[13] Gonzalez (1962, p. 2).
[14] Puerto Rico had a per capita net income of $1340 (U.S.) in 1970 as compared with $577 (U.S.) in 1960, see Government Development Bank for Puerto Rico (1970, p. 18).
[15] See Banco Central de Venezuela (1970, table A-VII-3, p. A-102).

During 1967, moreover, it is believed that the industrial sector passed petroleum for the first time as a factor in the country's gross domestic product. The year was also marked by the significant emergence of a heavy industrial "Ruhr" in the mineral-rich Guyana region of south-eastern Venezuela.

Industry's coming of age is a major economic milestone in this country, which formerly had a "one crop economy": oil. With an average growth rate of about 10 percent over a 10 year period, manufacturing now accounts for some 10 percent of the gross product . . . While the petroleum sector is still expanding, it has lost some of its former predominance; ten years ago, petroleum accounted for 23 percent of the gross product, while industry contributed only 13.4 percent.[16]

There were other indications of change brought about under the vigorous democratic leadership of Betancourt and his successors. In 1957, most Venezuelan agriculture was subsistence farming. Between 1957-67, the value of farm production rose 58 percent, and Venezuela estimated that it was near self-sufficiency in food production, and indeed was exporting some products like rice and sugar. Equally spectacular social advances were registered in education, social security, and housing. In the critical battle ground of the countryside, rice production increased tenfold between 1957 and 1967, egg production more than six times, poultry four times. Cotton production has tripled, and coffee and corn production have increased by two-thirds.

Reactive Nationalism: Reconstruction and Reorientation Through Planning

The Betancourt regime, however, had started in an atmosphere of crisis. The beginning of economic transformation in Venezuela was marked by the determination of the new leadership to initiate economic policies to counteract the crises of earlier years and eliminate the dangers of economic dependence on a single product. Under the new leadership, the economics of realism was substituted for the politics of *personalismo* which had characterized almost all Venezuelan leadership before the Betancourt regime.

The events of the years 1958-61 illustrate the adverse effects on internal development of a high degree of dependence on the external sector and on one major product, even though that product is petroleum. As we have seen, the economy had grown at a very high rate between 1950-58, a direct consequence of increased foreign earnings from petroleum exports, which permitted the maintenance of a sufficient volume of imports to cover investment and consumption needs. Between 1958-61, however, the terms of trade worsened for Venezuela when realized prices for petroleum fell when the Korean War ended, the Suez Canal reopened, and oil competition from other areas rose. The index of crude petroleum prices fell from 100.0 to 1958 to 91.8 in 1961, and exports expanded too slowly to compensate for this price decline. Venezuela's share of world petroleum exports dropped from 36.0 percent in 1958 to 32.8 percent in 1960 while import prices rose and external purchasing power declined.[17]

The situation was compounded by political factors. The abrupt transition from a dictatorship to representative government generated a climate of uncertainty, which was nourished by vested interests and heightened by the government's changed attitude toward the petroleum companies, and in turn

[16]Venezuela, Embassy of (1967).
[17]UNECLA (1963d, vol. 2, pp. 90, 91, 104).

by the petroleum companies' reactions to the new policies for the location and redistribution of their business.[18] Speculation filled the air. Pessimism and uncertainty spread and there was considerable disinvestment in petroleum and capital flight. The government obviously could not immediately fill this investment gap nor increase domestic production. The growth rate of the economy therefore dropped from the high level of 1950-58 to an average of only 3.6 percent for the period 1958-61.[19] In fact, the annual rate of increase of the GNP in 1960 and 1961 was only 0.9 percent and 0.2 percent, respectively—a decline of more than 2.5 percent per capita in each of the two years.

Every strategically vital indicator was down during the period 1958-61 because every one of these variables was largely dependent on the fortunes of the petroleum sector. Total investment fell by about 30 percent. The coefficient of total gross investment to the GNP fell from 27.4 percent in 1958 to 17.1 percent in 1961. The coefficient of fixed investment to the GNP fell from 25.8 percent to 15.8 percent, that of public investment declined by more than 50 percent, while that of private investment fell by some 33 percent.

Between 1959-62, an unfavorable balance of payments caused a drop in the international reserves of the Central Bank of Venezuela amounting to $412 million (U.S.) and a sharp fall in money circulating in the hands of the public from Bs. 4017 million in 1958 to Bs. 3579 million in 1960 (the lowest level in nine years). Bank deposits fell by some Bs. 650 million and liquidity was reduced to a critical limit following the reduction of bank deposits in the 13 months between August, 1959, and December, 1960.[20]

Despite the decline in petroleum investment, the high level of installed capacity enabled the industry to meet normal production requirements. But the average annual growth rate of industrial production fell from 10.8 percent in 1958 to 4.9 percent in 1958-61, and the volume of construction fell by some 12.1 percent a year over the three years. Agriculture, however, thanks to some effective agrarian reform efforts, maintained its pre-1958 growth rate of 5.7 percent during the period, and public utilities (electricity, gas, and water) expanded at 14 percent a year—thanks to government's determined efforts. Without these compensating factors, the fall in Venezuela's growth rate from 1958-61 and the resulting consequences would certainly have been worse. As it was, unemployment increased from 10.2 percent in 1958 to 14.3 percent in 1961.

It is out of these circumstances that Venezuela emerges as a clear case of "reactive nationalism" in Rostow's sense.[21] The reaction was against the uncertainties resulting from the traditional dependence upon one major product, the returns from which depended on factors outside Venezuelan control. The circumstances prevailing in 1958 and during the critical years 1959-61 made it clear that the kind of development required to transform the life of the

---

[18] See Banco Central de Venezuela (1968, p. 11).

[19] See UNECLA (1962, p. 111).

[20] See Banco Central de Venezuela (1968, pp. 11–12).

[21] See Rostow (1960, pp. 26–31). Cf. Glade's observations (1969, p. 485):

What has been sought in Mexico, Bolivia, Venezuela, and Cuba is the progressive socialization of economic life and, beyond that, the socialization of other areas of national relationships as well. The economic dimension is conjoint with important political and social dimension.

Venezuelan people could never be secured within the framework of the traditional underregulated economy. The new government of Venezuela, therefore, adopted a comprehensive planning approach as its basic instrument of economic and social change.

Planning Institutionalization

Planning is a deliberate and systematic attempt on the part of government to achieve predetermined and usually quantified goals through specific policies and instruments. Plans may differ in form, content, aims, time horizons, and so on, but in all planning, the government deliberately uses its influence to modify the behavior of the economy rather than trusting the free play of market forces.[22] The extent and character of government intervention depends on circumstances. Castro set up a complete command economy in Cuba, In Venezuela, national planning combines the stimulating of private enterprise and cooperation between the public and the private sector with the setting up of what government deems desirable boundary conditions on the operation of private enterprise.

Comprehensive planning can remain a mere proclamation of intentions on paper unless the planning is invested with authority and institutionalized at all levels of national, regional, and local economic activity. For comprehensive planning to be effective, it must also represent a rational, continuous, determined, and coordinated effort to bring about change. The plan adopted must satisfy the principles of consistency (anticipated manpower requirements must equal to the manpower available), efficiency (underutilization of resources must be eliminated), and optimality (the plan must represent the best of all alternative consistent plans and make the best possible use of the country's scarce resources).[23]

Planning was invested with authority, power, and permanence, and comprehensiveness when in December, 1958, Venezuela established a Central Office for Coordination and Planning (CORDIPLAN), placing it under the direct responsibility of the president and the council of ministers, but investing the president and the council with direct responsibility to initiate, supervise, and execute the national development plan. CORDIPLAN is not responsible for national planning; its assists the president and the council of ministers who therefore cannot abrogate the legal responsibility for comprehensive planning, although in reality CORDIPLAN does the job. In fact, CORDIPLAN was put under the control of a board of directors, with the executive director appointed directly by the president.

CORDIPLAN was given the responsibility of reviewing the development of the country, recommending projects and alternatives, evaluating development progress, and establishing cooperative links with private enterprise. Together with the Ministry of Finance, CORDIPLAN was given authority to prepare the

---

[22] The literature of planning is now enormous and planning is a word with many meanings. Cf. UN (1963a, p. 5): "In essence, a plan is a body of economic and social policies expressed in quantified targets and defined tasks." See Waterston (1966), Levy (1968, esp. pp. 135–136); Sirkin (1968, esp. pp. 1–6, 43–54), and Lewis (1966, pp. 13–24). For some general observations on Latin American planning, see UNECLA (1967b, pp. 1–17, 18–32).
[23] See Vernon (1967, pp. 102–103), Van Arkadie and Frank (1966, pp. 331–337), and Tinbergen (1958, pp. 9–11).

annual program budget. CORDIPLAN also enjoyed other responsibilities. These included initiating physical planning, coordinating urban planning with sectoral planning agencies, coordinating matters related to technical assistance, training planning personnel, and aiding the development of administrative planning techniques. CORDIPLAN includes five departments (economic development programming, short-term programming and evaluation, economic location, social and institutional programming and statistics and methodology) and several lesser but important bureaus.

Development institutions did exist in Venezuela before 1958, but they were narrower in their objectives and activities, insulated from one another, and unrelated to any broad-based, coordinated attack on the problems of the country. Their activities were governed by the caprices of small groups rather than by the determinations of the nation, and in most cases, their power and their support were simply castrated or destroyed under the Pérez Jiménez regime. In 1946, for instance, Venezuela created the autonomous National Economic Council (*Consejo de Economía Nacional*), to advise the government on coordination and development of the national economy, and the Venezuelan Development Corporation (CVF), to be the instrument for diversifying and developing national production.[24] Under Pérez Jiménez, CVF funds were simpliy slashed and parts of the organization destroyed altogether.[25]

The Betancourt government restored and revitalized some of these planning agencies, as well as establishing new institutions. The Ministry of Development (*Ministerio de Fomento*), created in 1863, for instance, was reorganized under coherent terms of reference and with the relations to the autonomous agencies shown in Figure 13.1. The isolation of the ministries and autonomous agencies was ended by the establishment of sectoral offices in each ministry and autonomous agency, under the authority of the ministry or agency concerned but dealing directly with CORDIPLAN; by the institution of committees, including representatives of the private sector, to coordinate the work of the ministers and the autonomous agencies and the plans of the public and private sector; and finally by the requirement that all planning at project, regional, or sectoral levels be consistently guided by and related to planning policies at the national level.[26]

We turn now to an examination of some of the achievements of the planning agencies. We will attempt to evaluate sectoral achievements and compare planned over-all growth rates with the actual rates of growth. We can then draw some conclusions on economic change during the period we are examining.

---

[24] See UN (1947, pp. 132–143). Unlike CORDIPLAN, the National Economic Council elected its own president.

[25] Alexander (1964, p. 39). See also Gonzalez (1962, pp. 4, 6, 7) and Friedmann (1965, p. 15).

[26] See UN (1962, p. 344). Here are a few examples of the committees through which the private sector was associated with planning activities: The Industrial Committee (created 1961) composed of presidents or directors of CORDIPLAN, the Ministry of Development, the Venezuelan Development Corporation, and the Venezuelan Guyana Corporation, and the directors of the industrial sectors of these agencies; and the Agricultural Planning Committee (created 1963) composed of representatives of the Ministry of Agriculture, the Agriculture and Livestock Bank, the National Agrarian Institute, and private sector organizations. The Social Committee and the Administrative Committee were established on the same principles. Cf. Griffin and Enos (1970, esp. pp. 203–204).

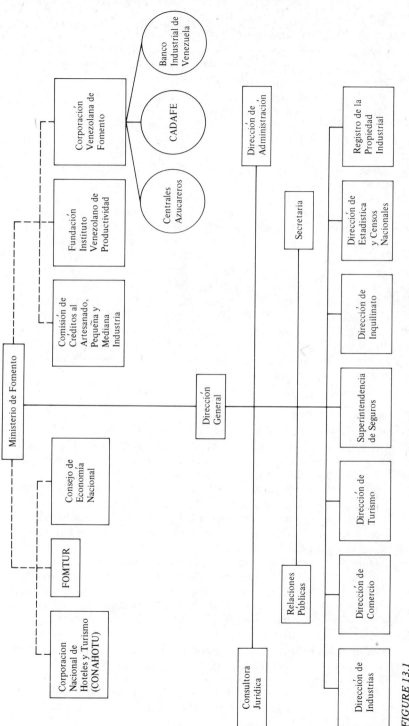

FIGURE 13.1

Reorganization of Ministry of Development in Venezuela, 1963. The dashed line indicates the autonomous organizations operating under the control of the Ministry of Development.[a]

[a]N.B.: The dashed line indicates the autonomous organizations oerating under the control of the Ministry of Development.

Source: Venezuela, Ministry of Development (1963).

CORDIPLAN and Venezuela's First Development Plans

Venezuela had the experience of three plans during the 1958–70 period. In each case, the plans were prepared by CORDIPLAN. Taken together, the continuity of these plans indicates a persistent official subscription to orderly development and continuing willingness to modify planning approaches and targets in the light of the experience gained.

In 1960 CORDIPLAN prepared a Four Year Economic and Social Development Plan (*Plan Cuatrenial*) for the period 1960–64. It was Venezuela's first comprehensive plan, but it proved abortive because of the critical external situation during 1959–61; the 1960–64 plan therefore had to be revised. In 1963 CORDIPLAN presented a new National Economic Development Plan for the period 1963–66. The 1963–66 plan emphasized planning as "an indispensable instrument of orientation and action" toward the best use of national resources under carefully established priorities which would make for rational development, counteract the previous vast wastage of national resources and economic distortion, and accelerate the process of economic and social development.[27] The 1963–66 Plan explicitly recognized the necessity for government, business, and workers to combine in a determined effort if the objectives of the plan were to be realized. The 1963–66 plan, however, fell short of anticipated targets, as we will see, so CORDIPLAN prepared a 1965–68 plan. Again the goals of the 1965–68 Plan were only partially realized, but the planning effort persisted. In 1969, CORDIPLAN was once more preparing a revised plan based on new priorities and on the reorganization of Venezuela into eight administrative regions, each with its coordination and planning office working under the authority of CORDIPLAN.

The Ministry of Development and the Autonomous Agencies

The new regime did not reject all inherited institutions. The Ministry of Development is an example of the pragmatic approach of the new regime. The Ministry of Development became the national executive agency charged with executing, directing, coordinating, and advising on planning and industrial development within the framework of the government's national economic policy. In general terms, Venezuela's industrial policy did not differ significantly in aims or in means from traditionally established import-substituting protectionist policies.

Associated with the Ministry of Development were a number of key autonomous agencies, including the Venezuelan Development Corporation, an inherited institution deliberately weakened under the Pérez Jiménez regime, which became the key autonomous institution for promoting Venezuela's new industrializing ambitions. During the period, the new regime also created or restored a number of other institutions, among them the Electricity Development Corporation (*Compania Anonima de Administracion y Fomento Eléctrico*) (CADAFE), the Venezuelan Petrochemical Institute (*El Instituto Venezolano de Petroquimica*) (IVP); the Venezuelan Petroleum Corporation (*Corporacion Venezolano de Petroléo*) (CVP); and the Venezuelan Guayana Corporation (CVG).

CADAFE is the key planning agency for the development of electrification. By 1969, the per capita output of electrical power production in Venezuela stood at 1190 kwh, over twice the average for Latin America, and the highest

[27]Venezuela, Central Office of Coordination and Planning (1963).

individual country average in Latin America.[28] We have already taken note of the role of the CVG in the development of the Guayana industrial complex. We will deal later in this chapter with the role of the IVP and the CVP in our evaluation of planned development in Venezuela and the role of the petroleum sector.

The Venezuelan Development Corporation

CVF, as we mentioned earlier, is the agency which is giving the principal push to Venezuela's industrializing ambitions. It is the chief source of medium and long-term credit in Venezuela. Although state-owned, the corporation does not compete with private enterprise; it provides financing to private enterprises which cannot for one reason or another secure accommodation from commercial banks. When it was established in 1946, CVF had an initial capitalization of 90 million bolivars (about $27 million (U.S.).[29] By 1968, CVF had a paid-in capital of 1.82 billion, bolivars and additional resources from bond issues and loans from abroad.

Between 1946–66, CVF concentrated on developing import substitution industries in the consumer field. During this period, CVF granted loans ranging from 25,000 bolivars to 28 million bolivars, at a rate of 6 percent to 7 percent, and for periods of up to 15 years. After 1966, CVF changed its objectives since import substitution had reached its saturation point. CVF now concentrates on intermediate and capital manufacture, and on agricultural industries, commercial fishing, and tourism with special emphasis on exportation.

CVF assists credit applicants to prepare for orderly business development by helping them with feasibility and market studies, labor, raw materials, taxation and legal questions, management problems, and problems involving financial risks. Since CVF works with private enterprise locally or internationally in the interests of advancing Venezuela's industrialization and growth rate, the evolution of CVF illustrates the flexible strategies adopted by Venezuela to move away from dependence on petroleum and to push economic growth through public incentives and private and international cooperation.

A few examples will indicate the flexibility of CVF strategy. In the Guayana region, CVF owns 50 percent of the $30 million (U.S.) aluminum reduction plant. Reynolds Metals, the other partner, supplies the technolgoy and management. In the Venezuelan sugar industry, CVF support has stimulated development to the point where Venezuela not only supplies its own needs and exports sugar, but has developed bagasse, a by-product of the sugar industry, for use in paper pulp manufacturing. CVF supported the development of a peanut and peanut oil industry in eastern Venezuela. This involved a loan of 10 million bolivars to the producing company, an initial planting of some 45,000 acres, and an oil-processing plant for annual yield of 8000 tons of peanut oil. In mining, CVF invested in 1967 seven million bolivars in preinvestment studies, research, and credit financing. Other CVF investments at the same time included 113 million bolivars in chemical projects; 93 million bolivars for tourism and national park development along the Caribbean coast, the Andes, and the Guayana region, and another 50 million bolivars for tourist development in eastern Venezuela.

---

[28] See U.S. Department of State (1971, p. 20). The estimated 1969 per capita output for 19 Latin American republics was 490 kwh. In 1960 the per capita output for Venezuela was estimated at 630 kwh, compared with the average of 320 kwh for Latin America.

[29] See UN (1947, p. 137). See also *New York Times* (1968).

CVF, the United Nations, the Ministry of Agriculture, and other agencies cooperated in making special studies of the fishing industry, and CVF financed part of a grant of 50 million bolivars to build 146 trawlers for tuna and shrimp fishing and to train fishing personnel between 1966–70. The effort included building and delivering the trawlers to private fishermen who would repay on easy terms, and the construction of new docks, refrigeration facilities, electrical and mechanical repair shops, a shipyard, and shrimp and fish-salting and other installations for the convenience and advance of the fishing industry. In the larger Latin American world of LAFTA, to secure better advantages for Venezuela CVF hired an American firm to assess the potentialities of this market for Venezuelan natural and semi-processed agricultural products. In the more limited but vitally important area of small and medium-size business, CVF developed a plan for the leasing of fixed assets with the option of buying, *Arrendamiento de Activos Fijos con Opcion de Compra* (Rental of Assets with Option to Buy). The plan aimed at increasing the ownership of industrial property among small and medium-size businesses, the state contributing the fixed assets—land, buildings, and machinery—and leasing these assets to business which had the option of buying them over the long run.

The principle was established in 1958 that Venezuelan industrial and economic development must be oriented to Venezuelan reality.[30] Obviously orientation patterns in Venezuela were highly diverse, in contrast to the monolithic course adopted in Cuba during the same period.

Institutionalization for Agrarian Reform

Agrarian reform was as critical to Venezuela in 1958 as it was to all Latin America. Latifundism had to be modified. On April 19, 1960, the state enacted the Law of Agrarian Reform (*La Ley de Reforma Agraria*), which recognized and protected the right of private property in land provided this right fulfilled a social function (*en cuanto esta cumpla su funcion social*). The principle of social function is, of course, the same as the famous Article 27 of the Mexican Constitution of 1917, with its emphasis on the harmonious use of property.[31] The provisions of the Venezuelan agrarian law were similarly inspired by a desire for both equity and economic efficiency. A reactivated and autonomous National Agrarian Reform Institute (IAN) was established to administer the new law.

Under this law, unproductive lands, farms worked by tenants, sharecroppers, and other nonowners, and lands used for large-scale cattle raising could be expropriated—but only where there were no uncultivated lands or other properties belonging to the state which could be used for resettlement. The law carefully classified land in terms of distance from consumption centers, water supply availability, and soil conditions, once again gaining from the recognized defects of the earlier agrarian revolution in Mexico.[32] The law protected profit-making enterprise. Farms in this category included farms with less than 150 hectares which could be worked profitably; farms of less than 300 hectares;

---

[30] See Venezuela, Ministry of Development (1963, p. 4).
[31] See Cline (1963, pp. 209–228). See also Venezuela, Central Office of Coordination and Planning (1962).
[32] Hanson (1949, pp. 68–73).

and grazing land of less than 2000 hectares in one category and less than 3000 hectares in a second category. Large landholders were given the right to reserve an area not subject to expropriation.

Institutionalization was once again rapidly built up to insure effectiveness and order in carrying through agrarian reform—another lesson learned from Mexico's mistakes in agrarian reform. The principal institutions set up or revamped in the agrarian reform program of 1958–61 in coordination with IAN included the Ministry of Agriculture; the agricultural extension services; *Banco Agricola y Pecuario*; and ADAGRO (*Almacenes de Depositos Agropecuarios C.A.*), which had a capital of 30 million bolivars and was empowered to set up and manage silos, warehouses, and cold storage plants conjointly with private capital if possible.[33] The cooperative movement included the Ministry of Public Works, the Ministry of Education, and a whole array of community development agencies and included the training of cooperative leaders. At the same time a National Irrigation plan was established with the responsibility of irrigating 230,000 acres by 1966.

The basic aim of the Agrarian Law of 1960 was to transform the agrarian structure of Venezuela and incorporate the rural population into the economic and social development process through substitution of a just system of property, tenancy, and exploitation of land for the latifundist system and to support any such reorganization by an adequate credit system and adequate technical help for rural agricultural producers. In consonance with this aim, the institutionalization described above developed while at the same time—between 1958 and mid-1962—1,480,649 hectares of land were immediately redistributed; 50,165 *campesino* families resettled; 140 technical assistance centers established; and 21,600 hectares irrigated. Between 1959–69, an estimated 4 million hectares of public and private land had been distributed to 165,000 families.[34]

The program of agrarian reform is in direct contrast to Cuban agrarian reform during the same period. In Cuba, the landless peon of the pre-Castro plantation system remained a landless peon of the state under Castro. In Venezuela, the landless under the latifundist system before Betancourt were becoming individual landowners in increasing numbers. In Cuba, a comprehansive command state allowed no room for group expression. In Venezuela, three presidents were elected during the period by popular suffrage. If the constitutional system continues, the landless have a chance to bring organized pressure to bear in the interests of protecting and promoting the continuation of agrarian reform.[35]

Planning: Estimated and Actual Growth Rates

Planning is an anticipatory exercise. Projections assume that other things will remain equal, but since the future is always uncertain, adjustments are anticipated in case other things do not remain equal. There is built-in realism in Venezuelan

---

[33] The Agricultural and Livestock Bank had been created in June, 1928.

[34] Central Bank of Venezuela (1969, p. 107). See also Venezuela, Ministry of Agriculture (1963aa).

[35] *Federacion Campesino de Venezuela* (FCV), a powerful peasant organization founded in the 1930s, performs this role. The FCV had an estimated 550,000 members in 1965 and 3500 local unions, of which 65 percent are affiliated to the *Accion Democratica* (AD), 25 percent to the *Social Christian Party* (COPEI) and 10 percent to the Democratic Republican Union (URD). See U.S. Senate (1969, p. 195).

planning. Plans are subject to year-by-year adjustment so that there is always a national four-year plan, and policies and targets for the next year are revised on the basis of the past year's experience. The element of uncertainty is therefore never discounted. Venezuelan planning experience amply illustrates that institution-building, target-setting, and even the most rational of planning approaches are not guarantees against uncertainty. What the Venezuelan experience does demonstrate is the capacity of the country to come to terms with realism and to adjust planning anticipations accordingly.

We have already seen that the 1960-64 plan had to be revised because of the change of data (largely exogenous) during the years 1959-61. Table 13.1 gives a limited picture of the targets planned for the years 1962-66. Even the deliberate driving forward of the economy (*impulsarlo deliberadamente*) failed to achieve the planned targets for the period as a whole. Nonetheless, the deliberate attempt to change the behavior of the economy went on. The 1963-66 plan was followed by a 1965-68 plan with revised targets, but the same basic goal of diversifying the economy and building up strong agricultural and industrial sectors. The expansion of the petroleum sector was still to be of central importance and petroleum was slated to advance at 4.2 percent a year. Agricultural output was to advance 7.7 percent a year; mining 13.7 percent; exports 8 percent; and manufacturing 10.5 percent. The GNP was to go up 7.2 percent. Again, actual achievements fell short of planned expectations. Over the period 1965-68, the total product grew only by 4.6 percent or so a year, little more than half the rate for the period 1951-59.

Venezuela, like Libya, because of its oil resources, can be categorized as one of the exceptional economies of the developing world, and the gap between anticipated and actual rates of growth in Venezuela cast significant light on the constraints to a more rapid acceleration of economic development.[36] The question of time horizons becomes important. Planning does not suddenly work the miracle of economic transformation. Venezuelan planning experience at the end of the 1960s was comparatively recent. Planning is a complicated political process and coordination between political groups, between economic agencies accustomed to work in isolation and even capriciously, between peasants and latifundists, between competitive regions and the center, does not suddenly evolve. Even if Venezuela with an oil resource base could be

TABLE 13.1

Venezuela: Planned and Actual Growth Rates of Gross Domestic Product

Periods	Total product	Agriculture	Petroleum and mining	Industry
Pre-plan (1951–59)	8.0	4.5	7.3	11.2
Plan (1962–66)	7.1	7.5	4.4	11.7
Actual rates (1963–66)	6.0	6.9	1.7	9.0

Sources: For Pre-plan and Plan periods: Venezuela (n.d., pp. iii, 1–3). For actual rates: *Economic Bulletin for Latin America* (1967, p.4).

[36] See Farley (1971).

regarded as financially well off in comparison with most developing countries, it was certainly not well off in terms of an adequate and increasing supply of trained manpower to carry the rough innumerable planning roles.[37] Improving the supply of trained manpower takes time. By definition, too, a developing country has only a small group of local entrepreneurs and increasing their number takes time. Limitations in the supply of high talent manpower imposes limitations on the speed of development. The training of planning administrators in Venezuela to match the expansion of planning agencies and activities remains a matter of concern. In fact, the shortage of trained manpower, according to the Committee of the Alliance for Progress (CIAP) accounted largely for the failure of the 1965-68 plan to achieve target goals.[38]

These facts were recognized and anticipated even in the 1963-66 plan.[39] Successful implementation of the plan, the 1963-66 planners foresaw, depended on the reform of public administration; clearer definition and distribution of agency functions; detailed studies of social and physical infrastructural needs; more effective financial administration and controls. the extension of the policy of administrative decentralization, particularly the strengthening of regional and municipal administration; and the extent to which government succeeded in building up an adequate supply of technically trained personnel qualified to carry through the planned programs of the government. To fulfill this objective, a School of Public Administration was set up in 1963 and provision was made for continuously expanded and supported higher education and specialized training at all levels, including vocational and adult education. The 1963-66 plan further recognized the necessity for state planning agencies to maintain permanent contact with the business sector, the worker, and the *campesino* to insure the effectiveness of their participation.

The 1963-66 plan further provided for systematic comparisons—every six months—between planned targets and the rate of implementation at macro, regional, sectoral, and project levels. Finally, the architects of the 1963-66 plan foresaw deviations from planning targets emerging from factors outside the control of the government, from data deficiencies, from difficulties in anticipating the response of the private sector to particular aspects of economic policies, and from external factors. Considering the ample resource basis for Venezuelan planning, the realism of the Venezuelan planning approaches, and yet the continuing gap between targets and actual growth rates, it becomes evident that even under conditions of financial affluence and determination economic transformation cannot be accomplished overnight, as the uninitiated might think.[40]

External Constraints: The Petroleum Sector

The continuing gap between targets and achievements casts light also on the difficulty of escaping from monoproduct dependence. In Venezuelan planning,

[37] See Pan American Union (1967d, pp. 96–97).
[38] See Inter-American Development Bank (1968, p. 320).
[39] See Venezuela Central Office of Coordination and Planning (1963b, pp. III4–4 to III4–7).
[40] Cf. Fei and Ranis (1966, p. 3):

The transferability of any particular set of concepts is circumscribed by differences in the social issues faced, in the tools available, and, consequently, in the vision of the future presented. Therefore, the usefulness of past theories is limited for examining the problems facing us now in the less developed world.

as we have seen, the rate of increase of petroleum exports and the level and stability of petroleum prices were key factors in the planning of targets.[41] Petroleum prices were, however, externally determined, and fluctuations in these prices continuously affected the attempt to change the structure and behavior of the Venezuelan economy.

The petroleum sector, expected to grow 4 percent a year under the 1963-66 plan and at about the same rate under the 1965-68 plan, grew only 2.6 percent for the whole period 1960-69 and the value of petroleum exports globally fell 2.1 percent.[42] Capital expenditures in petroleum declined between 1960-66. The contribution of the petroleum sector to capital formation declined by more than 50 percent during this period, weakening Venezuela's balance of payments structure. Since the importation of intermediate and capital goods and even raw materials was essential to support Venezuela's import substitution policy, the government had to resort to external borrowing to maintain the required flow of imports,[43] as we see from the following figures. Table 13.2 gives a few

Changes in the Percentage of Total Imports, 1960-69

	1960	1969
Final consumer goods	25.4	12.8
Intermediate goods	52.0	61.3
Capital goods	22.6	25.9
Total	100.0	100.0

indicators of the declining position of Venezuelan petroleum during the period.

Three major factors have contributed to the persistently declining position of petroleum. First, after 1958 Venezuela introduced new regulations subjecting the petroleum industry to national pressure for an increased share of the petroleum profits, to the right of the nation to terminate petroleum concessions upon legal expiration, to the right of the nation to participate more decisively in petroleum activity, and to the substitution of bargaining through Organization of Petroleum Exporting Countries (OPEC) rather than bilaterally with individual companies or groups of companies.[44] This continuing policy generated uncertainly, disinvestment, and flight from the petroleum industry. Second, the United States, the chief consumer of Venezuelan petroleum (42.8 percent of Venezuela's petroleum exports in 1969) has introduced a new system under which imports of crude oil are restricted to 12.2 percent of the internal production of the United States. In addition, the United States has begun to give preferential treatment to Canada and Mexico. Third, the position of Venezuelan

---

[41] Cf. Venezuela Central Office of Coordination and Planning (n.d., p. I-3): "En efecto, se contempla en el Plan que el producto petrolero aumentara a la tasa de cuatro por ciento anual. . . . Ciertamente el petroleo es aun el factor individual mas influyente en la dinamica de nuestro economic." Cf. the 1960-64 plan: "Los ingresos petroleros que se anticipan parecen lo suficientemente probables como para constituir la base financiera fundamental del Plan."

[42] See Banco Central de Venezuela (1970, p. 108).

[43] *Ibid.*, see chapter 10, "Sector Externo."

[44] See Maidenberg (1971, p. 1). Cf. Hirschmann (1969).

TABLE 13.2

Venezuela: Indicators of Changing Parameters in the Petroleum Industry

	1960	1961	1963	1965	1967	1969
Share of world exports (in percent)	33					16.8[a]
Share of supply of crude petroleum imports of						
United States	51.4[b]				37.3[c]	
Western Europe			25.2	18.8	25.0	21
Average FOB quoted prices						
For crude (U.S. dollars per barrel)		2.31			2.28	2.30
For derivatives			2.41			2.24
Average realized prices (U.S. dollars) per barrel)		2.19				1.85
Contribution to capital formation (in percent)	15.3				7.0	
Contribution of crude petroleum to GDP (in percent)	28.6					21.8

[a] 1968.
[b] 1959.
[c] 1966.

Sources: Banco Central de Venezuela (1969, 1970).

petroleum has been weakened by the new competition from the Middle East and Africa and by new technology in the form of supertankers which have reduced transport costs and given advantages to Middle East and Mexican petroleum in markets which formerly favored Venezuelan petroleum.

The State, the Petroleum Industry, and Foreign Investment

If one concentrates on growth rates one may be tempted to equate improved growth rates with economic progress. We have seen the error of this kind of economic perspective. In addition, more subtle objectives of development might be missed. For example, many countries seek through planning not only to change the structure of the economy but to subordinate economic decision-making by foreign vested interests to the sovereignty of the state and the local entrepreneur. In some cases, the change is abrupt and total, as in Cuba. In other cases, the transition evolves in a different manner as in Peru, Puerto Rico, and Mexico. In Venezuela, as in much of Latin America, planning is aimed at increased internalization of economic decision-making while maintaining both the established commercial relationships with foreign interests and the welfare of the private sector.

Although actual achievements fell short of the targets, discussion, legitimate bargaining pressures, and practical agreements resulted to a significant extent in the subordination of economic decision-making by foreign interests in Venezuela to the internal determinations of Venezuela and the objectives of Venezuelan development. More than this, institutionalization insured some significant national control of economic decision-making.

Because of the heavy dependence on oil, for instance, the government introduced measures to protect the economy from "disruptive fluctuations in revenue."[45] The income tax law was revised, raising the top income bracket to 52 percent, but tax deductions on new investment were maintained and new incentives were introduced to increase the over-all volume of exports within the petroleum program. To support price stabilization and to protect the government further against revenue fluctuations, government and the oil companies reached agreement on a basis for figuring out taxes and for the payment of back taxes. In 1966, through a new policy of service contracts, the government entered into fuller partnership and participation in the petroleum business, a distinct change from the old concession system.

The differences introduced in 1967 by the service contracts are significant. Under the old terms, concessions were granted for periods up to 40 years and, in return, Venezuela received taxes, levies, and royalties amounting, by 1958, to 60 percent of the total oil profits. In 1960, Government created the *Corporacion Venezolana Petroleo* (CVP), after announcing in 1959 the ending of new concessions. CVP was the instrument created by government to share in joint ventures with private enterprise. Under the new system, contracts are awarded by competitive bidding, and under special circumstances by negotiation. The maximum duration of the contracts is 20 years, modifications being made to 30 years under special circumstances. Realism, however, shone through. In adopting these new measures, it was officially stated, the government "was very careful to assure reasonable profits for the oil companies."[46] By 1970, the government's share of the petroleum profits amounted to 80 percent.

While expressing confidence that one major remaining problem would be resolved, Venezuela stimulated practical action to solve another. The first problem was the removal of restrictive U.S. import quotas for Venezuelan petroleum, and the second concerned the need for Venezuelan oil to be desulfurized in order to assist in the reduction of air pollution in U.S. cities. Desulfurization requires new and expensive technology, equipment, and time to install. To accelerate this development, Venezuela offered incentives to companies willing to set up desulfurization plants. One of the first companies, the Creole Petroleum Corporation, signed a contract for the building of a desulfurizing plant at Amuay at a cost of $114 million (U.S.), to be paid for jointly.

Petroleum also served as a base for new departures into petrochemical and gas. Significant developments were registered in these two areas between 1966–68.[47] The Venezuelan Petrochemical Institute (IVP), set out to attract private

---

[45] Venezuela, Embassy of (1968, p. 12).

[46] *Ibid.* The ratio of government share to net profit of the petroleum industry in 1950 was 51:49; in 1957 52:48; in 1959 68:32; in 1963 67:33; and in 1966 65:35. See Venezuela (1967, p. 10).

[47] Venezuela (1967, pp. 18–20). See also *New York Times* (1968).

capital to the petrochemical field. In 1966, the government appropriated to IVP 487 million bolivars for development capital. In 1966, joint projects were initiated with the foundation of a $3.5 million (U.S.) mixed capital company to produce 15 million tons of dodecil benzine a year. IVP holds 15 percent of the stock, a local Venezuelan group 55 percent, and Shell and Phillips Petroleum 15 percent each. Table 13.3 shows some indicative developments in this field. Eleven different petrochemical joint projects were entered into during 1968, three of which came into operation the same year, with the rest scheduled to be in operation in 1969 and 1970. Another was tentatively scheduled for 1971. These contracts involved an investment of $274.5 million (U.S.) excluding an IVP contribution of $130 million (U.S.). The accomplishments of 1968 represented an advance on those of 1967 when seven contracts were signed involving an investment of $152.5 million (U.S.). Generally speaking, the Venezuelan government holds a 55 percent share in the industry.

It was estimated that these developments in petrochemicals would give direct and indirect employment to 50,000 people and that industry would generate over $200 million (U.S.) of foreign exchange, 14 percent of the current total for the nation. Realizing that the companies would need credit financing, IVP successfully attracted both domestic and international capital. In addition to these indicative directions, IVP began combining with private companies, particularly with U.S. companies, to bring about major developments in natural gas.

Attitudes Toward Foreign Investment

While pursuing a planned path of economic nationalism, Venezuela firmly recognized the significance of private initiative even within a planned economy. "Industry in Venezuela," it was officially stated, "is predominantly private."[48] Government capital participated in electrical power, and gas, and in fields requiring heavy capital not readily available in the private sector. State agencies operate in a number of areas—airlines, railroads, steamshiplines, telephones and telegraph, ports and airports, steel, petrochemicals, sugar milling, credit, and development. Nonetheless, the declared general policy of the government is against a priori intervention in the private commercial and industrial sector.

Similarly in the area of foreign investment, official policy embodied a firm declaration in favor of all legitimate safeguards for foreign investment. Venezuela, according to official declarations, boasted of no discrimination against business or industrial operation "whether it is conducted by nationals or by foreigners."[49] Indeed, between 1961–66, U.S. investment in Venezuela practically doubled. In 1965, total foreign investments in Venezuela amounted to some $5 billion (U.S.), 67 percent of this coming from the United States. There were no restrictions on the repatriation of profits, dividends, and other transfers. There were however three areas of restraint influencing development in preferred directions. The government preferred to discourage portfolio investments and to encourage, through reduced duties and other incentives, foreign capital investment in the establishment, operation, and development of industries, agriculture and livestock raising, and mining. The government also preferred (under Venezuelan

[48] New York Times (1968, p. 18).
[49] Ibid., p. 14.

TABLE 13.3

Venezuela: Selected Developments in Petrochemicals

	Year start	Companies involved	Investment (in millions)	Percentage share of capital	Plant location	Output goals
Dodecil benzine	1966	IVP,[a] Sosa-Rodriguez (local), Shell, Phillips	$ 3.5	IVP 15 Sosa 55 Shell 15 Phillips 15		15 million tons a year
Low-density polyethylene	1969	IVP Union Carbide (N.Y.)	$ 29.5		Lake Maracaibo	50,000 tons a year
Aluminum sulpate, fluoridric acid, and refrigerants	1968	IVP Allied Chemical Corp., N.Y.	$ 5.5	IVP 50 Allied 50	Morom, Cordoba State	
Plyuron-chloride		IVP 2 U.S. firms 1 Japanese firm	$ 15			50,000 tons a year
Synthetic rubber	1969	IVP Goodyear Tire & Rubber	$ 25			50,000 tons a year
Ammonia	1969	IVP 3 U.S. oil companies 1 U.S. based independent oil producer 1 European financial organization	$120		Zuila State	4,000 tons a day (from 3 plants)
Dynamite (plant enlargement)	1968	IVP	60 bolivares	100	Morom	26,000 tons a year
Fertilizer (capacity expansion)	1968		$ 60			Expansion from 120,000 tons a year to 720,000 tons

[a] IVP (Venezuelan Petrochemical Institute).

Source: Venezuela, Embassy of (1968–1970) (Vol. 12, no. 8, Spring 1968).

Labor Law) that 75 percent of all employees in any business be Venezuelans—a preference subject to modification on technical grounds. In all this, a sensitivity to establishing the right climate for investment was not factored out and state agencies developed a growing sophistication in providing help and encouragement to prospective foreign investors prepared to work under Venezuelan norms.

Despite the continuing gap between planning and performance, Venezuela registered substantial gains in terms of the entrenchment of a development ideology, wedded not to inflexible political dogma, but to the realistic ideals of sound management of the economy and pragmatic relationships under a mixed enterprise system. Out of this conception emerged a clear recognition that "as has been the case for over 40 years, petroleum is still the cornerstone of Venezuela's economy," In an advertisement in the *New York Times* of January 22, 1968, Venezuela officially declared:

Not only does oil provide the Government with its principal source of revenue and foreign exchange, but under a policy of development and diversification it is reinvested in the vast industrial and social changes that are taking place. Oil is the motor behind Venezuela's progress and the key to a better future. Any tampering with this industry, therefore, is a threat to the well-being of the Venezuelan people . . . The value of these exports is in the neighborhood of 2 billion dollars or about 90 percent of all export income. Likewise, 90 percent of all foreign investment is represented by oil, 75 percent of which is American. It is obvious, therefore, that a continuing expansion of oil production and export is essential to Venezuela's overall prosperity and economic stability. [50]

Sectoral Changes

Concentration on the gap between growth expectations and performance can conceal significant sectoral shifts, however small, in desirable directions as well as significant dilemmas, particularly in the pursuit of import-substituting industrialization under planned development.

Between 1960 and 1969, for instance, the contribution of the primary sector to the GDP dropped from 36.0 percent to 28.4 percent, but it was the contribution of crude petroleum which dropped from 28.6 percent to 21.8 percent, while the contribution of agriculture remained steadily around 7 percent and minerals around 1 percent. [51] The contribution of the secondary sector rose from 19.8 percent to 20.2 percent and within this sector, manufacturing industry rose slightly, from 10.8 percent to 12.9 percent. The tertiary sector, however, increased its contribution from 44.2 percent to 51.4 percent. These were modifications, however slight, in monoproduct dependence. [52]

Agricultural growth over the period 1960–69 was higher in Venezuela than

---

[50] *Ibid.*

[51] See Banco Central de Venezuela, *Informe Economico* (1969, Table A-VII-2, p. A–102).

[52] There were equally significant changes in the formation of fixed capital. Within the structure of total investment for 1960–66, increases in investment were particularly due to the the significant expansion of urban house building, which doubled during the period. Investment in agriculture, however, grew at an average annual rate of 5.5 percent and in manufacturing industry at an average annual rate of 4.0 percent, while public administration and services registered a joint growth rate of 5.9 percent. Capital formation in urban housing increased its share of total capital formation from 9.7 percent to 15.7 percent between 1960–66.

anywhere else in Latin America, even though below the planned growth targets. From 1960–66, agriculture grew at an annual average rate of 6 percent, nearly double the growth rate of the Venezuelan population. In 1967, agriculture grew by 7 percent. Between 1960–66, the area under cultivation expanded at an annual average rate of 2.3 percent. In 1967, the area under cultivation increased by 7 percent. In 1967 agricultural production was 44 percent higher than in 1957, and Venezuela was 92 percent self-sufficient in agricultural production.[53] Traditional imports dropped from the import list with the achievement of self-sufficiency. Indeed, Venezuela has begun in recent years to be an exporter of agricultural products. Small farmers covered by the agrarian reform program started in 1960 contributed 20 percent of the total agricultural volume of the country in 1967 as against 3 percent in 1960.

The industrial sector over the last decade did not achieve the average annual growth rates projected under the plan for 1963–66 or the plan for 1965–68. Manufacturing grew at an average rate of 7.5 percent a year between 1960–69. But, except for water and electrical energy, this was the fastest-growing sector over the period. There are several other discouraging aspects to the rate of manufacturing growth for the period. The average rate of growth achieved for 1960–69 was less than the estimated rates of growth for the periods 1950–55 and 1955–60.[54] In addition, the average annual rates of growth for the period 1959–69 were highly erratic (see Table 13.4). Beginning with an explicable increase of 0.9 percent for the years 1959–61, the average rate of growth rose to 13.5 percent in 1963–64, dropping to 8.6 percent in 1964–65, and never again reaching the average level of any previous year during the period 1965–69.

Nonetheless, manufacturing during 1960–69 did register some achievements, in that diversification did advance and some significant growth did take place. On a base, for instance, of 1963=100, manufacturing production stood at 179.1 in

TABLE 13.4

Venezuela: Rates of Growth of Industry[a]

	Total	Total excluding refining	Durable goods	Nondurable goods
1959–60	0.9	0.6	-10.2	4.8
1960–61	6.6	6.5	4.2	6.9
1961–62	9.7	9.6	16.1	7.5
1962–63	7.7	8.5	9.9	6.9
1963–64	13.5	15.1	20.5	11.1
1964–65	8.6	9.2	16.8	5.7
1965–66	1.1	1.0	0.6	1.0
1966–67	6.3	7.0	6.2	5.8
1967–68	5.7	5.9	8.7	5.1
1968–69	4.5	5.2	4.3	4.5

[a] At 1957 prices.

Source: Banco Central de Venezuela (1970).

[53] Venezuela, Embassy of (1968, p. 16).
[54] UNECLA (1963a, p. 31) gives a figure of 11.7 percent for 1950–55 and 7.7 percent for 1955–60.

1957 and reached an index of 356.1 in 1966, nearly double. Again, by 1969, industrial production in Venezuela accounted for 69.3 percent of the national consumption of goods against a ratio of 59 percent for 1960 (see Table 13.5). The import content of the domestic supply of manufactured goods also declined, from a ratio of 37.2 percent in 1959 to 20.2 percent by 1966.[55] Moreover, between 1960–69, the economically active population in manufacturing nearly doubled—a contrast to declining numbers in agriculture, petroleum, and mining.[56]

	1960	1969
Agriculture	732	706
Petroleum	41	24
Mining	10	9
Manufacturing	253	496

Despite these achievements in manufacturing development, the fluctuating growth rates after 1965 are an indication of difficulties confronting an industrialization drive when economic nationalism requires the economy to pass from the import-substituting stage in consumer goods to the establishment of domestic intermediate and capital goods industries. This watershed stage is the great testing point of political and economic leadership and of national consensus. Retardation of the development drive at this stage is serious. In Venezuela, new policies were being forged at the end of the period to meet the problems of this transitional stage—policies which emerged from experience and policies inspired by the persistence of the Venezuelan development ideology.

Horizontal to Vertical Diversification: Problems of Transition

The fluctuating growth rates in industry, especially the deteriorating industrial growth rates after 1965, followed upon significant shifts in the character of the industrialization process in Venezuela. The first stage of the industrialization process primarily involved horizontal diversification—production of a larger and larger number of articles which were imported previously. This was a relatively easy stage but one which, because of the narrow domestic market, soon reached its limits. The second stage, vertical diversification or the deepening of the process, is much more difficult. This is the stage now being worked out in Venezuela. Horizontal diversification may be said to have reached its limits in 1965.

TABLE 13.5

Venezuela: Imports and National Production as Percentages of Total Consumption of Goods

		INTERNAL PRODUCTION		
	Importation	Agriculture	Industry	Total
1960	22.0	19.0	59.0	78.0
1969	10.7	20.0	69.3	89.3

Source: Banco Central de Venezuela (1970).

[55] See Venezuela (1967, p. 9).
[56] *Ibid.*

The shift in emphasis is reflected in the change in comparative growth rates of the two great aggregates in the industrial sector—durable and nondurable goods. In 1968–69, for instance, the durable goods production sector expanded by 4.3 percent, while the nondurable goods sector rose 4.5 percent (see Table 13.4). These rates obviously represented precipitous declines when compared with the rates of advance in 1963–64. The decline in the growth of the nondurable goods sector is indicative of the fact that import substitution had reached its limits. In fact, nondurable goods as a percentage of capital formation fell from 75.5 percent in 1961 to 71.3 percent in 1967.[57]

Accelerating the production of durable goods involved several new considerations. Intermediate and capital goods industries require lumpy investments and a longer period of gestation than nondurables. Attracting investment into this sector was more difficult since decisions to invest involve a far more cautious estimate of all factors, including the climate of confidence in the economic future. The advancement of durable goods manufacture was therefore slower than planned. These considerations in great measure explain why increases in gross fixed investment in manufacturing went from 31 percent in 1964 to 15.3 percent in 1965, to 2.1 percent in 1966, and to 8 percent in 1967, and why the export of manufactured goods declined 0.6 percent in 1966.

The government unhesitatingly pushed on in support of manufacturing development through protection, incentives, and institutional support. Nonetheless, although the coefficient of imports to gross domestic product declined from 13 percent in 1961 to 11 percent in 1967, external dependence was not at an end. Imports of consumer goods decreased 2 percent a year for 1961–67, but imports to support the industrial process increased an average of 8 percent a year, at almost the same rate as the increase in the growth of the domestic industrial sector.

At the end of the decade, while still adamantly guarding the national interest and seeking escape from monoproduct dominance and external dependence, Venezuela had begun making changes in its traditional policy of protection.. Emphasis was being placed on price, quality, and efficiency—on standards of performance which were to be competitive with international standards. At the end of the decade protection was contingent on capacity to penetrate the wider market of Latin America and beyond, on the extent to which the industry utilized agricultural and industrial raw materials of Venezuelan origin, and on the ability to meet the expectations of the Venezuelan consumer. The new policy embodied one final note of realism as an incentive to achieve these standards. Protection to industry was no longer to be extended for an indefinite period.[58]

CONCLUSIONS

On the whole, therefore, despite the lower aggregate growth of the economy between 1960–69 as compared with 1950–59, there emerged in the latter period immensely significant differences in the organization of economic activity and in the orientation and deployment of the nation's resources. The ideology of development persisted. The commitment to planning persisted. The response to

[57] Banco Central de Venezuela (1967, p. 95).
[58] See Banco Central de Venezuela (1969, pp. 116–119).

new situations which frustrated planned intentions was flexible. Concentration on safeguarding the national interest was unyielding. On the whole, a consistently practical management of the economy inspired, by reasonable determinations, was able to secure very practical achievements despite immense and many-sided pressures, including armed violence.

We do not attempt to forecast the future.   Major variables prevent sufficient certainty to make predictions. Political attitudes are mercurial. The world of oil—a world of complicated buyer and seller bargaining—is mercurial. International relations can be as changeable as internal attitudes and relations. "Contradictory economic interests," to use Felix's term, do not necessarily resolve problems with textbook rationality.[59] Honduras fought a war with El Salvador. Venezuela's neighborly relations with the independent Republic of Guyana and Venezuela's initial reservations about ANCOM are all part of the changing variables. Like most developing countries, Latin America, moving anxiously to new stages of national adjustment, has too many changeable elements to risk long-term predictions. There is, however, one nonvariable. It can safely be predicted for Venezuela, and for all of Latin America, that in economic development the national interest will continue to be the permanent criterion in all international arrangements and that internally there will be no retreat from the determination to escape from poverty and to retain the balance of decision-making to promote development.

We next make some concluding observations on the question of poverty and political leadership.

---

[59]Felix (1970, p. 99).

CHAPTER 14

THE POLITICAL VARIABLE: POVERTY
AND POLITICAL LEADERSHIP

Our concern in this book has been to supply perspectives on the dimensions of the Latin American development problem, the character and durability of the constraints, the successes achieved by counteracting policies, the complexity of the variables which affect predictions about the time it will take for the economy to be so transformed that there is a permanent and pervasive improvement in the quality of the life of the Latin American people.

THE UNIQUENESS OF LATIN AMERICAN DEVELOPMENT PATHS

Like every other country in the world, each country in Latin America has to take into account the peculiar circumstances which determine its own peculiar approaches to the problem of economic development. In turn, approaches to the development of the region as a whole must reflect the economic and social milieu of Latin America as a whole. Nationalism is a concrete reality and it is impossible to impose any model from one country on any other within the hemisphere, or to implant economic models imported from outside the hemisphere. The Mexican development approach is entirely different from that of Venezuela or Puerto Rico or the nondevelopment approach of Haiti. Cuba suffers from application of a dogma which is difficult to graft on to Latin American nationalist expectations. Even at the extreme political end of the continent, Allende's policies for the economic advance of Chile are likely to have boundary conditions set by his predecessor, Eduardo Frei, as well as by Chilean nationalism and Chile's determined espousal of a democratic political tradition. In the context of Latin America, development models must come to terms with the complex web of economic and social realities.

Nonetheless, history makes it clear that in the development experience principles are transferable and common situations abound. The Americas came together in an Alliance for Progress to share ideas and approaches, to discover differences, and to determine the degrees of moral, technical, and financial support which are possible and the degree to which differences could be accommodated for the constructive and more rapid development of Latin America. Changing the behavior of the Latin American economies is, however, an inescapable internal responsibility. Changing the economic orientation so that change remains consistent with normal democratic liberties is an integral part of development expectations.

The Venezuelan development experience and the Mexican experience, as well as the experience emerging from other development activity, may assist perspective on the important question of the time required for development in

Latin America. Despite consistent determination and ingenuity—over 50 years in the case of Mexico—these two well-endowed nations still have major problems to resolve before there is an over-all improvement in the quality of human life in these countries. With the population growth, the boundary conditions to more rapid change in every country in Latin America still remain formidable. But if the Venezuelan and Mexican experiences are regarded as relevant, they may help other Latin American countries to save time in eliminating development-inhibiting factors as they reveal themselves.

Poverty and Political Leadership

The question of redemption from poverty in Latin America is inseparable however from the question of political leadership and the political process. In the developing country, the economic and political wisdom of an effective political leader is of far greater importance to economic development than in a country like the United States, Canada, Denmark or Switzerland. In a developed country the development consensus is as universally established as devotion to the flag. In economically developed countries, an effective political leader who is indifferent to economic development is far less likely to ruin the economy disastrously than he would be in Latin America or in most developing countries. In the developed country, countervailing factors can be spontaneously mobilized, more frequently than otherwise, to counteract the effects of indifferent or inept economic and political leadership. In the developed country, business abilities are widespread; high talent manpower is normal in every subsection of organized life; and economic development institutionalization internally and international connections are well established. Economic life in the developed nation can endure until the incumbency of the wrong political leader runs its course. This is hardly the case in Latin America at this stage of the development process.

It is not difficult to identify the influence of the political leader in the economic development of most countries of Latin America today. At least, one important description of an economic model of development attempts to quantify the contribution of this variable to changing the course of economic development.[1] Interesting though this attempt is, empirical evidence makes this exercise superfluous for most of the less developed Latin American countries. Stagnation in Haiti can be attributed to the antidevelopment orientation of the Duvalier regime over the last decade. The transformation of Puerto Rico is clearly related to the determined pursuit of economic development inspired by Múñoz Marin.[2] It is doubtful whether the Venezuelan development push would have registered significant diversification from 1961 on without the overthrow of Pérez Jiménez

---

[1] Adelman and Morris (1968, pp. 1191, 1201, 1203, 1209).

[2] Cf. Observations on Puerto Rican political leadership before Múñoz Marin in Hanson (1955, p. 94):
They . . . were men of energy and integrity, passionate in their love for Borinquen, [but] they were also men of the nineteenth century who many times failed to understand the twentieth. . . . they could not hope to change . . . their own traditions and orientations which stemmed from centuries of relationships with Spain. Their language, their thinking, their sense of social values and human dignity, often clashed with the American go together spirit.

See also Anderson (1965).

and his replacement by leadership committed to broad and rapid economic advance for Venezuela.

Cuba is another outstanding example: economic orientation reflected the dominance of Batista as it does the dominance of his successor. Argentina still seeks to solve the economic development problems bequeathed by Perón. Alexander Bustamante and Norman Washington Manley, the two early premiers of a self-governing Jamaica, implanted the development ideology in modern Jamaica because of their dominant hold on the island. In the Republic of Guyana, economic acceleration depends on the influence of two leaders who dominated the political life of the country for the last 25 years—L.F.S. Burnham, the premier, and Cheddi Jagan, the former premier.

At a more advanced stage of economic development, when the supply of committed leadership expands, the influence of the effective political leader may not be as decisive or a less effective leader's indifference to economic development as a priority could be modified by the pressures from competitive leaders or by the fact that development has acquired a sufficiently on-going character to counteract the leader's negative effect. Most Latin American countries, however, are not at this stage so the development commitment of the existing effective political leader remains critically important. In writing of leadership in Latin America, Tannenbaum notes with contemporary relevance (1966, p. 118):

. . . the idea that the various cultures within the nation are equally legitimate . . . has found no Rousseau. It may be asking too much of national leadership to be sensitive and responsive to the needs and difficulties of all cultural groups. But these groups are the body of a nation in a country like Guatemala. If national leadership is to have any meaning it ought to be responsive to these groups.

Silvert makes a parallel observation (1968, p. 259):

Development is neither unilineal nor automatic. The choices of men and their ability to translate those choices into action constitute one of the determinants of whether the process will be expeditions and immediately fruitful or nasty, brutish, savage, and corrupt, and perhaps even a total failure. . . . These modern choices can only be made by modern men; any theory of development must obviously include a concept of developed persons.

Since most Latin American countries are still attempting to initiate the development process, the commitment of political leadership to development is much more than a mere marginal consideration. The question is of relevance to more than the psychologist, the sociologist, the political scientist, and the historian.

Even where political leadership is committed to development, in some cases it may not command the required backing because excessive social disaggregation and polarization constitute the order of the day. On the other hand, the universal desire for development might be there, but the leadership may be lacking or the government may be unwilling to give organized and decisive effect to this desire. The importance of political leadership in less advanced countries and the frequently dominant influence of the effective political leader make leadership attitude and popular support for economic development the most decisive factors in economic change.

Leadership commitment, however, like political independence, capital formation, and reactive nationalism, essential though they are as permanent attributes of a society, are not sufficient for economic development. None of these variables can contribute effectively to economic change until the basic political conditions include the right leadership combined with the right degree of development literacy and the right degree of social consensus. Haiti, for instance, has been independent since 1804; yet Haiti remains the poorest country in the hemisphere. Latin America has consisted of independent nations for well over 150 years, yet the Latin American economic dilemmas still persist despite significant instances of leadership commitment to development.

A CONCLUDING AXIOM

If the important question is not the emotional enjoyment of political independence and political leadership per se, but the inescapable question of economic transformation and the redemption of social despair in Latin America, a concluding axiom may now be propounded for a Latin America where development is the obvious priority. The great prerequisite for development in Latin America is the emergence at all levels of a political leadership with a decisive command of popular feeling, a political leadership precommitted to the economics of realism and determined to subordinate narrower political pursuits to realistic developmental achievements, a political leadership armed with the ingenuity to achieve the economic development needed to meet an obvious emergency situation.[3] Evidence shows that this is not too formidable a demand on the genius of the Latin American people. The great requirement in many cases will be a deliberate rechanneling of energies to the earthy job of engineering economic development so essential to increasing the sum total of human happiness in Latin America.

---

[3]Cf. Pinto (1969, pp. 21–22):

In fact it can be said that there is not one single political organization in the whole region which—as a body—has defined and adopted a "developmental ideology." . . . In all fundamental questions, the initiative still lies outside the political apparatus or—occasionally—within small enclaves inside the parties themselves. The ideological focus is still restricted to some small sectors of the progressive intelligentsia, a few technocrats, government advisers, and a handful of entrepreneurs.

Cf. also Myrdal (1964, p. 102):

All the underdeveloped countries are now starting out on a line of economic policy which has no close historical precedent in any advanced country. In the same way as the course of economic events and policies in advanced countries always gave rise to new realignments of social and economic theories better fitted to, and closely conditioned by, the immediate historical circumstances, it would be entirely appropriate if the very different events and policies in the underdeveloped countries today were accepted as a challenge to produce new and different theoretical frames for social and economic research.

APPENDIX A

STATISTICAL TABLES

TABLE A.1

Estimated Average Growth Rates of Developed and Less Developed Countries

| | 1966 region weight | PERCENT CHANGE IN TOTAL GROSS NATIONAL PRODUCT | | | | | | | | |
| | | | | Change from preceding Year | | | | | | |
		1950–55	1955–60	1961	1962	1963	1964	1965	1966	1967
LESS DEVELOPED COUNTRIES										
Latin America	33.2	5.1	5.0	5.1	4.0	2.5	6.5	5.1	4.3	4.5
Near East	14.0		5.9	4.8	7.1	7.3	7.3	6.1	7.1	5.0
South Asia	18.3	3.4	4.2	5.1	3.4	6.4	6.7	-1.8	2.6	8.3
East Asia										
Including Indonesia	13.4		3.8	4.6	3.2	5.5	5.2	4.4	6.8	5.5
Excluding Indonesia	9.8		4.9	4.8	4.9	8.2	5.3	7.7	7.7	6.1
Africa	11.1			0.4	4.3	3.8	3.5	5.2	3.4	4.3
Other[a]	10.0		3.4	10.6	7.7	7.6	6.6	7.4	7.6	4.0
Total[b]	100.0	4.7	4.5	4.9	4.5	4.8	6.1	4.2	4.9	5.4
DEVELOPED COUNTRIES										
United States	51.6	4.3	2.2	1.9	6.5	4.0	5.5	6.3	6.4	2.4
Europe	35.1	5.0	4.4	5.0	4.3	4.3	6.0	4.0	3.2	2.7
Other developed countries	13.3	6.2	6.1	8.9	6.1	6.8	10.2	5.3	7.7	8.9
Total including United States	100.0	4.7	3.4	3.9	5.6	4.4	6.3	5.3	5.4	3.4
Total excluding United States	48.4	5.2	4.8	6.0	4.7	4.9	7.1	4.3	4.4	4.4

PERCENT CHANGE IN GNP PER CAPITA

950-55	1955-60	Change from preceding Year					Current rate of population growth
		1963	1964	1965	1966	1967	
2.3	2.1	-0.4	3.5	2.1	1.3	1.5	3.0
	3.4	4.7	4.8	3.5	4.7	2.4	2.5
1.3	2.1	3.9	4.2	-4.1	0.1	5.6	2.5
	1.2	2.8	2.4	2.7	4.1	2.7	2.7
	2.1	5.2	2.4	4.7	4.7	3.1	2.9
		1.5	1.2	2.9	1.1	2.0	2.4
	2.4	6.5	5.5	6.3	6.5	2.9	1.1
2.8	2.2	2.3	3.6	1.7	2.4	2.9	2.5
2.6	0.5	2.5	4.0	4.9	5.1	1.3	1.1
4.3	3.6	3.3	4.9	3.0	2.4	2.0	1.0
4.4	4.6	5.4	8.8	3.9	6.3	7.6	1.4
3.5	2.2	3.2	5.1	4.1	4.3	2.4	1.1
4.2	3.8	3.8	5.9	3.2	3.4	3.5	1.1

Largely Spain and Puerto Rico.
These estimated growth rates for the less developed countries in total and by region are based on the trend data.

Source: U.S. Department of State (1968c, p.1).

11

Reduction in Death Rates in Relation to Goals of the Charter of Punta del Este

	UNDER 1 YEAR				1-4 YEARS			
	Death rate per 1,000 live births			Percent of Decrease Achieved	Death rate per 1,000 population			Percent of Decrease Achieved
	Average 1960-62	1966	1966 Goal		Average 1960-62	1966	1966 Goal	
Middle America[a]	71.3	63.4	53.5	44	14.0	11.6	10.5	69
Barbados	65.9	47.7	49.4	110	3.7	2.2	2.8	167
Costa Rica	66.1	65.0	49.6	7	7.5	6.0	5.6	79
Cuba	38.0	37.7[b]	30.4[b]	4	2.3	1.8[c]	2.0[c]	167
Dominican Republic	94.1	81.1	70.6	55	10.4	7.3	7.8	119
El Salvador	72.5	62.1	54.4	57	17.1	13.5	12.8	84
Guatemala	89.3	91.4	67.0	—	32.4	29.5	24.3	36
Haiti	—	—	—	—	—	—	—	—
Honduras	48.4	36.7	36.3	97	14.1	12.4	10.6	49
Jamaica	49.1	35.4	36.8	111	6.8	4.7	5.1	124
Mexico	71.4	62.9	53.6	48	13.8	10.9	10.4	85
Nicaragua	63.1	47.9	47.3	96	8.6	7.5	6.4	50
Panama	51.1	45.0	38.3	48	7.9	8.0	5.9	50
Trinidad and Tobago	42.9	42.8	32.2	1	2.5	2.0	1.9	83
South America[a]	83.9	73.6	62.9	49	13.3	10.2	10.0	94
Argentina	61.0	59.3	45.8	11	4.3	2.4	3.2	173
Bolivia	103.0	108.2	77.2	—	16.8	14.0	12.6	67
Brazil	—	—	—	—	—	—	—	—
Chile	117.8	101.9	88.4	54	8.2	5.0	6.2	160
Colombia	92.8	81.2	69.6	50	15.4	10.8	11.6	121
Ecuador	99.4	90.4	74.6	36	22.2	17.0	16.6	90
Guyana	—	—	—	—	—	—	—	—
Paraguay	89.7	69.6[d]	67.3	90	9.4	8.5	6.4	30
Peru	92.9	63.0[d]	69.7	129	15.7	10.5	11.8	133
Uruguay	44.6	42.7	33.5	17	1.3	1.3	1.0	—
Venezuela	52.1	46.7	39.1	42	5.7	4.9	4.3	57

[a] Regional rates based on data for the same countries as included in *Facts on Progress*, PAHO Misc. Pub. No. 81.
[b] 1965.
[c] 1964.
[d] Provisional

Source: Pan American Health Organization (1968b, p. 7).

TABLE A.3

Estimated World Population, 1960–2000 (In Millions)

	1960	Constant Fertility		High Variant		Medium Variant		Low Variant	
		1980	*2000*	*1980*	*2000*	*1980*	*2000*	*1980*	*2000*
MORE DEVELOPED COUNTRIES									
Europe	425	496	571	492	563	480	527	467	491
Soviet Union	214	295	402	296	403	278	353	296	316
Northern America	199	272	388	275	376	262	354	248	294
Oceania	16	22	33	23	35	23	32	22	28
LESS DEVELOPED AREAS									
Mainland China	654	942	1,811	971	1,345	850	1,045	782	893
Japan	93	114	127	117	139	111	122	108	115
Other East Asia	47	87	175	83	139	80	120	76	110
South Asia	865	1,446	2,702	1,448	2,444	1,420	2,270	1,378	1,984
Africa	273	458	560	463	864	449	768	434	684
Latin America	212	387	736	383	686	378	638	362	532
World Total	2,998	4,519	7,522	4,551	6,994	4,330	6,130	4,147	5,449

Source: Ohlin (1967, p. 22).

TABLE A.4

Life Expectancy at Birth, 1950–70

	Period[a] (1)	Life expectancy in years (2)	Life expectancy in Years 1965–70 (3)
Latin America			60.6
Argentina	1947	59.2	67.4
Barbados	1950–52	55.7	69 (1969)[a]
Bolivia	1949–51	49.7	45.3
Brazil	1940–50	42.4	60.6
Chile	1952	51.9	60.9
Colombia	1950–52	45.1	58.5
Costa Rica	1949–51	55.9	66.8
Dominican Republic	1949–51	62.1	52.1
Ecuador	1949–51	52.0	57.2
El Salvador	1949–51	51.2	54.9
Guatemala	1949–51	43.7	51.1
Haiti	1950	32.6	44.5
Honduras	1950	45.8	48.9
Mexico	1950	49.7	62.4
Nicaragua	1949–51	59.9	49.9
Panama	1950–60	56.1	63.4
Paraguay			59.3
Peru	1949–51	57.4	58.0
Trinidad and Tobago	1945–47	54.5	64 (1959–61)[a]
Uruguay	1949–51	68.8	69.2
Venezuela	1950–51	57.6	63.7

[a]Same source as that for Columns (1) and (2).

Sources: Columns (1) and (2): Inter-American Development Bank, (1969a). Column (3): Quoted from Latin American Demographic Centre (CELADE) in Prebisch, (1970b, p. 25).

TABLE A.5

Population and Growth Rates by Sectors

	1970 Popula-tion[a] (1)	1970 Urban Popula-tion[a] (2)	1970 Rural Popula-tion[a] (3)	1969-70 Urban Popula-tion Growth (in percent) (4)	1969-70 Rural Popula-tion Growth Rate (in percent) (5)	1965-70 Number of de-pendents per 100 persons of working age (6)
Argentina	24,089	16,978	7,111	2.4	0.7	57.3
Barbados	253	114	139	2.0	0.1	n.a.
Bolivia	3,956	1,002	2,954	2.4	1.0	82.7
Brazil	93,545	50,025	43,520	4.6	1.1	84.3
Chile	9,510	7,007	2,503	3.4	0.9	80.6
Colombia	21,168	11,648	9,520	5.0	1.4	98.6
Costa Rica	1,767	640	1,127	4.3	3.6	104.7
Dominican Republic	4,324	1,601	2,723	5.7	2.6	101.0
Ecuador	6,089	2,283	3,806	4.7	2.7	97.1
El Salvador	3,499	1,392	2,107	4.0	3.3	98.3
Guatemala	5,172	1,892	3,280	4.9	2.2	97.9
Haiti	4,856	857	3,999	3.8	1.6	82.0
Honduras	2,703	700	2,003	5.2	2.8	
Jamaica	2,020	727	1,293	4.3	1.2	
Mexico	50,624	29,468	21,156	5.2	2.1	97.8
Nicaragua	1,986	869	1,120	4.6	2.7	102.9
Panama	1,465	685	780	4.4	2.2	90.9
Paraguay	2,378	852	1,526	3.5	2.9	99.9
Peru	13,581	6,256	7,325	1.2	3.3	93.1
Trinidad and Tobago	1,106	589	517	6.0	0.3	
Uruguay	2,889	2,433	456	2.9	0.3	57.0
Venezuela	10,390	7,934	2,456	5.6	1.2	94.0

[a] In thousands.

Sources: Columns (1) through (5): Inter-American Development Bank, (1969a, p. 99). Column (6): Latin American Demographic Centre (CELADE) quoted in Prebisch, (1970b, p. 25).

TABLE A.6

New Patients, According to Method, Attending Public or Private Family Planning Clinics, 1965-69

	Women of fertile age (in thousands)	Number of private clinics	Number of public clinics	Intrauterine devices	Oral	Injection	Sterilization	Other	Total	Percent of women of fertile age protected
Argentina	5,611	6	20	12,669	17,102	421	–	153	30,345	0.54
Barbados	59	11	–	124	2,012	–	–	–	22,239	37.69
Bolivia[a]	983	2	1	2,251	–	–	–	–	2,251	0.23
Brazil	18,878	1	44	16,590	26,982	–	–	1,790	69,362	0.37
Colombia	4,150	26	33	59,514	8,735	529	–	3,000	71,778	1.73
Costa Rica	311	10	42	12,599	24,338	190	–	–	37,067	11.92
Cuba[a]	1,860	–	–	8,572	–	–	–	–	8,572	0.46
Chile	2,062	3	170	151,691	46,478	–	2,341	12,598	213,108	10.34
Ecuador[a]	1,117	29	1	18,496	–	–	–	–	18,496	1.66
El Salvador	635	–	59	21,184	12,725	367	–	–	34,216	5.40
Guatemala	972	10	23	10,095	7,940	1,900	–	–	19,875	2.04
Haiti	1,075	2	–	3,000	3,000	–	–	–	6,000	0.56
Honduras	483	1	61	12,162	10,815	194	–	–	23,171	4.80
Jamaica	450	160	–	828	9,856	2,047	–	–	12,731	2.83
Mexico	9,459	19	15	9,160	26,022	2,722	–	690	38,534	0.41
Nicaragua	369	–	25	1,415	948	51	–	2,000	4,406	1.20
Panama	264	1	5	9,988	713	54	–	–	10,755	4.07
Paraguay[a]	451	6	2	–	–	–	–	–	4,730	1.15
Peru[b]	2,590									
Dominican Republic	786	2	15	5,675	1,213	–	–	–	6,888	0.88
Trinidad and Tobago	216	12	17	7,286	11,334	50	–	5,041	23,711	10.98
Uruguay	680	–	15	5,200	1,800	–	–	–	7,000	1.03
Venezuela	1,971	9	30	20,875	4,010	–	–	–	24,885	1.26

[a]Data for 1969 not available.
[b]Estimated.

Source: Population Reference Bureau (1970, p. 3).

TABLE A.7
Estimated Birth Rates

	1860–64	1900–04	1920–24	1940–44	1950–54	1955–59
Argentina	46.8	41.8	34.3	25.7	25.4	24.1
Bolivia				45.1	42.4	
Chile	46.9	44.7	42.2	38.3	37.0	37.6
Colombia		43.0	44.6	42.4	44.0	45.1
Costa Rica		46.9	44.9	42.8	45.0	45.3
Cuba		44.6	36.7	31.9	30.0	
Ecuador			47.7	46.0	46.4	46.5
El Salvador		43.8	46.6	45.2	47.9	47.9
Guatemala		45.8	48.3	45.2	50.9	49.0
Honduras			44.3	43.8	46.0	46.0
Mexico		46.5	45.3	43.8	45.0	45.8
Panama		40.3	40.0	39.5	38.5	40.5
Peru		40.3	40.0	44.5	45.5	46.2
Venezuela		41.8	41.2	41.5	44.2	44.3

Source: Andrew Collver, *Birth Rates in Latin America* (1965, p. 26), quoted in Ohlin (1967, p. 15).

TABLE A.8
Agricultural Land and Agricultural Land Per Capita, 1967

	Agricultural land as percent of total area	Agricultural land per capita (in acres)
Unites States	47	5
19 Latin American republics	25	5
Argentina	50	15
Bolivia	13	8
Brazil	15	4
Chile	17	3.5
Colombia	17	2.6
Costa Rica	30	2.4
Dominican Republic	26	0.8
Ecuador	19	2.4
El Salvador	51	0.9
Guatemala	19	2.4
Haiti	31	0.4
Honduras	38	4
Mexico	52	6
Nicaragua	13	2.5
Panama	18	2.6
Paraguay	26	12
Peru	16	4
Uruguay	86	14
Venezuela	21	5
Jamaica	45	0.6
Trinidad and Tobago	35	0.4

Source: U.S. Department of State (1967e, pp. 10–11).

TABLE A.9

Illustrations of Demographic Disequilibrium, 1968

	Density per square mile	Selected regions	Percentage of area of country	Percentage of population of country
Argentina	22	Patagonia	28.3	2.5
Bolivia	9	Altiplano	16	60
Brazil	27	eight Atlantic coastal states	60	17.6
Chile	12 per sq. km.	central valley	14.4	60
Colombia	45.1	Antiquoia, Atlántico, Caldas, Cundinamarca, Cauca valley	11	53
Mexico	62	Federal District	16	50
Nicaragua	34.4	triangular area between Lake Nicaragua, Managua, and Pacific Coast	7	48
Peru	26	coastal region	11	40[a]
		jungle region	51	9[a]
Venezuela	27.9	Andean States and Federal Territories of Northern Andean Range	7	50
		Guayana region	45	3

[a] 1961.

Source: Inter-American Development Bank (1968).

Indicators of Disequilibrium in Value of Regional Production and Distribution of Income

	Percentage of contribution to country's industrial production	Index of average income per person in relation to the national average	Percentage contribution to gross domestic product
Greater Buenos Aires and Rosario (Argentina)	66		
São Paulo-Guanabara-Belo Horizonte axis (Brazil)	80		
Santiago and Valparaiso cities (Chile)	66		
Federal District and Monterrey (Mexico)	45		
Lima-Callao (Peru)	56		
Montevideo (Uruguay)	75		
Brazil			
Northeast		51	
North and central east		60	
East		96	
South		144	
Mexico[a]			
Pacific, south and central zones		35	
North and Gulf of Mexico		54	
North Pacific		93	
Greater Buenos Aires (Argentina)			45
Santiago province (Chile)			43
Federal District (Mexico)			35
Lima (Peru)			40

[a] In relation to average income per person in the Federal District.

Source: CEPAL (1970a).

TABLE A.11

Brazil: Selected Indicators of Uneven Industrial Growth (In Thousands)

	Estimated population	Employed in manufacturing
Six Amazon states (Amazonas, Pará, Amapá, Rondonia, Acre, Roraima)	3,300	18.5
Nine northeastern states (Maranhão, Pernambuco, Piauí, Paraíba, Rio Grande do Norte, Sergipe, Alagoas, Bahia, Ceará)	26,155	162
East (Minas Gerais, Espíreto Santo, Guanabara, Rio de Janeiro State)	22,500	451
South[a] (São Paulo,[b] Rio Grande do Sul, Paraná, Santa Catarina)	33,150	1,260
Sao Paulo		965
Midwest (Mato Grosso, Goias, Federal District)	4,500	13

[a] These four states with a population of just over one-third of the total for the country receive 65 percent of all industrial incomes and 48 percent of all farm income.
[b] The State of São Paulo receives around 55 percent of all industrial income in Brazil and about 21 percent of all farm income.

Source: Brazilian Government Trade Bureau (1968a). Data based on figures compiled by the Brazilian Geographical and Statistical Institute (IBGE).

TABLE A.12

Transportation

	Improved roads per 1000 square miles	Registered motor vehicles (in thousands) (1968)	Railroad passenger kilometers (in millions) (1967)	Railroad net ton kilometers (in millions) (1967)
Comparable United States	900	99,960	24,450	1,050,000
19 Latin American Republics (Total)	100	7,600		
Argentina	56	1,786	13,600	11,400
Bolivia	30	25	n.a.	n.a.
Brazil	156[a]	2,487	13,500	19,900
Chile	116[a]	233	2,000	2,500
Colombia	60	241	420	1,100
Costa Rica	194	51	26	28
Dominican Republic	274	20	n.a.	n.a.
Ecuador	88	54	53	66
El Salvador	314	44	n.a.	n.a.
Guatemala	148	57	n.a.	120
Haiti	51	16	n.a.	n.a.
Honduras	33	22	n.a.	n.a.
Mexico	54[a]	1,524	4,300	19,700
Nicaragua	62	33	41	14
Panama	65	47	n.a.	n.a.
Paraguay	22	19	14	17
Peru	28	203	250	650
Uruguay	76	197	n.a.	n.a.
Venezuela	66	524	39	17

[a] Includes all roads.

Source: U.S. Department of State (1969d).

TABLE A.13

Relative Position of the Latin American Road System, 1962

	All weather roads (in thousands of kilometers)	Percentage of world total	KILOMETERS OF ROAD NETWORKS	
			Per 1,000 kilometers	Per 1,000 inhabitants
Africa	775	6.0	26	3.0
Asia and the Middle East	1,820	14.1	128	1.9
Latin America	412	3.2	21	2.0
Oceania	658	5.1	77	38.6
World Total	12,926	100.0	130	6.3

Source: ECLA/OAS Transport Programme, quoted in UNECLA (1963a).

TABLE A.14

Selected Highways under Study and Construction

	Regions and countries linked up	Length on completion (in kilometers)
Pan American Highway System	All Latin America	76,161
Pan American Highway Proper	Most of Latin America	41,578
Carretera Marginal	Bolivia, Colombia, Ecuador, Peru, Venezuela, Paraguay, Brazil	9,200
Pan American Transversal Highway	Rio de Janeiro, Paranaguá, Asunción, La Pez, Lima	5,000
International Highway	Lima, Brasília, Rio de Janeiro	
Caribbean Circuit Highway	Colombia, Venezuela, (Santa Marta–Rio Hacha–Maracaibo–Caracas)	
Pan Amazon Highway	Amazon (through Patuinaya basin) and the Pacific (links with various centers in Colombia, Venezuela, Ecuador, and Peru)	
Central Trans-Andean Highway	Mandoza (Argentina) and Valparaiso (Chile)	430

Source: UNECLA (1964, pp. 300–302); (1967, pp. 234–237)

TABLE A.15

Road Construction and External Assistance

	Total road construction and improvement loans (in millions of U.S. dollars)	Recipient	Period
U.S. Agency for International Development	375	Latin America	1961–68
Inter-American Development Bank	160	Latin America	1961–68
Inter-American Development Bank	35	Brazil	1968
World Bank (IBRD)	350	Latin America	1961–68
	27.5	Mexico	1968
	17.2	Colombia	1968
	11.6	Chile	1968

Source: U.S. Department of State (1968d).

322

TABLE A.16

Communications

	Telephones (in thousands) (1)	Radio broadcasting transmitters (2)	Radio receiving sets (in thousands) (3)	Television receiving sets (in thousands) (4)	DAILY NEWSPAPERS	
					Number (5)	Copies per 1,000 population (6)
Comparable United States	93,700	5,470	n.a.	67,000	1,763	314
Canada (1964)	7,011		10,000	4,950	111	223
19 Latin American Republics	5,200	3,181				
Argentina	1,500	105	6,200	1,500	232	n.a.
Bolivia	25	75	500	n.a.	6	26
Brazil	1,300	944	7,500	2,300	255	54
Chile	260	133	1,500	60	46	118
Colombia	450	185	3,000	300	26	52
Costa Rica	25	40	123	35	6	77
Dominican Republic	31	137	139	19	5	27
Ecuador	45	220	510	8	27	52
El Salvador	25	67	395	30	15	47
Guatemala	25	71	210	50	8	31
Haiti	5	27	60	4	4	6
Honduras	10	51	128	7	7	19
Mexico	800	495	7,281	1,300	205	112
Nicaragua	15	63	100	10	9	49
Panama	50	84	225	48	10	75
Paraguay	15	19	160	n.a.	8	n.a.
Peru	140	201	2,000	175	53	47
Uruguay	200	97	900	175	35	314
Venezuela	280	169	1,651	591	27	78

Source: Columns (1), (2): U.S. Department of State (1969d). Columns (3), (4), (5), (6): U.S. Department of Commerce (1968aa).

TABLE A.17

Estimated Fixed Investment Requirements for the Guayana Region

	1963-66		1963-75	
	Millions of Bolivars	*Percent distribution*	*Millions of Bolivars*	*Percent distribution*
Total fixed investment requirements	3,166.2	100.0	15,281.2	100.0
Resource development	982.3	31.0	2,751.3	18.0
Industry	1,073.2	33.9	6,979.2	45.7
Heavy industries	966.2	30.5	6,031.2	39.5
Other manufacturing and construction	107.0	3.4	948.0	6.2
Housing	435.3	13.8	2,594.1	17.0
Public utilities	113.2	3.6	413.2	2.7
Transportation	450.3	14.2	1,743.1	11.4
City center	9.5	0.3	215.8	1.4
Other commercial centers	20.0	0.6	171.4	1.1
Other public facilities	77.5	2.4	408.2	2.7
Industrial estates	4.9	0.2	4.9	0.0

Source: Corporacion Venezolana de Guayana (1963, p. 54).

TABLE A.18

Venezuela: Exports, Present and Future

	Volume (in thousands of metric tons)		Value (in millions of dollars)	
	1960	*1975*	*1960*	*1975*
Crude petroleum	104,895	163,426	1,710	2,664
Refined petroleum	36,959	57,582	562	875
Coffee	25	39	30	47
Cacao	12	19	8	13
Other products	824	1,283	16	25
Traditional exports Total	142,715	222,349	2,326	3,624
Minerals				
Iron ore	19,422	25,000	142	182
Manganese, magnesite, asbestos and barite ores	–	60	–	20
Metals				
Iron and steel	–	1,320	–	264
Reduced iron ore	–	8,200	–	287
Aluminum	–	140	–	70
Manganese, magnesite, tungsten, and molybdenum	–	33	–	20
Heavy machinery	–	20	–	150
Chemicals				
Phosphorous	–	60	–	14
Ammonia	–	80	–	6
Guayana region exports Total	19,422	34,853	142	811
Total	162,137	257,202	2,468	4,425

Source: Corporacion Venezuela de Guayana (1963, p. 55).

Manufacturing Production by Economic Sector: Venezuela and Ciudad Guayana[a]

	Venezuela[b]		Ciudad Guayana[b]		Ciudad Guayana as percent of Venezuela	
	1960	1975	1960	1975	1962	1975
Foodstuffs	618	1,645	0.7	–	0.1	–
Beverages	260	744	–	183	–	6.5
Tobacco	135	419	–	–	–	–
Textiles	210	1,356	–	2	1.0	0.2
Footwear and clothing	290	855	0.7	39	0.2	4.6
Rubber products	47	308	0.1	1	0.2	0.3
Furniture	180	742	1.0	8	0.6	1.1
Leather products	35	176	–	–	–	–
Paper and by-products	66	587	–	83	–	10.4
Wood	67	210	2.1	–	1.9	–
Chemical products	185	1,058	0.3	72	0.2	6.8
Nonmetallic mineral products	228	695	0.5	77	0.2	11.1
Metal products	161	2,163	50.0	2,060	31.0	95.2
Machinery and transportation equipment	160	1,832	1.2	688	0.8	37.6
Graphic arts	173	1,296	0.2	15	0.1	1.2
Miscellaneous	131	1,377	0.1	13	–	0.9
Total[c]	2,970	15,463	56.9	3,241	1.9	21.0

[a] Value added.
[b] Millions of bolivars at 1957 prices.
[c] Excludes petroleum refining.

Source: Corporación Venezolana de Guayana (1963, p. 56).

TABLE A.20

Projection of Population and Labor Force in Cuidad Guayana (In Thousands)

	1966	1975
Heavy manufacturing industry	7.9	43.8
Metals	5.0	18.9
Heavy machinery	2.0	19.1
Chemicals	–	0.8
Construction materials	0.8	2.5
Pulp and paper and forest products	–	2.8
Total labor force	36.2	146.0
Mining	1.1	2.0
Agriculture	1.7	2.5
Other manufacturing	4.2	19.6
Construction	8.1	22.4
Trade	4.2	16.6
Transport	1.8	8.6
Services	7.2	30.6
Total population	115.0	415.0

Source: Corporacion Venezolana de Guayana (1963, p.57).

TABLE A.21

Housing Needs by Years by Family Income Groups, Guayana Region of Venezuela

	Reason for need	Total demand	MONTHLY INCOME LEVEL IN BOLIVARS				
			500 or less	*500 to 1,000*	*1,000 to 2,000*	*2,000 to 3,000*	*3,000 or more*
1962	present deficit	3,300	931	1,428	870	53	18
1963–65		15,167	4,555	6,103	3,170	989	350
	replacement	1,600	1,000	450	150	–	–
	migration	10,267	2,624	4,225	2,150	936	332
	1962 deficit	3,300	931	1,428	870	53	18
1966–70	migration	24,668	3,163	8,465	6,920	5,390	730
1971–75	migration	31,855	2,165	6,850	11,435	8,220	3,185
1976–80	migration	41,000	1,680	5,125	16,975	11,030	6,190

Source: Corporacion Venezolana de Guayana (1963, p.57).

TABLE A.22

Amerind Population

	Year	Amerind population as a percentage of total population
Mexico	1960	8.8
Costa Rica	1962	0.6
El Salvador	1961	0.4
Guatemala	1958	53.6
Honduras	1960	5.5
Nicaragua	1960	2.9
Panama	1960	5.8
Argentina	1960	0.6
Bolivia	1960	63.0
Brazil	1960	1.5
Chile	1960	31.8
Colombia	1961	1.6
Ecuador	1961	30.4
Guyana	1961	7.5
Surinam		2.3
French Guiana		6.8
Paraguay	1960	3.8
Peru	1961	46.7
Venezuela	1960	1.5
British Honduras	1961	22.6

Source: Roberts (1969, pp.686–688).

TABLE A.23

Deaths from Infective and Parasitic Diseases and from Gastritis, Enteritis, and so on, 1964

| | DEATHS FROM INFECTIVE AND PARASITIC DISEASES | | | DEATHS FROM GASTRITIS, ENTERITIS, AND SO ON | | | Percentage of total deaths from ill-defined and unknown causes |
	Number	Rate per 100,000	Percent	Number	Rate per 100,000	Percent	
United States	18,512	9.7	1.0	8,178	4.3	0.5	1.4
Canada	1,246	6.5	0.9	750	3.9	0.5	0.8
Argentina	6,216	31.9	3.7	4,807	24.8	2.9	20.2
Chile	8,925	106.4	9.5	5,743	68.4	6.1	6.8
Colombia	18,653	106.7	10.6	18,427	105.4	10.5	14.2
Costa Rica	1,106	79.7	9.0	1,898	136.8	15.5	10.9
Dominican Republic	1,295	37.1	5.9	3,442	98.5	15.8	47.6
Ecuador	10,080	206.5	17.1	5,876	120.4	10.0	22.6
El Salvador	3,228[a]	118.6	10.9	1,642	60.3	5.5	34.7
Guatemala	17,979[b]	430.5	25.2	9,561	229.0	13.4	15.7
Honduras	1,743	83.3	8.5	1,504	71.9	7.3	46.7
Mexico	39,427	99.5	9.7	44,064	111.2	10.8	17.6
Nicaragua	1,723	107.9	14.8	1,400	87.7	12.0	30.0
Panama	988	83.3	11.7	537	45.3	6.4	19.3
Paraguay	1,804[b]	81.5	8.1	818[b]	83.0	8.2	35.0
Peru	6,750	137.5	15.1	3,992	81.3	8.9	2.3[b]
Uruguay	816[b]	30.8	3.5	339[b]	12.8	1.4	6.7
Venezuela	4,716	56.0	7.7	4,028	47.8	6.6	27.4

[a] Statistic for 1964.
[b] Statistic for 1963.

Source: Pan American Health Organization (1965). The Pan American Health Organization notes that "the percent of deaths in the group from ill-defined or unknown causes is a useful index for measuring the availability of medical care."

TABLE A.24

Per Capita Daily Caloric Intake, 1966

	Calories per day (1)	Protein content of animal origin (in daily grams per person) (2)
United States[a]	3,200	
19 Latin American republics	2,550	
Argentina	2,920	58.7
Bolivia	1,980	13.2
Brazil	2,690	18.3
Chile	2,830	27.1
Colombia	2,200	22.6
Costa Rica	2,610	21.8
Dominican Republic	2,290	15.3
Ecuador	2,020	17.9
El Salvador	1,840	9.4
Guatemala	2,220	8.3
Haiti[b]	1,780	n.a.
Honduras	2,010	14.5
Mexico	2,550	15.2
Nicaragua	2,350	20.1
Panama	2,500	23.9
Paraguay[c]	2,520	23.7
Peru	2,340	19.9
Uruguay	3,170	67.1
Venezuela	2,490	26.4
Jamaica	2,260	
Trinidad and Tobago	2,470	

[a] 1967 data.
[b] Estimated.
[c] 1960–62 data.

Source: Column (1): U.S. Department of State (1969d). Column (2): Inter-American Development Bank (1969a).

TABLE A.25

Physicians, Dentists, Graduate Nurses, and Nursing Auxiliaries per 10,000 Population

	PHYSICIANS			DENTISTS			GRADUATE NURSES			NURSING AUXILIARIES		
	Year	Number	Ratio	Year	Number	Ratio	Year	Number	Ratio	Year	Number	Ratio
North America	1966	330,467	15.2	1966	115,723	5.4	1966	736,994	34.2	1966	844,607	39.4
Middle America	1966	42,841	5.2	1966	7,436	0.9	1966	28,690	3.5	1966	67,233	8.4
South America	1966	105,118	6.4	1966	46,280	2.9	1966	44,941	2.7	1966	114,846	7.2
Argentina	1968	37,732	16.4	1963	11,584	5.3	1964	22,903	10.4	1964	7,429	3.4
Barbados	1967	106	4.3	1967	17	0.7	1964	393	16.3	1964	420[a]	17.4
Bolivia	1966	1,187	3.2	1966	692	1.8	1964	411	1.1	1964	1,148	3.1
Brazil	1964	34,251	4.4	1964	22,000[b]	2.8	1966	8,212	1.0	1963	55,664	7.3
Canada	1965	23,990	12.2	1965	6,396	3.3	1964	115,818	60.1	1961	62,553	34.2
Chile	1964	4,842	5.8	1964	2,974	3.5	1965	1,780	2.1	1965	13,260	15.4
Colombia	1967	8,654	4.5	1962	3,400	2.1	1965	1,259	0.7	1965	10,818	6.0
Costa Rica	1967	858	5.4	1967	125	0.8	1967	787	4.9	1967	1,976	12.4
Cuba	1966	6,862	8.8	1966	1,451	1.9	1966	4,112	5.2	1966	5,663	7.2
Dominican Republic	1966	1,935	5.2	1964	479	1.4	1967	183	0.5	1967	2,172	5.6
Ecuador	1965	1,698	3.3	1964	518	1.0	1965	364	0.7	1965	1,849	3.6
El Salvador	1967	726	2.2	1967	246	0.8	1966	715[a]	2.4	1966	1,680[a]	5.5
Guatemala	1966	1,005	2.2	1966	281	0.6	1966	576	1.3	1965	2,289	5.2
Guyana	1966	197[c]	3.0	1966	36[c]	0.5	1966	929	14.0	1966	564	8.5
Haiti	1967	302	0.7	1967	169	0.4	1968	521[b]	1.1	1968	771[b]	1.7
Honduras	1966	466[a]	2.0	1966	78[a]	0.3	1966	251[a]	1.1	1966	1,288[a]	5.4
Jamaica	1964	854	4.9	1966	143	0.8	1964	3,799	21.8	1964	611	3.5
Mexico	1967	25,033	5.5	1965	3,463	0.8	1965	8,252	1.9	1965	40,000	9.4
Nicaragua	1965	698	4.2	1965	196	1.2	1965	353	2.1	1965	1,047	6.3
Panama	1967	644	4.8	1967	121	0.9	1967	875	6.6	1965	1,113	8.9
Paraguay	1968	1,344	6.0	1968	353	1.7	1966	226	1.1	1965	1,471	7.2
Peru	1967	6,223	5.0	1967	1,948	1.6	1965	3,600	3.1	1965	5,783	5.0
Trinidad and Tobago	1968	388	5.2	1968	62[a]	0.6	1967	1,240	12.1	1967	493	4.8
United States	1967	306,424	15.5	1965	109,301	5.6	1966	621,000	31.7	1966	782,000	39.9
Uruguay	1964	3,051	11.4	1962	1,250	4.8	1964	496	1.8	1964	3,756	14.0
Venezuela	1968	8,620	8.9	1968	2,229	2.0	1966	4,342	4.9	1966	12,574	14.1

Country	Year	No.	Rate	Year	No.	Rate	Year	No.	Rate	Year	No.	Rate
Antigua	1967	17	2.8	1964	4	0.7	1967	88	14.4	1967	60	9.8
Bahama Islands	1966	99	7.1	1964	17	1.3	1964	144	10.7	1964	190	14.2
Bermuda	1967	48	9.4	1964	25	5.2	1964	165	34.4	1964	49	10.2
British Honduras	1966	33	3.0	1966	5	0.5	1966	94	8.6	1967	68	6.0
Canal Zone	1967	100	17.9	1966	17	3.0	1966	233	41.6	1966	273	48.8
Cayman Islands	1967	2	2.2	1964	1	1.1	1967	6	6.7	1967	8	8.9
Dominica	1967	11	1.6	1963	2	0.3	1967	87	12.6	1967	13	1.9
Falkland Islands	1966	4	20.0	1966	2	10.0	1962	4	20.0	1966	4	20.0
French Guiana	1966	23	6.2	1965	7	1.9	1965	60	16.7	1965	71	19.7
Grenada	1967	18	1.8	1962	4	0.4	1967	105	10.6	1967	83	8.4
Guadeloupe	1966	149	4.7	1966	39	1.2	1966	269	8.4	1967	–	–
Martinique	1967	167	5.0	1962	59	2.0	1967	381	11.4	1967	151	4.5
Montserrat	1966	6	4.3	1966	1	0.7	1966	32	22.9	1964	–	–
Netherlands Antilles	1964	141	6.9	1964	31	1.5	1964	96	4.7	1964	60	2.9
Puerto Rico	1966	2,886	10.8	1966	455	1.7	1966	4,776	17.9	1966	6,653	24.9
St. Kitts-Nevis-Anguilla	1966	16	2.6	1966	3	0.5	1966	79	13.0	1966	5	0.8
St. Lucia	1966	17	1.7	1966	2	0.2	1966	65	6.3		–	–
St. Pierre and Miquelon	1966	5	10.0	1966	1	2.0	1966	11	22.0	1966	5	10.0
St. Vincent	1967	12	1.3	1962	3	0.4	1967	64	6.9		–	–
Surinam	1966	155	4.4	1966	21	0.6	1966	355	10.1	1966	455	13.0
Turks and Caicos Islands	1962	2	3.3	1963	1	1.7	1963	23	38.3	1963	15	25.0
Virgin Islands (U.K.)	1966	5	5.6	1966	1	1.1	1966	5	5.6	1966	15	16.7
Virgin Islands (U.S.)	1967	68	13.3	1963	13	3.2	1963	86	21.5	1963	116	29.0

[a] Government only.
[b] Estimate.
[c] Government and private hospitals.

Sources: Pan American Health Organization (1968). Inter-American Development Bank (1969a).

TABLE A.26

Construction and Ownership of Dwellings as Percent of Gross Domestic Product and Economically Active Population in Manufacturing and Construction

	Construction as percent of GNP (1967) (1)	Ownership of dwellings as percent of GNP (1967) (2)	Manufacturing as percent of GNP (1967) (3)	Investment of all kinds as percent of GNP (1968) (4)	Percent of economically active population in manufacturing (5)	Percent of economically active population in construction (6)
Argentina	4.9	3.9	31.3	19	24.9[a]	5.7
Bolivia	5.2	11.3	16.0	16	8.1[b]	1.9
Brazil	26.7	3.8	26.7	16	8.9[a]	3.5
Chile	4.6	2.7	25.9	16	17.2[a]	7.0
Colombia	4.9	6.0	17.2	22	12.8[d]	4.3
Costa Rica	4.5	8.0	18.8	23	11.5[e]	5.9
Dominican Republic	4.5	6.8	16.5	15	8.1	2.5
Ecuador	4.2[f]	6.6[f]	17.0	14	14.6[g]	3.3
El Salvador	3.2	3.8	19.6	13	12.8[h]	4.1
Guatemala	1.9	7.8	14.9	14	11.3[d]	2.6
Honduras	4.2	8.4	15.0	19	7.7[h]	2.0
Mexico	3.9	–[c]	26.5	23	13.7[a]	3.6
Nicaragua	3.2	7.0	14.8	19	11.7[e]	3.6
Panama	5.3	6.7	16.3	23	7.6[a]	4.3
Paraguay	3.0	3.2	15.6	15	15.1[g]	3.3
Peru	4.8	5.4	15.0	18	13.2[h]	3.4
Uruguay	3.5	2.5	27.6	12	21.0[e]	4.8
Venezuela	4.6	25.1	14.6	25	12.2[h]	5.6
Total share for 18 Latin American countries	3.5	4.5	23.3	19	–	–

[a] 1960.
[b] 1950.
[c] included in other services.
[d] 1964.
[e] 1963.
[f] estimate.
[g] 1962.
[h] 1961.

Source: Columns (1), (2), and (3): U.S. Department of State (1969d). Column (4): U.S. Department of State (1970). Columns (5) and (6): Pan American Union (1969).

TABLE A.27
Estimated Housing Deficit (In Thousands of Housing Units)

	Year	Total (excluding replacements)	Urban	Rural	Minimum annual building needs	Average number of units built per year
Argentina	1961	1,500	–	–	–	–
	1965	2,000	–	–	160	72 (1963)
	1968	2,300	n.a.	n.a.	n.a.	108,222
Bolivia	1961	384	100	284	–	–
	1965	–	–	–	29	–
	1966	615	486	128	40	2.5 (1965)
Brazil	1961	8,400	–	–	–	–
	1965	10,500	–	–	–	–
	1966	4,600[a]	–	–	630	–
Chile	1961	550	–	–	–	–
	1965	440	–	–	160	80
	1966	600	360	240	75	
	1967	630	–	–	–	–
Colombia	1962	280[b]	–	–	–	–
	1964	290	–	–	60	–
	1966	346.5	–	–	150	–
	1968	416.3[c]	–	–	60	–
Costa Rica	1961	98.8	32.6	66.2	–	–
	1966	100	–	–	20	less than 6.0
Dominican Republic	1961	206	58.7	147.3	–	–
	1966	297.065	92.320	204.745	16,894	very few
	1968	389	–	–	–	–
Ecuador	1950	322	–	–	–	–
	1960	580	–	–	–	–
	1966	325	–	–	28	6.0
El Salvador	1950	337	149	188	–	–
	1965	342	168	174	–	–
Guatemala	1949	377	–	–	–	–
	1966	600	150	450	30.5	17
Haiti	1950	107.515	–	–	–	–
	1965	392.053	–	–	–	974[d]
Honduras	1961	173	–	–	–	–
	1965	300	–	–	14 (1966)	7 (1966)
Mexico	1960	1,000	–	–	–	–
	1966	3,500	–	–	–	–
Nicaragua	1960	158	–	–	–	–
	1966	115	39	76	11.3	6.855 (1966)
Panama	1950	–	–	76	–	–
	1960	118	36	82	18	3.0 (1960–65)
Paraguay	1950	8	–	–	–	–
	1962	162	42	120	17.0 (1966)	very few
	1969	160	–	–	–	–
Peru	1961	2,000	–	–	–	–
Uruguay	1961	150	–	–	–	–
	1966	100	55	45	24	19.0 (1960–63)[e]
Venezuela	1961	540	–	–	–	–
	1964	800	–	–	–	–
Trinidad and Tobago	1960	–	–	–	6	3.5

[a] Revised estimate.
[b] For cities 10,000 and over.
[c] For 20 departmental capitals.
[d] Total of 1961–1964.
[e] Fewer for 1963–66.

Source: Inter-American Development Bank. (1961), (1962a), (1963b), (1965a), (1966), (1967), (1968a), (1969a).

TABLE A.28

Estimates of Income Distribution

								PERCENTAGE OF INCOME CORRESPONDING TO EACH GROUP						
	Country	Received by	1 10%	2 10%	3 10%	4 10%	5 10%	6 10%	7 10%	8 10%	9 10%	10 10%	5% highest	1% highest
1961	Argentine	persons	1.9	3.3	4.2	5.1	6.0	7.1	8.3	10.0	13.2	40.9	31.2	16.3
1960	Brazil	working population	1.8	2.4	3.1	4.2	5.3	6.0	8.1	10.3	13.8	45.0	33.0	18.0
1962	Colombia	active population	2.5	3.4	4.1	4.9	5.3	6.1	7.5	9.5	14.0	42.7	30.4	10.0
1961	El Salvador	active population	2.4	3.1	3.2	3.3	4.0	4.8	7.2	10.6	15.8	45.6	33.0	18.0
1962	Venezuela	families	1.4	1.6	3.0	3.7	4.6	6.0	8.3	13.4	17.3	40.7	26.5	9.0
1960	Panama	working population	1.9	3.0	3.7	5.9	6.0	6.5	7.0	9.4	12.6	44.0	34.5	16.5
1963	Mexico	families	1.5	2.1	3.1	3.8	4.9	6.0	8.1	12.0	17.0	41.5	29.0	12.0
1961	Costa Rica	families	2.6	3.4	3.8	4.0	4.4	5.4	7.1	9.3	14.0	46.0	35.0	16.0

Source: UNECLA, quoted in Centro Interamericano de Administradores Tributarios (1970, p.11).

TABLE A.29

Income Distribution According to Income Groups

Income groups	Percentage of the total income received	Index of average income (regional average = 100)	Average income per person (in dollars)
20 percent of the lowest	3.5	18.0	68.0
30 percent under the average	10.5	35.0	133.0
30 percent over the average class	25.4	85.0	322.0
15 percent under the higher groups	29.1	194.0	740.0
5 percent of the highest groups	31.5	629.0	2,400.0

Source: UNECLA, quoted in Centro Interamericano de Administradores Tributarios (1970, p.12).

TABLE A.30

General Wage Levels

	Year	Monetary unit [a]	Per hour	Per day	Per week	Per month
Bolivia	1957	bolivianos	–	5,848	–	–
Costa Rica	1960	colones	–	–	–	347.0
Dominican Republic	1961	pesos	–	–	–	109.0
Honduras	1960	lempiras	–	–	–	71.0
Paraguay	1961	guaranies	–	–	–	454.4
Peru	1961	soles	–	46.05	–	–
Uruguay	1957	pesos	–	20.42	–	–
Venezuela	1958	bolivars	–	22.11	–	–
Canada	1961	dollars	–	–	78.11	–

[a] 8565 bolivianos = $1 U.S. (1957); 5.615 to 6.65 colones = $5.93 (1960); 1 peso (Dominican Republic) = $1 U.S. (1961); 2 lempiras = $1 U.S. (1960); 126 guaranies = $1 U.S. (1961); 26.81 soles = $1 U.S. (1961); 1.504 to 6.11 pesos (Uruguay) = $1 U.S. (1957); 3.09 to 3.35 bolivars = $1 U.S. (1958).

Source: International Labor Office (1962).

TABLE A.31
Agricultural Wages

	Year	Monetary unit	Per hour	Per day	Per week	Per month	Type of workers
Chile	1959	escudos	–	0.62 (minimum)	–	–	permanent and nonpermanent
Colombia	1961	pesos	–	6.60 (men) 4.70 (women)	–	–	agriculture
Costa Rica	1960	colones	1.06[a] 0.91[b] (minimum)	–	–	–	general farm hands
Mexico	1960	pesos	–	9.38	–	–	day laborers
Peru	1959	soles	–	26.40	–	–	general farm hands
Canada	1961	dollars	–	7.60	–	–	general farm hands
United States	1961	dollars	0.834	–	–	–	all workers

[a] On coffee plantations.
[b] Agricultural and livestock production.

Source: International Labor Office (1962).

TABLE A.32
Average Wages per Hour by Field of Activity (In U.S. Dollars)

Activity	Average wages per hour
Total for industry	0.31
Beverages	0.34
Food	0.29
Printing and publishing	0.29
Transportation	0.29
Nonmetallic mineral products	0.28
Textiles	0.27
Clothing and shoes	0.26
Furniture and accessories	0.25

Occupation	Ordinary current wages per hour
Skilled worker	0.34–1.00
Semiskilled worker	0.21–0.50
Unskilled worker	0.13–0.27
Janitor	0.25–0.25
Watchmen	0.15–0.30
Packaging clerk	0.10–0.20
Mechanic for precision work	1.00–1.20
Radio-telephone	0.75–1.00
Heavy equipment	0.43–1.00
Lathe	0.40–0.85
Light equipment	0.39–0.61
Welder	0.35–0.93
Spinner-weaver finisher	0.35–0.70
Steel worker on constructions	0.35–0.45
Carpenter	0.34–0.60
Plumber	0.33–0.63
Cement worker	0.32–0.53
Driver of light trucks	0.32–0.45
Foreman and supervisors	0.30–0.75
Electrician	0.30–0.80
Mounter or installer	0.30–0.40
Boiler	0.30–0.50
Mason	0.25–0.53
Painter	0.25–0.50
Oven	0.25–0.30
Mixer	0.21–0.30
Mechanic	0.20–0.62
General assistance	0.20–0.40
Press	0.18–0.31
General service	0.17–0.20
Operators of machinery in general	0.15–0.40
Minimum wages	0.10–0.15

Occupation	Ordinary current monthly salaries
Engineer	400–650
Chemist	320–480
Plant supervisor (inspector)	300–450
Accountant	150–400
Cashier	150–240
Draftsman (designer)	100–250
Assistant accountant	100–225
Bilingual secretary	100–160
Bookkeeper	70–150
Stenographer	60–100
Reception	60–100
Messenger	60– 90
Chauffeur	50–150
Watchman-janitor	50–150
Office clerk	40– 60

Source: Central American Bank for Economic Integration (1967, pp. 32–33).

TABLE A.33

General Consumer Cost of Living Index, 1960-69 (Base 1963 = 100)

	1960	1961	1962	1963	1964	1965	1966	1967	1968	1969
Argentina	55.3	62.8	80.4	100.0	122.1	157.1	207.1	267.6	311.0	334.6
Bolivia	88.2	95.0	100.7	100.0	110.1	113.0	121.2	111.2	117.3	119.9
Brazil	27.3	37.8	57.6	100.0	187.0	302.4	443.4	574.4	713.5	879.3
Colombia	69.5	75.4	78.6	100.0	117.8	126.1	147.2	159.0	170.8	182.6
Costa Rica	91.5	94.6	97.1	100.0	103.3	102.7	102.8	104.0	108.2	111.1
Chile	56.5	60.9	69.3	100.0	146.0	188.1	231.1	273.0	345.7	451.7
Ecuador	88.1	91.8	94.4	100.0	104.0	107.2	104.1	108.1	112.8	119.9
El Salvador	101.1	98.4	98.5	100.0	101.7	102.3	101.1	102.6	105.2	104.9
United States	96.6	97.6	98.8	100.0	101.4	103.1	106.2	109.1	113.7	120.0
Guatemala	98.4	97.8	99.9	100.0	99.5	99.5	99.4	99.4	102.2	104.1
Haiti	93.0	96.4	95.9	100.0	109.3	111.7	120.1	117.4	119.0	122.6
Honduras	94.5	96.1	97.1	100.0	104.5	107.9	109.7	112.5	115.2	118.9
Mexico	96.7	98.4	99.4	100.0	102.3	106.0	110.5	113.8	116.5	119.8
Panama	99.0	99.1	99.5	100.0	102.4	102.9	103.1	104.5	106.2	108.1
Paraguay	179.8	–	–	–	100.0	103.8	106.8	108.3	109.0	111.2
Peru	84.4	88.2	94.0	100.0	110.5	129.3	141.4	109.8	130.8	138.9
Dominican Republic	88.2	84.5	93.4	100.0	102.0	100.5	100.5	101.8	101.8	102.7
Trinidad and Tobago	92.5	93.5	96.3	100.0	100.8	102.6	106.8	109.1	118.0	121.0
Uruguay	60.7	74.4	82.5	100.0	142.4	223.0	386.8	732.2	1650.0	1994.7
Venezuela	–	–	98.9	100.0	102.2	103.9	105.7	107.1	107.1	109.7
Guyana	93.8	94.8	98.7	100.0	100.8	103.0	105.5	108.3	109.3	124.7

Source: Inter-American Statistical Institute (1970).

Index of Cost of Living 1960–70 in Respect to Housing (Base 1963=100)[a]

	1960	1961	1962	1963	1964	1965	1966	1967	1968	1969
Argentina[b]	54.1	57.7	71.8	100.0	109.5	124.6	200.7	257.0	289.0	303.6
Bolivia[c]	102.4	98.3	104.9	100.0	102.7	105.2	115.5	116.1	124.7	127.3
Brazil[d]	27.3	36.8	54.0	100.0	175.5	302.4	440.1	595.1	735.3	856.3
Colombia	71.7	77.3	83.5	100.0	106.2	114.3	142.2	157.5	167.5	180.4
Costa Rica	91.5	93.6	96.1	100.0	100.8	101.1	101.0	101.6	104.2	105.9
Chile[e]	64.4	69.0	76.2	100.0	150.7	188.8	227.2	277.4	349.2	445.2
Ecuador	93.5	95.4	97.9	100.0	101.7	107.4	102.0	105.7	108.0	109.7
El Salvador	128.0	105.9	100.9	100.0	98.9	104.9	104.7	107.4	109.8	110.3
United States	97.3	98.0	98.8	100.0	101.3	102.5	104.9	108.0	112.5	119.7
Guatemala	99.7	99.3	99.8	100.0	100.5	100.9	101.4	101.5	102.9	103.1
Haiti	101.3	102.9	98.3	100.0	102.4	122.2	138.9	132.4	119.3	120.3
Honduras	97.7	98.9	99.7	100.0	100.3	100.8	100.6	101.4	108.5	111.5
Panama	100.2	100.0	99.6	100.0	100.5	101.3	102.0	103.6	104.7	105.6
Paraguay	146.2	–	–	–	100.0	103.9	105.8	104.9	105.6	108.6
Peru	95.0	97.0	98.0	100.0	102.1	117.6	127.5	–	128.4	139.3
Dominican Republic	97.9	82.0	95.5	100.0	99.9	99.4	100.7	101.0	97.8	100.6
Trinidad and Tobago	93.5	94.9	95.9	100.0	102.1	106.8	110.9	114.6	117.9	121.1
Uruguay	83.3	83.8	84.6	100.0	119.8	168.5	240.4	381.3	784.8	1229.3
Venezuela	–	–	98.9	100.0	100.7	102.4	103.2	104.1	104.7	106.3
Guyana	99.1	98.9	99.1	100.0	100.6	101.8	102.9	103.9	104.9	114.6

[a] Monthly average.
[b] for federal capital.
[c] cities of La Paz, Cochabamba, and Omro.
[d] São Paulo.
[e] Santiago.

Source: Inter-American Statistical Institute (1970).

TABLE A.35

Indicators of Educational Level[a]

	Percentage of illiterates in the population 15 and older (1)	Percentage of persons age 5–14 enrolled in primary schools (2)	Percentage of persons age 15–19 enrolled in secondary schools (3)
United States	3	88	60
Guatemala	71	22	7
Argentina	14	66	21
Bolivia	68	24	7
Brazil	51	26	10
Chile	20	66	18
Colombia	43	28	7
Costa Rica	21	49	7
Dominican Republic	57	40	7
Ecuador	44	41	9
El Salvador	61	31	4
Haiti	89	15	–
Honduras	65	22	3
Mexico	43	39	4
Nicaragua	62	23	3
Panama	30	54	24
Paraguay	34	51	9
Peru	58	44	–
Uruguay	15	62	17
Venezuela	48	40	6

Higher education per 100,000 persons (4)	Newspaper circulation per 1,000 persons (5)	Government expenditures in education c.1960 (in dollars per capita (6)	Government expenditures in education as percent of Gross National Product (7)
1,511	347	97	4.6
84	19	3	1.9
480	100	9	2.9
166	23	1	1.4
98	59	32	1.6
290[b]	76	10	1.7
94	55	14	4.0
192	92	14	2.3
106	24	4	1.4
127	49	3	1.6
65	35	5	2.7[c]
28	3	1	2.2
57	20	4	1.9
111	48	5	1.4
81	50	5	1.8[c]
190	118	13	3.3
121	12	2	1.7
193	39	4	2.9
484	197	6	1.0[c]
137	65	39	2.3

[a] Figures are for years c.1950.
[b] 1959 figures.
[c] GDP.

Source: UNECLA (1963d), vol. 2.

TABLE A.36

Education—Miscellaneous Indicators

	Year	Average level of education for whole population (in school years)	DROPOUT RATES IN PERCENTAGES			PERCENTAGE OF UNTRAINED TEACHERS	
			Primary (grades 1-6)	Secondary	University	Primary	Secondary
Argentina	1963	3.9^a	85^b	43.5	–	–	–
Bolivia	1964		70	80	–	46^c	–
Brazil		1.7^a	66^e	–	–	–	–
Chile	1965	6^c					
		3.5^d	70	–	–	42^f	50^a
Colombia	1964	6	84 / 99^d	80-99	–	–	–
Costa Rica	1965	3.2^a	88	85	–	–	–
Dominican Republic	1964	1.0^a	–	–	–	–	–
Ecuador	1964	3.0	86.5	–	96	–	–
El Salvador	1966	1.3^a	80	75	97	46	86
Honduras	1965	–	82	56	–	55^g	10
Mexico		2.3^a	–	–	–	–	–
Nicaragua	1965	1.4^a	–	–	–	66	95
Panama	1965	3.5^a	65	–	–	6	–
Paraguay	1965	–	84.5^g	67	–	35	–
Peru	1965	3	66^h	72^h	91	–	–
Venezuela	1966	3	–	–	–	–	–

[a] Statistic for 1950.
[b] North East.
[c] Urban.
[d] Rural.
[e] Grades 1-4.
[f] Statistic for 1960.
[g] Statistic for 1963.
[h] Statistic for 1964.

Source: Inter-American Development Bank (1966).

TABLE A.37

Central Government Expenditures on Education [a]

	Index of central government expenditures on education, 1967 (1961 = 100) (1)	Percentage of government expenditures on education, 1968 (2)
Argentina	147.1	13.8
Bolivia	195.1	30.5
Brazil	178.9	7.1
Chile	171.8	18.7
Colombia	132.5	14.5
Costa Rica	156.5	29.0
Dominican Republic	254.0	14.0
Ecuador	168.6	19.9
El Salvador	125.4	25.7
Guatemala	120.8	17.9
Honduras	185.6	22.3
Mexico	166.4	17.9
Nicaragua	306.8	21.8
Panama	173.4	28.2
Paraguay	170.0	15.7
Peru	167.1	26.2
Uruguay	143.6	23.9
Venezuela	157.4	14.1
Total 18 republics	161.8	

[a] Constant 1966 prices.

Source: Column (1): U.S. Department of State (1969b). Column (2): Inter-American Development Bank (1969a).

TABLE A.38

Industrial Origin of Gross Domestic Product, 1967 (In Percent)

Economic sector	Argentina	Bolivia	Brazil	Chile	Colombia	Costa Rica	Dominican Republic	Ecuador
Agriculture, forestry, and fishing	15.4	19.8	28.3	8.2	30.5	23.0	22.9	33.4
Mining (including petroleum)	1.9	13.5		10.5	2.0	18.8	1.3	1.9
Manufacturing	31.3	16.0	26.7	25.9	17.2		16.5	17.0
Construction	4.9	5.2		4.6	4.9	4.5	4.5	4.2[d]
Electricity, gas and water	2.8	1.3		1.6	1.5	1.5	1.2	1.5
Transport, communication and storage	9.4	7.1	8.4	4.7	6.6	4.0	7.0	4.1
Wholesale and retail trade	12.9		12.7	22.0	14.0	17.2	17.1	13.0
Banking, insurance, and real estate		9.8	e	2.8	3.3	2.6	2.1	2.8
Ownership of dwellings	3.9	11.3	3.8	2.7	6.0	8.0	6.8	6.6[d]
Public administration and defense	11.1	8.5[f]	7.0	5.7	6.3[f]	10.5[f]	12.2	6.6[d]
Other services	6.4	7.5	13.1	11.3	7.7	9.9	8.4	8.0[d]

El Salvador	Guate- mala	Hon- duras	Mexico	Nica- ragua	Pan- ama[a]	Para- guay	Peru[a]	Uru- guay[a]	Vene- zuela	Total[b]
26.4	27.3	38.4	15.9	28.7	21.7	33.0	19.9	15.6	7.4	20.2
0.1	0.1	1.8	4.7[c]	1.5	0.3	0.3	7.2 ⎫		26.0	4.9
								27.6		
19.6	14.9	15.0	26.5	14.8	16.3	15.6	15.0 ⎭		14.6	23.3
3.2	1.9	4.2	3.9	3.2	5.3	3.0	4.8	3.5	4.6	3.5
1.5	1.1	1.3	1.4	1.7	1.9	0.7	1.1 ⎫		2.5	1.9
								10.1		
4.3	5.5	6.2	4.1	5.1	5.8	4.1	4.4 ⎭		3.7	6.4
24.3	28.4	13.9	26.0	19.9	13.5 ⎫		15.3	15.1	16.1	17.3
						24.4				
1.9	2.4	1.9	e	2.4	3.0 ⎭		2.9	e	⎫	2.9
3.8	7.8	8.4	e	7.0	6.7	3.2	5.4	2.5		4.5
									25.1	
7.5	4.7	2.9	2.6	8.9	2.1	4.3	11.3	e		6.3
7.4	5.9	6.0	14.9	6.8	23.4[g]	11.4	12.7	25.6 ⎭	8.8

[a] 1966.
[b] Total of 18 countries listed.
[c] Includes petroleum refining and manufacture of coke.
[d] Estimate.
[e] Included in "Other services."
[f] Includes government services.
[g] Includes earnings of Panamanians working in the Canal Zone.

Source: U.S. Department of State (1970aa).

TABLE A.39

Population Density

	DENSITY OF POPULATION	
	National, per square kilometer, 1969	*Rural, per 1000 hectares, 1965*
Argentina	9	46
Bolivia	4	–
Brazil	11	335
Colombia	19	443
Costa Rica	34	632
Chile	13	216
Ecuador	21	620
El Salvador	155	1,673
Guatemala	46	1,442
Haiti	184	–
Honduras	22	410
Mexico	25	185
Nicaragua	15	558
Panama	18	489
Paraguay	6	118
Peru	10	314
Dominican Republic	87	1,480
Uruguay	16	47
Venezuela	11	153
Barbados	621	–
Guyana	3	–
Jamaica	166	–
Trinidad and Tobago	214	–

Source: CEPAL (1969e).

TABLE A.40

Total Gross National Product in 1967 Prices (In Millions of U.S. Dollars)[a]

	1950	1955	1960	1961	1962	1963	1964	1965	1966	1967	1968[b]	Current growth rate (in percent)	Exchange rate[a] per U.S. dollar
18 republics[d]	45,456	58,448	74,637	78,654	81,700	83,968	89,361	93,758	97,887	102,299	108,116	5.1	
CAEC[c]	1,858	2,321	2,900	2,997	3,185	3,390	3,576	3,822	4,009	4,187	4,402	4.8	
Argentina	9,200	10,625	12,420	13,225	13,030	12,575	13,570	14,835	14,685	14,945	15,650	3.3	350 pesos
Bolivia	n.a.	n.a.	510	521	550	584	610	644	690	712	760	5.0	12 pesos
Brazil	12,560	16,550	22,012	23,675	24,823	25,321	26,110	26,973	28,194	29,743	31,650	6.0	2.0 new cruzeiros
Chile	2,787	3,233	3,970	4,216	4,414	4,631	4,816	5,038	5,343	5,426	5,600	2.4	5.79 escudos
Colombia	2,609	3,403	4,125	4,321	4,535	4,663	4,958	5,113	5,379	5,534	5,872	4.5	14.06 pesos
Costa Rica[e]	258	373	468	482	506	538	539	594	635	671	720	6.5	6.65 colones
Dominican Republic	490	678	885	836	952	1,001	1,071	927	1,033	1,068	1,111	3.7	1 peso
Ecuador	615	797	996	1,009	1,058	1,108	1,188	1,224	1,283	1,350	1,420	5.2	18 sucres
El Salvador[e]	392	489	594	607	669	697	763	803	837	882	912	4.4	2.5 colones
Guatemala[e]	700	783	1,013	1,056	1,094	1,197	1,215	1,306	1,367	1,416	1,487	4.3	1 quetzal
Honduras[e]	265	333	431	433	453	462	487	520	555	577	606	4.5	2 lempiras
Mexico	8,705	11,750	15,734	16,347	17,058	18,144	19,989	21,091	22,639	24,112	225,820	6.8	12.5 pesos
Nicaragua[e]	237	343	394	419	463	496	536	599	615	641	677	4.9	7 cordobas
Panama	271	325	446	493	537	581	611	664	729	773	815	5.7	1 balboa
Paraguay	274	318	358	377	398	407	417	444	456	477	498	4.5	126 guaranies
Peru	1,588	2,123	2,616	2,830	3,092	3,209	3,429	3,594	3,799	3,974	4,055	3.3	38.7 soles
Uruguay	n.a.	1,476	1,473	1,518	1,484	1,470	1,508	1,518	1,555	1,483	1,483	-2.3	118 pesos
Venezuela	2,811	4,334	6,192	6,259	6,584	6,884	7,508	7,871	8,093	8,515	8,980	5.4	4.5 bolivars

[a]Data converted from national currency into dollars using exchange rates shown.
[b]Preliminary figures.
[c]Arithmetic average of percent change for 1968 over 1967 and 1967 over 1966.
[d]The 18 republics listed; excludes Haiti, for which trend data are not available.
[e]Central American Economic Community countries (CAEC).
N.B. GNP data are unadjusted for inequalities in purchasing power among countries.

Source: U.S., Department of State (1970aa).

TABLE A.41

Per Capita Gross National Product in 1967 Prices (in U.S. Dollars)[a]

	1950	1955	1960	1961	1962	1963	1964	1965	1966	1967	1968[b]	Current growth rate (in percent)[c]
18 republics[d]	310	347	384	393	396	396	409	417	423	429	441	2.1
CAEC[e]	231	248	264	265	272	280	286	296	301	305	311	1.6
Argentina	539	562	596	625	605	575	611	658	641	643	663	0.3
Bolivia	n.a.	275	138	138	142	148	151	156	163	164	171	2.4
Brazil	242	275	316	330	336	332	333	334	339	347	359	2.9
Chile	459	471	510	529	541	555	565	579	602	599	607	0.4
Colombia	230	258	268	272	277	276	284	284	289	288	296	1.2
Costa Rica[e]	300	363	373	371	377	387	375	399	412	421	439	3.2
Dominican Republic	230	267	292	266	293	298	309	258	278	278	280	0.4
Ecuador	190	212	229	224	227	230	239	238	241	245	249	1.6
El Salvador[e]	211	229	242	240	256	259	274	279	282	287	288	1.0
Guatemala[e]	250	237	259	261	262	277	280	284	289	291	297	1.4
Honduras[e]	183	200	222	216	219	216	220	228	235	236	239	0.8
Mexico	331	385	436	439	443	455	485	494	513	528	546	3.2
Nicaragua	224	280	279	288	309	322	337	365	363	367	375	1.6
Panama	341	354	420	451	475	498	507	533	566	582	594	2.4
Paraguay	196	203	204	209	215	213	212	219	218	221	223	1.2
Peru	187	242	261	274	291	293	304	308	316	321	317	0.2
Uruguay	n.a.	625	580	589	568	555	562	559	566	533	526	-3.6
Venezuela	567	712	843	822	836	845	891	902	596	911	927	1.7

[a] See Table A.40 for exchange rates used.
[b] Preliminary.
[c] Arithmetic average of percent change for 1968 over 1967 and 1967 over 1966.
[d] The 18 republics listed: excludes Haiti, for which trend data are not available.
[e] Central American Economic Community countries (CAEC).
N.B. GNP data are unadjusted for inequalities in purchasing power among countries.

Source: U.S. Department of State (1970aa).

TABLE A.42

Projections of Supply and Demand in Agriculture to 1980

	Projection for 1980
Total population	365 million
Additional population 1965–80	120 million
Income elasticity of demand for food products	
For low income groups	0.6
For higher income groups	0.33
Time required for low income half of population to reach food consumption levels of higher income groups (assuming past increases in 1965 of income, consumption, and distribution patterns)	100 years
Annual increase of per capita income to double per capita food consumption of low income group	6%
Average annual increase of per capita income for rest of population	1.5%
Average annual per capita growth rates in income	2.5%
Average annual per capita growth rate in demand for agricultural products	1.6%
Annual rate of population growth	2.9%
Increase in aggregate demand for agricultural products by 1980	4.6%
Cumulative annual rise in intraregional exports	10%
Annual growth rate of total exports	3.9%
Annual rate of increase of exports to countries outside Latin America	2.5%
Annual rate of decrease of imports from countries outside Latin America	3.3%
Annual rate at which agricultural production must expand	4.3%
Annual increase of rural population	1.5%
Annual average rise in per capita agricultural income (assuming constant relative prices)	2.8%
Average annual rise in per capita income for higher income group	0.8%
Annual rate of absorption of natural population in agriculture	2%
Average annual rise in productivity per worker	2.4%
Average annual rise in productivity per worker (rate of migration to towns remaining constant)	2.8%
Production increase from extending crop area	66%
Production increase from improving yields	33%
Extension needed for seeded area to attain 1980 goals	50%
Investment needed 1965–80 for extension of seeded area	$25,000 million
Average annual rate of increase in unit yields	2.8%
Increase in fertilizers required	5.5 million tons
Additional agronomists needed, 1965–80	40,000
Anticipated increase over 1960 in value nonfood manufacturers	30% to 40%
Average regional product-capital coefficient in agriculture	0.33
Average annual gross investment in agriculture	$3,600 million
Additional average annual investment required	$800 million
Additional resources required annually for land reform programs	$1,300 million
Additional capital needed 1965–80 for fertilizers	$1,500 to $2,000 million
Additional annual working capital requirements	$2,500 million
Agricultural import component as percentage of gross value of agricultural investment	15
Average annual value of imports of capital goods and imports required	$750 million
Annual external financing required	$700 to $800 million

Source: UNECLA (1964, pp. 357–396).

TABLE A.43

Agricultural Population and Population Economically Active in Agriculture (1965 Estimates)

	Agricultural population (in thousands)	ECONOMICALLY ACTIVE POPULATION			
		Total (in thousands)	In agriculture (in thousands)	Percent in agriculture	Percent in manufacturing industry
Costa Rica	720	425	205	48	11.3 (1963)
Dominican Republic	2,145	1,070	605	57	–
El Salvador	1,670	945	555	59	19.6 (1966)[a]
Guatemala	2,842	1,485	955	64	13.9 (1964)[b]
Haiti	3,728	2,630	2,070	79	2.7 (1960)
Honduras	1,405	645	420	65	–
Mexico	22,200	13,340	6,970	52	21.9 (1967)[c]
Nicaragua	960	510	300	59	12 (1965)
Panama	540	415	180	43	12 (1964)[a]
Argentina	4,470	8,350	505	18	34.3 (1966)
Bolivia	2,592	1,360	885	65	3.6 (1966)[d]
Brazil	40,726	26,175	12,565	48	13 (1966)
Chile	2,399	2,655	690	26	24.2 (1966)
Colombia	7,546	5,715	2,455	43	–
Ecuador	2,963	1,585	825	52	13.4 (1965)
Paraguay	1,018	680	345	51	–
Peru	5,825	3,470	1,635	47	13.2 (1965)
Uruguay	470	1,045	180	17	27.8 (1965)[a]
Venezuela	2,562	2,780	815	29	21.1

[a] Includes construction.
[b] Secondary sector.
[c] Includes mining, manufacturing, electricity, construction.
[d] Includes mining.

Source: UNFAO (1966). Statistics for the percent in manufacturing industry: Inter-American Development Bank (1967).

TABLE A.44

Indexes of Total Agricultural Production 1957–59=100

	Total production								Per capita production							
	1961	1963	1964	1965	1966	1967	1968	1969ᵃ	1961	1963	1964	1965	1966	1967	1968	1969ᵃ
Total 19 republics	111	119	117	131	127	133	133	136	102	103	98	107	101	103	100	99
CAECᵇ	120	136	143	144	145	155	152	152	109	116	118	115	112	116	110	107
Argentina	102	116	114	104	111	119	111	118	96	106	103	92	97	102	94	98
Bolivia	107	111	111	111	113	109	113	113	100	99	97	95	94	89	90	88
Brazil	114	119	109	141	126	135	135	140	104	103	91	115	100	104	101	101
Chile	102	108	111	112	113	115	119	112	95	96	97	95	94	94	96	88
Colombia	106	113	112	118	118	124	128	130	96	97	93	95	92	93	93	92
Costa Ricaᵇ	119	119	110	116	133	142	148	153	106	99	88	90	99	103	104	104
Dominican Republic	106	106	105	95	99	103	97	110	95	89	85	75	75	76	69	76
Ecuador	122	123	127	134	139	150	141	147	111	105	105	107	107	112	102	102
El Salvadorᵇ	123	138	142	124	129	142	132	146	112	118	118	99	100	106	96	102
Guatemalaᵇ	118	142	143	162	147	160	158	157	107	120	117	129	114	120	115	111
Haiti	110	91	90	91	85	85	80	83	103	81	79	78	71	69	63	64
Hondurasᵇ	112	117	128	137	139	143	145	135	102	100	106	109	107	107	104	94
Mexico	111	124	133	145	145	146	152	148	100	105	109	114	111	108	108	102
Nicaraguaᵇ	123	158	197	182	190	190	184	169	113	136	165	147	149	145	136	121
Panama	103	107	118	133	133	142	147	154	94	92	98	107	104	107	107	109
Paraguay	106	114	112	115	112	123	118	125	98	100	95	95	95	95	88	91
Peru	124	122	130	127	127	123	117	118	114	106	109	103	100	94	87	85
Uruguay	110	115	124	120	110	97	111	108	105	107	114	109	99	86	97	93
Venezuela	110	134	139	147	153	162	173	178	99	112	113	115	116	118	122	121
Other Latin American countries																
Guyana	124	114	117	130	124	123	126	133	114	99	99	107	100	95	94	97
Jamaica	108	115	119	125	125	115	108	104	103	106	107	109	106	96	88	84
Trinidad and Tobago	111	107	105	111	104	105	117	121	101	91	87	90	82	82	90	91

ᵃ Preliminary figures.
ᵇ Central American Economic Community countries.

Source: U.S. Department of State (1970aa).

Economic Growth and Market Groups

		POPULATION DISTRIBUTION[a]					
	1962	*1965*		*1975*			
				4 percent growth[b]		*6 percent growth*[b]	
Market group	*In millions*	*In millions*	*In percent*	*In millions*	*In percent*	*In millions*	*In percent*
Rural peer	90	93	36	88	27	80	24
Urban peer	60	70	28	82	25	67	20
Largely outside the market economy	150	163	64	170	52	147	44
Rural middle income	10	17	7	43	13	52	16
Urban middle income	50	63	25	97	29	108	32
Well-to-do	8	10	4	20	6	23	7
In the market economy	68	90	36	160	48	183	56
Total	218	253	100	330	100	330	100

[a] Population totals based on U.S. median estimates; urban-rural breakdowns assume a continuing trend of urbanization similar to previous years. Economic class estimates are based on first-hand observations and scattered demographic data for the area.

[b] Gross rates of economic growth. Assuming an annual population increase of 3 percent, the lower economic rate would mean a 1 percent increase in per capita income; the higher economic growth rate a 3 percent increase in per capita income. Higher rates of per capita income compounded annually are projected as having a twofold effect: (1) a greater shift of population from rural to urban areas, and (2) a higher proportion of middle income—both urban and rural—and of the well-to-do.

Source: Kriesberg (1968).

TABLE A.46

Central America: Indicators of Land Distribution

Size of holdings	Year	Percentage total farm holdings	Percentage total cultivated area
Costa Rica	1963		
4.89 hectares and less		36.0	1.9
1,001 hectares and over		0.4	25.7
El Salvador	1961		
Less than 3 hectares		78.3	11.6
Over 100 hectares		0.9	47.7
Guatemala	1964		
Less than 3,50 hectares		74.9	11.7
894.40 hectares and over		0.1	26.0
Honduras	1966		
Less than 3.50 hectares		47.2	5.5
700 hectares and over		0.1	19.7
Nicaragua	1963		
Less than 3.50 hectares		35.4	1.5
700 hectares and over		0.6	30.5
Panama	1961		
Less than 5 hectares		45.8	5.3
500 hectares and over		0.2	20.5

Source: Pan American Union (1968b).

TABLE A.47

Estimates Trained Personnel Needed in Agriculture, 1967

	Number of students pursuing agriculture in higher education institutions	Agricultural students as percent of university students	Agricultural students: adequacy in relation to need	Government policies	EXTENSION AGENTS		Projection of needs	Extent to which goals achieved
					Number	Quality		
Argentina	5,400	3	only 118 graduates 1962–67; 3,500 agricultural engineers in Argentina; 50 percent in productive work in agriculture; 15,000 to 20,000 professionals needed	reorganizing national university to produce efficient specialists; Land Grant College being set up	450	200 agricultural engineers or veterinary doctors	1,600 agents needed (1 for every 300 farms); would take 40 years	
Bolivia (1967)	406	3.6	inadequate	none	71	half university graduates with degrees; some 4 years university training (no degree); rest, paid appointees (no training)	needs recognized, but no allocated funds or priority projects	No money because of budget limitations for action
Brazil (1965)	4,935	2.7	total of 10,000 to 11,000 needed 1967–72	rush training at 4 rural universities and in secondary schools, special workshops, and short courses and graduate level instruction	1,350	20 percent not college graduates; rest have little extended training	5,000 needed by 1970	50 percent met by 1970

Country								
Chile	868 (1964)	0.1	no projections of need; 152 university graduates in agriculture in 1964	sweeping reforms in educational structure being planned				
Colombia	2,865 (1963)	8.8	adequate in number; deficient in competence	encouraging training abroad	2,500	of 1,177 in 1965, 241 were professionals	output of 200 a year needed	10 years required to produce 200 a year; only 3 people trained in Colombia (used elsewhere)
Costa Rica	131 (1965)	2.27	inadequate	active training encouragement	63	weak in methodology	20 more agents needed	to be met in 4 years
Dominican Republic	66 studying abroad		inadequate	encouraging training abroad	51	quality low; no graduates or extension experience	100 agents needed	will not have 100 agents in next few years
Ecuador	100 grads (1966)		830 needed in 10 years	pushing university and other training	341	training poor; best graduates leave country	374 more needed by 1973	needs met only if budgetary problems solved
Guatemala	186 (1966); 6 grads (1966)	less than 5 percent	inadequate	government cannot pay graduates; private sector not employing them	30	hope to have graduate degrees by 1973	110 by 1971	uncertain; no funds for salaries; foreign help changing picture
Honduras	no agriculture college—51 abroad	2.1	inadequate	none	47	satisfactory	need to double number by 1972	needs can be filled by internal and external training over next 5 years
Mexico	2,765 (1966)		1963-5373 graduated; number inadequate; 4 times as many needed by 1980	great encouragement of training and facilities	304	graduates; but scantily qualified for extension work	plan for total number of 800 now	not likely to be achieved in near future

TABLE A.47

Estimates Trained Personnel Needed in Agriculture, 1967 (Continued)

	Number of students pursuing agriculture in higher education institutions	Agricultural students as percent of university students	Agricultural students: adequacy in relation to need	Government policies	EXTENSION AGENTS		Projection of needs	Extent to which goals achieved
					Number	Quality		
Nicaragua	100 (at home) 50 (abroad)	2.7	55 needed each year for next 10 years	no new policies to encourage agricultural studies	45	10 with equivalent of B.S. degree–rapid turnover	program had 50 percent of personnel needed	no plans to extend program determinable
Panama	143 (1966)	2.1	inadequate	aggressively encouraging	200	of these 50 graduates; 40 secondary vocational; majority well trained	15 more needed (1967–76) with degrees; 30 secondary vocational	80 percent met by by 1976
Paraguay	300	3.2	less than 200 professionals; inadequate	no definite policy				
Peru	1,529 (1966)	2.6	inadequate		1,601	4,500 needed	4,500 needed	can possibly be met in 10 years; high turnover; poor pay
El Salvador	130 (1966)	3.25	inadequate	careful attention	80			
Uruguay	1,250	3.7 (1963)	inadequate		50	inadequate quality–salaries low, etc.	260 needed by 1974	fair chance of success

Source: U.S. House (1967).

TABLE A.48

Miscellaneous Indicators of the Status of Agriculture, 1966

	Dollar value of food imports (in millions of U.S. dollars)	Percent of food imports to total consumption	Percent of national budget devoted to agricultural development
Argentina[a]	66.5	2.0	2.16
Bolivia[a]	17.5	12.9	9.1
Brazil	183[a]	–	5
Chile	133.4		13.0[b]
Colombia	25[a]	6.0[a]	12.0
Costa Rica	14[a]	–	17.0
Dominican Republic	120.0[a]	–	7.0[b]
Ecuador	130	5	7.1
Guatemala[a]	12.968	–	10.0
Honduras	8.785[c]	4.5[c]	6.0
Mexico	209[d]		11.9[b]
Nicaragua	13.4[a]	5.0[e]	4.0
Panama	21.649[a]	4.2[a]	3.3
Paraguay		8.2	1.8[a]
Peru	110.547[c]		6.19
El Salvador	29.2[a]	32.0[a]	3.6 (current expenditures)[b]
			16.6 (capital expenditures)[b]
Uruguay	64.6[f]		3[a]
Venezuela[a]	174.533	24.0	11.3

[a] Data from 1965.
[b] Data from 1967.
[c] Data from 1964.
[d] Projected 1970.
[e] Data from 1962.
[f] Data from 1963.

Source: U.S. House (1967).

TABLE A.49

Composition of Imports as a Percent of Total

Categories of imports	1948–49	1959
Consumer goods	22.0	20.3
Nondurables	15.1	13.8
Durables	6.9	6.5
Fuels	7.4	10.2
Raw materials and intermediate products	30.1	34.4
Metallic	6.8	7.6
Nonmetallic	23.3	26.8
Capital goods	38.7	32.5
Building materials	6.8	4.2
Machinery and equipment for agriculture	3.4	2.5
Machinery and equipment for industry	19.7	17.0
Machinery and equipment for transport	8.8	8.8
Other	1.8	2.6
Total	100.0	100.0

Source: UNECLA (1963d, vol. 2).

APPENDIX B

DEVELOPMENT REPORTS

*PARTIAL TEXT OF THE AMERICAN CHIEFS OF STATE
MEETING, APRIL 12-14, 1967*[1]

Chapter 2: Multinational Action for Infrastructure Projects

The economic integration of Latin America demands a vigorous and sustained effort to complete and modernize the physical infrastructure of the region. It is necessary to build a land transport network and improve all types of transport systems to facilitate the movement of persons and goods throughout the hemisphere; to establish an adequate and efficient telecommunications system and interconnected power systems; and jointly to develop international watersheds, frontier regions and economic areas that include the territory of two or more countries. In Latin America there are in existence projects in all these fields, at different stages of preparation or implementation, but in many cases the completion of prior studies, financial resources, or merely the coordination of efforts and the decision to bring them to fruition are lacking.

The Presidents of the member states of the OAS agree to engage in determined action to undertake or accelerate the construction of the infrastructure required for the development and integration of Latin America and to make better use thereof. In so doing, it is essential that the groups of interested countries or multinational institutions determine criteria for assigning priorities, in view of the amount of human and material resources needed for the task.

As one basis for the criteria, which will be determined with precision upon consideration of the specific cases submitted for study, they stress the fundamental need to give preferential attention to those projects that benefit the countries of the region that are at a relatively lower level of economic development.

Priority should also be given to the mobilization of financial and technical resources for the preparation and implementation of infrastructure projects that will facilitate the participation of landlocked countries in regional and international trade.

In consequence, they adopt the following decisions for immediate implementation:

1. *To complete the studies and conclude the agreements necessary to accelerate the construction of an inter-American telecommunications network.*
2. *To expedite the agreements necessary to complete the Pan American Highway, to accelerate the construction of the Bolivarian Highway (Carretera Marginal de la Selva) and its junction with the Trans-Chaco Highway and to support the studies and agreements designed to bring into being the new highway*

[1] Pan American Union (1967g).

361

systems that will join groups of countries of continental and insular Latin America, as well as the basic works required to develop water and airborne transport of a multinational nature and the corresponding systems of operation. As a complement to these agreements, negotiations should be restrictions on international traffic and of promoting technical and administrative cooperation among land, water, and air transport enterprises and the establishment of multinational transport services.

3. To sponsor studies for preparing joint projects in connection with watersheds, such as the studies commenced on the development of the River Plate basin and that relating to the Gulf of Fonseca.

4. To allocate sufficient resources to the Preinvestment Fund for Latin American Integration of the IDB for conducting studies that will make it possible to identify and prepare multinational projects in all fields that may be of importance in promoting regional integration. In order that the aforesaid Fund may carry out an effective promotion effort, it is necessary that an adequate part of the resources allocated may be used without reimbursement, or with reimbursement conditioned on the execution of the corresponding projects.

5. To mobilize, within and outside the hemisphere, resources in addition to those that will continue to be placed at the disposal of the countries to support national economic development programs, such resources to be devoted especially to the implementation of multinational infrastructure projects that can represent important advances in the Latin American economic integration process. In this regard, the IDB should have additional resources in order to participate actively in the attainment of this objective.

Brazil: Principal Regional Development Institutions and Classification of Their Major Activities

| | AGENCY AND REGION | | | | | |
Major activity	DNCCS N and NE	CVSF E and NE	SUDENE E and NE	SPVEA N	SPVFS S and CW	CODESUL S
Development planning			X	X		
Natural resources surveys and improvement	X	X	X	X	X	X
Land	X	X		X		
Water	X	X				
Forestry	X	X		X		
Transportation	X	X	X	X	X	X
Road	X	X		X		
Air	X					
River navigation		X				
Electric energy		X	X		X	
Power production		X				
Rural electrification		X				
Agricultural development	X		X	X		X
Colonization				X		
Extension and experimentation				X		
Irrigation	X	X				
Industrial promotion			X	X		
Education		X	X			
Health	X	X		X	X	
Waterworks and sanitation	X	X	X			

N: North; NE: Northeast; E: East; S: South; CW: Central West

DNCCS: National Drought Control Department. Authorized 3 percent of federal tax revenues, subject to matching contributions by the states of the Drought Polygon.

CVSF: San Francisco River Valley Commission. Authorized 1 percent of federal tax revenues plus special appropriations by Federal Ministries (usually Agriculture). Embraces five states which participate only as "observers" in policy-making.

SUDENE: Northeast Development Authority. Authorized 6 percent of federal tax revenues, plus a wide range of funds from states, Federal Ministries, autonomous entities in the region. Has the authority to grant sizeable (60 to 100 percent) tax exemptions investing in its jurisdiction. Ten of the 20 members of its council are appointed by the state governors, six represent the federal ministries, three represent the San Francisco Hydro-electric Company (CHESF), with one representative of the Chief of Staff of the Armed Forces.

SPVEA: Amazon Economic Development Authority. Receives 3 percent each of federal, state and municipal revenues in its jurisdiction. 15 members—nine represent the three member states, which cover more than one-half of Brazil.

SPVF: Southwest Frontier Economic Development Authority. Includes four states, and its authority derives from the principal Federal ministries. (No data on finances.)

CODESUL: Council for the Development of the Extreme South. No specific operational data.

Source: Inter-American Development Bank (1965a).

BIBLIOGRAPHY

Ackley, Gardner (1966) *Macroeconomic Theory*. New York: Macmillan.

Adams, Mildred, ed. (1963) *Latin America: Evolution or Explosion?* New York: Dodd, Mead.

Adams, Richard N., et al. (1960) *Social Change in Latin America Today*. New York: Random House (Vintage Books).

Adelman, Irma (1967) *Theories of Economic Growth and Development*. Stanford, Calif.: Stanford University Press.

Adelman, Irma, and Cynthia Taft Morris (1968) "An Econometric Model of Socio-Economic and Political Change in Underdeveloped Countries," *American Economic Review*, vol. 58 (December 1968), pp. 1184–1218.

Adelman, Irma, and Erik Thorbecke, eds. (1966) *The Theory and Design of Economic Development*. Baltimore: John Hopkins Press.

Aleman, Roberto, et al. (1967) *Economic Development Issues: Latin America* (Prepared for the Committee for Economic Development). New York: Praeger.

Alexander, Robert J. (1962) *Labor Relations in Argentina, Brazil and Chile*. New York: McGraw-Hill.

Alexander, Robert J. (1964) *The Venezuelan Democratic Revolution*. New Brunswick, N.J.: Rutgers University Press.

Alexander, Robert J. (1968) "The Import-Substitution Strategy of Economic Development." New Brunswick, N.J.: Rutgers University Press. Reprinted from *Journal of Economic Issues*, vol. 1, no. 4 (December 1967).

Anderson, Charles W. (1967) *Politics and Economic Change in Latin America*. Princeton, N.J.: Van Nostrand Reinhold.

Anderson, Robert William (1965) *Party Politics in Puerto Rico*. Stanford, Calif.: Stanford University Press.

Bach, George Leland (1966) *Economics, An Introduction to Analysis and Policy*. Englewood Cliffs, N.J.: Prentice-Hall.

Baer, Werner (1965) *Industrialization and Economic Development in Brazil*. Homewood, Ill.: Irwin.

Baerwald, Friederich (1969) *History and Structure of Economic Development*. Scranton, Pa.: International Textbook.

Bailey, Helen Miller, and Abraham B. Nasatir (1960) *Latin America: The Development of Its Civilization*. Englewood Cliffs, N.J.: Prentice-Hall.

Baldwin, Robert E. (1966) *Economic Development and Growth*. New York: Wiley.

Balogh, Thomas (1965) "Land Tenure, Education and Development in Latin America," in Lyons (1965), pp. 67–72.

Banco Central de Venezuela (1968) *Síntesis de la economía venezolana 1961–1967*.

Banco Central de Venezuela (1969) *Revista del banco central de Venezuela*, no. 29 (January–June 1969), pp. 287–292.

Banco Central de Venezuela (1970) *Informe económico correspondiente al año 1969*.

Banco de Guatemala (n.d.) *Investing in Latin America*.

Banco de Mexico (1968) *Annual Report, 1967*.

Banco do Nordeste do Brasil S/A (1968) Departamento de Estudios Economicos do Nordeste, *Abacaxi No Nordeste: Tendencias da producão e do mercado*.

Banco do Nordeste do Brasil S/A, 1967–1969, Departamento de Estudios Economicos do Nordeste, Consumo de productos industrias do nordesta (series): *Resumo do pesquisas em quinze cidades* (1967), *Cidade de Teresina* (1968), *Cidade de Natal* (1968), *Cidade de Joã o Pessoa* (1968), *Cidade de San Luis* (1968) and *Cidade de Caruarú* (1969).

Bank of the Republic (Colombia) (n.d.) *Guia para el inversionista.*

Baranson, Jack (1968) "Integrated Automobiles for Latin America?" *Finance and Development Quarterly,* no. 4, 1968, pp. 25–29.

Barraclough, Solon L. (1970) "Agricultural Policy and Land Reform," in "Key Problems of Economic Policy in Latin America," supplement to *Journal of Political Economy*, vol. 78, no. 4 (July/August 1970), pp. 906–947.

Beckerman, W., and R. Bacon (1966) "International Comparison of Income Levels: A Suggested New Measure," *The Economic Journal*, vol. 76, whole no. 303 (September 1966), pp. 519–536.

Belassa, Bela (1964) *Trade Prospects for Developing Countries.* Homewood, Ill.: Irwin.

Belassa, Bela (1970) "Industrial Development in an Open Economy: The Case of Norway," *Finance and Development*, vol. 7, no. 1 (March 1970), pp. 28–33.

Bell, John Fred (1967) *A History of Economic Thought*, 2d ed. New York: Ronald Press.

Bell, P. W., and M. P. Todaro (1969) *Economic Theory*. New York: Oxford University Press.

Benham, F., and H. A. Holley (1960) *A Short Introduction to the Economy of Latin America*. New York: Oxford University Press.

Benton, William (1961) *The Voice of Latin America*. New York: Harper & Row.

Berstein, Marvin D., ed. (1966) *Foreign Investment in Latin America*. New York: Knopf.

Beyer, Glenn, H., ed. (1967) *The Urban Explosion in Latin America*. Ithaca, N.Y.: Cornell University Press.

Bhatt, V. V. (1965) "Some Notes on Balanced and Unbalanced Growth," *The Economic Journal*, vol. 75, whole no. 297 (March 1965), pp. 88–97.

Blanshard, Paul (1947) *Democracy and Empire in the Caribbean*. New York: Macmillan.

Blasier, Cole, ed. (1968) *Constructive Change in Latin America*. Pittsburgh: University of Pittsburgh Press.

Blaug, M., ed. (1968) *Economics of Education*. Baltimore: Penguin.

Blitz, Randolph C. (1965) "The Role of High-Level Manpower in the Economic Development of Chile," in Harbison (1965), pp. 73–107.

Bloom, Gordon F., and Herbert R. Northrup (1965) *Economics of Labor Relations*, 5th ed., Homewood, Ill.: Irwin.

Boorstein, Edward (1968) *The Economic Transformation of Cuba*. New York: Monthly Review Press.

Boskey, Shirley (1959) *Problems and Practices of Development Banks*. Baltimore: John Hopkins Press.

Boulding, Kenneth E. (1970) *Economics as a Science*. New York: McGraw-Hill.

Brandenburg, Frank (1962) "A Contribution to the Theory of Entrepreneurship and Economic Development: The Case of Mexico," *Inter-American Economic Affairs*, vol. 16, no. 3 (Winter 1962), pp. 9–11.

Brandenburg, Frank (1964) *The Development of Latin American Enterprise*. Planning Pamphlet No. 121, Washington, D.C.: National Planning Association.

Brazilian Government Trade Bureau (1968) "Free-Trade Boom Enlivens Manaus, 'Jungle Capital'," *Brazilian Bulletin*, vol. 26, whole no. 494 (July 1968).

Brazilian Government Trade Bureau (1968a) *Brazilian Bulletin*, vol. 26, whole no. 493 (June 1968).

Brazilian Government Trade Bureau (1970) "Brasilia Marks Tenth Anniversary," *Brazilian Bulletin*, vol. 25, whole no. 515 (April 1970).

Brenner, Y. S. (1966) *Theories of Economic Development and Growth*. New York: Praeger.

British Guiana (Guyana) Development Program (1966–1972) (n.d.) Georgetown, Guyana: The Government Printery.

Brown, Robert L. (1966) *Transportation and the Economic Integration of South America*. Washington, D.C.: The Brookings Institution.

Browne, Malcolm W. (1968) "Uruguayan Emigration Rises Fourfold in Growing Inflation," *New York Times* (May 4, 1968), p. 20.

Bruchey, Stuart (1965) *The Roots of American Economic Growth, 1607–1861*. New York: Harper & Row.

Bruton, Henry J. (1965) *Principles of Development Economics*. Englewood Cliffs, N.J.: Prentice-Hall.

Burnett, Ben G., and Kenneth F. Johnson (1968) *Political Forces in Latin America: Dimensions of the Quest for Stability*. Belmont, Calif.: Wadsworth.

Cale, Edward G. (1969) *Latin American Free Trade Association: Progress, Problems and Prospects*, Office of External Research, U. S. Department of State, May, 1969. Washington, D.C.: Government Printing Office.

Cameron, Rondo (1967) "Economic Development: Some Lessons of History for Developing Nations," *American Economic Review*, vol. 62, no. 2 (May 1967), pp. 312–324.

Cárdenas, Jose C. (1968) "Latin American Experience in the Multinational Investment Field," in Inter-American Development Bank (1968), pp. 311–381.

Carranza, Roque (1967) "Development and Stabilization Policies in Latin America: Some Problems," in UN, Committee for Development Planning (1967), pp. 112–155.

Castro, Fidel (1968) "Speech of Fidel," Havana, January 14, 1968; reproduced in *Granma*, year 3, no. 2.

Center for Inter-American Relations (1969) *Brazil 1969*.

Central American Bank for Economic Integration (1967) *Investment Opportunities in the Central American Common Market*.

Centro Interamericano de Administradores Tributarios, *Informative Newsletter*, vol. 2, no. 11 (July 1970), p. 11.

CEPAL (1968a) *Notas sobre la economía y el desarrollo de America Latina*, no. 4 (October 15, 1968).

CEPAL (1968b) "El problema del subempleo," *Notas sobre la economía y el desarrollo de America Latina*, no. 7 (November 30, 1968).

CEPAL (1969a) *Notas sobre la economía y el desarrollo de America Latina*, no. 10 (January 16, 1969).

CEPAL (1969b) *Notas sobre la economía y el desarrollo de America Latina*, no. 12 (February 16, 1969).

CEPAL (1969c) *Notas sobre la economía y el desarrollo de America Latina*, no. 13 (March 1, 1969).

CEPAL (1969d) *Notas sobre la economía y el desarrollo de America Latina*, no. 16 (April 16, 1969).

CEPAL (1969e) *Notas sobre la economía y el desarrollo de America Latina*, no. 20 (June 16, 1969).

CEPAL (1969f) *Notas sobre la economía y el desarrollo de America Latina*, no. 22 (July 1969).

CEPAL (1969g) *Notas sobre la economía y el desarrollo de America Latina*, no. 23 (August 1, 1969).

CEPAL (1969h) *Notas sobre la economía y el desarrollo de America Latina*, no. 26 (September 16, 1969).

CEPAL (1969i) *Notas sobre la economía y el desarrollo de America Latina*, no. 27 (October 1, 1969).

CEPAL (1969j) "Regionalización de las politicas de desarrollo en America Latina," *Notas sobre la economía y el desarrollo de America Latina*, no. 27 (October 1, 1969).

CEPAL (1970a) *Notas sobre la economía y el desarrollo de America Latina*, no. 35 (February 1, 1970).

CEPAL (1970aa) *Notas sobre la economía y el desarrollo de America Latina*, no. 37 (March 1, 1970).

CEPAL (1970aaa) *Notas sobre la economía y el desarrollo de America Latina*, no. 34 (January 16, 1970).

CEPAL (1970b) *Notas sobre la economía y el desarrollo de America Latina*, no. 39 (April 1, 1970).

CEPAL (1970bb) *Notas sobre la economía y el desarrollo de America Latina*, no. 38 (March 16, 1970).

CEPAL (1970c) *Notas sobre la economía y el desarrollo de America Latina*, no. 41 (April 1970).

CEPAL (1970d) "Planificación de recursos humanos," *Notas sobre la economía y el desarrollo de America Latina*, no. 54 (September 16, 1970).

Chamberlain, Neil W. (1965) *Private and Public Planning*. New York: McGraw-Hill.

Chase Manhattan Bank (1962) "The Central American Common Market," *Latin American Business Highlights*, vol. 12, no. 3, pp. 1–9.

Chase Manhattan Bank (1967a) "Urbanization in Latin America," *World Business*, vol. 5 (March 1967), pp. 5–8.

Chase Manhattan Bank (1967b) "Latin American Integration," *World Business*, vol. 6 (May 1967), pp. 10–11.

Chase Manhattan Bank (1967c) "Inflation in Latin America," *World Business*, vol. 7 (July 1967), pp. 6–7.

Chase Manhattan Bank (1967d) "Special Report: Colombia," *World Business*, vol. 9 (November 9, 1967), pp. 3–14.

Chase Manhattan Bank (1968a) "Central American Common Market," *World Business*, vol. 10 (January 1968), pp. 14–16.

Chase Manhattan Bank (1968b) "Mexico," *World Business*, vol. 13 (October 1968), pp. 19–20.

Chase Manhattan Bank (1969a) "Report on Copper," *World Business*, vol. 15 (April 1969), pp. 10–12.

Chase Manhattan Bank (1969b) "The Central American Common Market," *World Business*, vol. 15 (April 1969), pp. 13–14.

Chase Manhattan Bank (1969c) "Report on Coffee International Agreement Extended," *World Business*, vol. 14 (January 1969), pp. 15–16.

Chemical Bank (1970) *International Economic Survey: Puerto Rico* (June 1970).

Chilcote, Ronald H. (1969) "Brazil and Portuguese Africa in Comparative Perspective," University of California Colloquium, January–March 1968, *Latin American Research Review*, vol. 4 (Spring 1969), pp. 125–136.

Cline, Howard F. (1963) *Mexico: Revolution to Evolution, 1940–1960*. New York: Oxford University Press.

Coale, Ansley J. (1964) "Population and Economic Development," in Novak and Lekachman (1964), pp. 125–140.

Coale, Ansley J., and Edgar M. Hoover (1958) *Population Growth and Economic Development in Low-Income Countries. A Case Study of India's Prospects*. Princeton, N.J.: Princeton University Press.

Cohen, Benjamin I. (1968) "The Less-Developed Countries' Exports of Primary Products," *The Economic Journal*, vol. 78, whole no. 310 (June 1968), pp. 334–343.

Cohen, Sanford (1966) *Labor in the United States*. Columbus, Ohio: Charles F. Merrill.

Cole, J. P. (1965) *Latin America: An Economic and Social Geography*. London: Butterworth.

Commission on International Development (1969) *Partners in Development*. New York: Praeger.

Committee for Economic Development (CED) (1967) *Cooperation for Progress in Latin America*. New York.

Committee for Economic Development (CED) (1964) *Economic Development of Central America*.

Corporacion Venezolana de Guayana (1963) *Guayana: Cornerstone of the Development of Venezuela*. Corporacion Venezolana de Guayana.

Corporacion Venezolana de Guayana (1968a) *La Agricultura CVG–1968 Informe Anual Separata*.

Corporacion Venezolana de Guayana (1968b) *GURI*.

Corporacion Venezolana de Guayana (1968c) *La Programa Economico CVG–1968 Informe Anual Separata*.

Crow, John W. (1966) "Economic Integration in Central America," *Finance and Development*, vol. 3, no. 1, pp. 58–66.

Cumberland, Charles C. (1968) *Mexico: The Struggle for Modernity*. New York: Oxford University Press.

Currie, Lauchlin (1966) *Accelerating Development: The Necessity and Means*. New York: McGraw-Hill.

Currie, Lauchlin (1967) "Economics and Population," *Population Bulletin*, vol. 23, no. 2 (April 1967), pp. 25–38.

Daland, Robert T. (1967) *Brazilian Planning: Development, Politics and Administration*. Chapel Hill: University of North Carolina Press.

DANE (Departamento Administrativo Nacional de Estadistica) (1967) *Informe Al Congreso Nacional*. Bogota, Colombia: DANE.

Davis, Harold Eugene (1968) "The History of Ideas in Latin America," *Latin American Research Review*, vol. 3 (Fall 1968), pp. 23–44.

Davis, Kingsley (1968) "Demographic Aspects of Economic Development in India," in Falkus (1968), pp. 269–298.

Davis, Stanley M. (1969) "U.S. Versus Latin America: Business and Culture," *Harvard Business Review* (January–February 1969), pp. 88–98.

Denton, Charles F. (1969) *La política del desarrollo en Costa Rica*. San Jose, C.R.: Edition, Novedades de Costa Rica.

DESAL (1967) *Reportaje DESAL* (International Edition, Santiago, Chile), vol. 1 (October 1967).

DESAL (1968) *Reportaje DESAL* (International Edition, Santiago, Chile), vol. 3 (March 1968).

Domar, Evsey D. (1957) *Essays in the Theory of Economic Growth*. New York: Oxford University Press.

Dorselaer, Jacques (1967) "Quelques aspects régionaux du phénomène urbain en Amérique Latine," *Civilisations*, vol. 17, no. 3, pp. 263–279.

Drucker, Peter F. (1962) "Marketing and Economic Development," in Walters, Snider, and Sweet (1962), pp. 783–784.

Ducoff, Louis J. (1960) *Human Resources of Central America, Panama and Mexico 1950–1980 in Relation to Some Aspects of Economic Development*. New York: UNECLA.

Duncan, W. Raymond, and James Nelson Goodsel (1970) *The Quest for Change in Latin America*. New York: Oxford University Press.

Economic Bulletin for Latin America (1967) "The Economic Policy of Colombia 1950–66" (October, 1967), pp. 90–106.

Edelman, Alexander T. (1965) *Latin American Government and Politics*. Homewood, Ill.: The Dorsey Press.

Ellis, Howard S., ed. (1963) *Economic Development for Latin America*. London: Macmillan.

Enke, Stephen (1963) *Economics for Development*. Englewood Cliffs, N.J.: Prentice-Hall.

Enke, Stephen (1966) "The Economic Aspects of Slowing Population Growth," *The Economic Journal*, vol. 76, whole no. 301 (March 1966) pp. 44–56.

Enke, Stephen (1969) "Economists and Development," *Journal of Economic Literature*, vol. 7, no. 4 (December 1969), pp. 1125–1139.

Fabricant, Solomon (1969) *A Primer on Productivity*. New York: Random House.

Falkus, Malcom E. (1968) *Readings in the History of Economic Growth*. New York: Oxford University Press.

Farley, Rawle (1956) "Aspects of the Economic History of British Guiana 1781–1852, a Study of Economic and Social Change on the Southern Caribbean Frontier." Ph.D. thesis, University of London.

Farley, Rawle (1958) "Economic Change on a Caribbean Frontier," *The Caribbean*, vol. 2, no. 9 (April 1958), pp. 194–199.

Farley, Rawle (1962) "Education for a World of Uncertainty," *Extra-Muros*, vol. 1, no. 1 (1962), pp. 49–58.

Farley, Rawle (1967) "Puerto Rico, Development, Urbanization and Integration," in International Institute of Differing Civilizations: *Urban Agglomerations in the Countries of the Third World: Their Political, Economic and Social Role*. Brussels: Editions de L'Institut de Sociologie, Université Libre de Bruxelles, pp. 610–635.

Farley, Rawle (1971) *Planning for Development in Libya: The Exceptional Economy in the Developing World*. New York: Praeger.

Fei, John C. H., and Gustav Ranis (1964) *Development of the Labor Surplus Economy: Theory and Policy*. Homewood, Ill.: Irwin.

Fei, John C. H., and Gustav Ranis (1900) "Agrarianism, Dualism, and Economic Development," in Adelman and Thorbecke (1966), pp. 3–41.

Felix, David (1970) *The Political Economy of Regional Integration in Latin America*. New Brunswick, N.J.: Studies in Comparative International Development, Rutgers University.

Fillol, Tomas Roberto (1961) *Social Factors in Economic Development: The Argentine Case*. Cambridge, Mass.: M.I.T. Press.

First National City Bank (1969) *Argentina: An Economic Study* (February 1969).

Fleisher, Belton M. (1970) *Labor Economics: Theory and Evidence*. Englewood Cliffs, N.J.: Prentice-Hall.

Flores, Edmundo (1967) *On Financing Land Reform: A Mexican Casebook*. St. Louis: Social Science Institute, Washington University.

Friedmann, John (1965) *Venezuela: From Doctrine to Dialogue*. Syracuse, N.Y.: Syracuse University Press.

Fulton, David C. (1968) "The Ex-Desert of Northwest Mexico," *Finance and Development*, vol. 53 (September 1968), pp. 2–9.

Furtado, Celso (1965) *The Economic Growth of Brazil: A Survey from Colonial to Modern Times*. Berkeley: University of California Press.

Furtado, Celso (1967) *Development and Underdevelopment: A Structural View of the Problems of Developed and Underdeveloped Countries*. Berkeley: University of California Press.

Furtado, Celso (1970) *Obstacles to Development in Latin America*. New York: Doubleday.

Gill, Clark C. (1966) *Education and Social Change in Chile*. U.S. Department of Health, Education and Welfare, Office of Education. Washington, D.C.: Government Printing Office.

Gillin, John P. (1960) "Some Signposts for Policy," in Adams et al. (1960), p. 14–62.

Glade, William P., Jr. (1969) *The Latin American Economies*. New York: American Book, Van Nostrand, Reinhold.

Glade, William P., Jr., and Charles W. Anderson (1963) *The Political Economy of Mexico*. Madison, Wisc.: University of Wisconsin Press.

Gonzalez, Godofredo (1962) "Venezuela y La Alianza para El Progreso," speech delivered by Minister of Public Works, Chief of Venezuelan Delegation, at first meeting of Inter-American Economic and Social Council, October 24, 1962.

Gouveia, Aparecida Joly (1967) "Education and Development: Opinion of Secondary School Teachers," in Lipset and Solari (1967), pp. 484–510.

Government Development Bank for Puerto Rico (1970) *A Special Report on the Commonwealth of Puerto Rico*, September 1970.

Great Britain, Colonial Office (1948) *Report of the British Guiana and British Honduras Settlement Commission*. London: His Majesty's Stationery Office, Cmd. 7533.

Griffin, Keith (1969) *Underdevelopment in Spanish America: An Interpretation*. Cambridge, Mass.: M.I.T. Press.

Grunig, James E. (1969a) "Economic Decision Making and Entrepreneurship Among Colombian Latifundists," *Inter-American Economic Affairs*, vol. 23, no. 1 (Summer 1969) pp. 21–46.

Grunig, James E. (1969b) "The Minifundio Problem in Colombia: Development Alternatives," *Inter-American Economic Affairs*, vol. 23, no. 3 (Winter 1969), pp. 3–24.

Guyana Ministry of Information (1968) *Guyana: Two Years of Independence and Progress*. Georgetown, Guyana.

Habakuk, H. J. (1968) "The Historical Experience on the Basic Condition of Economic Progress," in Falkus (1968), pp. 33–48.

Haberler, Gottfried (1963) "Terms of Trade and Economic Development," in Ellis (1963), pp. 275–307.

Hagen, Edmund Edward (1966) *Highways into the Upper Amazon—Pioneer Lands in Southern Colombia, Ecuador, and Northern Peru*. Gainesville: University of Florida Press.

Hagen, Everett E. (1962) *On the Theory of Social Change*: How Economic Growth Begins. Homewood, Ill.: Irwin.

Hagen, Everett E. (1963) *Planning Economic Development*. Homewood, Ill.: Irwin.

Hagen, Everett E. (1968) *The Economics of Development*. Homewood, Ill.: Irwin.

Hanke, Lewis, ed. (1967) *History of Latin American Civilization: Sources and Interpretations*, vol. 2. Boston: Little, Brown.

Hanson, Earl Parker (1955) *Transformation: The Story of Modern Puerto Rico*. New York: Simon and Schuster.

Hanson, Simon G. (1951) *Economic Development of Latin America*. Washington, D.C.: Inter-American Economic Affairs Press.

Hanson, Simon G. (1967) *Five Years of the Alliance for Progress: An Appraisal*. Washington, D.C.: The Inter-American Economic Affairs Press.

Harbison, Frederick H., and Charles A. Myers (1959) *Management in the Industrial World: An International Analysis*. New York: McGraw-Hill.

Harbison, Frederick H., and Charles A. Myers (1964) *Education, Manpower, and Economic Development: Strategies of Human Resource Development*. New York: McGraw-Hill.

Harbison, Frederick H., and Charles A. Myers (1965) *Manpower and Education: Country Studies in Economic Development*. New York: McGraw-Hill.

Hauch, Charles C. (1963) *The Current Situation in Latin American Education*, Bulletin No. 21, U.S. Department of Health, Education, and Welfare. Washington, D.C.: Government Printing Office.

Heilbroner, Robert (1963) *The Great Ascent: The Struggle for Economic Development in Our Time*. New York: Harper & Row.

Heller, Walter (1962) "Fiscal Politics for Underdeveloped Economies," in Okun and Richardson (1962), pp. 448–468.

Herrera, Felipe (1960) "Financing Inter-American Development," address before National Academy of Economics and Political Science at Brookings Institute, Washington, D.C., May 11, 1960.

Herrera, Felipe (1965) *Latin American Economic Integration*. Inter-American Development Bank, September 1965.

Herrera, Felipe (1966) *Economic and Political Bases for a Latin American Common Market*. Inter-American Development Bank, 1966.

Herrera, Felipe (1969) "Nationalism and Economic Integration in Latin America," lecture delivered at Georgetown University, October 30, 1969.

Herrera, Felipe (1970) *Survey of International Development*, vol. 7, no. 4 (April 1970), p. 2.

Herrick, Bruce H. (1965) *Urban Migration and Economic Development in Chile*. Cambridge, Mass.: M.I.T. Press.

Higgins, Benjamin (1968) *Economic Development Problems, Principles, and Policies*, rev. ed. New York: Norton.

Hilton, Ronald, ed. (1969) *The Movement Toward Latin American Unity*. New York: Praeger.

Hirschmann, Albert O. (1963) *Journeys Toward Progress: Studies of Economic Policy-Making in Latin America*. New York: Twentieth Century Fund.

Hirschmann, Albert O. (1964) "Population Pressures as a Force for Development," in Novack and Lekachman (1964), pp. 140–146.

Hirschmann, Albert O. (1969) "The Political Economy of Import-Substituting Industrialization in Latin America," in Nisbet (1969), pp. 237–266.

Hirschmann, Albert O. (1969) *How to Divest in Latin America and Why*. Essays in International Finance, no. 76 (November 1969). Princeton, N.J.: International Finance Section, Department of Economics, Princeton University.

Hopkins, John A. (1969) *The Latin American Farmer*, U.S. Department of Agriculture Economic Research Service (August 1969), Washington, D.C.: Government Printing Office.

Horowitz, Abraham, and Burke, Mary H. (1966) "Health, Population and Development," in Stycos and Arias (1966), pp. 145–195.

Hoselitz, Bert F., ed. (1960) *Theories of Economic Growth*. New York: Free Press.

Hoselitz, Bert F. (1962) "Noneconomic Factors in Economic Development," in Okun and Richardson (1962), pp. 337–348.

Huberman, Leo (1963) "Which Way for Latin America?" in Sweezy and Huber-
    man (1963), pp. 48–56.
Huberman, Leo, and Paul M. Sweezy, eds. (1968) *Cuba: Anatomy of a Revolu-
    tion*, 2nd ed. New York: Monthly Review Press.
Huizer, Gerrit (1969) *Peasant Organization in the Process of Agrarian Reform
    in Mexico*. St. Louis: Social Science Institute, Washington University.
Humphrey, Hubert H. (1963) *A Report on the Alliance for Progress, U.S. Senate
    Committees on Appropriations and on Foreign Relations*, 88th Cong., 1st
    sess., Sen. Doc. No. 13 (April 11, 1963).

Institute of International Studies and Overseas Administration of the University
    of Oregon (1960) "Problems of Latin American Economic Development," in
    the U.S. Senate (1960a) Committee on Foreign Relations, pp. 545–684.
Inter-American Development Bank (1961) *Socio-Economic Progress in Latin
    America*, Social Progress Trust Fund, 1st Annual Report.
Inter-American Development Bank (1962a) *Socio-Economic Progress in Latin
    America*, Social Progress Trust Fund, 2nd Annual Report.
Inter-American Development Bank (1962b) *Private Enterprise and Latin Ameri-
    can Development*. Buenos Aires (April 25, 1962).
Inter-American Development Bank (1963a) *Medium-term Financing of Latin
    American Exports*. Washington, D.C. (February 1963).
Inter-American Development Bank (1963b) *Institutional Reforms and Social
    Development Trends in Latin America*. Washington, D.C. (March 1963).
Inter-American Development Bank (1963c) *Financial Aspects of Economic Inte-
    gration in the Hemisphere*. Caracas, Venezuela (April 1963).
Inter-American Development Bank (1965a) *Socio-Economic Progress in Latin
    America*, Social Progress Trust Fund, 5th Annual Report.
Inter-American Development Bank (1965b) *Proposals for the Creation of the
    Latin American Common Market*. Washington, D.C.
Inter-American Development Bank (1966) *Socio-Economic Progress in Latin
    America*, Social Progress Trust Fund, 6th Annual Report.
Inter-American Development Bank (1967) *Socio-Economic Progress in Latin
    America*, Social Progress Trust Fund, 7th Annual Report.
Inter-American Development Bank (1968a) *Socio-Economic Progress in Latin
    America*, Social Progress Trust Fund, 8th Annual Report.
Inter-American Development Bank (1968b) *Multinational Investment in the
    Economic Development and Integration of Latin America*. Bogota, Colombia
    (April 1968).
Inter-American Development Bank (1969a) *Socio-Economic Progress in Latin
    America*, Social Progress Trust Fund, 9th Annual Report.
Inter-American Development Bank (1969b) *The Process of Industrialization in
    Latin America*. Guatemala (April 1969).
Inter-American Development Bank (1970) *Socio-Economic Progress in Latin
    America*, Social Progress Trust Fund, 10th Annual Report.I
Inter-American Development Bank (n.d.) *Tax Systems of Latin America*. Joint
    Tax Program OAS–IDB. Washington, D.C.: Pan American Union.
International Bank for Reconstruction and Development (1966–1967) *IDA
    Annual Report.*
International Bank for Reconstruction and Development (1968) *IDA Annual
    Report.*
International Bank for Reconstruction and Development (n.d.) *World Bank
    Atlas: Population, Per Capita Product and Growth Rates*. Washington, D.C.
Inter-American Statistical Institute (1970) *Boletin Estadistico* (July 16, 1970).
International Labor Office (1962) *Yearbook of Labor Statistics*.

Jaguaribe, Helio (1968) *Economic and Political Development: A Theoretical Approach and a Brazilian Case Study*. Cambridge, Mass.: Harvard University Press.

Jamaican Ministry of Development and Welfare (n.d.) *Five Year Independence Plan 1963-1968*.

James, Preston E. (1969) *Latin America*, 3rd ed. London: Cassell.

James, Preston E. (1964) *Introduction to Latin America: The Geographical Background of Economic and Political Problems*. New York: Odyssey Press.

Johnson, Harry G. (1968a) *Economic Policies Toward Less Developed Countries*. New York: Praeger.

Johnson, Harry G. (1968b) "Towards a Generalized Capital Accumulation Approach to Economic Development," in Blaug (1968), pp. 34-44.

Kaldor, Nicholas (1964) *Essays on Economic Policy*, vol. 2. New York: Norton.

Kalijarvi, Thorsten V. (1962) *Central America: Land of Lords and Lizards*. New York: Van Nostrand.

Kanner, Lee, ed. (1968) *The New York Times World Economic Review and Forecast 1968*. Princeton, N.J.: Van Nostrand.

Keesing, D. B. (1967) "Outward-Looking Policies and Economic Development," *The Economic Journal*, vol. 77, whole no. 306 (June 1967), pp. 303-320.

Kerr, Clark, et al. (1964) *Industrialism and Industrial Man*. New York: Oxford University Press.

Killick, Tony (1970) "Commodity Agreements as International Aid," in Meier (1970), pp. 533-538.

Kindleberger, Charles P. (1963) *International Economics*, 3d ed. Homewood, Ill.: Irwin.

Kindleberger, Charles P. (1965) *Economic Development*, 2nd ed. New York: McGraw-Hill.

Kitty, Daniel R. (1967) *Planning for Development in Peru*. New York: Praeger.

Klaasen, L. H. (1967) *Methods of Selecting Industries for Depressed Areas, An Introduction to Feasibility Studies*. Paris: OECD.

Kohler, Heinz (1968) *Scarcity Challenged: An Introduction to Economics*. New York: Holt, Rinehart & Winston.

Kolbeck, Gustavo Romero (1967) "Economic Development of Mexico," in Committee for Economic Development (1967), pp. 177-214.

Kreisberg, Martin (1968) *Food Needs and Market Demands in Latin America— A Fresh Appraisal*, U.S. Department of Agriculture, Society for International Development (March 7, 1968). Washington, D.C.: Government Printing Office.

Krueger, A. O. (1968) "Factor Endowments and Per Capita Income Differences Among Countries," *The Economic Journal Journal*, vol. 78, whole no. 311 (September 1968), pp. 650-651.

Kuznets, Simon (1950) "International Differences in Income Levels," in Okun and Richardson (1962), pp. 3-26.

Kuznets, Simon (1960) "Population Change and Aggregate Output," in National Bureau of Economic Research (1960).

Latin America (1969a) (January 3, 1969).

Latin America (1969b) (February 28, 1969).

Latin America (1969c) (April 18, 1969).

Latin America (1969d) (February 21, 1969).

Latin America (1969e) (April 14, 1969).

Latin American Free Trade Association (LAFTA) (1970) *Newsletter* (issues of July, September, and December 1970).

Latin American Reports (1964) *Latin American Report: The Central American Isthmus*, vol. 5, no. 7 (April 1964).

Leff, Nathaniel H. (1968) *Economic Policy-Making and Development in Brazil, 1947–1964.* New York: Wiley.

Leibenstein, Harvey (1957) *Economic Backwardness and Economic Growth.* New York: Wiley.

Leontieff, Wassily (1963) "The Structure of Development," in *Scientific American* (1963), pp. 105–124.

Lernoux, Penny (1967) "Venezuela's Miracle in the Countryside," *Venezuela Up-to-Date* 127 (Summer–Fall 1967).

Letvin, William (1964) "Four Fallacies About Economic Development," in Novack and Schackman (1964), pp. 23–29.

Levy, Fred J., Jr. (1968) *Economic Planning in Venezuela.* New York: Praeger.

Lewis, W. Arthur (1962) "Economic Development with Unlimited Supplies of Labor," in Okun and Richardson (1962), pp. 279–303.

Lewis, W. Arthur (1964) "Is Economic Growth Desirable?" in Novack and Lekachman (1964), pp. 10–22.

Lewis, W. Arthur (1966) *Development Planning.* New York: Harper & Row.

Lewis, W. Arthur (1969) *The Principles of Economic Planning.* New York: Harper & Row.

Lipset, Seymour Martin, and Aldo Solari, eds. (1967) *Elites in Latin America.* New York: Oxford University Press.

Lipsey, Richard G., and Peter O. Steiner (1972) *Economics*, 3rd ed. New York: Harper & Row.

Llosa, Jorge Guillermo (1960) "A Map of Peru," *Las Americas*, June 1960.

Lockley, Lawrence C. (1963–1964) *A Guide to Market Data in Central America.* Tegucigalpa, Honduras: Central America Bank for Economic Integration.

Lopez, Enrique Perez, et al. (1967) *Mexico's Recent Economic Growth: The Mexican View.* Austin, Texas: University of Texas Press.

Lotz, Jorgen R., and Elliott R. Morss (1967) "Measuring Tax Effort in Developing Countries," *IMF Staff Papers*, vol. 14, no. 3 (November 1967), pp. 478–499.

Lourié, Sylvain (1965) "Education for Today or Yesterday?" in Lyons (1965), pp. 28–41.

Ludwig, Armin K. (1969) "The Kubitschek Years, 1956–61: A Massive Undertaking in a Big Rush," *Cultural Change in Brazil*, Midwest Association for Latin American Studies (October 30 and 31, 1969), pp. 101–113. Muncie, Ind.: Ball State University.

Lyons, Raymond F., ed. (1965) *Problems and Strategies of Educational Planning Lessons from Latin America.* Paris: UNESCO, International Institute for Educational Planning.

Maddison, Angus *Economic Progress and Policy in Developing Countries* (New York: Norton, 1970).

Macario, Santiago (1964) "Protection and Industrialization in Latin America," *Economic Bulletin for Latin America*, vol. 4, no. 1 (March 1964), pp. 63–101.

McGann, Thomas F. (1966) *Argentina: The Divided Land.* Princeton, N.J.: Van Nostrand.

McNamara, Robert S. (1968) Address to the Board of Governors by the President of the World Bank Group, Washington, D.C., September 30, 1968.

McNamara, Robert S. (1970) "The Time Dimension of the Task," *International Development Review*, vol. 1 (1970), pp. 3–8.

Maidenberg, H. J. (1971) "Venezuela Receiving Signals for Change," *New York Times*, February 28, 1971, sec. 3, p. 1.

Mamalakis, Markos J. (1969) "The Theory of Sectoral Clashes," *Latin American Research Review*, vol. 4 (Fall 1969), pp. 9–46.

Mansfield, Edwin (1968) *The Economics of Technological Change*. New York: Norton.

Maritano, Nino, and Antonio H, Obaid (1963) *An Alliance for Progress: The Challenge and the Problem*. Minneapolis: T. S. Denison.

Matthews, Herbert L., ed. (1963) *The United States and Latin America*, American Assembly series. Englewood Cliffs, N.J.: Prentice-Hall.

May, Herbert K. (1968) *Problems and Prospcets of the Alliance for Progress: A Critical Examination*. New York: Praeger.

Meade, J. E. (1967) "Population Explosion, the Standard of Living and Social Conflict," *The Economic Journal*, vol. 77 whole no. 306 (June 1967), pp. 233–242.

Meade, J. E. (1968) *A Neo-Classical Theory of Economic Growth*. London: Unwin University Books.

Meier, Gerald M. (1970) *Leading Issues in Economic Development: Studies in International Poverty*, 2nd ed. New York: Oxford University Press.

Meier, Richard L. (1965) *Development Planning*. New York: McGraw-Hill.

Mesa-Lago, Carmelo (1970) *Ideological Radicalization and Economic Policy in Cuba*. New Brunswick, N. J.: Rutgers University Press.

Michaelis, Michael (1968) "Technology for Society," *American Economic Review*, vol. 58, no. 2 (May 1968), pp. 492–501.

Millikan, Max F., and Donald L.M. Blackmer (1970) "The Desirability of Social Change," in Spiegelglas and Welsh (1970), pp. 142–152.

Millikan, Max F., and David Hapgood (1967) *No Easy Harvest: The Dilemma of Agriculture in Underdeveloped Countries*. Boston: Little, Brown.

Ministerio de Economia, Guatemala (1966), *Analysis of Mineral Samples of Guatemala* (July 1966).

Mintz, Sidney W. (1962) "The Role of the Middleman in the Internal Distribution System of a Caribbean Peasant Economy," in Walters, Snider, and Sweet (1962), pp. 786–799.

Moore, John D. J. (1962) "The Mobilization of Foreign Private Resources," in Inter-American Development Bank (1962), pp. 37–47.

Moore, Wilbert E. (1951) *Industrialization and Labor*. Ithaca, N.Y.: Cornell University Press.

Mora, Jose A. (n.d.) *From Panama to Punta del Este: Past Experience and Future Prospects 1956–1968*. Washington, D.C.: Pan American Union.

Morgan, Theodore, George W. Betz, and N. K. Choudbury, eds. (1963) *Readings in Economic Development*. Belmont, Calif.: Wadsworth.

Mörner, Magnus (1967) *Race Mixture in the History of Latin America*. Boston: Little, Brown.

Musgrave, R. A., and Alan J. Peacock, eds. (1958) *Classics in the Theory of Public Finance,* International Economics Association, London: Macmillan.

Myers, Charles A. (1959) "Management in Chile," in Harbison and Myers (1959), pp. 169–184.

Myint, H. (1971) *Economic Theory and the Underdeveloped Countries*. New York: Oxford University Press.

Myrdal, Gunnar (1964) *Economic Theory and Underdeveloped Regions*. London: Methuen University Paperbacks.

National Advertising Co. (n.d.) *Guyana: A Nation on the Move*. Barbados: National Advertising Co.

National Bureau of Economic Research (1960) *Demographic and Economic Change in Developed Countries*. Princeton, N.J.: Princeton University Press.

Navarro, Moises Gonzalez (1969) "Mexico: The Lopsided Revolution," in Veliz (1969), pp. 206–229.

Nehemkis, Peter (1966) *Latin America, Myth and Reality*, rev. ed. New York: Mentor.

Newsweek (1967) "Mexico: An Economy Comes of Age" (August 7, 1967), pp. 60–66.

New York Times (1968) "The New York Times Survey of the Economy of the Americas" (January 22, 1968).

New York Times (1970a) "Three Communists Given Key Economic Posts in Chilean Cabinet" (October 31, 1970), p. 1.

New York Times (1970b) "Peru Laws Forcing Out Foreign Firms" (October 31, 1970), sec. c, p. 39.

New York Times (1971a) "Venezuela Receiving Signals for Change" (February 28, 1971), sec. 3, p. 1.

New York Times (1971b) "Allende, in Interview, Bars Any Base Imperiling U.S." (March 28, 1971), p. 1.

Nisbet, Charles T., ed. (1969) *Latin America: Problems in Economic Development*, New York: Free Press.

Novack, David E., and Robert Lekachman, eds. (1964) *Development and Society: The Dynamics of Economic Change*. New York: St. Martin's Press.

Nurske, Ragnar (1955) *The Problems of Capital Formation in Underdeveloped Countries*. Oxford: Basil Blackwell.

Nutter, Warren G. (1957) "The Measurement of Income and Income Change," *Journal of Political Economy*, vol. 10 (February 1957), pp. 51–63. Reproduced by Morgan, Bety, and Choudbury (1963), pp. 25–38.

Nystrom, J. Warren, and Nathan A. Haverstock (1966) *The Alliance for Progress*. New York: Van Nostrand.

Ohlin, Goran (1967) *Population Control and Economic Development*. Paris: Development Center for the Organization for Economic Cooperation and Development.

Okun, Bernard, and Richard W. Richardson (1962) *Studies in Economic Development*. New York: Holt, Rinehart & Winston.

Oliver, Corey J. (1968) "Education in the Alliance for Progress," speech delivered to Foreign Policy Association of Minnesota, April 11, 1968.

Organization for Economic Cooperation and Development (1968) *The Food Problem of Developing Countries*, Paris: OECD.

Organization for Economic Cooperation and Development (1969) (December 1969, pp. 269–270).

Organization for Economic Cooperation and Development (1970) *OECD Observer* (February 1970).

Ostos, Raul Martinez (1962) The Mobilization of Domestic Private Financial Resources and the Role of National Development Institutions," in Inter-American Development Bank (1962), pp. 17–35.

Oxley, G. M. (1968) Private Enterprise in Latin America," Stanford Research Institute *International*, vol. 9 (1968), pp. 13–17.

Pan American Coffee Bureau (1967) *Annual Coffee Statistics, 1967*.

Pan American Health Organization (1965) *Health Conditions in the Americas 1961–1964.*

Pan American Health Organization (1968a) *Annual Report of the Director.*

Pan American Health Organization (1968b) *Facts on Health Progress.*

Pan American Union (1965) *Public Administration in Latin America.*

Pan American Union (1966aa) *La administración pública como instrumento del desarrollo*. Uruguay.

Pan American Union (1966b) *Profile of Progress of Social and Economic Development and Integration in Central America and Panama*. Alliance for Progress.

Pan American Union (IA-ECOSOC and CIAP) (1967a) *Domestic Efforts and the Farming Sector of Nicaragua* (1967).

Pan American Union (1967b) *Evolución reciente de la economía de America Latina* (May 12, 1967).

Pan American Union (IA-ESOCOC and CIAP) (1967c) *Domestic Efforts and the Needs for External Financing for the Development of Chile* (September 1967).

Pan American Union (1967d) *Progreso de la administración para el desarrollo en America Latina*.

Pan American Union (1967e) *La Alianza para el progreso y las perspectivas de desarrollo de America Latina* (Examen del primer quiquenio 1961–1965). Washington, D. C.

Pan American Union (CIAP) (1967f) *El esfuerzo interno y las necesidades de financiamento externo para el desarrollo del Brasil*. Washington, D. C.

Pan American Union (1967g) *Declaration of the Presidents of America*. Meeting of American Chiefs of State, Punta del Este, Uruguay (April 12–14, 1967).

Pan American Union (CIAP) (1967h) *The Frontiers of South America* (Document presented at meeting of Inter-American Committee on the Alliance for Progress, Washington, D. C., October 3–6, 1966).

Pan American Union (IA-ECOSOC) (1967i) *Industrialization in Latin America*. Washington, D. C.

Pan American Union (IA-ECOSOC and CIAP) (1968a) *Domestic Efforts and the Needs for External Financing for the Development of Colombia* (January 1968).

Pan American Union (1968b) America en Cifras 1967–1970 (Annual). Washington, D. C.

Pan American Union (IA-ECOSOC and CIAP) (1968c) *Domestic Efforts and Needs for External Financing for the Development of Guatemala* (1968).

Pan American Union (1968d) *An Evaluation of the Department of Natural Resources of SUDENE* (March 26, 1968). Washington, D. C.

Pan American Union (1968e) *Development Administration Program*.

Pan American Union (1968)f *The Alliance for Progress and Multilateral Economic Cooperation*, Washington, D. C.

Pan American Union (1969) *Statistical Compendium of the Americas*. Washington, D. C.

Pan American Union (1969a) *Boletin Estadistico* (September 1969).

Pan American Union (1969aa) *Alliance for Progress Weekly Newsletter* (April 14, 1969).

Pan American Union (1969b) *Alliance for Progress Weekly Newsletter* (November 24, 1969).

Pan American Union (1970) *Alliance for Progress Weekly Newsletter* (March 2, 1970).

Papanek, Gustav F., ed. (1968) *Development Policy: Theory and Practice*. Cambridge, Mass.; Harvard University Press.

Pegrum, Dudley F. (1968) *Transportation Economics and Public Policy*, rev. ed. Homewood, Ill.: Irwin.

Pepelasis, Adamantios, Leon Meara, and Irma Adelman (1961) *Economic Development: Analysis and Case Studies*. New York: Harper & Row.

Phelps, Edmund S., ed. (1962) *The Goal of Economic Growth*. New York: Norton.

Pinto, Anibal (1969) "Political Aspects of Economic Development in Latin America," in Veliz (1969), pp. 9–46.

Plaza, Galo (1969) in Pan American Union (1969aa).

Political Quarterly (1950) (April-June, 1950).

Pollack, James McKenzie (1966) "Health Sector Planning and National Planning," *International Development Review*, vol. 8, no. 4 (December 1966). pp. 14–17.

Poppino, Rollie E. (1968) Brazil: The Land and People. New York: Oxford University Press.

Population Reference Bureau (1968) *Population Bulletin*, vol. 24, no. 1 (February 1968).

Population Reference Bureau (1969) *1969 World Population Data Sheet*. Washington, D. C.

Population Reference Bureau (1969aa) *Desarrollo urbano en America Latina.* Washington, D. C.

Population Reference Bureau (1970) *1970 World Population Data Sheet*. Washington, D. C.

Powelson, John P. (1964) *Latin America: Today's Economic and Social Revolution*. New York: McGraw Hill.

Powelson, John P. (1968) "Towards an Integrated Growth Model," in Blasier (1968), pp. 57–85.

Prebisch, Raul (1969) "La marcha hacia el mercado comun latino americano," *Notas sobre la economia y el desarrollo de America Latin, no. 23 and no. 24* (August 1 and 16, 1969).

Prebisch, Raul (1970a) *Survey of International Development*, vol. 7, no. 5 (May 1970), p. 2.

Prebisch, Raul (1970b) *Change and Development: Latin America's Great Task* (July 1970). Washington, D.C.: Inter-American Development Bank.

Prieto, Luis B. (1963) "Education for Latin America," in Adams (1963), pp. 169–177.

Quintana, Carlos (1969) "Latin America Development in the Present Decade," *Inter-Economics*, vol. 1 (January 1969), pp. 18–22.

Ragatz, Lowell Joseph (1963). *The Fall of the Caribbean Planter Class in the British Caribbean 1763-1833: A Study in Social and Economic History*. New York: Octagon Books.

Randall, Laura (1964a) "Economic Development Policies and Argentine Economic Growth," in Randall (1964b), pp. 123–142.

Randall, Laura, ed. (1964b) *Economic Development: Evolution or Revolution?* Boston: D. C. Heath.

Reid, P. A. (1966) "Investing in Agriculture," *Finance and Development*, vol. 3, no. 3 (September 1966), pp. 202–211.

Reynolds, Lloyd A. (1969) "The Content of Development Economics," *The American Economic Review*, vol. 59, no. 2 (May 1969, pp. 401–408.

Reynoso, Placido Garcia (1969) "Government Policy and Business Responsibility in the Process of Industrial Development and Economic Integration in Latin America," in Inter-American Development Bank (1969b), pp. 3–29.

Riggs, Frederick W. (1956) "Public Administration: A Neglected Factor in Economic Development," *Annals of the American Academy of Political and Social Science: Agrarian Societies in Transition* (May 1956), pp. 70–80.

Roberts, C. Paul (1969) *Statistical Abstract of Latin America*, 1968. Berkeley: University of California Press.

Roberts, Paul O., and David T. Kresge (1968) "Transport for Economic and Social Development Simulation for Transport Policy Alternatives for Columbia," *American Economic Review*, vol. 58, no. 2 (May 1968), pp. 341–359.

Robinson, Harry (1967) *Latin America: A Geographic Survey*. New York: Praeger.

Robock, Stephan H. (1962) "Recent Economic Trends in Northeastern Brazil," *Inter-American Economic Affairs*, vol. 16, no. 3 (Winter 1962), pp. 65–89.

Rockefeller, David (1967) "Economic Development: The Banking Aspects," address by President of Chase Manhattan Bank, N.A., at International Monetary Fund Meeting, Rio de Janeiro, September 22, 1967.

Rodwin, Lloyd, and Assoc. (n.d.) *Planning Urban Growth and Regional Development*, Cambridge, Mass.: MIT Press.

Roper, Penelope (1970) *Investment in Latin America*, QER Special no. 6 (April 1970). London: The Economist Intelligence Unit.

Rostow, W. W. (1960) *The Stages of Economic Growth*. New York: Oxford University Press.

Ruttan, Vernon W. (1968) "Growth Stage Theories, Dual Economy Models and Agricultural Development Policy," J. S. McLean Visiting Lecture, January 20, 1968, Guelph, Canada, University of Guelph, Department of Agricultural Economics, Publication No. AE 1968/2.

Saavedra, Sergio Updurraga (1967) "Key Factors in Chilean Economic Development," Committee for Economic Development (1967) pp. 59–137.

Samuelson, Paul A. (1961) *Economics: An Introductory Analysis*. New York: McGraw-Hill.

Sayigh, Yusif (1964) "Nationalism and Economic Development," in Randall (1964b), pp. 9–130.

Schmid, Lester (1968) "The Productivity of Agricultural Labor in the Export Crops of Guatemala: Its Relation to Wages and Living Conditions," *Inter-American Economic Affairs*, vol. 22, no. 2 (Autumn 1968), pp. 33–34.

Schmidt, Orvis A. (1966) "The World Bank Group in Latin America," (Address before Canadian Inter-American Association, Montreal, March 2, 1966).

Schultz, Theodore W. (1962) "Investment in Human Capital," in Phelps (1962), pp. 106–120.

Schwartz, Norman B. (1970) "Limited School Progress and Institutional Incompatibility: A Guatemalan Case," *Civilisations*, vol. 20, no. 2 (1970), pp. 240–260.

Scientific American (1963) *Technology and Economic Development*. New York: Knopf.

Scitovsky, Tibor (1969) "Prospects for Latin American Industrialization Within the Framework of Economic Integration: Bases for Analysis," in Inter-American Development Bank (1969b), pp. 30–48.

Scobie, James R. (1964) *Argentina: A City and a Nation*. New York: Oxford University Press.

Sedwitz, Walter J. (1968) "La America Latina adolece de muchos vacíos gerenciales," *International Management*, McGraw Hill (May 1968), vol. 23, no. 5, pp. 32–33.

Seers, Dudley, ed. (1964) *Cuba: The Economic and Social Revolution*. Chapel Hill, N.C.: University of North Carolina Press.

Seers, Dudley (1969 "The Meaning of Development," *International Development Review*, vol. 4 (December 1969), pp. 2–6.

Shaffer, H. G. (1968) "A Critique of the Concepts of Human Capital," in Blaug (1968), pp. 45–57.

Sheahan, John (1968) "Imports, Investment and Growth," in Papanek (1968), pp. 93–114.

Siebert, Horst (1968) *Regional Economic Growth: Theory and Policy*. Scranton, Pa.: International Textbook Co.

Sigmund, Paul E., Jr. (1963) *The Ideologies of the Developing Nations*. New York: Praeger.

Silvert, Kalman H. (1965) *Chile: Yesterday and Today*. New York: Holt, Rine-hart & Winston.

Silvert, Kalman H. (1968) *The Conflict Society: Reaction and Revolution in Latin America*. New York: Harper & Row.

Simon, Julian L. (1970) "Family Planning Prospects in Less-Developed Coun-tries, and a Cost-Benefit Analysis of Various Alternatives," *The Economic Journal*, vol. 80, whole no. 317 (March 1970), pp. 58–71.

Simonsen, Mario Henrique (1963) "The Role of Government and Free Enter-prise," in Adams (1963), pp. 123–142.

Simplicity, Richard P. (1970) "The Bogota Saga of Malcolm Springsteele," *World-Wide Land and Planning*, vol. 4, no. 4 (July–August 1970), pp. 22–31.

Singer, Hans W. (1964) *International Development: Growth and Change*. New York: McGraw-Hill.

Singer, Hans W. (1967) "Social Development: Key Growth Sector," *International Development Review*, vol. 8, no. 1 (March 1965). Reprinted in Tangri and Gray (1967), pp. 3–8.

Sirkin, Gerald (1968) *The Visible Hand: The Fundamental of Economic Plan-ning*. New York: McGraw-Hill.

Skidmore, Thomas E. (1967) *Politics in Brazil 1930–1964: An Experiment in Democracy*. New York: Oxford University Press.

Smith, John (1969) "The Campesinos, Perspectives in Latin America," *Inter-American Economic Affairs*, vol. 23 (Summer 1969), pp. 47–66.

Smith, Robert Freeman, ed. (1966) *Background to Revolution: The Develop-ment of Modern Cuba*. New York: Knopf.

Smith, T. Lynn, ed. (1965) *Agrarian Reform in Latin America*. New York: Knopf.

Snow, Peter G. (1967) *Government and Politics in Latin America*. New York: Holt, Rinehart & Winston.

Society for International Development (1970) *Survey of International Develop-ment*, vol. 8, no. 3 (March 1970).

Sommerfield, Raymond M. (1966) *Tax Reform and the Alliance for Progress*. Austin: University of Texas Press.

Spengler, Joseph J. (1960) "John Stuart Mill on Economic Development," in Hoselitz (1960), pp. 118–124.

Spiegelglas, Stephen, and Charles J. Welsh, eds. (1970) *Economic Development: Challenge and Promise*. Englewood Cliffs, N.J.: Prentice-Hall.

Stark, Harry (1963) *Social and Economic Frontiers in Latin America*, 2d ed. Dubuque, Iowa: Wm. C. Brown.

Stavenhagen, Rodolfo (1970) "Marginality, Participation and Agrarian Structure in Latin America," *International Institute for Labor Studies Bulletin*, no. 7 (June 1970), pp. 57–92.

Stein, Stanley J., and Barbara H. Stein (1970) *The Colonial Heritage of Latin America: Essays on Economic Dependence in Perspective*. New York: Oxford University Press.

Stokes, William S. (1967) "Social Classes in Latin America," in Snow (1967), pp. 51–70.

Straetzel, Donald S. (n.d.) "Go South, Young Man," *Reader's Digest* (January 1966), pp. 2–6.

Street, James H. (n.d.) "Latin American Economic Integration: Some Historic Guideposts," in Hilton (1969).

Street, James H. (1967) *The Latin American Structuralists and the Institutional-ists Convergence in Development Theory*. New Brunswick, N.J.: Rutgers Uni-versity Press.

Streeten, Paul (1968) *National Coffee Policy: Industrialization and Development.* Institute of Development Studies at the University of Sussex, Mimeo Series no. 11 (May 13, 1968).

Stycos, J. Mayone (1969) *Fe, Ideologia y Crecimiento de la Poblacion en America Latina.* Washington, D.C.: Population Reference Bureau.

Stycos, J. Mayone, and Jorge Arias (1966) *Population Dilemma in Latin America.* Washington, D.C.: Potomac Books.

Suits, Daniel B. (1970) *Principles of Economics.* New York: Harper & Row.

Sunkel, Osualdo (1966) "The Structural Background of Development Problems in Latin America," in Nisbet (1969), pp. 3–37.

Sweezy, Paul M., and Leo Huberman, eds. (1963) *Whither Latin America?* New York: Monthly Review Press.

Tangri, Shanti S., and Peter Gray, eds. (1967) *Capital Accumulation and Economic Development.* Boston: D.C. Heath.

Tannenbaum, Frank (1966) *Ten Keys to Latin America.* New York: Random House.

Time (1970) Chile: "The Expanding Left" (October 19, 1970), pp. 23–32.

Tinbergen, Jan (1958) *The Design of Development.* Baltimore: Johns Hopkins Press.

Tinbergen, Jan, and H. C. Boss (1962) *Mathematical Models of Economic Growth.* New York: McGraw-Hill.

UN (1947) *Economic Development in Selected Countries: Plans, Programs and Agencies.*

UN (1950a) *Domestic Financing of Economic Development.*

UN (1950b) *The Economic Development of Latin America and Its Principal Problems.*

UN (1951) *Land Reform Defects in Agrarian Structure as Obstacles to Economic Development.*

UN (1955) *Processes and Problems of Industrialization in Underdeveloped Countries.*

UN (1959) "Statistical Series for Use of Less Developed Countries," in *Programs of Economic and Social Development*, Statistical Papers, Series M., No. 31.

UN (1961) *Foreign Private Investments in the Latin American Free-Trade Area.*

UN (1963a) *Planning for Economic Development.*

UN (1963b) *Report of the Latin American Seminar on Housing Statistics and Programs, 1962.*

UN (1965) *External Financing in Latin America.*

UN (1966) *The Process of Industrial Development in Latin America.*

UN (1967) *Trade Expansion and Economic Integration Among Developing Countries.*

UN (1968) *Latin American Economy in 1967.*

UN, Committee for Development Planning (1967) *Planning and Plan Implementation.* New York.

UN, Conference on Trade and Development (1968) *Toward a Global Strategy of Development.* Geneva.

UN, Department of Economic Affairs (1951) *Measures for the Economic Development of Underdeveloped Countries.*

UN, Economic and Social Council (1963) "Toward a Dynamic Development Policy for Latin America," 10th sess., Mar de Plata, Argentina (May 1963).

UN, Economic and Social Council (1963aa) *Financing of Industrial Development.*

UNECLA (1953) *Economic Survey of Latin America.*

UNECLA (1955) *Analyses and Projections of Economic Development.*

UNECLA (1958) *Economic Survey of Latin America.*

UNECLA (1959) *The Latin American Common Market.*

UNECLA (1960) *Relation to Some Aspects of Economic Development.*

UNECLA (1961) *Foreign Private Investments in the Latin American Free Trade Area.*

UNECLA (1962) *Economic Survey of Latin America 1964.*

UNECLA (1963a) *Economic Survey of Latin America 1965.*

UNECLA (1963b) *Financing of Industrial Development.* Export Credit Systems and Institutions (March 28, 1963).

UNECLA (1963c) "The Cuban Economy in the Period 1959-1963," in UNECLA, *Economic Survey of Latin America 1965.*

UNECLA (1963d) *The Economic Development of Latin America in the Post-War Period,* 2 vols.

UNECLA (1963e) *Towards a Dynamic Development Policy for Latin America.*

UNECLA (1964) *Economic Survey of Latin America 1966.*

UNECLA (1964aa) "The Growth and Decline of Import Substitution in Brazil," *Economic Bulletin for Latin America,* vol. 9, no. 1 (March 1964), pp. 1-59.

UNECLA (1965) *External Financing in Latin America.*

UNECLA (1966) *Statistical Abstract of Latin America.*

UNECLA (1966aa) *Evaluacion de la Integracion Economica en Centroamerica.*

UNECLA (1967a) *Economic Survey of Latin America 1969.*

UNECLA (1967aa) *Economic Bulletin for Latin America* (October 1967).

UNECLA (1967b) "Income Distribution in Latin America," *Economic Bulletin for Latin America,* vol. 12, no. 2 (October 1967), pp. 38-60.

UNECLA (1968a) *Education, Human Resources and Development in Latin America,* New York.

UNECLA (1968b) *Economic Survey of Latin America 1966.*

UNECLA (1969a) *Economic Development and Income Distribution in Argentina.*

UNECLA (1969b) *Economic Survey of Latin America 1967.*

UNESCO (1961) *International Yearbook of Education.*

UNESCO (1965) *International Yearbook of Education.*

UNFAO (1965) *Accion de la FAO in America Latina.*

UNFAO (1966) *FAO Production Yearbook.*

UNFAO (1967) *A Strategy for Development.*

U.S. Department of Agriculture (1966) *Agricultural Credit Programs in Latin America,* Report on First Meeting of U.S. Agricultural Credit Technicians in Latin America. Guatemala City, Guatemala (August 8-10, 1966).

U.S. Department of Agriculture (1967) *International Agricultural Development,* selected issues.

U.S. Department of Agriculture (1967aa) *The Western Hemisphere Agricultural Situation.*

U.S. Department of Agriculture (1969) *The Latin American Farmer,* Foreign 257, Economic Research Service.

U.S. Department of Commerce (1960) *U.S. Business Investments in Foreign Countries.*

U.S. Department of Commerce (1968) *Survey of Current Business* (November 1968).

U.S. Department of Commerce (1968a) *Survey of Current Business* (October 1968).

U.S. Department of Commerce (1968aa) *Statistical Abstract of the United States.*

U.S. Department of Commerce (1969) *Statistical Abstract of the United States.*

U.S. Department of Labor (1963) *Forecasting of Manpower Requirements,* BLS Report no. 248, Bureau of Labor Statistics (April 1963).

U.S. Department of State (1965) Agency for International Development, *The Alliance for Progress: An American Partnership*.

U.S. Department of State (1967a) *Commitment for Progress: The Americas' Plan for a Decade of Urgency*, Declaration of the Presidents' of America, Punta del Este, Uruguay (April 12–14, 1967).

U.S. Department of State (1967b) Agency for International Development, *A Blueprint for Action*, Final Report, Fifth Conference of the Americas on Malnutrition as a Factor in Socio-Economic Development (September 24–29, 1967).

U.S. Department of State (1967c) *1967 Year End Review of the Alliance for Progress*.

U.S. Department of State (1967d) Agency for International Development, *U.S. Foreign Aid and the Alliance for Progress* (May 10, 1967).

U.S. Department of State (1967e) *Latin American Economic Growth Trends*.

U.S. Department of State (1968a) "U.S. Foreign Aid and the Alliance for Progress," in *Agency for International Development, Proposed Foreign Aid Program, Fiscal Year 1968*.

U.S. Department of State (1968b) Bureau of Inter-American Affairs, *Latin American Economic Growth Trends, Seven Years of the Alliance for Progress* (April 1968).

U.S. Department of State (1968c) Agency for International Development, *Gross National Product Growth Rates and Trend Data by Region and Country* (July 25, 1968).

U.S. Department of State (1968d) *1968 Year End Review of the Alliance for Progress*.

U.S. Department of State (1968) *The Woven Strands*. Washington, D.C.: Government Printing Office.

U.S. Department of State (1969a) "Problems of Population Growth." Reprinted from *The Department of Labor Bulletin* (August 11, 1969); Department of State Pub. 8510, General Foreign Policy Series, no. 241, pp. 1–3.

U.S. Department of State (1969b) *A Review of Alliance for Progress Goals*.

U.S. Department of State (1969c) Bureau of Inter-American Affairs, *Toward a Decade of Progress, 1969 Year-End Review of the Alliance for Progress*.

U.S. Department of State (1969d) Agency for International Development, *Latin American Economic Growth Trends*.

U.S. Department of State (1970) Agency for International Development, *Selected Economic Data for the Less-Developed Countries*.

U.S. Department of State (1970aa) Agency for International Development, *AID Economic Data Book—Latin America*.

U.S. Department of State (1971) (January 1971).

U.S. Department of State (n.d.) Agency for International Development, *Profile of Social and Economic Development and Integration in Central America and Panama*.

U.S. House (1966) "The Charter of Punta de Este Establishing an Alliance for Progress within the Framework of Operation Pan American," 89th Cong., 2nd sess., in *Regional and other Documents Concerning the United States' Relations with Latin America* (January 28, 1966), pp. 101–114.

U.S. House (1967) Subcommittee on International Finance, *Food for Progress in Latin America, A Report on Agricultural Development in Latin America Pursuant to House Resolution 1043*, 89th Cong., 2nd sess., by Henry S. Reuss, Chairman, Subcommittee on International Finance.

U.S. House (1969) *A Review of Alliance for Progress Goals*, a report by the Bureau for Latin America, Agency for International Development, 91st Cong., 1st sess., (March 1969). Washington, D.C.: Government Printing Office.

U.S. Senate (1960a) Committee on Foreign Relations, Subcommittee on American Republics' Affairs, *United States/Latin American Relations*, 86th Cong., 2nd sess., doc. no. 125.

U.S. Senate (1960b) "Development of Latin American Political Thought," in U.S. Senate (1960a), pp. 62–69.

U.S. Senate (1967a) Committee on Foreign Relations, *Latin American Summit Conference*, Hearing on S.G. 53, 90th Cong., 1st sess. (March 17 and 21, 1967).

U.S. Senate (1967b) Committee on Foreign Relations, Subcommittee on American Republics' Affairs, *Survey of the Alliance for Progress–The Political Aspects*, 90th Cong., 1st sess. (September 18, 1967).

U.S. Senate (1967c) Committee on Foreign Relations, Subcommittee on American Republics' Affairs, *Survey of the Alliance for Progress–The Latin American Military*, 90th Cong., 1st sess. (October 9, 1967).

U.S. Senate (1967d) Committee on Foreign Relations, Subcommittee on American Republics' Affairs, *Survey of the Alliance for Progress–Foreign Trade Policies*, 90th Cong., 1st sess. (October 30, 1967).

U.S. Senate (1967e) Committee on Foreign Relations, Subcommittee on American Republics' Affairs, *Survey of the Alliance for Progress–Problems of Agriculture*, 91st Cong., 1st sess., doc. no. 91-17 (December 22, 1967); study prepared by Professors William C. Thiesenhusen and Marion R. Brown, University of Wisconsin.

U.S. Senate (1968a) *Amendments to the OAS Chapter*, Hearing before Committee on Foreign Relations, 90th Cong., 2nd sess. (February 6, 1968).

U.S. Senate (1968b) *Inter-American Development Bank Capital Stock*, Hearing before Committee on Foreign Relations on H.R. 15364, 90th Cong., 2nd sess. (March 25, 1968).

U.S. Senate (1968c) Committee on Foreign Relations, Subcommittee on American Republics' Affairs, *Survey of the Alliance for Progress–Inflation in Latin America*, 91st Cong., 1st sess. (February 29, 1968), statement by Professor Raymond F. Mikesell, University of Oregon.

U.S. Senate (1968d) Committee on Foreign Relations, *Survey of the Alliance for Progress–Insurgency in Latin America*.

Urquidi, Victor L. (1964) *Free Trade and Economic Integration in Latin America: Toward a Common Market*. Berkeley: University of California Press.

Urquidi, Victor L. (1967) "Fundamental Problems of the Mexican Economy," in Lopez (1967), p. 181.

Urquidi, Victor L. (1968) *El Desarrollo Economico y el Creciemiento de la Poblacion*. Washington, D.C.: Population Reference Bureau.

Van Arkadie, B., and C. Frank (1966) *Economic Accounting and Development Planning*. New York: Oxford University Press.

Vanek, Jaroslav (1962) *International Trade: Theory and Economic Policy*. Homewood, Ill.: Irwin.

Veliz, Claudio, ed. (1969) *Obstacles to Change in Latin America*. New York: Oxford University Press.

Venezuela (1967) *Basic Data for Venezuela*. Washington, D.C.: Embassy of Venezuela (May 1967).

Venezuela, Central Office of Coordination and Planning (1962) "La reforma agraria," *Informaciones de Venezuela* (November 1962), pp. i, 13–15.

Venezuela, Central Office of Coordination and Planning (n.d.) *Plan de la Nación 1963-1966*. Prefacio y puntos salientes del Plan.

Venezuela, Central Office of Coordination and Planning (n.d.) *Plan de la Nación 1965-1968*. Vivienda rural.

Venezuela, Embassy of (1967) Information Service, *Venezuela's Hard Currency*.
Venezuela, Embassy of (1968–1970) *Venezuela Up-to-date*.
Venezuela, Ministry of Development (1963) *Desarrollo Industrial de Venezuela*.
Venezuela, Ministry of Agriculture (1963aa) *Reforma agraria y desarrollo Agro-pecuario en Venezuela*.
Vernon, Raymond (1963) *The Dilemma of Mexico's Development*. Cambridge, Mass.: Harvard University Press.
Vernon, Raymond, ed. (1964) *Public Policy and Private Enterprise in Mexico*. Center for International Affairs series. Cambridge, Mass.: Harvard University Press.
Viner, Jacob (1964) "The Economics of Development," in Novak and Lekachman (1964), pp. 4–9.

Wagley, Charles (1964) *Amazon Town, a Study of Man in the Tropics*. New York: Knopf.
Walters, S. George, Max D. Snider, and Morris L. Sweet, eds. (1962) *Readings in Marketing*. Cincinnati: South-Western.
Waterson, Albert (1966) *Development Planning: The Lessons of Experience*. London: Oxford University Press.
Whitback, R. H., and Frank E. Williams (1940) *Economic Geography of South America*. New York: McGraw-Hill.
Whyte, William F., and Lawrence K. Williams (1968) *Toward an Integrated Theory of Development*, ILK Paperback No. 5 (February 1968). New York: Cornell University, New York State School of Industrial and Labor Relations.
Williams, Eric (1944) *Capitalism and Slavery*. Chapel Hill: University of North Carolina Press.
Wionczek, Miguel S. (1963) "Incomplete Formal Planning: Mexico," in Hagen (1963), pp. 150–182.
Wolfe, Marshall (1965) "Social and Political Problems of Educational Planning in Latin America," in Lyons (1965), pp. 73–75.
Wright, A. C. S., and J. Bennema (1965) *The Soil Resources of Latin America*, UNFAO.

Yudelman, Montague (1966) *Agricultural Development in Latin America: Current Status and Prospects*. Washington, D.C.: Inter-American Development Bank (October 1966).

Zea, Leopold (1968) "Philosophy and Thought in Latin America," *Latin American Research Review*, vol. 3 (Spring 1968), pp. 3–16.

INDEX

INDEX

72 73 74 75 76 9 8 7 6 5 4 3 2 1